BUCK CLAYTON'S

JAZZ WORLD

BUCK CLAYTON'S
JAZZ WORLD

by

BUCK CLAYTON
assisted by
Nancy Miller Elliott

Discography compiled by
Bob Weir

NEW YORK
OXFORD UNIVERSITY PRESS
1987

© Buck Clayton 1986

First published in 1986 by
The Macmillan Press Ltd
London
England

Published in 1987 in the United States by
Oxford University Press Inc
200 Madison Avenue
New York
NY 10016

ISBN 0-19-520535-9

Printed in Great Britain by
ANCHOR BRENDON LTD
Tiptree, Essex

Typeset by Rowland Phototypesetting Ltd
Bury St Edmunds, Suffolk
in 10/11½pt Caledonia

The publishers gratefully acknowledge permission to reproduce
in this book photographs from the collections of Buck Clayton
and Nancy Miller Elliott.

Contents

Foreword

It was the French musician and critic André Hodeir who wrote that, with a tiny number of exceptions, jazz musicians reach the end of their musical life around the age of forty. Ironically, the book in which he made the sweeping diagnosis—*Jazz: its Evolution and Essence*—came out in the mid-1950s, at exactly the time that the development of the long-play record and the revival of interest in so-called mainstream jazz were combining to cast doubt on his theory.

Among the considerable body of mature musicians who showed themselves in this period to be playing as well as ever, one at least went far beyond that. I can remember to this day the particular record—a 78 rpm single, as it happens—which opened my ears to the existence of a "new" Buck Clayton. Ever since he first recorded with Count Basie in the late 1930s, Buck had made his mark as a player of great style, sensitivity and elegance with, as we then believed, a penchant for the cup mute. *Wrap your troubles in dreams*, recorded with Mezz Mezzrow's band during a 1953 European tour, revealed a new dimension to his playing—a "presence," if you like, compounded of majestically sweeping phrases, passionate attack and a tone of deeply burnished gold.

When we first met, and played together, in 1959, and in subsequent tours during the 1960s, I gained an insight into why, despite the dramatically heightened authority in his playing, Buck was still spoken of by the jazz writers in terms more appropriate to a fashion model or an ice-skater. Considering the risks that he was always willing to take, his trumpet-playing was, to be sure, remarkably poised, elegant, immaculate, polished and the rest. Why did they not hear what I heard, night after night—the excitement, inventiveness, passion and reckless daring?

The answer lies, I believe, in a couple of facts about his tours with my band. Buck did a lot of writing for our concerts and recordings. He invariably wrote himself the *second* trumpet part, on the grounds, first, that it was my band and not his and, secondly, that he could then trim the arrangement so that we could continue to play it after he returned to the States. Then again, when I suggested initially that he should come on in each half for a special feature spot, in the manner of most of the star American visitors, he showed no enthusiasm for it. He wanted to play all through the session as a member of the band, taking his solo turn with the rest of us.

Now, this is not the way that exciting, passionate and reckless jazz giants normally behave. For such larger-than-life performance we accept, and indeed expect, the hair-trigger temperament, the protruding ego and the dominating personality. Faced with a persona of reticence and reserve, we take a bit more time to assess accurately the musician underneath. It helps to have stood next to him on the stand for a whole string of dates and to have realized very soon that, while he clearly subscribed to the "consensus" rather than the "confrontation" policy in musical performance, the way that he not only maintained but raised his own standards at every session itself presented a formidable challenge.

During a close friendship which I value more than anything else in my musical life, we have maintained a running joke about the "wrestler's tricks" he used to pull on me, getting me to lower my guard by pleading some disadvantage ("I've left my jockstrap in the hotel" was the most blatant) and then overwhelming me with a burst of unfettered power! On his visit to us in the autumn of 1985, we had evidence that the capacity to pull wrestler's tricks is not only undimmed but unconscious. During a rehearsal at which we played through some of the many pieces he's written for my band, Buck stood up while one number was in progress, walked over to where saxophonist John Barnes was standing, picked up his baritone sax part and, having studied it closely for a few seconds, put it back without a word and returned to his seat. At the end of the number, a somewhat demoralized J. B. asked, "What's the matter, Buck? Was I playing something wrong?" "What's that?" said Buck. "No, no—I'd forgotten about that tune and just wanted to see what it's called."

Like the full splendor of Buck's music, the reminiscences in this book have taken a long time to come out. Characteristically, they are not startling or sensational. Perhaps the most shocking to fans of long standing is the revelation that he hated that cup mute with which he became so closely identified in the early Basie years! But one thing is certain—the book will demand the same reassessment of Buck Clayton, jazz musician, as did those eye-opening records thirty-odd years ago.

But I still think there's a wrestler's trick in there somewhere . . .

Humphrey Lyttelton
London, 1986

Introduction

Before beginning this story of my life, I'd like to give credit to so many guys who encouraged me to do things. These people include, here in New York: George Avakian, Brick Fleagle, Rev John Garcia Gensel, Cliff Glover, John Hammond, Nat Hentoff, Dan Morgenstern, Sy Oliver, Hank O'Neal, George Wein and Ben and Jeanne Wright; elsewhere in the USA and Canada: Hughie Clairmont, Stanley Dance, Schifford Garner, Nat Pierce and Pat Scott; in England: Max Jones, Humphrey Lyttelton and Steve Voce; in Europe: Yannick Bruynoghe, John Darville, Felix Debrit, Charles Delaunay, Hugues Panassié, Johnny Simmen and Jack Armitage; and, last but not least, Dr Roger Currie in Australia and Yasuo Segami in Japan.

I should like to make honorary mention of some of my friends who have passed on since I began the book, all of whom have been part of my story: Willard Alexander, Count Basie, Eddie Beal, Kenny Clarke, Bill Coleman, Vic Dickenson, George Duvivier, Clarence Glass, Jr, Earl Hines, Helen Humes, Harry James, Budd Johnson, Dill Jones, Jo Jones, Kenny Kersey, Ed Lewis, Dan Minor, Benny Morton, Bill Pemberton, Peppy Prince, Gene Ramey, Ernie Royal, Zoot Sims, Joe Turner, Dick Vance, Dicky Wells, Cootie Williams and Trummy Young.

Buck Clayton

One morning in Parsons, Kansas

It was swinging one morning in Parsons, Kansas, around ten o'clock on November 12th 1911, when I was born. This is my story, the life of a jazz musician. My father, Simeon Oliver Clayton, in his youth played cornet in Rockwall, Texas. Texas in those days had quite a few good musicians, almost as many I think as there were in New Orleans, but New Orleans had the fame for jazz. He told me many times of an old cornet that he once had but did not have a case for. He would just stick it in his overcoat pocket and carry it with him wherever he went. It was only natural that he would teach me to play trumpet. As Dad got older he finally ended up playing a sousaphone, which suited him, as he was a big man weighing about two hundred pounds. Dad was real talented and at an early age became interested in both music and writing. He was a very good poet and writer and once owned and was the editor of a newspaper called *The Blade*.

He had one of the greatest singing groups in the territory. It was a quartet in which he sang bass and was very popular in southeast Kansas. They called themselves Clayton's Imperial Four and used to travel all over the state singing at county fairs, concerts and various programs. When someone wanted to hire my Dad's quartet they'd say, "Let's call Sim Clayton" (or S. O. Clayton). I named my son Steven Oliver. I didn't want to put Simeon on him because it's not a modern name, so I named him Steven Oliver and he too was known as S. O. Clayton. Many traveling quartets had to take second place when they arrived in Parsons and were confronted by my Dad's quartet. Clayton's Imperial Four was highly regarded by all as one of the leading quartets at the time.

All four of the guys were wonderful singers. The baritone singer in the group was Walter Davis, who had a beautiful, rich voice. Walter Davis was the father of Wild Bill Davis, the great organist who played so many years with the Duke Ellington band. He was one of the few people who came out of Parsons that made a name in the jazz world. There were other musicians to come out of Parsons that I'll speak about later on.

My home town was a small town of about 11,000 people. When I was a kid it was mostly a railroad town. There was the MKT line—Missouri, Kansas and Texas line, known also as the Katy line. The Katy line ran north and south from Texas, Oklahoma and Missouri. There was also the Santa Fe line, which ran east and west.

My home was a little dull to me. I spent all of my school days there, up through high school. My mother, Aritha Anne Dorsey, was a schoolteacher when I was born. She was also a pianist and vocalist. She was born of Creole heritage of slave parents, a descendant of a French Huguenot slave owner named Howell Chastain. She always said that the fact that I had a Frenchman as a forefather was nothing to be proud of, because he had seduced one of his slaves.

I was named Wilbur after the inventor and aviator Wilbur Wright. My mother wanted me to have a name that wouldn't have a nickname, like Bill for William, Bob for Robert or Eddie for Edward. However, she defeated her own purpose by nicknaming me Buck. When I was about twelve years old little wild Indian boys were known as bucks. She always said that I was a pretty wild kid so she named me Buck, because of being part Cherokee Indian on my Dad's side of the family.

Mom was born in Stonewall County, Texas, on June 14th 1876 and moved to Parsons at an early age. She received her early education in the public schools of Parsons and was graduated from the beauty academy at Joplin, Missouri. She owned and operated the first beauty parlor in Parsons. She was a teacher in the public school systems of both Joplin and Parsons. She married my dad on June 28th 1910. Both were members of the Brown Chapel African Methodist Episcopal Church and prominent in music circles. My father was president of the AME church council. My dad just barely missed being born a slave as he was born on December 24th 1865, the year of emancipation—which must have been a great joy for my grandparents. Dad always complained of not getting any birthday presents because of being born on Christmas Eve. He was born in Rockwall, Texas.

When I was a kid of about seven years old many of the toys that I played with, when I could afford them, were degrading to black people. I once had a toy called the "Alabama Coon Jigger." When you wound him up he would dance. He was blue-black and had great big white eyes and great big red lips. Even though Dad wrote many poems condemning prejudice, those were still some pretty rough times for black people.

My mother never did like jazz, especially when she first heard it. She liked classical music. Once she offered me fifty dollars if I'd learn Rachmaninoff's Prelude in C sharp minor for piano, which I promptly did. Mom used to say that jazz was for lowlife people, and sometimes in those days it would seem that she was right. In Kansas City there was a place called the Yellow Front where every weekend somebody would get knifed or shot. Murders every week and sometimes more than one—maybe two or three. And all this was happening in other Kansas City joints too. The same thing was happening in New Orleans among prostitutes and pimps. Louis Armstrong used to tell me later how many people he knew had been killed in little clubs while listening to jazz by somebody that was either jealous or drunk. Louie told me that even he had once been cut.

That was not the kind of life my mother wanted me to get into—those little what we call "bucket of blood" places where you go in and never know whether you're going to come out alive or not. She never asked me not to play jazz, but she really didn't like it too much. My father had a little liking for jazz and his favorite jazzman was Fats Waller. He used to say to me, "Just listen to ol' Fats play this," or "Just listen to ol' Fats play that." It wasn't until I played Carnegie Hall that my mother eased up on jazz. She thought, "Well, if jazz has come along so far that it can be played in Carnegie Hall, then it must be alright." She never bothered me anymore.

The very first inkling of jazz music in my home, as I recall, was two piano sheets that were bought by my older two cousins, Aritha Dorsey, who later became married and lived in St Louis, Missouri, as Mrs Aritha Spotts, and Lucille Dorsey, who later married and became Mrs Lucille Kerford of Atchison, Kansas. They were the daughters of my mother's brother, Monroe Dorsey. The two piano sheets were *Arkansas Blues* and *Darktown Strutters' Ball*. Both songs have since become jazz and dixieland standards. Jazz was just beginning to become the "in" thing when my cousins bought the piano sheets, and as they were in their teens they wanted to be in on the latest fad. I was about six years old myself. When I was about seven years old my mother bought an Edison phonograph, but there wasn't a single jazz record in the house nor anything that even resembled a jazz record. I don't think Edison made jazz records. Later, however, they did make a vocal recording of *Yes sir, that's my baby*. We had a few records of Bert Williams, the great negro comedian, but all the rest was classical music.

I remember when I was a small boy musicians used to come through my home town riding freight trains, with saxophones, trumpets, etc., on their way to Kansas City to try to get work in the Kansas City bands. Migrating musicians who didn't have the train fare. In Parsons, as in several other small towns in the Midwest, there was the Holy Roller church. People who worship with such spirit and enthusiasm that the music they create makes you want to dance whether you're religious or not. Many Sunday nights I used to go to the Holy Roller church at 22nd and Morgan Avenue in Parsons and swing with the Holy Rollers, who used to play tambourines, trombones or anything else that could be used for rhythm. The songs they played and sang were natural swingers, such as *When the saints go marching in*. The Holy Rollers had more pep than our ordinary churches.

One time at this church I was sitting in the second balcony with some more little guys, and I had some sand in my shoe that was bothering me and kept distracting me from the swinging rhythm that was going on around me. The preacher, a one-legged little fat man, was delivering a sermon that had everybody so full of gospel that they were talking in tongues, when I decided to empty my shoe of the sand that was bothering me. I took the shoe off to shake the sand out of it, and someway it slipped out of my hand and fell down below to the first floor and hit one of the ladies on the head—or rather on her hat. That brought the whole thing to a halt. The preacher looked up in the second balcony and saw me and said, "Come on down, son, and get that shoe. Every time I seem to get a sermon going the devil has to stop it."

Dad's chapel orchestra practiced at my home every Sunday afternoon. Some of the members would leave their instruments at my home until the following week when they would rehearse again, so I had access to all kinds of instruments. Sometimes I would play trombone, saxophone, cornet or anything that I felt like playing because of these instruments lying all around my house. I could play the scales on every instrument, but I couldn't play songs. When I was about ten I used to play the old piano rolls on a neighbor's player piano. I believe some of the piano rolls were made by Fats Waller, J. P. Johnson, Jelly Roll Morton and others. I'd tire myself out pumping on those old music-roll player pianos.

As a boy, during the twenties, it was my good fortune to meet many of the civil rights leaders of that era through my mother, who had been a freedom fighter from the day she was born. My parents were equally involved in absolute freedom for black people. My mother, as choir leader, and my father, as bass singer in the choir and president of the church council, were always in demand to host the visiting dignitaries who happened to be visiting my home town as speakers, singers and all other forms of advancement for black people. We were fortunate in having a nice home and it was perfect for the visiting dignitaries to stop at our house as in those days it was impossible to stay at the white hotels. My mother had been a NAACP member for as long as I can remember. I used to read *The Crisis* at an early age. I also was an admirer of the *Kansas City Call* and at times was one of the *Call*'s newsboys.

I remember a time when Mr W. E. B. DuBois, the great United States author, educator and advocate of negro rights, stayed at my home and I was quite interested in his conversations with me. Being a young boy, I considered him to be a real hero and I was also fascinated by his beard guard that he would put on every night to keep his beard neat. Every morning when he would arise his beard was just as neat as it was when he went to bed.

Roland Hayes, one of the greatest black singers in the world, was once our guest and he too impressed me very much. Mr Hayes, a United States concert tenor, became known for his persuasive interpretations of negro spirituals. To have these great people sleep under the same roof as I was something that I never did forget, and sometimes they would eat pig's feet just as we did.

Roy Wilkins's father, Reverend Wilkins, was transferred to Parsons as our minister and at once became one of my father's great friends. Roy Wilkins was attending school at the time in Kansas City. He later became a United States negro leader and a social welfare executive who was prominent in the civil rights movements. In 1923 he became the managing editor of the *Kansas City Call*.

In Topeka, Kansas, where I was attending the Federation of American Negro Women as a baritone singer in a juvenile quartet, I was selected to fan Mrs Mary McCleod Bethune, the very great educator and special advisor on minority affairs to President Franklin D. Roosevelt. That really impressed me quite a bit. I was determined to keep her cool as in those days air conditioning had not yet appeared on the scene. The affair was a big dinner where Mrs Bethune was guest of honor and I kept her "cool."

As I mentioned before, Mom was what we call a "freedom fighter" from way back. Even before the civil rights movement started. The theaters in Parsons were prejudiced and black people had to sit in what we called the "crow's nest," which were seats way up in the balcony where the projector was—so far back you could hardly see the screen. Well Mom decided one day to go see a certain picture that she had been wanting to see. So she went to this theater, the Best Theater, and walked in and deliberately sat down in the seats for the white clientele. One of the ushers approached Mom and said, "You can't sit there, mam." Mom didn't even answer him so he went to the front office and came back with the manager. "Madam," he says, "you know that you can't sit there. Your seats are upstairs." Mom sat right there. Finally the manager, now quite confused, went into the street and came back with two policemen. They all tried to get Mom to move up to the crow's nest but Mom held her ground and told all of them, police included, "The only way you're going to get me out of this seat is to carry me out bodily." So they huddled around for a few seconds and finally decided it was best to let Mom alone, and she went on and enjoyed the rest of the movie.

I don't think that my parents were ever too severe with me for some things that perhaps they should have been, but then the times that I knew I was going to get a whipping were the most severe times in my life. Because of the fact that Parsons was such a quiet little town, I was always in the lead of my gang in doing everything, good or bad. In fact from the time I was ten until the time I was fifteen I did quite a few pretty bad things. My father always planted vegetables in our vacant lot next to our home and one of the vegetables would always be corn on the cob. Now I loved corn so much, and still do, that I just couldn't wait for it to fully grow and become ripe. Dad would go out to harvest his corn at the end of the season and he'd find half of the stalks stripped because I had eaten the corn before it got a chance to ripen. I'm sure he knew I did it but he never said anything to me about it.

When I was a teenager I learned to drive a model-T Ford. My Dad, among all of his other occupations, was also a masseur and used to give sweat baths and massages to local people at our home. He had installed a sweat bath cabinet, an Indian tent sweat system with certain herbs for vaporizing, and massage tables. Naturally many of his clients would drive to our home for the treatments. In Parsons at the time was another minister's son, Charles Owens. His father was Rev L. H. Owens, who was then pastor of the AME Church. They were good friends, his father and mine, and Charles and I were best of friends, but Charles was one of the worst boys to be a preacher's son that I ever saw. In comparison to him I was an angel. When Dad's customers would drive their cars to our home for Dad to give them the treatments and the baths they would leave their cars parked in front of our house. One day Charles and I decided to take one of the cars and drive it around a bit while Dad was working on the customer. We did, then later we took more and more cars and would drive them until almost all of the gas was gone and we'd get them back just a little before my Dad finished with his clients. Dad never caught on but sometimes he wondered why the customers had just enough gas to get back home after a visit to see him. That was how I learned to drive.

Sometimes on summer evenings I'd become so bored at having nothing at all to do that me and my bunch would go out and just make something happen, and at times it wouldn't be all good. Simon Long and I were the first black boy scouts in Parsons to become Eagle Scouts under the leadership of the scoutmaster Mr Van Hoose, and I was also leader of the Wolf Patrol.

When the wrestling promoters were scouting young wrestlers for the preliminary bouts at the wrestling events, Herman Higgenbotham and I were the first and the only two kids to become wrestlers. I used to admire a wrestler in Parsons—Billy Hallas, a professional Greek wrestler and one of the best. I used to go to all of his matches and root for him to win over his competitors, especially one named Dutch Mantell. While attending one of his matches one evening, a fellow came up to me and asked me if I would like to participate in one of Billy's matches on the preliminary card. I said, "Of course I would." So then he went to find an opponent for me. He chose another guy who liked to wrestle—about my age but bigger than I was. Herman Higgenbotham. At the time I weighed about seventy pounds and Higgie weighed about eighty-five, so the match was arranged. I was billed as "Clever Clayton" and Herman was billed as "Husky Higgenbotham." The night of the match my Dad went along with some of his friends to see me win, but I didn't win that night and Dad was sad for a while but he still encouraged me to continue. Dad was a sports fan and he also liked baseball. In fact he formed a baseball team, Clayton's Colts. I was too small to play on it, though. Getting back to wrestling, ol' Herman had put a "flying mare" on me and all I could remember was the theater going round and round in my head, and when he dumped me I couldn't get up. The second match was different, though, and Higgie didn't win; we wrestled to a tie and my Dad had something to brag about. Herman Higgenbotham died in Denver, Colorado, a few years back. At the time of his death he weighed about five hundred and eighty-five pounds and was known as the Denver Fat Man.

Some of the things that we did out of boredom didn't set too well with my Mom and Dad, especially as they were high in the church circles of the Brown Chapel church. Once when I was about twelve my Dad beat hell out of me for fighting, which I didn't think was quite right because he didn't even know what we were fighting about, whereas if he had only stopped to find out what it was all about he might have agreed with me. This guy, William Barclowe, had called me a son of a bitch and a few other things that my father would not have liked, but still I got my butt whipped by him for resenting these remarks. But I was in such pain from the fight that I didn't need any more punishment. My right arm, I thought, was broken because, even though I won the fight, I had been hit on my right arm with a brick as the fight was being broken up by Royter Cherry (who later became my brother-in-law) and Wesley "Snip" Cole. I don't think Dad approved of fighting in general. I was cleaning myself up to go home and look presentable and had my back turned to this guy with whom I'd been fighting, when this brick hit me and I went on home half crying from the pain and ran into my Dad, who proceeded immediately to give me another pain, one that I could have done without.

My Dad, though, as a rule, didn't like to whip me. Sometimes he would whip me halfheartedly at my mother's insistence and then take me outside and give me enough money to go buy some ice cream. One of my teachers, Mr R. F. Miller, and my Dad were the only two men to whip me. Mr Miller of course had permission to whale on me anytime that I got out of line. He had a hickory paddle that I'll never forget and when he'd say, "Mr Clayton, will you step out into the hall please?" I knew I was in for it. To the other kids in the class it was like a show as they could hear every lick that he gave me with that hickory paddle. Mr Miller had a way of grabbing you in the seat of your pants and making it tight over your butt so that it hurt more and sounded louder. The rest of the class would have a field day at my expense. Every time they would hear the paddle, "whap," they would count, "One, whap . . . two, whap . . . three . . ." and so on, until it was over.

My mother was the dangerous one. When she got ready to punish me there was no fooling around. Most of Mom's whippings came from not washing the dishes. If it was my time to do the dishes (us kids all had turns), I was supposed to have the breakfast dishes all clean and finished by the time that Mom got home from the beauty parlor at noon. Sometimes some of the kids would come by to play and dishes were forgotten for the moment. I'd be having a ball sometimes playing in our yard when out of nowhere I'd see Mom coming down the street, and too late I'd realize that I hadn't done the dishes yet. Sometimes I could see Mom turn the corner of 21st Street and Grand Avenue on her way home as she passed New Hope Baptist Church, but even then it was always too late. Mom would come home, take off her gloves and say, "I thought I told you to have those dishes washed when I got home." As usual I didn't have any kind of an excuse. Mom would say, "Go on out and get your switches 'cause you know you're going to get it." We had peach trees in our yard and the branches from a peach tree hurt more than any other kind of branch from any tree; they hit you like a knife, then they continue to wrap around you. These peach tree switches and a little psychology were Mom's favorite weapons. I'd go out in the yard and cut maybe four or five little scrawny branches and bring them in to Mom. She'd take one look and, knowing that I had deliberately brought in some weak branches, go out and cut her own and come back in the house with some of the biggest and longest branches that she could find. They looked to me like young trees. Now this is where the psychology came in. Mom would go slow in selecting the branches that she wanted, knowing all the time how I was suffering in the house watching through the window. And believe me I was suffering. When she finally finished and came back inside all hell would break loose. It seemed to me that she'd never stop, and those peach branches were cutting me like nothing else in this world. Finally she'd stop, but in this case there would be no money to go buy ice cream.

Helen Humes the vocalist once told me that she'd bet that I was spoiled and pampered because I happened to be the only boy in the family. I never thought so. My parents were not overly strict with me, neither did they pamper me. Most of the little arguments I had at home were the kid type arguments. I dared not argue with Mom nor Dad. Always with my sisters, Jean and Margery. Nearly all the time with Jean about one thing or another. Usual kid's stuff, "He hit me," or "She hit me," or "He's got the biggest piece" (of pie), or "She's got the biggest piece," etc. My Dad had a terrible temper but I never saw it come to the surface. Maybe it was because he was a deacon in the church, but he never argued with Mom. Mom had the sharp tongue. I remember just once she gave Dad hell for going on strike at the MKT railroad. Dad had walked out with the rest of the strikers and Mom couldn't see that at all. The last time Dad gave me a whipping was when I was about fourteen years old. I was beginning to feel like a man then and I kinda' resented Dad's whipping me. I thought that I had become too old for that. As usual Jean and I had gotten into an argument about a piece of strawberry shortcake: "His piece is bigger than mine." So finally this argument came to an end with my piece of shortcake, cream and all, right in Jean's face. Right away she runs to Dad with all this cream on her face and strawberries in her eyes. Dad gets mad as hell at me even though I didn't hurt her. So in anger he starts to look for something to whip me with. Usually it was a razor strop or something else, but this time he picked up an electrical extension cord, hauled me into the back room and lit into me. Well by this time, with my new-found manly feeling, I was beginning to get mad myself, so I said to myself, "I'm not going to cry this time. I don't care what he does, I'm not going to cry." Dad starts whalin' away and, though it hurt like hell, I wouldn't cry. Finally Dad noticed that I wasn't crying and he got madder and started to whip harder, and that extension cord was really getting to me. Then I noticed Dad breathing heavier and heavier and I still hadn't cried. He gave me a long look and said, "OK, I guess you're a man now." He never whipped me again, nor Mom either.

When I was about fourteen years old I was known to be a pretty good artist in school. One day some men who hung around the barbershop arranged a contest between me and another fellow, Dan Tucker, who was also a pretty good artist. They gave us both a picture of a big boat and we were to paint it in watercolors. We were given one week to do the job and then bring it back to the barbershop to be judged by these men. They gathered around the pictures and after about twenty minutes declared me the winner. I also won first prize in a contest given by the city of Parsons for making a picture for the community chest drive. I liked drawing very much and in fact I was once thinking of becoming a commercial artist, but jazz got in the way. I used to draw pictures of bands and hoped to have my own band someday.

My first athletic coach was Ben Preston, who coached me in my early track days. My first basketball coach was Thomas D. Early, who always had a winning team until we ran into that Fort Scott team. We could never beat those guys. Laddie Perry was a man that used to race against horses for a certain distance at Marvel Park. Mom was a church lady in all respects but I think she liked the horses a little bit. She used to take me to the trotters' races in Marvel Park when I was about fifteen years old and make small bets on horses owned by her friend Sam White, who was a dairy farmer—the only black dairy farmer in town who owned race horses. Sometimes I'd hear her yell, "He broke, he broke." I didn't know what she meant at first but later I learned that the horse had broken his pace and was lost to the race.

My mother, being a schoolteacher, taught me to read and write when I was four years old, and when I went to school at age six they just passed me right into the third grade because of my previous learning. I could read the comics of the *Parsons Daily Sun* at the age of four. I was learning to play piano at six and I ran about three piano teachers crazy, literally crazy. Then my mother decided for me to go to one of her friends, Mrs Mineola Walker, who became my main teacher, and she developed me into being a pretty good pianist. I took piano from the time I was six to the time I was eighteen.

Mrs Walker had a piano recital one night which featured all of her students. We had been given special piano solos to learn. Me and my two sisters practiced so hard for the concert knowing that a lot of people were going to be there. It was in the summer time and the weather was hot and the church windows were all raised for fresh air. I had practiced every day for my part of the concert but I had never practiced without the music being in front of me. The night of the concert everybody before me had played well, including my sisters, and my turn was next. I went to the piano, opened my music sheet and began playing. Just about the time I was half way through a gust of wind came through one of the windows and blew all of my music down on the floor. I got a little panicky at first but I didn't stop playing. I just let it lay there and somehow I finished the song without reading the rest of the music. My Mom and Dad saw what happened and were pretty proud of me. Mrs Walker also took a little notice of me and seemed to think that I was a little bit ahead of the others.

Of all the musicians who came from Parsons only a handful ever became known in jazz circles. Notably Sir Charles Thompson, Wild Bill Davis, Norene Tate, Clarence Taylor, Clarence Trice and myself. We had a very talented drummer, about ten years older than I, who lived in Parsons— Heywood Bryant. He was really an outstanding drummer. He left Parsons with a carnival and later became a circus musician. Sir Charles ran away from home by slipping through a window at night when his parents were asleep. He had been encouraged to leave by tenor sax man Wild Bill Moore.

My mother and father both had relatives who were in show business, though it wasn't well known. My mother was related to the famous Whitman Sisters and my father was a relative of the famous Chicago comedian Marshall "Garbage" Rogers. I always did want to run away from home after I became a certain age, but I was partially inspired by the mother of one of my best friends, Allen Jones. His mother Nettie had run away from Parsons to become a chorus girl with the Drake and Walker minstrel show after it had played in Parsons, leaving Allen, husband and everybody. She was a beautiful lady, too beautiful for Parsons I thought.

I didn't know too much about jazz even at the age of fifteen. In the theaters at home they always played records of these bands that I didn't know the names of. I found out later that Wilbur Sweatman's was one of them. One of the things that influenced me on trumpet was a jazz number. I don't recall the name of it, but years later in talking to a friend, Jimmy McPartland, I learned that he was the guy who played the trumpet solo on this record that I used to hear so much as a kid in the local theaters.

I was interested in the bands out of Kansas City: Bennie Moten, Coon Saunders, George E. Lee and quite a few others. Kansas City was a hotbed for jazz then and had many big bands. The first jazz recording that I ever heard was at an early age. It was the *Empty Bed Blues* by Bessie Smith with J. P. Johnson on piano. In my home all I ever heard was my Dad singing bass solos: *Asleep in the Deep, When you come to the end of a perfect day* and similar solos.

My two sisters Jean and Margery were never interested too much in music, although they took piano lessons. They really never did develop too much. There was a girl in Parsons, Norene Tate, who had a cousin, Lucille Holland. Both of those girls were exceptionally gifted on piano and Norene influenced me very much. I used to listen to her play when I was very young. Sometimes in school they would let Norene practice in the gymnasium for an hour, and there I was in class trying to learn geography, arithmetic, algebra, etc. I could hear Norene at the piano. I was supposed to be studying but the windows would be up and I could hear Norene in the gym. I couldn't get anything together. I couldn't study. All I could do was listen to her play. Two of the songs I remember that she used to play that I liked so much were *Hard-to-get Gertie* and *'Deed I Do*. I still like *'Deed I Do* and play it often.

Sometime later Norene joined a little combo of local musicians which included a wonderful musician. His father, Clarence Glass, Sr, was a good friend of Dad's, and Clarence Glass, Jr, was taught by his father to play saxophone and trumpet. Clarence is now superintendent in one of the Kansas City schools, I believe. That little band influenced me also. It had two other good musicians in it: Danny Shakespear on drums and Fred Henderson on banjo and guitar.

One day I read a poster that said the George E. Lee band of Kansas City was coming to Parsons and was going to play for a dance about a month from the time that I read the poster. Everybody was excited. That was the biggest band to play Parsons as far as I knew. I couldn't dance very well. I wasn't interested in dancing. We were all one hundred percent boys, you know, into football, baseball and basketball, and we had just started to like girls. There was a little girl, Sarah Bright, who lived across the street from me and, knowing that we were going to the dance, we decided to practice on how to dance two or three weeks before the band got there, so we could dance a little bit at least. We practiced for days, one-step, two-step, waltzes and all the dances of those days. Hour upon hour. Finally the big day came.

George E. Lee rolled into town in a fleet of beautiful automobiles. Cords, I believe, were the names of the cars.

We all went to the dance and as soon as I entered the hall I saw all of those beautiful instruments standing on the bandstand and I flipped. In the band was a saxophonist, Clarence Taylor, known professionally as Tweety Taylor, whose father and family had lived in Parsons. There was also Baby Lovett on drums, Herman Walder on alto sax, George Lee and his sister Julia. The rest of the band I didn't know. I stood in front of this band and watched them as they began to tune up. I became rooted right to the spot. I didn't see anybody as all I could see was the band. I didn't know what people behind me were doing and cared less. I didn't dance one single dance during the whole four hours that the band played. I didn't even see the little girl, Sarah, that had spent so much time learning to dance with me. All I could see were trumpets, saxophones, trombones and all the other instruments while listening to this beautiful jazz music. When the band left town Sarah didn't speak to me for weeks because I had sabotaged all of her dancing plans, aside from it being very embarrassing to her. Some of the songs that George sang that night I still remember, although it was my first time hearing them. He sang *Chloe, If I could be with you, Eleven-thirty Saturday Night* and *Mississippi Mud*. He looked so sharp in his Oxford-gray coat, pearl-gray vest and gamble stripe pants. When he sang he snapped his fingers. He had a beautiful voice, a strong voice, that could fill up the hall without a microphone. He used a megaphone. He was really sharp.

During the dance, however, I talked with one of the trumpet players in the band, Bob Russell. He was one cool cat and so sharp. He had four or five different kinds of horns in front of him. He took me under his wing a little bit and told me how much money they made, what nice times they had, and how he enjoyed playing. He had just joined George's band and was a well-known trumpeter among the "territory bands," as they were called. The territory bands were mostly southern and midwestern bands that were nearly always on the road. I think Bob later moved out to Seattle or Oregon.

After talking to Bob I said to myself, "This is it! I'm going to get a trumpet." I'd not yet heard of Louis Armstrong nor Duke Ellington. My Dad wanted me to get a trumpet too because he wanted me to play in his church orchestra, which I couldn't do playing piano. I couldn't join my high-school band because I only played piano. I finally bought a trumpet and I was so happy with it. With a trumpet you can carry it with you, take it to bed with you if you feel like it, polish it, keep it clean and tune it up, whereas with a piano you can't tune it yourself unless you happen to be a piano tuner. Sometimes you play on a piano that can cut all of your fingers up because the ivory on the keyboard is broken and jagged. With a trumpet you can take it out on a field and play it out there all by yourself. So I got the trumpet and, boy, was I happy. The first song I learned to play was *Five Foot Two, Eyes of Blue*.

I began practicing with my Dad, who taught me the scales. There was another kid in Parsons who had been playing a few years and also played with my Dad's chapel orchestra—Clarence Trice. Between Clarence and my father I learned all of the scales on the trumpet. Clarence later played with big Kansas City bands, notably Andy Kirk's great band. By having played piano I could already read music. That was no problem. I just had to learn the fingering to the trumpet. I practiced and practiced while all the time doing other little jobs around town. I set pins in a bowling alley for an Italian guy, John Delesega. I shined shoes, I sold papers.

About the time I was seventeen a band came through my home from Cherryvale, Kansas: Hoot and Stomp Bailey's band was nothing like George E. Lee's band as there were only about seven musicians. They had one trumpet player and he had taken ill that night and couldn't play. They asked all over town, "Do you know anybody that can play trumpet tonight in our trumpet player's place?" Naturally everybody said, "Yeah, get that little Clayton boy. He's learning to play cornet." So they hired me as there was no one else around that could play anything at all. All night long we played four songs because that was all that I knew: *Five Foot Two, Eyes of Blue, Hard-to-get Gertie, 'Deed I Do* and *Dinah*. We played these four songs over and over again, but just the same I made five dollars for that gig. It was the first time that I had ever made any money playing trumpet in my life.

When I was much younger I used to play little jobs on the piano for house parties and I'd make three or four dollars. Later I formed a little band in which nobody could play a real instrument but me on the piano. There were two little guys playing tissue paper over combs. They would hum and buzz the songs while I played them on piano, with another little cat playing on a snare drum. That was our band and I was the leader. Later we strengthened the rhythm section by adding a ukulele.

I used to watch the bands come through my home town on the way from Texas and Oklahoma up to Kansas City, and I met many more musicians. Count Basie played through my home town but nobody in Parsons knew who he was then. Just another piano player in a traveling band, probably Gonzelle White's band. I went to Forest Park one night and listened to a band that I thought was great. I found out years later that the trumpet player in that band was Joe Keyes, the same Joe Keyes that was first trumpet player in Count Basie's band when I joined them in Kansas City years later. I admired that little band a lot and especially their arrangements. That was the first time I ever thought of arranging music. I couldn't understand how anyone could write for an instrument without being able to play that instrument. How one could write for a saxophone or trumpet or trombone and then put them all together and make it sound like one big instrument. I already knew all of the chords and changes on piano but I didn't start writing until later when I was in California.

One evening, when radios had just come out and were quite popular, about 6.30 or seven o'clock, I was walking down Belmont Avenue in Parsons and I heard some jazz music coming out of a lady's house. She had her windows up and I could hear a jazz band playing. I stopped right in my tracks and started listening to this band. I didn't move. I was just frozen there as long as that band played. It was the Coon Saunders band broadcasting from the Mulbach Hotel in Kansas City. What I didn't know was that there had been some prowlers in this same neighborhood where I was listening to the music. Pretty soon, after listening to several numbers, I looked down the street and saw a police car full of police. They all jumped out and started running towards me. I thought, "What the hell is this?" I temporarily forgot about the music when I saw these cops coming and thought to myself, "Well, I'd better get out of here." So I started to run. There was one old cop that I especially didn't like, and he didn't care too much for us kids. We called him Peek-a-Boo and we'd had trouble with him before. I was leaving him far behind as they chased me because I was on the track team at the time and was pretty fast. I ran over to Main Street and was running west on Main Street. I knew he was behind me, but I was leaving him so fast that I would have gotten rid of him in a couple of minutes more. As I was running on Main Street, of all the people in Parsons, I ran head on into my father. He had just taken my mother to a Parent-Teachers Association meeting and was on his way home when he spied me running like hell down the street. "What's the matter, son?" he asked me, "where are you going?"

I said, "Pop, I gotta meet somebody and I ain't got time to talk right now."

He said, "Now wait a minute. Why are you running so fast? Just look at you, all out of breath."

I said, "Dad, I tell you I'm late. I'm supposed to be somewhere and I'm late already." As I was standing there arguing with my Dad, up comes Peek-a-Boo and grabs me right in the collar, right in front of my Dad. Poor Dad almost had a heart attack, being a minister. He really didn't know yet what was happening. I still hadn't told him when Peek-a-Boo says, "I got ya!" They put me in a car and took me down to jail and my father naturally went with me. As it turned out they found out that I wasn't a prowler, but I still had to stay in jail for about a half an hour while I was trying to explain that I was only listening to that music coming out of this lady's window. So Tom Coulter, the local jailer, let me out after they found out that I was from a respectful family and was an Eagle Scout in the boy scout troop.

Even later, when I saw Pee Wee Erwin, I told him that he was one of the reasons that I was put in jail in front of my father, because I know that he used to play with Coon Saunders when he was a kid. I'm not sure that he was with the band at that time, but I told him the story and blamed him jokingly just the same.

I had two buddies, Jack Medlock and Simon "Paye" Long. They were wonderful athletes. Best athletes in town in anything you wanted to play, football, basketball, track meet, swimming. They couldn't run faster, though, than Royter Cherry as Royter was as fast as a greyhound when it came to racing. Jack and Simon wanted to play some kind of instrument because I was playing one. Simon could play a little piano, Jack couldn't play anything. One day Jack hustled up enough money to buy a used E-flat alto saxophone and I taught him how to play one song, *Song of the Wanderer*. Jack practiced this song and I'd practice it with him. After a few weeks he got up enough nerve to play this song in church as an alto solo, and the only reason he did that was because there were a lot of pretty little girls in this church, New Hope Baptist Church. He played it alright and was pretty happy with himself. Simon's father offered him a suit of clothes or a saxophone as a Christmas present, and he chose the suit of clothes. He never got another chance to get a saxophone so he never learned to play anything else aside from the piano. Jack never learned anything else either.

My greatest buddy on saxophone was Schifford Garner. Schiff and I really started exactly together. We were about the same age, went to the same school, graduated together, and both played in a little band in Parsons called Mouse and his Music. Mouse was a violin player whose real name was Raymond Jones. He had played in Kansas City at the Eblon Theater with many big names, but had come back to Parsons to live. I don't know why, as he was a good violinist. Schifford and I were about the best in the Mouse and his Music band except for Mouse himself. One day Schiff and myself got an offer to go to Bella Vista, Arkansas. We thought, "That's great! We're going to make ten dollars." At that time when we went to school with ten dollars in our pockets we were big shots. This was just a little bit before the Depression, in 1929, and ten dollars meant quite a bit. So we drove down to Bella Vista in a car and when we got there we were hungry. We went to a restaurant, a white restaurant, and sat down, and some old lady yelled at us, "Hey, you can't sit in here. Get out of here and go in the back yard." We went out in the back yard and there were old hound dogs laying all around on the ground. They put up a plank on top of two big oil-drum cans for us to eat on, which we didn't do because we were getting pretty mad ourselves. We could hear other local people imitating crows at us, "Caw! Caw! Caw!" That turned us off of Arkansas. Arkansas was a pretty mean state in those days. There were no civil rights and black people were still being lynched.

Finally the manager, the fellow who hired us, came over and picked us up in his car, as he knew the prejudice was there. He took us to this cave where we were to play. It was a cavern way deep down in the mountains that in earlier days had been used as a hide-out for Jesse James and his gang. It was about one hundred and fifty feet below ground, right down in the mountains. You had to go down winding stairs, right through the rock and everything, to get to where the dance hall had been built. We went down and very soon the place filled up with real Ozark hillbillies. They started dancing and also started drinking Ozark moonshine. After about two and a half hours they started getting drunk, whoopin' and hollerin'! Then they started unscrewing the light bulbs and smashing them up against the rock walls just to hear them break and burst. Finally it got to the point where one little redneck jerk came over to me and said, "Hey, boy, what time is it?" He saw that I was wearing a wristwatch. I didn't answer him because I'm salty anyway by this time, and when he called me "boy" I really was hot. I just clammed up because we were way down there and there was no way we could get out. There were about five hundred of them in the hall, so I just didn't answer. Then he got mad because I didn't answer him. He said, "God dammit, if you don't tell me what time it is, I'll go get my brother and we'll beat hell out of you." The manager of the place saw what was happening and came up and pulled this guy away before anything happened, because the whole place could have blown right up and me with it. He made this guy go out, made him go upstairs outdoors to cool off, and when he did that all the guy's buddies got mad. About this time, fortunately, there was only about twenty more minutes to play, so the manager asked us to play *Home, Sweet Home* as the closing number of the evening. We played the last number and they all went up topside. The manager followed them upstairs and when he came back down he said, "Fellows, I'm sorry but you can't leave right now. You'll have to stay down here for a couple of hours because they're waiting for you to come out." So we waited. We waited for about an hour and he went up to check again. He would check about every half hour and there would still be a few of them hanging around the entrance to the cave. Finally he made a check and the last of them had gone home and we could come out of that place safely. Schifford and I said goodbye to the other local guys that we had been playing with and wasted no time in getting back to Parsons. We both said, "To hell with Bella Vista, Arkansas. You can have it."

By this time I was getting kinda sick of Parsons because there was nothing to do. Nothing exciting ever happened. The only thing we could do was to go down to the railroad station about eight thirty in the evening and watch the trains come through, because sometimes there would be some pretty little girls on the train going from Texas or Tulsa, Oklahoma, to Kansas City, and they had to stop in our town for about twenty minutes. Sometimes we'd talk to these little girls if they'd talk out of the car windows. We'd get their addresses and sometimes write them down. That's about all there was to do, just go down and look for girls on these trains. That was the biggest thing to do in Parsons. No baseball games except the ones we played ourselves, and at that time there were no televisions, so I was beginning to get fed up.

I had a friend, Theodore Booker, that had moved out to Los Angeles and he used to write back to me and tell me how beautiful Los Angeles was. This was around 1928 or 1929 and it really was beautiful then. No smog at that time. I began to get the urge to go to California and I convinced Jack, the one who was trying to play saxophone, to go with me as he too was getting kinda bored with Parsons. We couldn't think of a way to go without upsetting our families. We never had any money so our plan was to tell everybody that we were going to run off and go to Los Angeles, but really not go at that time. We'd say that we were going the next week and then we wouldn't go that week. We'd put it off for a month and then we wouldn't go again. We did that for about a year until nobody believed us. Finally one day we said, "Well, goodbye, we're leaving. We are going to catch a freight train and go to California."

They would say, "Aw, shut up, Buck. You've been saying all that crap before. You'll be here till you're eighty years old." Finally Jack and I really did decide to go. Naturally I told my mother, but she didn't take me seriously as I told her that we were leaving.

One night soon after I met Jack at 11.30 at his house, and we went to the Santa Fe railroad and caught a train going west to Wichita, Kansas. Then from Wichita we caught another train going straight out to California. I think I had about seven dollars. Jack didn't have a penny, but he knew that as long as I had something he had something. We rode on going west until we got to La Junta, Colorado, where we got off the train to get something to eat. We knew that we were going to catch the same train again after it had taken on some water. We went into a bakery and bought a couple of pies, a can of baked beans, some pickles and candy. The usual hobo menu. We went back to catch the train and we got on and were riding about an hour when we saw another old hobo on the train. Trains were full of hobos in those days. Sometimes they would talk to us, and they didn't know nor care where they were going. We knew that we wanted to go to Los Angeles, but some of those guys would just get on a train and go anywhere. Old men that just ride. They don't care where they're going nor where they've been. They asked Jack and me where we were going and we told them, Los Angeles. One guy says, "Well, what the hell are you doing on this train?"

We said, "We're going west."

He says, "The hell you are. This train is going south." We had made a mistake and caught the wrong train out of La Junta. So Jack says to me, "Look, we'd better get off here at the next stop." But by this time we had crossed the Texas border line. We decided to get off of this train and catch another one back to La Junta and get the right train going on out to California.

OK. We jumped off of the train as it slowed down in a little town somewhere in Texas, and had to wait about three hours before there would be another train back to La Junta. So Jack and I waited on the outskirts of this town, laying under some trees, waiting for the next train going north again to La Junta, when a big car-load of big fat red-faced detectives and police drove up to us. The first thing they said was, "Ah ha, you're them two niggers that raped that white woman over in such-and-such a county day before yesterday."

I thought, "Oh shit, here we go."

They repeated, "Yes, you're the same two niggers." So they threw us in a car and took us to some little town. I never did find out the name of it, didn't really want to know. This was about seven o'clock in the evening. They took us to the railroad station, downstairs in the basement. About nine of these guys followed us to the bottom of the station. They formed a circle, then they all picked up those big flags that trainmen use to flag down trains. They rolled them up until they were like clubs and they made Jack and me get in the middle of the circle. They told us to dance and threatened to hit us across the head if we didn't. "Buck dance" they called it. Jack and I started dancing the best as we knew how and then Jack started crying. I'll never forget that. He's a great big old cat, a football player and everything, crying like he was sure that they were going to shoot us. When they asked us where we were going we said, "We're trying to get to California."

They said, "Oh no, don't give us that." They never did hit us but they had these clubs and we did everything that they said. So we danced and we danced, and about two o'clock in the morning they stopped molesting us. They all went outdoors except a couple, and these two took us up to the top of this broken down railroad station and showed us a road. They said, "Now hit the road. Get the hell out of here."

We said to ourselves, "Oh well, we're free anyway." So we started walking. It was dark. We walked down the road and in about ten minutes we were completely out of the town and found ourselves on a lonely country road. We still planned to return to this town and catch another freight back to La Junta, so we walked and walked.

After about ten more minutes Jack turned around and said, "Buck, look at this." I looked back and saw about five cars that had been following us. We knew that these cars were full of these big rednecked Texas guys that were supposed to be police. All we could see were their headlights. Suddenly I felt a cold chill. We were really afraid but we continued to walk and the cars continued to follow us. I said to Jack, "We're in a hell of a fix. Here we are on a dark lonely road, we don't even know where. It's about three o'clock in the morning somewhere in Texas and there's five cars following us."

He said, "Yeah, I know. But what can we do to get out of this mess?"

I said, "I don't know. Because if we keep walking we're going to be in still another territory where we aren't known." The small towns in any southern state then were the worst ones. We couldn't stop, though, nor start running, because that would have given these guys a reason to swoop down on us. So we walked and thought, "How in hell are we going to get out of this?" The lights continued to follow us about half of a mile behind. We just knew what was going to happen. They were just waiting until we got far enough out of town.

Suddenly the cars stopped. We continued to walk and look back. For some reason which I'll never know they stopped for about five minutes. Then they all turned around and went back in the direction of the town. My belief is that someone in that group, probably one of the leaders, convinced them not to go through with what they had planned. I'm sure they wouldn't have followed us seven miles out in the country for nothing, especially at three o'clock in the morning. We breathed a big sigh of relief and said, "Thank God." Still, the only way we could get back to La Junta would be to wait for the next train leaving that small town, so we waited about an hour and then we sneaked back into this same town and caught the next train to La Junta. God knows what would have happened to us if we had been caught again by those same people. However, we found ourselves at last on our way back to La Junta.

There was one more perilous situation that we found ourselves in where we might have disappeared and no one would have known what happened to us. We had caught a train and the car we caught had been a vegetable car; it still smelled like celery. We were way up in the Rockies and it was getting terribly cold. We knew that in vegetable cars there is an ice compartment to keep the vegetables cold while being shipped, and as this car was empty we planned to use this little compartment to sleep in and at the same time to keep warm. So we slid down into the compartment and said, "We'll sleep here in this car and tomorrow, who knows, we may just wake up and be in California." So we went to sleep.

We slept all night. When we woke up the car wasn't moving. It was dark in the compartment and we couldn't see our hands before our eyes. We wondered why we were not moving. We thought that the train had stopped to refuel or something. So we decided to open the door and peep out and see where we were, if we were in a city or something like that. We pushed up on the door and it wouldn't open. We pushed and we pushed, but the door just wouldn't open. We both tried. We pushed together and it wouldn't open, so then we got panicky. We started pounding on the walls of the car. We pounded and beat on the walls with our fists and feet hoping that someone would hear the pounding and investigate.

After beating on the walls for about four hours we just gave up, and just as we stopped beating and kicking we heard someone on top of the car. It was a little Mexican fellow that just happened to be walking down the tracks and heard our kicking and beating coming from the car. Knowing that someone was in there, he climbed up on top of the car and found that someone had locked the car with a steel wire. He broke the lock and looked down in there and saw us. We were overjoyed at seeing him peering down at us. We found out later from one of the yard men that that certain car had been sidetracked. It had been put on another track and was not to have been used for three months. If this little Mexican guy hadn't came along at the right moment, we would have been trapped in that car for three months and nobody would have known what happened to us until they looked down in there and saw what remained of Jack and myself. Very few people fool around with those cars that are temporarily out of use, but we thanked God for that little Mexican fellow who just happened to be there.

Sometimes Jack and I would catch a train where the only cars we could catch were boxcars, where the doors were locked and we couldn't get inside. So we would have to run on top of these boxcars, maybe twelve or fifteen of them, to find one coal car in which we could sleep. At times the smoke from the engine would lay so close to the tops of the boxcars that it would come directly in our faces and we were hardly able to see. We were lucky that we didn't make a mis-step and fall off. So when we would find one of these coal cars we'd go to sleep in it along with all the coal dust and grime, but at least we were warm. We still had to contend with those railroad bulls—the guys who kick tramps off of the trains, sometimes breaking their arms and legs, even killing them occasionally. They would throw you right off the top of a speeding train sometimes. I guess there must have been some with a little pity, but I sure as hell never saw any. We were chased by these bulls with dogs in Flagstaff, Arizona, but we happened to be on the ground at the time and we caught another train. Before the bulls and the dogs could get to us we were long gone. After we crossed the Rocky Mountains we could tell we were getting into California by the scenery and the smell of orange groves.

Everything began to get beautiful and after a few more hours we were in California. It had taken us six days to make that trip by freight train, and we both felt like kissing the ground as the old freight finally rolled into the Los Angeles rail yards. I made an oath when we stepped on the ground. I swore that I'd never again in my life ride another freight train for anything in the world. My face was so full of coal dust, soot and grime, that it took me about three weeks before I could get it clean again.

TWO

Los Angeles and the West Coast

The first thing that we did on arriving in Los Angeles was to look up Charlie Long, the brother of Simon Long in Parsons. He was a very prominent prizefighter then and he remembered us from his visits to Parsons. After looking for hours in Los Angeles we finally found him and we were all glad to see each other. He got us a room in the Orange Blossom Hotel on Central Avenue. He paid our rent for four weeks and then he got us a job working in a pool hall. Our hotel room was directly over the pool hall. This pool hall job was just a temporary job, and since our rent was paid for four weeks we went on out to look for other and better jobs. I didn't have my trumpet as I had left that at home: I sure couldn't hobo with a trumpet in my hand. So we looked for other jobs.

I found a job in a barbershop that was a little bit better than the pool hall. The boss of the barbershop had a nephew that had just arrived in Los Angeles and he wanted the job too, but since the boss had hired me first I got the job. About the same time I had met some young fellows about my age that wanted to be musicians—Ellihue Watson, Luke Jones and Oscar Bradley. Ellihue went by the name of Duke Ellihue. I guess he wanted his name to sound like Duke Ellington, who was just beginning to become popular in Los Angeles. Then he was also the leader of the group. A trumpet player, Luke Jones, was the alto sax man, and Oscar Bradley was the drummer.

One night after finishing work at the barbershop I went to a park where all the young kids used to go, and I was tinkling on the piano amusing myself. These little guys heard me and thought that I was a pretty nice piano player. Then I told them that I played trumpet but I didn't tell that I was a good trumpet player. I just left them guessing about that. However, Ellihue asked me if I could come by their rehearsal the following night at eight o'clock and naturally I said I'd be glad to. At the barbershop the day ended at eight o'clock and I was supposed to mop the floor after closing time. Now this night that they had asked me to come to their rehearsal was the night that I was supposed to do my customary mopping job, and all that day I tried to think of a way to get out of it. If I had mopped after eight o'clock I would have been late for my first rehearsal date with this little band and I sure didn't want that, so after thinking a long time about it I decided that I just wouldn't mop that night. I thought, "Maybe if I sweep it up real good the boss won't notice the difference." So I didn't mop. I swept it so clean that to me, at least, it looked like it had been mopped, but I guess it didn't look that way to the boss. The next morning after our rehearsal I showed up at the barbershop as usual and the boss says to me, "You're fired."

I asked, "Why?"

He said, "Now you know that you didn't mop the floor last night, did you?"

I said, "Well, no, I didn't."

He then said, "Well that's why you're fired." Before I could even get my gear out of the shop his nephew showed up and was on the job, which I believe is what he wanted all the time. So now I was out of a job and I still couldn't play trumpet well enough to earn a living at it.

One day after losing my job I met two brothers who were near my age and who had two more brothers a little older: the Willis brothers, Sentel, Val, William and Horace. They asked us if we would like to live with them at their home in Boyle Heights, a suburb of Los Angeles. Since I was out of a job and Jack didn't have one yet we said we'd be happy to, since our rent at the Orange Blossom Hotel was still going on and we could save money by living with the Willises. So we moved out to Boyle Heights. Mrs Willis was a real Christian woman and she took Jack and me in just as if we were her own sons. She let us have an apartment in the basement of her home and it was pretty neat. Our rent was only three dollars a week, which was quite a reduction from the Orange Blossom Hotel, so we moved in, bag and baggage.

The young musicians, however, didn't forget me and they got me a trumpet from somewhere so that I could practice while I was looking for another job. I thought that was so nice when Ellihue gave me the trumpet; he didn't really have to do it as he was the trumpet man himself. I accepted the trumpet and immediately started to practice on it. I was also looking for other jobs but found it kinda rough. It seemed that we went daily to every unemployment office in town with no good results. It was so tough there for a while that at paying three dollars a week rent I got twenty-seven dollars behind. However, I continued to practice and Jack and I continued to look for jobs.

We finally got a job in a garage greasing cars with a grease gun. I didn't know anything about greasing cars. Neither did Jack, but we took the job anyway. I'd go to work in the morning and Jack would come on in the evening. This went pretty well for about four days. One morning I showed up for work and I was met with those drastic words again, "You're fired."

I said, "Now what?" I found out that during the night Jack had accidentally shot grease all over one of the patrons and had ruined his new suit besides shooting grease all over the inside of his car, so we were both fired. In a few days, though, I was back working in another pool hall. The pool hall was owned by Mr Watson Burns in partnership with Mr Jim Akers, who owned a restaurant almost side by side on 12th Street and Central Avenue. I first started washing dishes in the restaurant but I didn't like that, washing dishes, peeling potatoes, making the salads and all that jazz, so I jumped at the chance when Mr Akers asked me if I would rather work in the pool hall. I found out later that the pool hall was the worst of the two. I was to receive fifteen dollars a week and my first duty after coming to work was to feed a pack of dogs. Mr Burns was a dog lover and had many pedigree dogs. I had to feed them all about six in the morning. Then, after feeding the dogs, I had to clean twenty-one full-sized pool tables. You had to brush the tables with a stiff brush in both hands and it really took quite a time to clean up all of the chalk marks made on the tables by the cats that were shooting pool. It was also pretty tiring. Next I had to clean twenty-one spittoons and that was the worst job of all. What a nasty job that was. Ughh. Those damn spittoons were always filled with tobacco juice and everything else that turned my stomach. Boy, was that nasty! Then the rest of the day I had to rack balls for the players who shot pool all day. My buddy who racked balls with me was a guy named Melvin. Melvin had been around and was one pretty tough cat that seemed to have been born and lived all his life in the street. He had consumption so I never would get too close to him, although I liked him. He was a nice cat and showed me a lot of things that I didn't know about working in a pool hall. He showed me how to break someone's neck by using karate, even how to do it with a common belt. He also told me one day that if I ever wanted to leave a big scar on someone's face after cutting him, to rub garlic on the blade of my knife. Of course that part didn't interest me one bit as I didn't have any intentions of cutting somebody with a knife, although I always carried one for protection. I was always allergic to knives, guns and razors. On Saturday nights, though, Melvin and I had to wear hatchets in our belts to break up fights. That was part of our jobs too. I was still about eighteen or nineteen years old and pretty athletic and I had to break up fights with these big old rough guys, some drunk or sore losers. Anyway, we had to break them up whenever they started. I never did chop anybody with the hatchet but sometimes I was tempted to. Pretty soon all of these same characters began to really know me and they came to like me, but I still carried my hatchet on Saturday nights as a deterrent. They'd think twice about starting a fight just seeing the hatchets that Melvin and I carried.

It was while working in this pool hall that I began to think of going back to Parsons and finishing my senior year in high school. I had always planned to go back to Parsons and graduate from high, but I had planned even then to return to Los Angeles afterwards and re-open my career as a jazz musician. I began saving my money and by the time September came along I had my bus fare and was ready to go. I had swore that I'd never again in life ride another freight train. So I went home and said goodbye to all of the Willises and caught the Greyhound bus to Kansas. When I got on the bus in Los Angeles I was alone as Jack hadn't yet saved up enough to get back home. He was saving his money by working in another pool hall across the street from the Dunbar Hotel, which was in a better part of town than where I'd been working.

When I got on the bus everything was peaches and pie. Everybody was so friendly. I got a nice seat near the front and I quickly became friends with two little white boys about my age. We laughed and talked for quite a few miles after leaving Los Angeles, but I found later that my ticket to Kansas was through a southern route that took me down into Texas, then up to Oklahoma and then on into Kansas. So as I said, these little kids were so friendly at first, but I noticed that the farther we got down in the southern part of the country, their attitude started changing, little by little. They became less and less friendly and when I had to go take a seat in the back of the bus when we got to the state of Texas, they became almost hostile. One day, seeing that I had a trumpet (which they had already seen as far back as Los Angeles), one of them hollered at me and said, "Hey, play us a tune on your trumpet." I answered him by saying that I couldn't play on the bus because we were like to hit a bump or something and it might hurt my lip. Then a few miles later he said, "Listen, you're down here in Will Rogers country now, and if you don't play that trumpet we'll tie you to this bus and drag you behind it." That made me mad and I told him to go to hell. I didn't say it loudly, but as soon as I did say it a big old bastard way up in the front seat jumped up and screamed, "Hey, God dammit, there's women on this bus." So I didn't say any more. Then this little kid, who considered himself insulted by me for having told him to go to hell, said, "I ain't never took that off of a nigger before and I ain't going to take it again." The bus got real quiet. I didn't say anything, but boy I was fuming. I don't know what might have happened if we had not drove up into a Greyhound station at that time to pick up new passengers. That was the stop where I was to get off of the bus and catch a train going the rest of the way to Parsons. I was hot as hell under the collar about the whole business, and when I got out of the back of the bus I slammed the door so hard that all the glass in the door shattered. Right away here comes another redneck station policeman and wanted to put me in jail. He had to have a complaint from the bus driver, however, before he could do that, so he asked the bus driver to sign a complaint. But the bus driver was a real nice guy and told him that as long as I didn't get cut by the glass there was nothing else to worry about. The bus company would pay for the glass so he had to let me go. I'm really hot by then, so I picked up my baggage and stalked into the train station and I hear this damn cop yelling again at me. He says, "Get the hell out of here. Can't you read?" I looked up and saw a sign that said "FOR WHITES ONLY." I thought, "For God's sake, please hurry and get me back to Kansas." Finally, after waiting a little while, the train for Kansas came and I got on it and I was almost as glad to get on it as I was to get out of that small town in Texas.

My mother, father, and two sisters were all so happy that I had returned home. In fact the whole town seemed to be happy to see me again. My mother was particularly glad to see me because she never did know for sure if the reason that I had ran off was because I felt that I had been mistreated in some way at home; she was more concerned that her friends may have thought I left for that same reason. After assuring her and all of my neighbors that I ran away simply because I wanted to go to California, she felt so much better. I always considered my family to be one of the best a guy could ever have, and all the time I was in California I never knew that Mom even thought that I may have left home from being mistreated.

After the big greeting at the railroad station we all piled into a friend's car and we drove home to 2313 Grand Avenue, where we found still more wellwishers and friends waiting. We had a party which lasted until about three o'clock in the morning, which is pretty late for a party in Parsons. Everybody had a swingin' time. I kinda missed Jack not being there with me, but he was still in Los Angeles saving up his fare home by bus as I had done.

The next day I walked around town and nothing seemed to have changed, except there were more little pretty girls there than when I left. All of the guys were exactly the same and still doing the same jobs. When I saw them it was hard for me to realize that I had been over fifteen hundred miles away and had come back to find them doing exactly the same things that they were doing before I left. It was as if the world had stopped for them, or rather time had stopped. Shoeshiners were still shining shoes even in the same shoeshine parlors; window washers were still washing the same windows in the same stores; and railroad workers were still working on the railroad.

When school started shortly after I was glad to get back into it. I had told my stories over and over again about our experiences on the road. You might have thought that I had really done something big the way I was treated by everybody, but I really hadn't done anything except work in garages and pool halls and wash dishes. My enthusiasm for jazz hadn't been changed, though, not one bit. I soon was diggin' all of the bands that I could. There was more bands now in Kansas City than before, and every weekend I'd buy a three-day excursion ticket and go up and listen to the bands at the Paseo Dancing Academy: George E. Lee, Jap Allen, Andy Kirk, Thamon Hayes and many more. I'd always have to be back, though, by Sunday night in order to make school Monday morning. I used to listen to Lips Page when he'd be playing in the Yellow Front.

I studied pretty hard in school for the whole nine months. I found myself back on the basketball team too, but I never played like Paye Long or Jack, nor Kado Cullem who was a great guard. And I was on the track team. So the year passed pretty quick for me and soon it was time to graduate. My graduating class was with friends that I had known all of my life, except for a few that had come to Parsons from some other city. Mom and Dad naturally were proud when I accepted my diploma.

Just as soon as school was out I started planning to go back to Los Angeles. Jack, by the way, had returned to Parsons about three months after I had started back to school. He looked good and sported a very pretty sweater from California which was the talk of the town. I had to find a job to get back to California as I couldn't make any money while I was in school, not enough to buy a bus ticket anyway. I had a cousin, Lucille Kerford, who had married the owner of a rock quarry in Atchison, Kansas, and she had asked me if I would like to come to Atchison and work until I had enough money to get back to LA. I told her that I'd be very glad to, so she told her husband,

Lloyd Kerford, and he talked it over with his brothers, George and Clarence. They all accepted me, even though I had never worked in a rock quarry before and didn't know a damn thing about it. I packed my little cardboard suitcase and lit out for Atchison. This time I took my trumpet, because I had been writing to my little young friends in Los Angeles and I was sure of working with them at least one day a week. So I arrived in Atchison and went to work at the quarry, and they really put me through the mill when they saw that I knew absolutely nothing about rock quarries. They played all the tricks on me that they play on people who don't know anything about quarries when they first arrive. One day the foreman sent me about three miles to pick up a left-handed monkey wrench. When I got there I was told that someone else had borrowed it, and I had to walk about three more miles to get there. At sundown I was still looking for that left-handed monkey wrench. Finally some kind soul took me aside and told me that there was no such thing as a left-handed monkey wrench. Even at that I still didn't dig a lot of things. They repeated the same trick on me a few days later, only this time I was sent out to find a can of striped paint and I fell for it again. However, the job was nice and I enjoyed it. It was the hardest work that I'd done since I laid track in Parsons years before on the MKT railroad line. In the rock quarry it was mostly blasting rock with dynamite and then breaking up the large boulders into smaller ones so that they could be shipped to various parts of the country. Finally, when I had enough loot to get my ticket on the Greyhound bus, I said goodbye to my cousin, her husband Lloyd and all of the guys that I had worked with. They wished me the best of luck and off I went to Los Angeles.

Nothing happened on the bus trip, except I saw quite a few sights that I hadn't been able to see when I was riding the rods: Indians selling beads and trinkets on the highways, cowboys, Mexicans selling tamales and other things like that. Finally we pulled into Los Angeles near 5th Street and, as I got off the bus and had walked about fifteen feet, my cardboard suitcase split right down the middle and all of my clothes, toothpaste, soap and everything fell out on to the street right in the middle of the traffic. I was so embarrassed. I had to pick everything up and put them back in the suitcase, but I couldn't close it. I had to walk for blocks carrying that damn suitcase in my arms like a baby. I registered at a little cheap hotel on 5th Street and immediately started calling all of my young musician friends. They were glad to know that I had returned, and it wasn't long before I checked out of that hotel and went to live with another young musician, Ronald Wharton, whose mother let me have a small apartment in her home on 43rd Street, near Central Avenue.

Mr and Mrs Wharton, Ronald's parents, were two of the nicest people that I ever met. I guess Mrs Wharton looked on me as a son like Mrs Willis had done when I was living in Boyle Heights. I seemed to be lucky like that. There were two girls that lived upstairs also, Faye Tillman and another girl named Thelma. Sometimes the upstairs apartments would be swingin', but Mrs Wharton never complained about the noise that was going on right over her head. Ronald was a banjo player that was just beginning to learn guitar.

I would rehearse two or three times a week with Luke Jones and Oscar Bradley. I don't know what had become of Ellihue but he was no longer around. Just Luke, Oscar, and some more fellows that I didn't know when I was there the year before. We were playing about one or two gigs a week —sometimes three. But anyway, I was making enough to pay my rent at least. Mrs Wharton's home was just about three blocks from the Dunbar Hotel, which was the center of entertainment life in Los Angeles. Every day I would just walk down to the Dunbar and look at different people, actors, musicians, and it was during this time that I first laid eyes on the great Louis Armstrong. I still hadn't realized just how great he was, as I still hadn't heard any of his early recordings that seemed to be known by every trumpet player but me. *Cornet Chop Suey, Heebie Jeebies, Potato Head Blues, Mahogany Hall Stomp*—I hadn't heard even one of these recordings. But I used to run around with another young trumpet man, Allie Grant. Allie, it seemed, knew every solo that Louie had ever made and he would sing Pop's solos to me. I guess if people ever saw us—Allie singing to me and gesturing with his hands, and me listening—standing on a street corner all by ourselves, they might have thought that we were two pretty nutty musicians.

When I saw Pops for the first time he was going to a rehearsal at Frank Sebastian's Cotton Club in Culver City. He had just come out of the hotel and he looked awfully sharp. His hair looked nice and shiny and he had on a pretty gray suit. He wore a tie that looked like an ascot tie with an extra-big knot in it. Pops was the first one to bring that style of knot to Los Angeles. Soon all the hip cats were wearing big knots in their ties. We called them Louie Armstrong knots. I only saw him for a few minutes but he sure impressed me just by his appearance. He got into a little old model-T Ford with Stuff Crouch, who was his right-hand man, and drove off to the Cotton Club. He was playing there as star soloist with the Leon Herriford band with the Caroline Snowden Revue.

Luke, Oscar and myself continued to rehearse with new enthusiasm every day after seeing all of these big-time people, and we would imagine that we were big-time too. We'd go on out to our little one or two jobs a week, and try to act like we were big-time musicians just off of Broadway and from New York City . . . such dreamers. We would play mostly for parties or for recreation centers and sometimes for small clubs. It was a thrill to pull up at a club like big musicians and find the people all waiting for you.

I had also begun to meet different little girls—one in particular. Her name was Rosalie Penn. I don't remember where I met Rosalie but she was the beginning of my girlfriends out there. I don't think Rosalie was more than sixteen when I met her but she was a pretty little girl with big expressive eyes. She always wore a French beret and tight skirts and was as tough as nails—not with me of course as she was always good company, but brother she was tough and was already drinking and smoking. She used to run around with another girl, who must have weighed two hundred pounds, named Big Emma. Rosalie and I became pretty tight. She'd come down to my apartment and teach me the facts of life, and pretty soon I began to like her, not love her, but I liked for her to be around. I wasn't the only one, though, that she was hanging out with, as sometimes I'd see her with prizefighters and other guys. But she didn't claim to be anything to them and I'm sure that she spent most of her time with me. She was a real flip chick and always chewed gum. I learned too, later, that she had one hell of a temper and was insanely jealous.

One night our little band had a gig out in Watts, California, which is a suburb of Los Angeles, at a place called Blainell's Club. Rosalie wanted to go along with me so, since she liked jazz, I made the preparations for her to go in the car. Now Blainell's was a club that was famous for being a rough place to be whether you be a musician or not. Several musicians wouldn't play the joint because they were afraid of being cut or shot or something like that. It was way out on a dark road, and if you had wanted a policeman for anything, well, there just wasn't any to be had. Every Saturday night was bloody. The kind of place that my mother used to preach to me about when she didn't want me to play jazz. So Rosalie and I and the rest of the band arrived at Blainell's and soon we were making with the music. Things went OK for the first two hours; nobody had been shot yet, nor cut. Rosalie seemed to be content listening to the music. Then a little Mexican girl came in and started making eyes at me. She was a pretty girl and I wasn't blind. I saw her digging me as she danced around in front of the bandstand, but knowing Rosalie was there I didn't retaliate. I just noticed her but Rosalie had seen her. When I came off of the stand for intermission Rosalie accused me of flirting with this girl. I told her she was crazy as really I hadn't done anything. I may have made a couple of winks at the chick but I know damn well that Rosalie didn't see me. She continued to raise hell with me about the girl and I kept telling her that it was all her imagination, but she didn't believe a word I was saying. Finally it was time for me to go back to the stand as intermission was over, so I left Rosalie at the table fuming. I had been playing about twenty minutes and I didn't see Rosalie when she sneaked into the kitchen and somehow stole a long butcher knife, about eight inches long. She came through the kitchen, which was behind the bandstand, and I didn't see her. I knew that she had left our table but I thought that she probably went to the ladies' room. I was playing a solo and I couldn't see that Rosalie had slipped up to the bandstand and was behind me. She had this knife raised up and she had thrust it down towards my back. My drummer naturally could see what was happening because he sat directly behind me. He was Logan Eubanks and had taken Oscar Bradley's place for some reason that particular night. So when he saw the knife he grabbed her arm, just as the knife was about three inches from my back, and somehow took it away from her without cutting himself.

By this time I'm as nervous as hell and really all shook up. Rosalie still wanted to fight but I just stayed away from her. When time came for us to go home I didn't even bother to take her back to Los Angeles. She did get home, though. I suppose she hitched a ride from someone going back to Central Avenue. I thought of Mom when I got home myself that night. I said to myself, "It almost happened this time, Mom, like you said, but not quite." Needless to say that was the end of Rosalie as far as I was concerned. She did, however, come by my apartment sometime later to make up with me, but I had had it and wasn't going to take any more chances with her. And I did continue to play gigs at Blainell's, as there just wasn't that many places that I could play. We were amateurs at the jazz business and hadn't even as yet joined the musicians' union. Sometimes the business at clubs like Blainell's was good and sometimes bad. When on a bad night with no business we would sit around the club playing cards or doing other things, as there wouldn't be a soul in the place. Then if someone saw a car coming down the road that appeared to be coming to our place, we would all run and jump on the bandstand and start playing like hell so as to make the people in the car think that the joint was really jumping by hearing all of this jazz. I played like this for some time. Sometimes good, sometimes bad.

One day a fellow that had known Ronald Wharton came to me and said, "Son, I hear you play trumpet pretty good."

I said, "Well, I try."

He then said, "Do you think you could come by my home tomorrow? We are going to open a new taxi dance hall, and if you can play as well as some people say you can I'd like to hear you."

"Certainly, I'll be there," I told him. That night I could hardly sleep for thinking about that proposition and I was up so early the next day practicing on my trumpet that I must have awakened the neighborhood about six o'clock in the morning. At two o'clock, the time for the audition, I was ready. I was there before all of the other musicians. I didn't know but one of them, and that was Ronald because he had also been asked to come with his banjo.

After being introduced to the other musicians we finally got around to playing. It was easy. We only had to play stock arrangements and no more than one chorus to a song. That's the way it was in the dime-a-dance business: one chorus, one dime for the girl, who in turn gave part of that to the owners of the dance hall. We rehearsed about two hours and the leader, whose name was LaVern Floyd, came over to me and said, "You know, son, I think you're going to be alright." Those words were very, very important in my life and I'll never forget them. It meant that at last I was going to have a regular job playing trumpet in a band. Not a big band yet, but a band. We had six pieces and my salary was going to be thirty-five dollars a week. I almost kissed LaVern. This was the very first band that I ever worked with and LaVern was really my first bandleader.

One of the musicians who was also going to work in the dance hall was a fellow that became one of my very best friends: Pete Kinard, who played tenor saxophone. Pete would invite me to come to his house and we would practice together. He had a small record player and we would learn all of the solos that we possibly could of different musicians. At that time I was crazy about Cootie Williams with Duke Ellington. I still am, but then I still didn't know about Louie Armstrong. We would rehearse for hours, Pete and myself. I learned as many of Cootie's solos as I possibly could, playing the record over and over again until I got it almost perfect. Solos like *Dukes, Rockin' in Rhythm, East St Louis Toodle-oo, Drop me off in Harlem* and so many others. The only thing I couldn't do with Cootie's solos was to growl like he did, because at this stage of my playing I didn't know how to growl, neither could I understand how anybody did it. But just the same I was playing Cootie's solos, growl or not.

Pete's favorite soloist on tenor sax was Prince Robinson, who at the time was with McKinney's Cotton Pickers out of Detroit. He would learn all the solos of Prince Robinson's that he could play. The ones that he couldn't play were put aside until later when he became better on the sax. The same thing went for me too. If I couldn't play a certain solo of Cootie's I'd put it aside and say to myself, "You just wait, I'll get you later." The first afternoon of Pete's and my rehearsals, I went out and bought a red rubber plunger —the kind that Cootie used when he growled on the trumpet. And I felt kinda good just having the plunger like Cootie had, even if I couldn't growl.

The big night came for the opening of the dance hall, the Red Mill dance hall. It was on north Main Street in Los Angeles, near the City Hall. It was a rather large hall owned by two fellows in partnership. The girls were beautiful for the most part and came to work in their dancing gowns. I was impressed. They all seemed glamorous to me because I had never played a dance or a gig where people wore evening gowns. The night went off without a hitch and the bosses were happy; so were we, especially me.

When I started in the Red Mill with LaVern I was naturally pretty green and inexperienced as far as trumpet players go. But there must have been a spark of something there as all of the guys liked me, and soon Pete Kinard and myself became the main soloists in the group. LaVern took me under his wing and showed me how that on weeknights we would play one chorus, which would be one dime ticket for the girls, and on Saturday nights we would play only one half of a chorus, for which the guys paid the same as the weekdays, but they didn't know the difference. Whenever the chorus stopped, as far as they knew it was a dime gone whether it was a full or a half chorus. Most of the clientele was Filipino fellows. They would wear some of the neatest clothes that I ever saw. They really dressed beautiful and I admired their taste so much.

One of my biggest troubles with the stock arrangements that we were playing were the famous Archie Bleyer arrangements. They used to turn me every way but loose. I could see then that I had a hell of a lot to learn. *Business in F* and *Business in Q* were two particular stocks that used to hang me every night. Another was *Mule Face Blues*. It sure was tough on a trumpet man of one year's experience, but before long I was playing them all with practice and work together. Another hindrance, which I did not realize at the time, was that I was playing trumpet incorrectly. I was playing on the inner flesh of my bottom lip and I wasn't corrected on this until I met trombonist Parker Berry, who straightened me right out.

During my stay at the Red Mill I met Mutt Carey—Papa Mutt, the famous New Orleans trumpet player, who had moved out to Los Angeles. I was always around Papa Mutt as much as I could possibly be because he used to tell me different stories about some of the old New Orleans musicians. He would also talk about Louie Armstrong when he was a young kid in New Orleans. We became friends but he never taught me anything. It's been said that he taught me to play trumpet but that isn't true. We were friends and I liked his vibrato on trumpet, but that's about all. I'd listen to him every chance I'd have to hear him play, but my father and Clarence Trice were the only ones that taught me to play anything on the trumpet.

I stayed at the Red Mill for over a year, and as we played non-stop my lips became pretty strong. I had learned so much, too, just from working there. I had become friends with one of the hostesses at the hall by the name of Irene King, Irene Faith King from Indianapolis. Irene was married to a fellow named Dutch who pressed pants for a living, but she would hang out with me so much sometimes that I used to wonder how she could get back home. She had her own little car and used to come by my apartment after work and stay until the next day. She later divorced and met a rich Frenchman who set her up in business. He bought her a restaurant in Hollywood which she named the Moviola Grill.

One night, after being at the Red Mill for over a year and a half, Ronald and I went to work as usual. We drove to work in Ronald's car and we found the Red Mill dance hall in ashes. It had burned down from a cigarette that hadn't been extinguished and had smouldered in one of the big soft seats of the hall. After closing time it had ignited and burned the place completely down. The instruments that were left there as usual at night, such as the drums and the bass and piano, were completely burned to ashes, but Pete, Ronald and myself had ours as we took them home with us every night. I was pretty sad about that as I had grown to love the Red Mill, even though I wasn't playing the kind of music that I would have liked to play. I wanted to play some special arrangements and also to play in a trumpet section. However, I was glad to have worked at the Red Mill and to have met some nice musicians playing in and around Los Angeles.

So I was out of a job. But I had bought some new clothes while I was at the Red Mill and I used to hang out with other musicians on Central Avenue, and I began to know a lot of entertainers. Not just the musicians themselves, but dancers, singers and all kinds of different people that were in the world of entertainment. We would put on our latest clothes and get sharp as a tack and meet on corners of Central Avenue and try to out-dress each other. Musicians at that time took pride in their clothes and always tried to look as immaculate as possible, and I can't understand how some of today's musicians can go on the bandstand with sweat shirts and even sneakers on. Maybe it's the generation gap, but I liked our times better. All musicians that were able to looked like fashion plates at that time. So we'd meet on these corners on Central Avenue and talk about the latest things happening. I met Willie Jones, drummer with Curtis Mosby's Blue Blowers, Teddy Eubanks, drummer (who was related to Logan Eubanks, the drummer who stopped Rosalie from knifing me), Sam Harris, a dancer, and Bad Boy Bobby Frazier, a dancer from Chicago. And there was one little young cat that always loved to hang out with musicians and entertainers. He was a few years younger than we were—and we were not too old ourselves. He'd get sharp like all the rest of us and stand on the corner with us big boys. I guess he must have been about fifteen years old at the time, but sometimes he would stay out too late hanging out with us, talking and jiving, and every time he'd get home late for the family supper he'd get his butt whipped. Steve Lockett was his name, and that same Steve Lockett is now assistant to the vice-president and general sales manager of the Seagram Distillers Company on Park Avenue, New York.

Paul Howard had the greatest little swing combo that I had ever heard, in Los Angeles or anywhere else. The Paul Howard Quality Serenaders really made an impression on me. At the time I heard them I hadn't as yet become familiar with the musicians and didn't know their names, but I believe that he had Harvey Brooks on piano, Lionel Hampton on drums, George Orendorff on trumpet and Lawrence Brown on trombone. Paul himself was on tenor sax. The rest of the group—I'm sorry, but I don't remember who they were. I could listen to them for hours. Later I became a fan and a friend of Paul's and he encouraged me as well as inspired me.

The Erwing Brothers band was another swinging group that played mostly taxi dances. Los Angeles was full of taxi dance halls at that time and the Erwing Brothers were one of the best bands that you could hear in a taxi dance hall. They didn't play stock arrangements like we did at the Red Mill but had their own special arrangements. They were originally from Texas but had moved out to LA. There were three brothers, James, piano, Dorchester, guitar, and Harris, saxophone. The rest of the band, as I recall, were not related. Harris Erwing was one of the world's best baritone saxophone players. The four greatest baritone sax players in my estimation are Harry Carney (with Duke Ellington), Harris Erwing, Jack Washington (with Count Basie) and Gerry Mulligan. All four were great.

One day, shortly after the Red Mill burned down, I was approached by Harris Erwing and was told that their trumpeter, a guy called "Fats," was temporarily away from the band. He asked me if I'd be interested in taking his place. He had heard of me through the grapevine and wanted me to play in Fats's place. Now Fats was what we call a growler. I had heard him play and he used to use an empty coffee can and a plunger to get the growl effect. I think that his idol was also Cootie Williams and he was trying to growl like him with these tin cans and stuff. I still hadn't learned yet how to growl, but I just couldn't pass up this chance to play with Harris Erwing so I accepted the job anyway, knowing that I couldn't growl. I liked Harris quite a bit as he was always a cheerful guy and knew a lot of pretty girls and they all liked him. I used to watch him when he'd be kidding a chick about something and the chick would just melt. He seemed to know every girl on the dime-a-dance circuit, so I thought, "Hell yes. I'll work with Harris." I not only liked his playing so much but I liked just about everything he did.

I went to work at the hall where the Erwing Brothers were playing and, to make a long story short, I lasted just about four days. It wasn't that I couldn't play the music but I couldn't play it the way that Fats played it. The rest of the brothers were so accustomed to hearing all of that coffee-can crap that they felt uneasy with me playing straight solos, so they let me out.

I couldn't have growled if they were going to kill me, so pretty soon I was back hanging out on the corners with all of the guys on Central Avenue. Shortly after that I decided that I'd better learn how to growl, which I did, finally.

So, as I was walking around Central Avenue, back to playing just gigs here and there, I met Peppy Prince, a drummer who at the time was working with Charlie Echols's band—a big twelve- or fourteen-piece band that had been playing all over LA and up and down the West Coast. Peppy had heard me play somewhere, probably at the Red Mill, and as the Echols band needed a third trumpet player at the time he thought he'd sound me out to see if I'd be interested in playing. First he said to me, "Hey Buck, do you like Charlie Echols's band?" I told him I did, as I had heard the band at two occasions and really did like it. It was a big band of at least fourteen pieces, and had a good sound. Then Peppy asked me if I would be interested in playing with the band as they needed a third trumpet player. I really was so happy to hear this, but at the same time I was just a little bit afraid of playing with such a big band. I wouldn't know what to do playing with so many men at the same time. I thought about it for a while, for about two minutes to be exact, then I told Peppy, "Hell yes! Why not?" I had wanted to play with a big band all my life and here was the opportunity. Sure I'd like to play with the famous Echols band. So Peppy said, "Good, I'll see what I can do."

He then went to Echols and said, "Hey, Ech, I found a little young cat that can play hell out of trumpet and he's fairly new in town. Why don't you sound him out on third trumpet?"

Echols said, "You really like him?"

Peppy said, "Sure do, and I don't think you can go wrong in listening to him sometime."

So Echols said, "Well, bring him down and I'll have a talk with him." The next day Peppy took me over to Echols's apartment and I was introduced to him. We talked for about fifteen minutes before he asked me the big question, would I like to play third trumpet in his band. I could not say a thing for about three minutes, it seemed, before I blurted out, "Yes I sure would, Mr Echols."

So then he said, "Well, come to rehearsal at Solomon's Dance Hall at a certain time and date and we'll start you in on third trumpet chair." I was ecstatic. Here was my chance to play in a real live big band. I had never been happier and for the rest of the day I was walking on clouds. Me, playing with a big band. It seemed too good to be true. So I thanked Peppy for introducing me to Echols. In a way he introduced me to the real life of a big band member.

The rehearsal was at two o'clock on a Friday afternoon at the Solomon's Dance Hall and I went with Peppy. I'll never forget meeting the guys in the Echols band. Some that I can remember were Jim Wynn, saxophone, Scottie, saxophone, Country Allen, trombone, Joe Lewis, guitar, and on bass was Reginald Jones, who had just left playing at the Cotton Club. Then there was a guy called Puss Wade on saxophone. The first man on trumpet was named Pee Wee Brice, I believe. He was originally from Texas and he took a liking to me right away for which I was glad, because by him being first trumpet player he could have made it hard for me if he had not liked my playing. So pretty soon rehearsal started and for the first time in my life I was actually playing with a section of three trumpets, even if it was only a rehearsal. I never felt so good in my whole life as I could remember. We rehearsed about seven new arrangements and not once did they tell me that I had made a mistake or a wrong note. What impressed me was the way the guys joked with each other. They had all known each other for years, I guess, so it was only natural. Country Allen, a green-eyed trombone man, joked more than all the rest.

Echols himself never played with the trumpet section. He always stood in front of the band and directed or played trumpet only on solos. He was not a hell of a trumpet player and he knew it, but he was more of a showman than anything else. He would stomp his feet and dance around in front of the band, throw his trumpet up in the air and catch it as it came down, sing and make funny noises on his trumpet. All in showmanship. One time, though, he threw his trumpet about fifteen feet in the air and missed it coming down and that trumpet was a wreck. The next day he had another one. He was really original in his dress as sometimes he'd wear Russian pyjamas to work, with a short billed white cap on his head. The Russian pyjamas were always silk but he wore regular pants under the tops of the Russian pyjamas. Echols was a nice cat, though, I must say that. Everybody liked him and especially the women. He must have had them in droves as they all liked the way he would stomp his feet and screw around on the bandstand. Then he was a pretty nice looking guy, too.

I stayed with Echols for more than a year and I became one of the regulars in the band. Soon they were featuring me on certain numbers where I could really let myself go. We traveled up and down the West Coast, which was new to me as I had so far never been out of Los Angeles. For my first time I saw Santa Barbara, Pismo Beach, Oxnard, Oakland, San Francisco, Seattle, Portland, and Vancouver. How I enjoyed traveling up and down the West Coast and through the mountains. We would travel in cars and we would put the music, our arrangements, on top of the cars. One night we had an engagement to play in Sacramento and when we got in town we found that all of our arrangements had blown off the tops of the cars. We tried to go back and find them but we didn't have that much time before the dance was to start. We went back a few miles but were only able to find a third alto sax part here and a trombone part there, so all we could do was to go back and play "heads" all night. Heads are arrangements made on the spur of the moment with no music. Someone, say in the reed section, sets a riff under someone playing a trumpet solo, for example, and the whole band can play and to an outsider it looks as if the whole band is playing special arrangements. But actually we didn't have one note to play as all of our music was somewhere between Los Angeles and Sacramento laying somewhere on the highway.

I met more and more musicians during my stay with Echols. I met Red Mack, whose real name was McClure Morris. Red was a youngster like myself, about the same age and a trumpet player, but what a trumpet player. He was everything in a trumpet player that I could imagine. I heard him at the Appomattox Club for the first time and I couldn't believe anyone could play like that. He had the most beautiful tone I'd ever heard. I really couldn't understand how he could play like that, so much better than I, and still be the same age as me. But Red had started playing early and I was a rather late beginner as I didn't even pick up a trumpet until I was about seventeen, which is a little late. I met Red and we got along just fine. I considered him to be the champion trumpet player in Los Angeles, but I never once got the chance to work with him as we were always in different bands. There were some more "hellions" in California that I met also. There was Claude Kennedy from Texas, one hell of a fine trumpet player who could play fast and make difficult passages seem easy; and then he could play "dirty" when he wanted to. There was Lloyd Reese, who I think was one of the best technicians on trumpet I'd ever seen or heard. I met Teddy Buckner, who was a great jazzman and was also about my age, but more advanced than I was. In my estimation these were the top trumpet players in Los Angeles at the time, but none of them could play with as pretty a tone as Red Mack.

After staying with Charlie Echols and company for over a year, I met one day a fellow who had just blew in from New York—the great Earl Dancer. Earl had been Ethel Waters's partner and manager and he really fell in Los Angeles like a real big-time New Yorker. He wore his light gray felt hat cocked on one side like all of the big-time entertainers did. He looked like a million dollars to me. He would smoke his cigarettes French style, he told me, that is, to inhale the cigarette, blow a smoke ring, and then inhale the smoke once again. Earl was a big name in show business and everybody was falling all over themselves trying to meet him. I don't know how I met him as I didn't know anything about him and I sure wasn't trying to meet him, but somehow someone introduced me to him and I took a liking to him. He was big-time and glamorous. Earl was also, as I found out later, a bit of a con man. He could talk himself into something very good and then continue to talk until he had talked himself right out of it. By being from New York and from Broadway he had several connections out in Hollywood, and it wasn't long before he was in the offices of some of the most influential directors and producers in Hollywood.

About this time Louis Armstrong made a return trip to California. This time he was to play again at Frank Sebastian's Cotton Club, only this time he was to play with Les Hite and his orchestra. Broomfield and Greely headed the revue. Les Hite had a good band. There were only two big bands in LA at the time, our band (Charlie Echols) and the Les Hite band. The first time I heard Louis play was on a recording coming out of a shop window as I was walking down Central Avenue. I just stopped still and stood listening to that golden tone. I had never heard anyone play with such soul. I really had expected to hear Louis play "hot jazz" and I didn't know that he could play with so much expression. My first hearing of Louis's playing was on *I'm confessin' that I love you*. The wonderful introduction that C. L. Burke made on guitar knocked me out even before the recording had got to the first chorus. Then Pops came in and sang it and played it so beautifully. I guess I was spellbound. I said, "Gee-zus, that's who I want to play like." Pops was the highlight of my career. I listened to other recordings such as *Ding Dong Daddy from Dumas, Sweethearts on Parade, Just a Gigolo* and *Body and Soul*. Now there was a beautiful piece of work. *Body and Soul* happens to be my favorite ballad and Louie did it so beautifully. When Louie sang the vocal to *Body and Soul* there was a trumpet solo behind him, just a straight melody played by George Orendorff of the Hite band. The way he played that solo so straight and muted was also a highlight of the record. I began to gather all of Louie's recordings that I could get my hands on, and I would listen to him every night when he would broadcast from the Cotton Club.

One night he did something on the radio program that I had never heard anyone do before on a trumpet, which was to make a gliss. A gliss means to slide from one low note to a high note without any in-between notes, in other words like a trombone would do. But a trombone is made with a slide so it's only natural, but to hear a trumpet do that with three valves, I just couldn't understand how that was possible. I thought to myself, "Louis has got to be playing a slide trumpet, because I don't believe he can be doing that with an ordinary trumpet." And then I had seen some pictures of Pops actually playing a slide trumpet. I talked with some fellows who were working at the Cotton Club with Pops—the famous Berry brothers. Nyas Berry was a good friend of mine and I asked him, "Is Pops playing a slide trumpet?"

He said, "No, Buck, he's playing a trumpet just like yours."

I said, "But how does he do that? How does he make a gliss like that?"

He said, "I don't know how he does it but he does. His horn is exactly like yours."

I said, "I don't believe it."

So then Nyas and James, one of the other brothers, said, "You meet us here tomorrow at six o'clock and we'll take you out to the club and you can see the show and talk to Pops."

"Beautiful," I said, "I'll be there."

I was there at five o'clock waiting for them to show up at six. They came and picked me up and took me out to Culver City. I was impressed by the Sebastian Cotton Club. It was a huge green and white club and Frank was very nice also, a nice looking Italian guy. I went with the Berry brothers to their room first. Then they said, "Now come on, we'll take you to Pops's dressing room."

When they took me in Louis's room it was so full of admirers and fans that I could hardly find Louis in there himself. Finally they got to Pops and said, "Pops, here's a little young cat that wants to play trumpet and he wants to talk to you." Louis was so nice, he said, "Oh that's nice, nice, nice."

I said, "Mr Armstrong, will you show me how you do this on your horn?"

He said, "Do what?"

I said, "Well, how do you make it sound like a soprano trombone? How do you make it slide up and down?" He took his horn out of his case. With

all these people making noise in his room he says, "Now, this is my horn."
And he showed it to me. He had a Conn horn at the time, a gold
Conn trumpet. He showed me his mouthpiece and he also pulled out a
picture of himself and autographed it to me and I was so thrilled. Then
he said, "I'll show you how I do it, but if we were down in New Orleans,
I wouldn't. In New Orleans whenever I did it, I'd put a handkerchief
over my valves so nobody could see how I did it, but you follow me and
I'll show you."

He left the room with all the noise and the bunch of people in there and
walked down the hall. I followed him, right behind him, and I found out
later after I got in the hall that he was going to the john. We went to the
toilet and Louis sat down on the stool to do whatever he had to do. He had
a white handkerchief tied around his head and he said, "Now I'll tell you."
Then he said, "Wait a minute. Here." And he gave me a cigarette. It was a
brown cigarette, not the kind that I had been used to seeing. I looked at the
cigarette and I guess he knew that I didn't know just what it was, so he said,
"Here, let me have it." So he sat on the stool and lit it. He puffed on it and
then he said, "Now I'll tell you." Then he puffed again and handed it to me,
kinda grinnin' like. I took it and I puffed on it too. I thought right away of
my mother who used to talk about dope fiends and coke heads and everything
that she didn't want me to be. She had impressed so much on me about
taking narcotics, but with Louis Armstrong I would have done anything. So
I puffed on it again and give it back to Pops, he puffed on it again and gave
it back to me. This went on until the whole cigarette was gone. Then Pops
said, "Now here's how you make the gliss." He told me, "You push your
valves half way down, not all the way down. All three valves. You push 'em
half way down and tighten up your lips, then you'll be able to make the
gliss." I later learned to do it. I did it very well after Pops showed me, but
when Louis finished with the toilet and we went back into the room again
with all the noise and the people, I didn't see him too much more that night
because he had to run out and do his show.

That night I went home and I got down on my knees and I prayed to God.
I said, "Oh God, now that I'm a dope addict, please forgive me. Please don't
let me become a real habitual dope addict. I just did it one time, please stop
me now. Please God, please stop me, I don't want to end up being a junkie."
I just knew that I had done the worst thing in the world, which really it
wasn't because I found out from later use that pot never affected me in any
kind of way except that it makes one feel elevated. It never affected Louis
either. It's not like being drunk where you may develop into being an
alcoholic. With pot you just smoke it without it becoming a habit. If you
have it, OK, if not, OK. It never did anything to me. Sometimes I'd take it
like a drink or cocktail just to perk me up, and it usually made me more
attentive to what I was doing.

I listened constantly to Louis and he made more recordings out there with
Les Hite. Pops had previously recorded with Leon Herriford the first time
he was in LA. Leon was a saxophone player and leader who had a tone on
his saxophone that reminded you of the Guy Lombardo reed section. Pops

was doing wonderful in California, breakin' it up and exciting the whole town.

One night a detective that had been hanging out with Pops all this time, a little young guy that Louie thought was a jazz fan, searched Pops's overcoat that was hanging in the dressing room and found a little part of a cigarette, marijuana, which we call a "roach." So when Louie got off the bandstand the guy apologized to Pops and said, "I'm so sorry, but I've got to take you in." So he arrested Pops. That left a big hole in the show, you know, with no Pops. Frank Sebastian didn't know what to do with Pops gone, especially for the broadcasts. Who could they get to fill Pops's shoes for the broadcasts? None other than my little young friend Red Mack. Red had a tone like Louie's and he could sing like Louie. He didn't look like Pops, but on the radio he sounded so much like Louis that many people hardly knew the difference really. Red Mack made a big name for himself when he took Pops's place till Pops got out. Louie stayed there until he left for the East and I believe that was the last time he played the Cotton Club.

Fats Waller came to the Cotton Club after Louie and was a success also, but I don't think anyone in the world could have had the success that Pops had. Fats was funny, jolly, and one hell of a pianist and did very well in Los Angeles. As for myself, I was crazy about almost everything that he composed. Eddie South came next to California and he was great too. I met Milt Hinton who was with him on bass. Milt is now one of the top bass players in New York City and about the swingin'est bass man anywhere. Later we worked together in New York. In fact we still work together. Milt met a little chorine out there who fell in love with him but at times used to bug him. Since she was the big-time chorus girl I used to call Milt Mr Woodson.

One night we had an engagement in San Pedro, so I thought that it was time that I should go to the barbershop and get spruced up a bit—get my hair conked and the whole bit. My favorite barber was Jimmy Brown, Barber Brown we called him. He was the best barber in Los Angeles and did a lot of work on entertainers and musicians. I went to the shop where Jimmy worked, in the Dunbar Hotel, and got in his chair to get a gas. Gas was another name that we called conk, but the whole process involved some lye that was mixed with other ingredients that, when put on your hair, makes it soft and silky. Really beautiful, but it has to be done rather quickly because if it stays too long in your hair it burns your scalp. Burns hell out of you. I think the formula for conk is about seventy-five percent pure lye, so you don't mess around too long with it.

So this day I walked in to get gassed, and the barbershop was full of guys talking about prizefights, girls, shows, dances and all the things that guys talk about when they hang out in barbershops. Jimmy started putting vaseline on my scalp as vaseline eases the burn from the lye. The way Jimmy conked your hair you didn't feel a thing, no burns nor anything, because he knew how to grease your scalp and then do it quick before it burned. As Jimmy was putting the vaseline on my head, the radio which was always on in the shop made an announcement for the following tune to be played. The disc jockey said, "And now, our next number will be Bing Crosby singing *I may never pass your way again."* By this time Jimmy had got my head full of this lye and I was preparing myself to listen to the radio. Just as the music started for the song I heard a rumbling noise. I didn't know what it was but it sounded like a freight train. It continued to rumble and it got louder and louder. Then all of a sudden the mirrors started falling off the walls. My barber chair was going from side to side. The chandeliers started swaying and the whole barbershop just shook—shook like crazy. Nobody said a word until a fellow who happened to be in the shop at the time, Alex Lovejoy, a well-known comedian, yelled out, "Earthquake!"

Everybody ran to the door to get out of the shop, including Jimmy. I didn't know what was happening, as we don't have earthquakes in Kansas, none that I knew of anyway. Everybody hit the door in all that flying glass so I decided I'd better get the hell out too, so I split with all of those big white barber towels around my neck. As I ran through the door there were bricks falling from the roof of the hotel, but luckily nobody was hit. There were also live wires falling and breaking above our heads. If the wires fell into a puddle of water you could see the steam come up. We ran out to the streetcar tracks and the tracks were buckling up and down like a roller coaster. Jimmy said, "This isn't the spot yet for us." So we ran over to a vacant lot where nothing could fall on us. There was confusion everywhere, confusion and panic. As I was sitting in this vacant lot I felt my first twinge of pain from that lye still in my hair. I said to Jimmy, "Look, man, how are we going to get this crap out of my hair? It's starting to burn."

Jimmy said, "I don't know, Buck, but we sure as hell can't go back in there now. We'll just have to wait until things calm down a little and then we'll try to get back in there and get it out of your hair."

So I thought to myself, "Of all the times for me to be in my first earthquake, it had to be when my head is full of lye."

I noticed too, for the first time, people looting stores during the quake. There were women chasing chickens down Central Avenue; they had broken into the poultry store across the street from the Dunbar and were chasing chickens everywhere. They would put them in their skirts and then pull their skirts up over their shoulders, full of chickens. More people were looting the bicycle store, and you could see brand new bicycles going down the street with brand new riders. By this time my head was getting hotter and hotter. I said to Jimmy, "Look, man, I can't take too much more of this."

He said, "Well, it should ease up pretty soon and we'll run back into the barbershop and I'll try to wash it out as much as I can." So we waited some more and finally it did ease up a bit. "OK," Jimmy said, "let's go." So back into the empty barbershop we ran. Luckily the water was still on and right away Jimmy started washing my hair. He must have washed it about three minutes when the earthquake started up again and we had to run out again. He had washed about half of it out and it was still burning. Again the quake stopped for a few moments and I said to Jimmy, "OK, Jimmy, let's get at it." Again we went back into the shop and stayed as long as we could before the quake started up again. Finally after so many trips in and out of the shop, we got it all washed out. I don't think I looked any better when we went to

San Pedro that night than I would have if I'd just stayed in bed. By the way, we got to San Pedro only to find out that the gig had been canceled because of the quake. Even then I wasn't finished with the quake yet as a wall in San Pedro almost fell on Peppy Prince and myself, missing us only by inches.

I continued on with Echols and it was just about this time that I began learning how to arrange music. Parker Berry was playing at the Cotton Club with Les Hite's band, but he was also sharing an apartment with me and another good friend, Eddie Beal. I'd watch Parker when he would be making an arrangement for the Hite band or for the movies or for some individual artist, and one day I asked him if he'd show me how he did it. He was happy at the thought of teaching me and began right away to show me how he did it. He and Eddie had moved in with me at the same apartment which I had at the Wharton's home, and by being around Parker day and night I began to make a little sense in arranging. I think he tried to teach Eddie a little too, but I don't think Eddie was too interested in anything but playing the piano. I'd stay up sometimes all night learning how to put notes together and for different instruments. My eyes would be blurred when I'd stop somewhere around eight o'clock in the morning. I liked arranging and I have thanked Parker Berry many times since he gave me my first lesson.

About this time I was running around with a young man from the South, Charlie Barnet. He had just come up from Texas, had a big pretty Cadillac and always had money. His family was very wealthy. He loved to hang around us guys in Echols's band. In fact he wanted to take some coffee grounds and rub them in his face to make him look like a black guy so he could play in our band. I dug Charlie and he dug me and our whole time was just one jam session after another. A friend of Charlie's that we also met was Jack Purvis. Purvis was an excellent arranger besides being able to play almost every instrument. We all used to go out to Watts together and Charlie would always pay the bill for everything. We'd jam until six or seven o'clock in the morning, then we'd drive back to LA and stay up until noon. He'd pay for everything, even girls if we brought any back with us from Watts.

Maceo Sheffield, a big 250- or 260-pound police detective from Seguine, Texas, was the baddest cat in Los Angeles. Everybody was afraid of him, but he loved musicians. Whenever he would raid a joint that wasn't supposed to have been open, he'd always open a back window and tell the musicians who happened to be in there, "Get the hell out of here." Then he'd arrest everybody else. Count Basie recorded a number which is called *Every Tub*. Sheffield was the originator of that name because, before he would break down the door on a raid, he would always ask, "Is my mother in there?" Usually no one would answer but at times someone would say, "No, Mr Sheffield."

Then he would say, "Well, if my mother's not in there, then every tub stand on its own bottom." That was eventually shortened to "every tub."

Sheffield used to take me on rides all around the outskirts of Los Angeles and we'd listen to his car radio. We used to listen to Duke Ellington records, such as *Drop me off in Harlem, In the shade of the old apple tree* and others that were being broadcast. I had never seen the Duke, but I knew that he was on schedule to come to California to make a movie.

Of all the characters who hung out on Central Avenue the most colorful and notorious in his escapades was, without a doubt, Stepin Fetchit, the big movie star at the time. Clarence Muse was a big man in the movies too at the time, along with Rex Ingram. Clarence Muse was in so many movies but he was a hell of a lot more conservative than Stepin Fetchit. Step was always raisin' hell on Central Avenue. Sometimes he'd go to work at the studios in five different Cadillacs like a big parade, right down Central Avenue. People used to say, "There goes ol' Step," when they'd see all of these Cadillacs. The five chauffeurs for the five Cadillacs were Filipino guys and they all wore expensive leather coats. The first two Cadillacs were for friends that Step would be taking to the studios to see him work. The third and fourth were for the clothes that he was to wear and the fifth was for Step all by himself.

There was also a guy named Frenchie who was once a prizefighter but was now just a bit punchy. He used to walk on his heels all of the time but he stayed sharp. He always had a carnation in his lapel and always wore the latest-style suits. There was "Soldier Boy" who was so crazy about Louis Armstrong that he would have done anything in the world that Louis asked him to do. There was Stuff Crouch, who was also a Louis Armstrong man, who owned an after hour joint. There was Gorilla Jones, a prominent fighter who used to walk down Central Avenue with a lion cub on a leash, a gift from Mae West. Some of the other prominent fighters were Mack House (a heavyweight from Buffalo, New York), Dynamite Jackson, Charlie Long, Ace Hudkins and Chalky Wright.

When they were making the first *King Kong* movie, the casting people came down to Central Avenue to hire all of the black people they could to use as natives in the movie. I wasn't doing anything regularly as Echols was just gigging here and there, so I decided that I'd go down and apply for a job as an extra. They were going to pay everybody seven dollars a day, everybody they could find. The next day we all went to Hollywood and the casting people asked us to all line up. We got in line and they began selecting people from the line. It seemed to me that they were taking everybody until they got to me. They looked at me and saw that I had gray eyes and then, too, I wasn't dark enough. Now I know I'm black and there is nobody on this earth any prouder of his black heritage than I am, but this casting company couldn't have cared less about my black heritage. They just didn't want any light complected, gray-eyed natives running around in the *King Kong* movie, so I was probably the only person on Central Avenue that didn't get a job in the picture. That really hurt me. Too light to be black and too black to be white.

Shortly after *King Kong* I was walking down Central Avenue and I saw a cute little chick in a riding habit. She had been riding with some more girls from the chorus line at the Cotton Club and had just got back from the riding stables. I was introduced to her and I found her to be a real cute little girl, and nice. Before long we were dating but there was only one hang up: she had been going with a musician in Les Hite's band and was, in a way, a childhood sweetheart. The girl's name was Gladys Henderson, but was called "Derb" by all the show people because she danced in the style of Derby Wilson, a prominent New York hoofer. I liked Derb but I think she was confused now about her former sweetheart and didn't really know just who she wanted to be with, him or me. It seemed to be me, but I don't think she really knew herself. Before long we became pretty tight and soon had an apartment together. We didn't stay too long, though, in the apartment because we had heard that Derb was to be in the upcoming movie that Duke was to make, and then we also learned that Earl Dancer was going to open up a nightclub under the Dunbar Hotel. So we soon moved out of the apartment into the Dunbar. Just in case we ever worked with Earl we would be right above the club.

Shortly after, Earl Dancer did begin to make his movies. He had been out to Hollywood and had convinced some of the directors and producers that he had a band and had signed a contract to do some movie work with his band, which he didn't have. So he began to talk to people that he figured he could use in a band, and I was asked by him if I'd be interested in joining a band that he planned to organize. I thought about it for a while, in fact I thought about it for a long time, and little by little I began to like the idea of working with Earl Dancer and making some movies with him. And then I'd also be working close to Derb as he was trying to get as many of the best dancers and singers that he could for his nightclub show.

In the meantime I worked with various bands, as Echols was not doing too much, gigging here and gigging there. I worked with one guy who became a friend and one that I'll never forget, Elmer Fain. We worked in the Paradise Club for a short time. Fain was a tenor saxophone player who is now an official in the Los Angeles Musicians' Union. I remember Fain as one guy who led his band and never gave the musicians hell about anything probably where he should have. After work we would go to an orange-juice bar where we would meet the chorus girls as they got through work at the Cotton Club. By this time prohibition had just been repealed and beer parlors were flourishing everywhere. Beer parlors and miniature golf courses. There were a million beer parlors where they served beer and pretzels, and all Los Angeles was happy that President Roosevelt had turned things around. Shortly after in came whiskey, and that was the red letter day in LA. My favorite whiskey at the time was Williken Family whiskey, which I don't think is made anymore. We were all happy that we didn't have to buy the stuff from bootleggers anymore. One night I got carried away and overdid it. I drank too much of something when I was working with Elmer Fain and the next day at noon I woke up with the sun shining in my eyes, my head splitting open and vomit all over my brand new tuxedo. I had gone to sleep in a big card box, and luckily my trumpet was under my body and nobody could see it so it was still there when I woke up. Such a hangover I'd never had in my life. I finally got up and got a cab and went home and tried to clean up, but my hangover seemed as if it would never go away. I hadn't been used to whiskey and that was my initiation, one that I'll never forget.

One night I had a date to meet Derb in an orange-juice bar that now sold anything you wanted. I was to have met her after she had finished work at the Cotton Club. When I got to the bar it was packed with girls, musicians, singers, dancers and about everybody in show business. I saw a lot of my pals there and everybody was having a ball. I looked for Derb but didn't see her anywhere. I just thought that I was there a bit early so I decided to wait for her. Derb was still undecided as to just who she was going with, me or the other boyfriend that she had been going with before me. Anyway, I waited and talked with all of the people that I knew and I knew quite a few of them by now. Eddie Beal was there and just about everybody. I began to walk around the room to see if I had missed Derb anywhere and I came to an empty table, but what confused me was that Derb's top coat was draped over one of the chairs of the table, so I knew that she had to be there. I started asking questions. I asked everybody, "Have you seen Derb?"

Everybody said, "No, Buck, I haven't seen her." I asked everybody, even my apartment mate or roommate, Eddie Beal, and he said, "Nope, I haven't seen her." I then began to think that she had gone away for a short while and had left her coat and would return to get it. After a few minutes of that, I threw that out of my mind and started asking questions again. Nobody knew where she was even though her coat was still there draped over that chair. I was perplexed. At this point one of the bartenders called me over to the bar and said, "Buck, nobody will tell you where she is, but I'll tell you. She was here when you first came in but she wasn't alone. She was with her boyfriend, the fellow from Les Hite's band, and when you came in they saw you and they both ducked into that closet over there in the corner." I felt like a damn fool. Everybody in that damn place knew she was there, but they all lied to me until the bartender told me what I wanted to know.

The next thing, the bartender pulled me up close to the bar and slipped a thirty-eight caliber pistol in my hand. Now the bartender didn't like the guy that she had come in with, so much that he would have liked to have seen him dead. He said to me, "Now they're both in there." I took the pistol in my hand and walked over to the closet where he had told me they were. The closet wasn't more than three feet wide. I walked over to it and stood in front of the door a moment. By this time you can imagine what it was like in that room. Everybody saw the pistol in my hand and they also knew that Derb and her friend was in there. It was so quiet that you could have heard a mouse piss on cotton. All of a sudden, they, the people, were the audience, the closet was the stage, and I was one of the principal actors, but I wasn't thinking about that now. I was mad alright, really mad. So I called through the door, "Derb!" There was no answer. I called again, "Derb, are you in there?" Still no answer. Then I said, "Well, if you're not in there and I shoot through this door, then I won't hit anybody, will I?" Still no response. So then I said, "OK. I'm going to count to three, and if that damn door isn't open I'm going to shoot right straight through it." I started counting, "One . . . two . . .," and just as I was going to say three the door cracked open a little bit, then it opened fully and there was Derb and her boyfriend. They were both scared as hell. Derb was crying and said that her friend had put his hand over her mouth and threatened to hit her in the mouth if she answered me, but he had changed his mind when I threatened to shoot through the door. By this time there was a deathly silence in the whole room. I stood there with this big thirty-eight in my hand but I didn't know just what to do. My mind was saying, "Don't shoot, don't shoot," and I was saying to myself, "It's not worth it. If you shoot and kill somebody, then you'll go to San Quentin probably for the rest of your life for murder. It's not worth it, don't shoot." So I hesitated a few seconds, then I turned away from the two of them and walked back over to the bartender who had given me the pistol and slapped the pistol down on the bar. Then I was mad at him for trying to get me to do his dirty work. He wanted me to kill Derb's friend because he didn't like him. I never liked him after that.

After laying the pistol on the bar, I walked out and Derb followed me, crying all the way home. I think that incident showed the way that Derb and I felt about each other. We liked each other but were not really in love. So she followed me home crying all the way and the next day things were almost normal, but I still was mad. And even after all that I still married her later.

The next week Earl Dancer came to our room in the Dunbar and asked me if I had considered working with him in Hollywood making movies. I wouldn't have to leave Echols's band, at least not yet, as I could work with Ech at night and make movies in the day. Earl was pretty desperate because he had promised to have a band in Hollywood for those big producers and had already signed contracts for a band that he was to be the leader of. The Fourteen Gentlemen from Harlem was his name for the band, although not a single one of us had even seen Harlem. So since I didn't have to leave Echols I promised Earl that I would work with him. For the movie work he didn't hire an organized band; everybody was from other bands but we were to work under the Earl Dancer name. Sometimes there would be Marshall Royal and Parker Berry from the Les Hite band, me and Peppy Prince from the Echols band and other different guys from other bands. Earl had put together a pretty damn good band, I thought, and when he showed us the contracts that he made in Hollywood we all were ecstatic. Hollywood at last.

We went to Hollywood to make a picture called *Broadway Bad*, though I think the title was changed to something else later. I had never been in a movie studio before until I met Earl. My first impression of Hollywood was like being in a dream world because there before me were all of the movie stars that I had seen in Parsons, Kansas, walking around and talking just like ordinary people. I used to think that they were all gods. Some of them looked like themselves, others didn't, especially if I'd see them without their makeup on. I was thrilled even being around these movie stars and when they'd talk to me I'd feel like sinking in the ground. In the picture *Broadway Bad* there was Ginger Rogers, who had just begun to make her name in movies. She was so pretty and I believe that she had been a dancer before coming into the movies. If I'm not mistaken I think *Broadway Bad* was one of her first movies. One time during the making of the picture she heard me tinkling around at the piano on our lunch break and she came over to me and said, "Would you please play *Am I Blue?*" Ethel Waters had just made this wonderful recording of *Am I Blue* and Ginger Rogers was trying to sing it, or rather she wanted to sing it, so I told her that I'd be happy to. I sat down at the piano and she sat next to me, and I played *Am I Blue* and she sang it during the whole lunch break.

In the picture there was Ginger Rogers, Joan Blondell, Jack Oakie and Arline Judge, and later I met Glenda Farrell, Spencer Tracy, Ramon Navaro and many others. Ramon Navaro was sure a sharp-looking guy. I had never seen Rudolph Valentino but I couldn't see how he could be much more good looking than Ramon. They would wear tuxedos if it was called for in the script, but what puzzled me was that their white ties were bright yellow along with their shirts. I learned later that yellow shows up whiter on the film than real white, also that thin people always look heavier on screen than they do in real life. When I'd walk down Hollywood Boulevard I was all eyes. It was just like now when I see people come to New York from Nebraska, Oklahoma or Kansas and they see these tall buildings in New York, they stand right in front of them and gape. They look straight up in the air for hours as they can't believe these buildings could be so tall. Well that's the way I was in Hollywood looking at all of these movie people. Later I met Jack LaRue and Warren Hymer, who was always portrayed as a dumb gangster. Sometimes he'd bring his Cadillac down to Central Avenue, fill it up with chorus girls and go out and spend the whole night together. He'd always leave them with the Cadillac, which naturally they'd run all over Los Angeles until it ran out of gas, and he'd come pick it up the next day. We were in many more pictures, such as *Lady for a Day*, *42nd Street*, and so many others that I've forgotten the names of many of them. One day I was late getting on the set after the noon break for lunch. I had been walking down Hollywood Boulevard, naturally looking at everything I could see, when I passed a tailor shop that had the most beautiful clothes in it that I'd ever seen in my life. It was the famous McIntosh Tailors of Hollywood who made many of the suits for some of the most prominent actors. I just stood there and looked and my mouth watered. I couldn't afford one of those pretty suits yet, but I swore that one day I'd get one. Even while I was looking in the windows I could see Joel McCray in there, and they were fitting him in a beautiful blue suit. When Duke Ellington came to town later and found McIntosh Tailors he would buy suits by the dozen and more than that. When he was on the road he used to send back to Hollywood for more suits as they had his measurements and had a special form made to fit them on. As I turned to leave I ran into Max Baer, who was then heavyweight champion of the world. He was going in to order some more suits and I'll never forget the suit that he had on. It was a dark plaid with special vents in the back of the coat.

All of a sudden I realized that I was late getting back to the studio so I ran like hell to get there as fast as I could, but even at that I was late. Everybody had changed into costume and was on the bandstand and the dressing room was completely empty except for me. I began to undress to put on my costume and run out on the stage as quickly as I could, and just as I had gotten down to nothing on except my drawers the dressing room door opened and in walked Loretta Young thinking that the dressing room was empty. She looked at me and flew out of there. I think if anyone ever asked me what my most embarrassing moment was, I'd have to say that was it. Later we worked at Graumans Chinese Theater, and I wanted to put my hands and feet prints in the cement plaques that were reserved for the super-great stars of the movies. We worked at a club called the Hollywood Barn—a big club where all the chorus girls were men. It was there that once again I saw Max Baer in that same beautiful suit that I had seen him wear the day I was looking in McIntosh's Tailors. It was there also that I saw James Cagney's brother, who looked so much like James that I thought they were twins; in fact they may have been, as I never knew nor never found out later.

Our next job with Earl was at a club called the Plantation Club, which was owned by the biggest gangster in Hollywood. The theme song of this club was *Lady of the Evening*. We were supposed to be paid on Saturday nights as usual, but on this particular Saturday night, just before we went to work, I took my last eight dollars and bought a pair of white shoes. Tom McCanns being so sure that I was going to get paid that night, my last quarter went into those white shoes. I've always had a yen for white shoes in summer, even now, so with my last loot I bought these beautiful white shoes and prepared to go to work. We all met at our usual meeting places with the guys that had cars to go out to the Plantation Club. Just as soon as we arrived at the club we were met by six guys with machine guns. They greeted us with these words, "Just get right back in your cars and get the hell out of here."

We asked, "Why? What happened?" We found out that during the night before, Earl had been out there and had done something that wasn't quite kosher during the game and had been kicked out and lost our job at the club. They didn't have to tell us twice, as these big gorillas looked like they meant business and those machine guns looked pretty menacing.

After that I did more work with Echols, as I found him to be a little more secure than Earl. I was walking around with these pretty white shoes on but with no money. After some more months with Ech, Earl Dancer hit upon the idea of having his own club. So, along with some of his New York connections, he obtained a corner on 42nd Street and Central Avenue under the Dunbar Hotel, which was an ideal place for a club. The Club Alabam was just up the street a few doors but the 42nd Street corner was the most ideal place to be found. Jack Johnson had tried to run it as a club but didn't have the know-how that Earl had and it had folded. So Earl went to work and had the club changed all around. It looked elegant when he finished it. By this time I could see that I would have to leave Echols if I intended to work with Earl at the club, so with a sad heart I said goodbye to all of the guys in the Echols band. My first big band.

Earl named the new club the Club Ebony. Everybody was still struck with Earl's New York background and his big-time associates, so he had no trouble getting the best entertainers, singers, dancers and musicians in town. People were flocking around Earl to meet him and to try to work in the new club. I agreed to work with him, Derb came in from the Cotton Club along with several other of the chorus girls, and in a few weeks he had about the best musicians and entertainers in Los Angeles and we went into rehearsal. The band was his biggest thing, as he figured if he had a good band he had already won half the battle. After the band came the chorus girls and he really had the best. I had become like a brother to nearly all of the chorus girls as they knew that I was going with Derb, so they all used to talk to me and they taught me so many things. Things that I didn't even know happened in this world. There was Ruth Scott, who was married to my friend skeleton brother, Harold Scott. She later divorced Harold and married Harry Mills of the Mills Brothers quartet. There was Alice Keyes, a beautiful green-eyed, red-haired, vivacious chick that was always the life of every party. There was Maudine Simmons, another green-eyed beautiful girl, who later married Nelson Sykes, a prominent bar owner of Chicago. There was Rosa Lee Lincoln, a real beauty who had the biggest dimples I had ever seen. She used to tease me in public by telling me that she was always jealous of my dimples. There was Marcita Gault, who was my secret love because she had the most beautiful shape in the world and such legs! I would never say anything to Marcita except "hello" or "goodbye," because to me she was too much in demand by all of the other guys and, although she was a good girl, I guess I was too shy to say anything else to her. I didn't figure that I could get past all of those other guys who used to admire her. There was also Juanita Moore, who has become a big actress on her own. She made *Imitation of Life*, which was to lead her to other successful movies. Today I see her on many TV commercials. These were most of the chorus girls and, along with Derb, they were one hell of a beautiful bunch of girls. Patsy Hunter was the choreographer of the group and soon had them in shape. One of the first dance routines she taught them was Bill Bojangles's dance of the stair steps.

There was a beautiful lyric tenor singer, Sally Harper, who impressed me so much with his voice. Unfortunately he died at an early age but not before he had upset the world with his rendition of *Ace in the Hole*. There was Alma Travers, who reminded me of today's Pearl Bailey. Alma was a great blues singer who once made Ripley's *Believe it or not* because she could, and sometimes would, sing with her mouth full of pins. There was the dance team of Rutledge and Taylor—Junie Rutledge and Johnny Taylor—a hell of a duet. Their favorite number was on the famous song *Me and my Shadow*, where they would dance so close together that you could only see one shadow. Eddie Anderson, who later became the world famous Rochester with the "Jack Benny Show," was the comedian and at times worked with the Rutledge–Taylor team. We tried to get the beautiful Mae Diggs to sing with the show along with Mary Richards and Daisey Boone (two beautiful girls), but we were not successful as they had other commitments.

We rehearsed the show practically every day for about three weeks until we knew every step, every note and every joke. The band became sharper than ever, I guess from really working hard and daily. Earl really knew what to do in the show business and we had taken on an air that would have done credit to any show in any city, including New York. I was living upstairs in the Dunbar and could see the show becoming more and more attractive to the general public as everyone began to ask the question, "When is it going to open?"

About this time a violin player came to Los Angeles from Chicago. At first nobody knew who he was but we soon found out that he was a pretty prominent violinist in Chicago and had just finished a long engagement at the Vendome Theater under Erskine Tate. He had played there with Louis Armstrong in the pit along with several other big time Chicago musicians, including Teddy Weatherford and Jimmy Bertrand. We had previously had no reason to have a violin in our band but we thought that, since we were putting on a show, we could use him so we asked him about joining up with us. He agreed quickly and we had ourselves a violin player. His name was Joe McCutchin. Joe was a friendly type of a guy and told us many stories of Louis when he first arrived in Chicago from New Orleans to play with King Oliver. We wrote him some parts to play in the show and it really added quite a bit to the band—more like classical, under the vocalists especially. Of course there wasn't much he could do when we were playing a really hot jazz number but when it came to sweet music and obligatos he was right there on the ball. We wrote him some special parts and our band was now more first-class in a way.

Finally the day came for the big opening of the Club Ebony. We had costumes galore. The band was in tuxedos and Earl looked like a million dollars in his full dress suit. He bought a brand new baton to direct the band but he didn't know a damn thing about how to use it and I guess it didn't make much difference. We in the show knew that he didn't know what the hell he was doing, and I guess the general public didn't know one way or the other what he was doing, but he did look good, which was half the battle. The big opening night was quite a success. It seemed that half of Hollywood came in their big cars, minks and jewelry. The waiters were decked out in formal clothes and it really looked like something that you'd see in the movies. The show went down without a hitch and got good reports in the papers the next day. The band, the cast, the waiters, the chefs, and I guess just about everybody was happy for Earl and for us too, as we figured we had a home now for a while and wouldn't have to be looking for work.

For the first few weeks everything went well. More and more movie stars came in and soon we became familiar with quite a few of them. Sometimes they'd pass money up to the band, to which we wouldn't object. George Raft came in often with his parties. He was a big hit with all of the chorus girls. One night he came in with a party and was having a ball. Some fellow came over to his table and wanted to fight him about something. George tried to fluff him off but the guy was insistent. By him being half loaded, he wanted to fight George for something that he didn't like that George had done in a movie. His own party tried to tell him that it was just a role that George had to play in the movie, but the cat was so drunk that he couldn't understand that and still wanted to fight George. This went on for some time and it began to annoy the patrons who were trying to enjoy the show. Finally George stood up at his table and was just about to take a poke at the guy, when some of the waiters and some of the patrons who had been watching grabbed the guy and threw him out of the club onto the street. He was lucky. He never got beat up but just thrown out on his ass. The show and the band kept clicking and the whole thing was forgotten in a few minutes. The drunk was mad at George because George had slapped some lady in a movie, and I guess he figured it was his duty to protect all ladies.

After about three weeks of successful shows came Saturday night, the night we were to be paid. As we went to Earl after the last show he gave us some kind of crap where the money had to be used for something else, and we only got paid one half of our salaries. He did promise us to pay the rest in three or four days so we let it pass, but frankly I hadn't forgotten the Plantation Club incident, where Earl had gotten into that poker game and had lost our job by pulling some kind of crap in the game. But I didn't say anything. I figured he just might pay everybody later and things would be back in order again. After about two more weeks he did pay us back in bits and pieces and the show went on. Then, about a month later, the same thing happened again, only this time we didn't get any money at all. Earl had gone out to Hollywood with our salaries and had gotten into another poker game and lost everything. He tried to explain his way out of this but nobody wanted to hear anything that he had to say. Alma Travers, who was pretty tough when she wanted to be, wanted to grab Earl in his collar as well as a lot of others, but Earl, being the con man that we all soon found out, explained his way out of this too and promised to pay us. We didn't have anything else to do at the time so we continued on with the show. The club was still doing very good business, however, so we stuck with it, and Earl would give us five dollars and ten or fifteen dollars on different occasions. Finally we all didn't know just how much he did owe us, but we kept working. Working and grumbling.

I had bought a little Boston bull terrier named Ghandi that I used to keep in my room in the Dunbar. A cute little dog, and I was quite fond of him and would leave him in the room while Derb and I went down to do the show. Then about a week after I bought him, Earl goofed up again. He just couldn't stay away from those Hollywood poker games and once again we had no salaries coming at the end of the week. Well this time he was in trouble from the whole cast. Half of them quit on the spot. It was so disgusting, as there was really no reason for all this when the club was going along so nicely from outward appearances. The waiters quit, half of the show quit, and I really couldn't find any reason for me to continue to work like that. That night, when I went upstairs to try to think about what to do, of all things there was a padlock on my door. I hadn't been able to pay my rent because of Earl's gambling in Hollywood and, to make it worse, my little dog was inside and I couldn't get in to feed him nor give him any water. Then I got mad. I had to go with Derb to her mother's home for that night and get up the next day and go out and try to hustle up enough money so that I could get Ghandi out of that room.

After a few pawn shops and loan sharks, I got enough money for the management of the hotel to open the door and I got my dog, but I still was mad as hell at Earl. Everything that a few weeks before seemed to be so good now seemed to be a whole lot of crap, simply because of Earl's weakness for gambling. So I decided I was through. I was completely fed up and wasn't going to take any more. Earl tried to continue but he did it without me, and soon the linen napkins on the tables became paper napkins, the waiters were just whoever he could find to work, the show went down to nothing and soon the club folded. Earl had done exactly in Los Angeles what he had done before in New York. Goofed up. So that was the end of my bit with Earl Dancer along with the Club Ebony.

Now that we had no band, no club, no nothing, we didn't know what to do next. I didn't see Earl for quite a few days after the downfall of the Club Ebony but when I did see him he looked like a beaten man. He was still playing poker if he could find a game but he no longer had the air of a big shot. Although I really had been angry about his handling of business at the club, I felt kinda sorry for him. It wasn't long before he was asking people for money, even me.

Our band was in doubt as to what was going to happen next, so before everybody started looking for other bands to join we decided to have a meeting and decide on whether to break up or not. The band was too good just to break up, as the time that we had spent in the Club Ebony at least had improved us to the point that we were very near being the best band in Los Angeles, barring none. So we had a meeting and we decided to appoint a new leader and continue on. There were only two members of the band that were under consideration for being leader, myself and Jack Bratton, because we had been doing all of the arranging. Jack was my friend and I was his friend and we promised each other that no matter what happened we would still work together. So a day of election was planned and everybody in the band, with the exception of Jack and myself, attended. After the votes were counted I had been chosen to be the leader. I don't know what the margin was but anyway I was the new leader. This was a brand new experience for me as I certainly had no desire at that time to be leader of a band. Later on perhaps, but not now, as I thought that I was too young. I was only twenty-three years old and quite inexperienced in being a band-leader and then, too, everybody in the band was older than I. However, I accepted and Jack was true to his promise and helped me very, very much get the band on the track again. So there I was, leader of a big band before I had planned on it.

I soon found out that being a bandleader is tough, especially if your band is not working. I had absolutely nothing to offer the guys except my arrangements, but we also had hope. I think the reason that I was elected leader was because I conformed more with the guys. Jack was studying to be a pharmacist and his family was fairly well-to-do, whereas I was all musician and had no other way to go. Jack was a good musician, a good

trumpet player, but he had such a strong family that he didn't have to pay
the dues the rest of us had to pay. The first thing that I had to do was to find
some kind of work for the band, so Jack, myself, and trombonist Happy
Johnson formed a trio to look for work. Many a day we would get in Jack's
car at ten o'clock in the morning and look for work until six or seven in the
evening. We had decided that we were not going to miss one single club in
asking for work. We went to clubs that already had bands working, for which
we didn't make ourselves too popular. We went to clubs that had been closed
for some time. We were pretty desperate. We even went to a couple of
hot-dog stands to try to influence the owner to use jazz. One of these owners
says, "Are you crazy? Just how in hell do you think I can use a fourteen-piece
band in a hot-dog stand?"

We said, "Well, we'll just bring our band out here and set up and play
music and attract people, and you'll sell more hot dogs."

His only answer was, "You get the hell out of here."

Once in a while we'd get a gig here and there, but not enough to keep a
band together. Happy Johnson was more like a business manager than Jack
and I and always had a briefcase in his hand to make him look like he was
all business. He really was a good man to have on the business end but he
never had a damn thing in that briefcase except blank contracts and empty
papers.

About this time I met Teddy Weatherford, who had just arrived from
Shanghai, China. He had been sent over to hire a band and take it back to
Shanghai. The records of Duke Ellington were just beginning to become
popular over there and black bands were the big thing at the time. Teddy
had been sent over to the States by the Tung Vong Company of Shanghai,
who owned the Canidrome Ballroom. Actually Teddy was supposed to have
visited Los Angeles, Kansas City, Chicago, St Louis, New York and even
Topeka, Kansas, in search of a band to take back to China. It wasn't long
before I was telling Teddy about our band or, rather, my band. He wanted
to hear it so we set up an audition especially for him. On the day or night
that he was to hear the band he discovered his old buddy Joe McCutchin,
with whom he had worked in Chicago at the Vendome Theater with Erskine
Tate, and that did it. Talk about two guys being glad to see each other,
because Teddy had been in the Orient for years and it wasn't long before
they were reliving all the old times in Chicago. So he heard our band and
liked it as we really did have a pretty sharp band, and the fact that Joe
McCutchin was with us made it almost a cinch. Les Hite was at the Cotton
Club and couldn't have made it even if he wanted to, which made it better
for us. So after hearing our band and finding his old pal Joe McCutchin, he
just cut out the rest of his trip to the other cities and decided to ask us,
would we go to Shanghai. Not as his own band but as Buck Clayton and his
Harlem Gentlemen. He was acting only as an agent for the Tung Vong
Company.

I was so glad to hear this, as probably if he had gone east he would have
found another band that he may have liked, as there were so many eastern
bands out of work at the same time. Musicians were still feeling the effects

of the Depression and struggling like hell to make a living. You'll never know how glad I was that Les Hite was working at the Cotton Club at that particular time, even though I thought that we had the best band. Les Hite had many good arrangements, sharp uniforms, big cars and the prestige of having worked with the biggest names like Armstrong and others. Anyway he asked us to go and we all agreed to go right on the spot. I saw it as an end to going out looking for jobs in such ridiculous places as hot-dog stands, so we planned to leave Los Angeles for Shanghai in a few weeks.

The conditions under which we were to go to China were not so hot compared to today's standards but at that time it was considered pretty fair, as we didn't have anything in the first place and had nothing to lose. The fellows in the band were to receive fifty dollars a week, which was equivalent in Chinese money to about two hundred dollars a week. I was to receive one hundred per week. Our transportation was to be paid one way by boat. We all agreed to that as we figured to stay there at least a year. Things were so cheap in China that fifty dollars stretched a long way compared with American currency. Teddy explained to us that tailor-made suits could be had for fifteen or twenty dollars. A maid or butler could be had for as little as three dollars a month, which included cooking, making heat in the morning in the winter, and many other things that we didn't even dare think of in the States. So we all signed up to go.

Next came the problem of Derb. She wanted to go too, especially after she heard that she could buy a sequin dress for as little as twenty dollars, but in order to go she had to be married. We talked about it but we didn't decide anything because we both were shying away from being married. We still only liked each other; being in love was something we wouldn't have known if it had hit us in the face, so we forgot about it for the time. We still had some weeks to decide what to do.

Duke Ellington rolled into town about this time to make the movie that he was contracted for, *Murder at the Vanities*. Derb was scheduled to work in the movie with Duke along with all of the best chorines in Los Angeles. He was contracted to play a theater for a couple of weeks before the beginning of the picture and it was at the theater, the Orpheum I believe, that I first saw him between shows. He needed a shave but had put on a lot of makeup to cover his beard. He was a good looking cat, I thought, every bit as good looking as all the photos that I had seen of him.

Someone introduced me to Duke and it was like meeting royalty. He seemed so regal. Not because his name was Duke but because of the air of regency that he projected. He had a big appetite, as while I was just looking at him he ate six hot dogs, but he wasn't fat. In his dressing room there were so many musicians and composers that wanted him to record their works— Leon and Otis Renee, California brother composers, among them. They were trying to interest him in doing their composition *When it's sleepy time down South*, which wasn't Duke's style of music, where on the other hand it was perfect for Louis Armstrong, who later made it his theme song. There was so many composers and would-be composers bugging Duke that day that I felt sorry for him and wondered if he ever had any time to himself. Later I met all of Duke's men: Freddie Jenkins, Johnny Hodges, Cootie, who was one of my idols, Sonny Greer, who had so much personality it just oozed out of him. I met them all—Harry Carney and all the rest—and you can't imagine how I was impressed by being among all of these really big-time people. Ivy Anderson knocked me out too.

The Dunbar Hotel was jumping, as almost every day there would be loads of people hanging around the front doors trying to get a glimpse of the Duke. After the theater engagement they went to work at the Paramount Studios making the movie, and every night in the Dunbar Hotel there would be parties thrown by Duke and his guys and there was chicks and champagne everywhere. The parties wouldn't last too long, though, as the band had to report to the studio at six o'clock in the morning. Sonny Greer was the one hit hardest by that early morning time but still he made it, with help.

I'll never forget one day when I happened to be in a restaurant in the Dunbar and most of Duke's guys were in there too and they were all listening to the jukebox. It was the first time since leaving the East that they had heard their recording of *It don't mean a thing if it ain't got that swing*, and that restaurant was swinging like crazy. So much rhythm I'd never heard, as guys were beating on tables, instrument cases or anything else that they could beat on with knives, forks, rolled-up newspapers or anything they could find to make rhythm. It was absolutely crazy. I found out one more thing about Duke's band being in a restaurant. If there is fifteen musicians that enter a restaurant they take up fifteen tables as everybody takes a table for himself. I never knew why, but everybody wanted and got his own table.

Our trip to China was to come up in about three more weeks and Derb and I still hadn't made up our minds as to what we were going to do in the marriage department. We actually didn't know what to do, so finally we hit on a plan. We said, "Well, since we can't decide right now what to do, let's go down and apply for the licence even if we don't use it. If we do decide to get married we'll already have the licence and we can get married in a few minutes, even if we wait until a few minutes before the boat leaves. We'll save time if we go now as at least we can get married in a couple of minutes if we still want to." So we did just that. We went down to City Hall and took out a licence to get married. A little bit in a fog but at least we had the licence. Whether we would use it or not we still didn't know.

Shortly after getting the licence I was in an after-hour joint one morning with Freddie Jenkins and some more guys shooting craps. George Raft was in there too, as he liked to hang out in after-hour joints on Central Avenue and gamble with the dice. He was with his buddy Lyle Talbot, and we were all trying our luck with the galloping dominos when I think Freddie Jenkins forgot and almost let the cat out of the bag. He said to me as the game was about to come to an end, "Buck, don't you forget to be there at ten o'clock."

I thought to myself, "Now where am I supposed to be at ten o'clock?" So I asked Freddie, "Be where?"

Then he caught himself and didn't say anymore. I was still trying to think where I was supposed to be and was wondering if I had forgotten a gig or something, which I certainly didn't want to do. Still later, as I was putting on my coat to go home, George Raft made a crack like, "Well, you better make a good night out of it because after tonight you won't have any more." That started me thinking again. What the hell did they mean, both he and Freddie? Anyway I went on home about five o'clock. During the following days I found out with a bang just what they meant.

Duke had bought a newspaper at the studio one day and had given it to one of the chorus girls to read while he was doing something else with the band. She was casually reading the news until she came to the section for obituaries, weddings and intentions to wed, and saw my name and Derb's under intentions to wed. Naturally she showed it to everybody except Derb and finally Duke saw it. "Ah ha," he said, "Buck and Derb think they're going to pull something over on everybody. They slipped off and got a marriage licence and didn't tell anybody about it. Looks like they are trying to pull a fast one on us." Then he says, "I tell you what we'll do." Then he went to the captain of the chorus girls and showed her the article. He said, "Buck's a bandleader and Derb's one of the chorus line. Let's give them a wedding that they'll never forget." So, without Derb knowing about it, he and the captain of the chorus went to the executives of the studio and planned a wedding that I never would have dreamed of. Everybody knew about it except Derb and me, and that is what Freddie Jenkins and George Raft meant that night when we were gambling in that after-hour joint. I was supposed to be at the Paramount Studio at ten o'clock to be married whether I wanted to or not.

That morning before ten o'clock I was called by the studio and told what was to happen, only the hour was to be one o'clock instead of ten. Invitations had been made to nearly everybody in Los Angeles, it seemed, and it seemed also that everybody had accepted, because they knew that if Duke had anything to do with it, it would be a swinging affair. Naturally Derb had been notified but we didn't talk about it. I just knew that I was to be married at one o'clock and I didn't have too much time to think about it. The more I thought of it the more I didn't want to get married. No offense to Derb, I just wasn't sure of myself. I was moving around like a robot until I noticed that it was eleven o'clock and I had hardly put on more than my socks. In those days, before the freeways, it took about forty-five minutes to get from Los Angeles, Central Avenue, to Hollywood. The next time I dug the clock it was eleven-thirty and I had at least put on my pants. I was almost broke as I had just got my laundry out and I found myself at twelve o'clock, noon, standing on a corner on Central Avenue trying to think what to do. I was leaning against a telephone post smoking cigarettes like they were going out of style, and at the same time looking at nearly all of Central Avenue going out to Hollywood to my wedding. It was like a Roman holiday. Everybody was going, and I was the one leaning against this telephone pole trying to decide what to do. They would say, "Hey, Buck, are you going to make it?"

I'd say, "I don't know yet."

Then they'd say, "Well, we're going on out anyway, 'cause it's going to be a ball."

So as I stood there I looked at my watch and it was one o'clock already, and I was still puffing on one cigarette after another. I was all by myself as it seemed that all the crowd that had passed me were already out in Hollywood. All of a sudden a car pulled up in front of me with a few of the members of my band in it and I was pulled into it. They said to me, "Well, if you can't make up your mind, we'll make it up for you." So away we went to Hollywood. I don't know, but if they hadn't come by and got me I might have stayed right there leaning against that post and missed the wedding. Anyway it was after one o'clock when we started for Hollywood and it was about two-thirty when we pulled up at the studio.

Duke was about to go crazy in a silent kind of way. Duke never showed his expressions too much. He had his head down in his hands like he was crying on the piano. He must have been thinking, "If this little young jerk don't show up, I'm in trouble." It was because of Duke that the studio had closed up for the whole afternoon and, at the salaries they were paying the stars, there was quite a bit of money involved, aside from the fact that they had made some pretty elaborate plans, such as building an entire bandstand for the Duke's band and a special seating capacity for the guests. Everybody was off for the afternoon, including such people as Mae West, George Raft, Carl Brisson and everybody, so that they could attend the wedding that Duke's band was going to play for. Duke was about to go crazy, Derb was embarrassed, and I was an hour and a half late when I walked in. She was crying, her mother was crying and it seemed that Duke himself was on the verge of tears when they looked up and saw me come in. Everything came to life, Duke started smiling, the newsreel cameras started getting in position and the Reverend Napoleon P. Greggs, who had been there for such a long time holding his Bible, started beaming. Duke's band played a number and then out comes all of the chorus girls. Some of the members of my band were there along with so many other people sitting in the special seats made especially to accommodate the guests. They passed out rice to everybody to throw, Duke played another number, then came the ceremony and I found myself married. Carl Brisson, star of *Murder at the Vanities*, gave the bride away. All the officials were there. Jack Bratton was my best man and actually knew in what pocket he had put the wedding ring. Cootie and Tricky Sam Nanton growled the wedding march as the cameras clicked away. I never had any idea they could make the wedding march sound like something right out of Harlem, but they did. Somehow it was in good taste and had the Duke Ellington flavor about it. When the ceremony was over Sonny Greer went into *Ring dem bells* and everybody went into the studio commissary, where there was the biggest cake I ever saw made for me and my wife. The festivities took place there. Ivy Anderson sang, Duke did a concert of numbers, and many other entertainers performed and in general everybody had a ball. My mother wasn't too crazy about the whole thing, though, as she said it was too much glitter and not enough sincerity. She was right, but I couldn't get out of it after Duke became involved in the plans, although I almost did. I don't really know what would have happened if the guys in my band hadn't come along and jerked me in that car. A couple of weeks later, as we were getting on the boat to leave for China, Duke came down to the boat to wish us a good trip and took several pictures of us.

THREE

Shanghai

Shortly after our wedding, which I must admit felt to me like a shotgun wedding, we packed our bags and caught the "President Hoover" of the Dollar Line ships for Shanghai, China. The personnel of the band was Teddy Buckner, Jack Bratton, myself (trumpets), Happy Johnson, Duke Upshaw (trombones), Arcima Taylor, Caughey Roberts, Hubert "Bumps" Myers (saxophones), Eddie Beal (piano), Baby Lewis (drums), Frank Pasley (guitar), Reginald Jones (bass) and Joe McCutchin (violin). We met at the pier and, with quite a few of our friends, had some bon voyage parties along with three wives who went with us. I was knocked out from the very start at the cleanliness of the boat and the friendliness of the passengers. I enjoyed listening to the little Chinese fellows ringing the bells announcing meal time. Naturally the bar was one of our favorite hangouts and sometimes some of the guys would play, just for the fun of it. We met and made many friends. Joe E. Brown, the famous movie actor with the big mouth, was aboard and we enjoyed talking to him. It's a funny thing, but when you're out on a boat everybody seems to be your friend, even people that you don't think you'd like to be associated with will become friends. We spent a pretty good time talking to people who were going to China for the first time and also to people who had been to China before and enjoyed telling us all about it.

I never once got seasick but I saw some people on the boat that were sick even from the second day out of California, including Derb. They really suffered. They lost weight and some of them in a few days didn't even look like the same people that got on the boat a few days before. There was a baseball player on board who at times would be so seasick that he really wanted to die. Many times I'd go into the dining salon for breakfast after a storm the night before and there would be perhaps only three or four people in the whole dining room, which was made to accommodate at least three or four hundred people. I'd always be there as my stomach was pretty good at that time. Everybody else seemed to have nurses bringing their meals to their cabins, but I was stuffing myself in the dining room at every meal. The trip went usually pretty calm for the whole three weeks. Nothing really happened that I hadn't seen before except that I had never seen flying fish and that used to amaze me—seeing the fish really fly out of the water, up into the air and back into the water. Sometimes we'd run into a school of whales and that too was something new to me, but other than that the trip was pretty routine. We were five days getting to Hawaii, eighteen days to

Japan and twenty-one days to China. When we were in Japan we were the only ones allowed to disembark. All the white passengers had to remain aboard while the ship was in dock while we Blacks were allowed to go ashore and have a ball. We could come and go as we pleased as long as we didn't miss the boat when it prepared to leave. We went ashore at Kobe, Yokohama and Nagasaki, and I must admit at times it was pretty hard to go back to the boat, especially after being in Kobe. There was really some pretty attractions there, all of them about four feet tall.

When we finally pulled into Shanghai harbor we were met by the bosses of the Canidrome Ballroom, Mr Tung and Mr Vong. They were two very rich Chinese, one fat and the other skinny, but both were very nice people. They greeted us with a huge welcoming committee and soon we were at a banquet that was really something else. I didn't know what I was eating and I couldn't eat with chopsticks but I was happy. We hadn't even had time to see the city yet, but the banquet was very friendly and Mr Tung and Mr Vong had gone all-out to make our arrival as enjoyable as possible. After the banquet Teddy reached over to me and said, "Buck, they don't think you enjoyed your dinner."

I asked, "Why?"

He said, "Well, in China you're supposed to splatter soup and everything all around your plate. When you do that they know that you enjoyed it." By me keeping clean they didn't know that I did enjoy it or, rather, most of it. From then on I just splattered soup and everything all around my plate. When I got up from my place it looked like a pig had just eaten dinner at my seat. There was, however, some things that I never could get with. For example, they served eggs that had been buried in the ground for twelve years. There was no shell on them. When they dug them up they were hard like hard-boiled eggs but they had turned purple. I couldn't eat 'em. They had a soup that was composed of four ingredients that were hard to obtain: the claws of a certain kind of bear that were ground into powder, a bird's nest from a certain kind of bird, the fin of a shark, and the fourth I don't remember, but actually when all of these things were put together it made a pretty nice soup. I enjoyed that, but I couldn't get with those twelve-year-old eggs.

After the banquet we were assigned to our living quarters. The band members were to stay in a large house where there were plenty of servants and house workers to take care of our needs. There were also cooks that knew how to cook American food. They had been taught by members of American bands that had been to China before us. For example, Valaida Snow, who had been there with the Jack Carter band, had taught them how to cook real soul food. The band boys were lucky: they could have fried chicken, yams, bacon and eggs and everything that they had been used to having at home, whereas for me and Derb, we had an apartment and had to do most of our own cooking. They figured that since we were newly married we would rather be together in an apartment, which was OK, but at the same time we didn't have the cooks that the boys had in the big house.

The next day we went out to look at the city of Shanghai and I was very much impressed with so many people in the street and so many different odors coming from the cooking done by the Chinese. There seemed to be millions of people all in the area of one block. I knew that the Chinese population exceeded all others, but I would have never in life imagined so many people. They were everywhere—in the streets, on the sidewalks, in alleys—and they would jostle you around so much that it was really a relief to get out of the way of them. Some of them hardly wore any clothes at all and others had on tattered rags. There were rickshaws everywhere with the little rickshaw coolies running, always running. I don't think I ever saw a rickshaw boy walking. Their feet must have been made of leather as they could withstand the heat of summer and the cold of winter in nothing but hand-made bamboo shoes. People, people, people, nothing but people. I walked around or, rather, I tried to walk around, but after being bumped into by so many different kinds of people I was glad to get back to my apartment. I think that I must have become accustomed to the population later, as the longer I was there the less I seemed to notice all of these people. I would see sometimes twenty or thirty coolies pulling a big huge heavy cart that in America would be pulled by a truck or horses. These people seemed to be really nothing but human horses and all they would be paid for at the end of the day was just enough to get a couple of bowls of rice and a place to sleep. I don't know how they did it.

We went farther downtown in the business district and found many foreigners there doing business. Companies from all over the world did business in Shanghai and you could see all kinds of nationalities—Indians, French, Russian, English, Americans and people from all corners of the world. We lived in the international settlement where most people were English, French, Russian and American. Bubbling Well Road was one of my favorite streets in Shanghai and I used to go shopping there many times. We were introduced to many American musicians who at the time were playing different hotels. The American musicians were particularly glad to meet this new band from the States and soon introduced us to all the hot spots in Shanghai. At night they would take us to the jai alai games and we'd watch the South American guys do their thing. Jai alai was something new to us, as we had never seen it before. We also met and made friends with many American marines who were stationed there. They were anxious to know what was happening stateside and we were glad to meet them. We were friendly, too, with the exiled White Russians living in China. It was then that I was introduced to vodka. Because of so many White Russians being in Shanghai it was almost a national drink—years before it was introduced to the United States. At one time I was beginning to learn Russian but later gave it up. I never tried to learn Chinese because there were so many different dialects. All I ever learned was how to call a rickshaw boy.

There were nightclubs galore in Shanghai and all of them had many pretty little Chinese hostesses. Dried watermelon seeds were sold in the nightclubs like popcorn is sold in theaters in the States. There were many bands of different nationalities: Filipino bands, Russian bands, East Indian bands and of course the oriental bands. They all played on so many different kinds of instruments. The only music that we could really understand was naturally the American music, especially the jazz. I liked the Russian music too and would have liked to have learned more about it.

The following day we went over to the Canidrome Ballroom to have a look at our new place of employment and at the same time have our first rehearsal. We found the ballroom to be in a huge white building that must have covered several acres of land—spacious grounds that included several green lawns where the tea dances were held. In the back of the huge building there was a greyhound racecourse where every night there would be racing. I used to watch the pack of greyhounds chase the electrical rabbit night after night. I never bet on the dogs but I found the Chinese to be big gamblers. Every night in one of the several gambling rooms in the Canidrome there would be a lottery (the kind of lottery that we have in the States perhaps once or twice a month the Chinese had every day). I don't believe that the whole time I was in the Canidrome I was in every gambling room in the building as there was so many. The word Canidrome means in some way "dog racing," from which came the name. There was no parking lots on the grounds but every car was assigned to a stall; in other words every car was assigned to its own private little garage. There were other ballrooms in the building but we occupied the largest and the most popular one. Everything was spick and span as there must have been gangs of ground-keepers and people who took care of the ballroom, including light technicians for the shows, and so many people in the big kitchens. All this was new to us. The dancing floor of the ballroom was as big as some entire clubs in the States. There were other clubs in Shanghai but the Canidrome topped them all. There was the Little Club, which was frequented mostly by Americans, especially the marines; there was the Ambassador Club, which sent for an American band after we arrived; there was the Santa Anna Club, which later sent for Earl Waley's band out of Seattle, Washington. So after our arrival it wasn't long before Shanghai clubs were hiring more black bands from America. The booking agents were doing a fabulous business in bringing over new acts demanded by the Chinese club owners.

Our first rehearsal was like being in a different world. We found the entertainers to be very friendly and helpful in many ways. The Mistress of Ceremonies was Ursula Preston from Britain, who aside from being Mistress of Ceremonies did a ballroom dancing act with a British partner who I believe was a Mr J. A. Andrew. Derb had been asked to perform in the show because of her background at the Cotton Club in Los Angeles. Thelma Porter, the wife of trombonist Duke Upshaw, was also in the lineup as a singer and there were also the people that we were just beginning to meet: Fay Courtney, Harlan and Janet Milner, Marya and Marta, Murry and Harris and others. Teddy Weatherford was playing four different nightclubs each night, so he could only play with us on one number before he would have to leave for another club to be in time for his show there. He would play one half hour in each club, running from one club to the next, but at the end of the week he had four salaries coming to him. His specialty with our band was *Rhapsody in Blue* which, by the way, was my first time to really direct a number. With the help of Joe McCutchin, who had done so much work in the pit of the Vendome Theater in Chicago, I became pretty good at it and really liked directing. Ravel's *Bolero* was another number that I liked to direct. We started the evening off with classical music from nine o'clock to nine-thirty and after that it was back to Harlem. The menu was just unbelievable. There was a fourteen-course dinner for four dollars beginning with queen olives, stuffed roast capon and ending with coffee. Just four dollars.

As soon as we hit Shanghai we were smothered with tailors who made suits, hand-made suits, for such ridiculous prices that we were ordering them like we were millionaires. All the tailors needed was a suit that you liked for them to use as a model, and they would have a brand new suit in two or three days at the most and made of beautiful material. One of the first tailors that we met was a little Chinese tailor named Pingee. By the time we were in Shanghai two months we had all sorts of uniforms and I wouldn't be exaggerating if I said that I believe that we had more uniforms than Duke Ellington. We had tuxedos of different colors, we had full dress suits both in black and in gray colors, we had many white suits of different materials and loads and loads of other style suits and combinations, besides our own personal suits. The good thing about all this was that you didn't have to pay for the suits right away. There was the chit system in China where you could order anything you wanted and not get the bill or part of the bill until the end of the month—just sign your name. But still at these low prices you could pay for everything you ordered in almost one payment. The chit system went for everything: nightclubs, restaurants, clothing stores, theaters and even prostitution houses. Many a chit went to these whorehouses and you'd be surprised at how much the bill was for some of the guys. By the way, speaking of prostitution houses, we hadn't been in Shanghai ten minutes it seems before half the band was going to the doctor with VD. Everybody would get a rickshaw and go to the doctor at the same time and it looked like a parade of Buck Clayton's band lined up in these rickshaws going to the doctor. We had a German doctor by the name of Dr Borovika who had been an ace in the First World War, and he was our man any time we had girl problems.

The opening night at the Canidrome was fantastic. There were so many fellow Americans who were glad to see us there along with many other people who were dignitaries from other countries. The show went down like we had been doing it for years and the next day we got raves in all of the Shanghai papers. We felt pretty good about it and I still say today that the two years I spent in China were the happiest two years of my life. My life seemed to begin in Shanghai. We were recognized for a change and treated with so much respect. However, later on we were to run into some southern prejudice, but that can never erase the really good times that we had in China. On our opening night Madame Chiang Kai-shek was there with a big party, including several beautiful Chinese ladies with the slits in their dresses, a style that I liked very much. She was with her sister, who insisted on learning tap-dancing from my trombonist Duke Upshaw, and really did take lessons from him every Saturday afternoon for a while. The joint was packed every night and we soon were the envy of all of the other bands in Shanghai. The guys held their heads, though, and took it all in stride.

The first ugly incident came after we had been working for about a month. I happened to be walking down the street one afternoon and I saw some of my guys all going down the street and they seemed to be looking for somebody. I wondered who they were looking for as nobody even mentioned that they were looking for someone. I just assumed that they were looking for some girls as they kept telling me to go on home to Derb. I said, "No, whatever you guys are looking for I want to be in on it too." So I kept on with them. Still they never mentioned anything about any girls, but I was just sure that's what it was all about; they were looking for some chicks and didn't want to tell me, so I presumed that they had already seen the girls and in some way had lost them in the streets and were trying to find them again. So I wouldn't go home, I just stayed with them until we turned a corner and I see about four rickshaws coming down the street with some white American marines in them. The next thing I heard was the white guys saying, "There they are. Niggers, niggers, niggers!" And before long one of them threw a brick that they had piled up in the rickshaws. I thought to myself, "I should have went on home." Obviously these guys were the ones who had called my guys niggers before and had ran off in their rickshaws and my guys were looking for them. They jumped out of their rickshaws and soon fists were flying everywhere. I hadn't hardly had a chance to realize what was happening before one of them came up and took a swing at me. I ducked the blow but he had knocked off my brand new Stetson hat, and as I saw my pretty new Stetson lying there on the ground I got mad as hell and it wasn't long before me and this guy were mixing it up. I still hadn't forgotten my wrestling days in Parsons, and being only twenty-three years old I grabbed this cat and put a headlock on him and proceeded to run his head into a brick wall, the way wrestlers today run their opponent into the ring-post. I guess the guy was pretty surprised. Everybody was fighting like hell—Baby Lewis, Frank Pasley, Joe McCutchin—and in about five minutes it was all over. I remember the guy that I had run head-on into the brick wall was bleeding from the ears and started to run away. Just as a last gesture I kicked him in the butt as he ran, but I had on a pair of patent leather shoes and I hurt my foot from kicking him and had to limp around for a few days.

The next day some of the southern newspapers wrote it all up as we were hoodlums and gangsters from the States and that we had used brass knucks in the fight, which we didn't. Nobody had any brass knucks, but Baby Lewis had wrapped a handkerchief around his fist to fight with and that was all. When it was all over the Chinese onlookers treated us like we had done something that they had always wanted to do and followed us all the way home cheering us like a winning football team. I guess they figured it was something that should have been done a long time before, because I remember one time I saw a marine fall off a bicycle and he promptly got up, went over to a Chinese coolie and kicked him in the ass and then got back on his bicycle and rode on off. That didn't affect our business at the Canidrome at all because we had already made many friends in the Marine Corps there.

Sometimes we would play for the marines for their dances and also we would play many benefits for them. We had one special marine friend, who always hung out at the Little Club, called Murphy. He was really a good friend and he used to call all of those kind of trouble-making marines "mavericks."

We bought all of our food from the American boats as they came to Shanghai. We had our reasons for doing that. The Chinese government didn't have regulations on their food as we have in America. As you know, in the USA there is government regulations on such things as eggs, milk, meat and practically everything. In China people just grew the vegetables or raised the stock and ate it without being tested. Also the Chinese farmers used human waste as fertilizer; they didn't use such things as cow manure as Americans do. I'll use the word "dung" for the human waste because it sounds a bit like a Chinese word, but it means human waste and, though I could still use another word for it, I prefer the word dung. The Chinese farmers would spread it over their vegetables for fertilizer and in some cases would dig wells and fill them up with dung so it would seep into the ground and still fertilize the farms. In the residential sections of Shanghai, where the poor people had no toilets, they would fill up huge pots of this waste and set it out on the streets to be picked up early in the morning by people who used to gather up this mess like we have garbage trucks to gather up garbage in the USA. We called them "honey wagons" and they would be drawn by old men and old women who I guess couldn't find any other kind of work. Sometimes after leaving a nightclub early in the morning you could smell these honey wagons coming from a distance of two miles away, and eventually you would see them coming in groups. Sometimes as many as ten or twelve of them would be on their way to the country to be spread over vegetables. I never could understand how the Chinese could stand that themselves, but China was a pretty old country and I guess that had been going on for quite a long time. These old men and women pulling these wagons like horses.

Speaking of horses, we used to go horseback riding almost every week. Eddie Beal, Bumps Myers and myself were the most consistent. We all had sharp riding habits, naturally, and would go out and ride early in the morning. I didn't know until later that nearly all the horses that we rode had been racehorses at one time and when they knew it was time to return to the stables they would run like crazy getting back home. They knew when it was time to go home and, believe me, they ran faster than the wind going back home. I had one of these horses once and he rode just fine until it was time to go back to the stables. You'd have to be a damn good rider to stay on one of these horses when they knew the ride was over, but I didn't know this at the time. So, when the ride was almost over and I had stopped the horse to talk to Eddie about something, he bolted for home and threw me out of the saddle, except that my foot had caught in the stirrup and he was dragging me. He dragged me about two and a half miles and there was nothing I could do. I couldn't stop him, but luckily Bumps and Eddie were with me and trying to catch up with him to stop him. I was trying desperately to keep away from his feet and hooves and was fortunate in doing so. Finally Eddie and Bumps caught up with my horse and grabbed his reins and stopped him.

My riding habit was in shreds and I was bruised a bit but I had managed to stay away from his hooves. I was so mad at the damn horse that when they caught him I tied him up to a tree, went and found me a club and beat hell out of him. I really tried to annihilate that damn horse, then I got back on him and rode him on back into the stable. Another time I was riding a horse and he did the same thing almost. He put his head down and almost threw me over his head but I didn't quite go over. I caught hold of his mane and held on, but if I had not held on I would have gone right into one of those wells that were filled with dung for fertilizer as he was less than a foot away from the edge of one. I hate to think what would have happened to me if I had been thrown into that well.

Another incident concerning horseback riding occurred when Eddie Beal and myself went riding. Eddie and myself had never been circumcised when we were babies and one day we thought it would be a good idea to get circumcised—better for our health and everything—so we went to see Dr Borovika and he agreed to fix us up. We both were circumcised the same day and were recuperating. After a few weeks I was able to go horseback riding again, which I did with no trouble. Eddie, seeing that I went riding, thought that he too was ready to go, but it wasn't like that. He went riding with me the next time I went, but he was not as well healed as I was and a day or two after the ride his sex organ became infected. Dr Borovika was called in again and for a while things were pretty serious as we all waited for news of Eddie's condition. We waited around and finally Dr Borovika declared Eddie to be back in good condition. We weren't sure if he'd ever have any success with his sex organ again or not; we thought that perhaps he'd lose it but he came through alright and we were all happy. Eddie was pretty lucky as he came out of it with only some scars. I guess he kept those scars, but he must have been alright as he had a very talented daughter who is now in California.

We were informed of a new act from Los Angeles that was coming to work with us. We were glad to hear the news, naturally, as the idea of seeing someone from home really knocked us all out. On the date of their arrival we went down to the boat to greet them and, after waiting a long time to get a glimpse of them, we finally saw them. They were the raggedest bunch of guys we ever saw. One of them even didn't have a seat in his trousers. They were so ragged and tattered that if the wind had blown on them they would have whistled like a peanut stand. We thought to ourselves, "Damn things sure have gotten worse in the States since we left." The act was called the Chocolateers and was composed of three guys of which I knew only two —Esmond Mosby, who was related to the nightclub owner and bandleader of the Curtis Mosby Blue Blowers, and a little guy that I knew only as Gyp, who came from a theatrical family who once had a traveling show called Gibson's Hot Chocolate Box Revue. The third member I didn't know and still can't remember his name. Gyp was only twelve years old and was a very likeable little guy. I remembered him as being one of the best street corner dancers in Los Angeles. Sometimes the dancers would have jam sessions among themselves and dance under the street lights until wee hours of the morning, and Gyp was one of the best, even if he was only twelve years old. The guys were so poor and raggedy that we had to lend them some of our costumes so that they could make the first show. They had absolutely nothing and I don't know how they got booked over there in such bad condition. Anyway, we saw to it that they opened the show. They did have a pretty good act and after we put them in touch with Pingee they had everything they needed in a couple of weeks.

Our next visitors were really a first-class act and came to China via Europe. They were the Five Hot Shots, who originated in New York. They had played in all the big cities of Europe—Paris, Vienna, Cannes—in Egypt and just about everywhere. They had made quite a bit of money since they left New York, sometimes as much as a thousand dollars a week each and sometimes more. They had worked with Louis Armstrong and Fats Waller in Europe and they were all so impressed with Louis that they all went out and bought trumpets and included trumpet playing in their act (all except Emile who preferred the trombone). These were the famous Five Hot Shots: Sneaks, who looked so much like Louis Armstrong that he could have passed for his brother; Walter, the little sharp pretty one; Herbie, the quietest one; Emile, the trombonist and business manager; and Clarence, the tall one. They really had a big-time act and looked good when all five did their act on the floor. I'll never forget the first time when I went to meet them at the club where they were working, the Paramount I believe. As I walked down the hall to their rooms all I could hear was trumpets and when they met me it wasn't long before we became real friends. Even today when there is only one of them left we are the greatest friends.

We continued on at the Canidrome Ballroom with more and more success, but little did we know that we were soon to become victims of one of the biggest frame-ups in theatrical history. The management had booked twelve little girls from California known as the Hollywood Blondes. They were very nice and pleasant to work with. We soon had their music down perfect and they proved to be a big hit. They were all pretty and real blondes and were all good dancers. All of Shanghai turned out to see these little girls from Hollywood: the French, English, Japanese, Russians and especially the Americans. And of course the wealthy Chinese. You were not allowed in the Canidrome unless you had some kind of stature. You had to be either rich or be a dignitary of some kind. Poor people couldn't afford to even look in the Canidrome.

One night, about a week after the opening of the Hollywood Blondes, there were two little Russian girls in the audience and one asked me for my autograph. I signed my name on a piece of paper and gave it to her and then she jerked a monogrammed handkerchief out of my coat pocket that had my intitials, B. C., on it along with an embroidered trumpet that I had made special by a special seamstress. I thought a lot of that handkerchief and I didn't like it too much when she jerked it out of my pocket and ran away with it. However, I soon forgot about it as I had several more and I didn't think I'd miss one too much. But it broke up a set: I did have a dozen of them, now I only had eleven. That night when I went home I forgot about the whole thing as being of any importance. Just another little nutty chick that wanted a souvenir from me.

The next night, as the show was about to begin, I noticed these same two girls who had been there the night before and had taken my handkerchief, only this time they came in with a big guy. All three of them were shown to a table and the two girls sat down. The big guy didn't sit down but just stared at me. Miss Preston, the Mistress of Ceremonies, went into her introduction to the Hollywood Blondes. I was next supposed to give the downbeat to the band for the music for the blondes, but I couldn't help but look at the big guy who came in with the two girls. He was looking at me with such hostility, no longer staring but now glaring. He was still standing and just as the Mistress of Ceremonies finished her introduction he crossed his arms and yelled out at me, "Turn your eyes the other way, you black son of a bitch." I was so surprised. The guy had said it in such a loud voice, such language in such an elegant club like this, and in front of so many respectable people. I could see he was a hoodlum. I turned to the band and gave the downbeat for the blondes, and then I decided to go over to this cat's table and ask him what was wrong or ask him to go outdoors. He still hadn't sat down. I left the bandstand just as all of the blondes were running out on the floor and went around to his table. Before I could get to his table he took a Sunday punch on me and hit me right between the eyes. I didn't know that this guy had been a marine prizefighter or else I would have taken a little more precaution in going over to his table. I didn't expect a Sunday punch. I went down on one knee and was trying to shake the cobwebs out of my head, and when my head did clear a little I could see that the whole band had jumped off the stand and was beating him up. Then I blanked out again and when I came to myself I found that the band had stopped pummeling him and he and I had fought all across the ballroom right in the middle of the Hollywood Blondes and out into the men's room. I was sitting on top of this guy—Jack Riley was his name—and I was trying to do as much bodily harm to him as I could. Every time I hit him in the face the back of his head would hit the cement floor in the men's room. I tried my best to really kill this guy and he was hollering, "Why don't some of you white sons of bitches help me?" Nobody came to his aid because everybody had seen that he started the whole thing. After hitting him so many times in the face and the back of his head hitting the cement floor, you couldn't tell which part of his head looked the worst, his face or the back of his head. It looked like a big watermelon. There was an American correspondent there who came up and tapped me on the shoulder and said, "Buck, that's enough, that's enough."

So I said, "OK, OK," and got up off of him. He was still cursing out the white people because nobody came to help him. Everybody's attitude seemed to be, "It's good enough for you. You got what you deserved."

The next day the whole colony of people from Georgia sent Mr Tung and Mr Vong a telegram saying that if I came to work that night I would be met with a hail of machine-gun bullets. So we were laid off for the time. We hadn't planned on returning to work for at least two weeks but we never did return to work there after the southern crackers raised so much hell and threatened to bomb the place. I was assigned a bodyguard by the Shanghai police and couldn't go anywhere for two weeks without this bodyguard going everywhere I went—nightclubs, restaurants, everywhere. And besides, I had two big beautiful black eyes.

Later, with regret, Mr Tung and Mr Vong told us that, in fear of harm coming to the Canidrome Ballroom, we had lost our job. Jack Riley then sued the operators of the Canidrome for five thousand dollars damages for the brawl, which by the way occurred on my birthday, November 12th. One of the witnesses, Monte Berg of the Little Club, testified that he happened to be seated so he couldn't see the bandstand, but that he heard an epithet and turned and saw me on the floor, then he saw me strike Jack Riley. Elsie Soong, the sister of Madame Chiang Kai-shek, testified in our behalf, which meant quite a bit to us. We put in a countersuit and Jack Riley's suit was rejected and he was directed to pay court costs. However, the frame-up had been successful: we had lost our job due to the other local nightclub owners who had been suffering from loss of business and also to booking agents who were not receiving a cent from us in booking-agent fees. The whole thing was a conspiracy by both to get us out of the Canidrome, and it was successful.

After our dismissal from the Canidrome we found that all of us had not saved our return fare home and as you know we had accepted the job under the condition that our fare was to be paid one way only. Then came the awful realization that we were stranded—stranded in Shanghai, China. I had paid some dues in my short life in show business but I had never paid those kind of dues. Stranded half way around the world. Those were really some dues. We were questioned by Felthan Watson, the United States District Attorney, and were advised to leave town as soon as possible, but we were never really ordered to leave officially. The repercussions at home must have been tremendous. Jack Bratton's family sent him a ticket right away to come home. Teddy Buckner had his fare and decided to leave to be with his family in Los Angeles. In fact one half of the band were making preparations to leave when we were asked to open at another nightclub in Shanghai. I think that most of the people of Shanghai realized that we had been the victims of a raw deal, especially the Americans, who were used to prejudice.

So we were soon working at the Casa Nova Ballroom—not quite as elegant as the Canidrome, but at least a job where we could prove ourselves. We could only use half the band that we had at the Canidrome so it was better in a way that the other half had departed for Los Angeles. Derb booked passage on a Japanese boat that was due to take a month to get back to LA. So we found ourselves with a band of six or seven pieces but we were highly respected in the new club and went on about our new job. We found that on this new job we were obliged to play Chinese music so we began to learn how. I sketched out some of the most popular Chinese songs at the time and after a few rehearsals we were playing it like we had been doing it a long time. It wasn't too much different from our own music except the Chinese have a different scale tone, but as long as it could be written in on the American scale it could be played.

I learned shortly after beginning at the Casa Nova that some of our true friends in the Marine Corps had caught Jack Riley early one morning, had labeled him as a rat, and had given him a second beating that was even worse than the first one we had given him. He was found unconscious, draped over the steering wheel of his car, which made me feel a little better.

Our new boss at the Casa Nova was half-American and half-Chinese and he was a great guy to work for. He never bothered us and we had our living quarters right in the club in an apartment on the upper floors. I enjoyed it from the start. There was Russian hostesses there and we got along just fine. There was one Russian girl there, named Luda, that I thought was the most beautiful woman that I had ever seen. I never knew that they made those kind of women in Russia. We became friends but that was all, nothing more. There was, however, one American girl, who was in China with her mother, that I thought was a real nut. She was the daughter of an American diplomat from Ohio and she took a liking to me, but I could never get with her. She used to bug me so much that at times I had to actually run away from her to get away. One time she started a hassle with me and I saw that I'd have to leave, so I started walking away rather fast. She started walking fast too, and soon I decided to run. Then she decided to run to keep up with me. I ran until her heel broke and she had to stop. I felt so foolish running down the street with a girl running after me like that, but that was the only way I could get rid of her—literally run away from her. Really a foolish feeling. That night, when I went to work, she was there sitting in the balcony with her mother. She sent word for me to come up to the balcony but I didn't want any part of that and didn't go. She sent for me a second time after about a half hour had passed and I refused again. The third time she sent a message that if I didn't come up there she was going to kill herself. I thought to myself, "This is a lot of bullshit," and I didn't go. I went on back to the bandstand, and was in the middle of playing *The Very Thought of You*, when I noticed a commotion up in the balcony. Everybody was grouped around the place where she had been sitting and I ran upstairs at the end of the number and found that this crazy chick had taken a lot of sleeping pills as I was playing and was lying on the floor. Someone had called an ambulance and soon they were taking her to the hospital. After being in the hospital a few hours they brought her around and she was OK. I never saw her again as I think her mother sent her back home to the States.

We continued at the Casa Nova for some time, but this time we were pretty careful to save our fare back home. My biggest concern then was the Japanese Army. They were becoming more and more open in their contempt for the Chinese government and I saw many things that disturbed me. They would hold maneuvers early in the morning right in the middle of the main streets of Shanghai. One morning they were having firing-range practice and the target was a Chinese flag. Another time, as I was coming out of a nightclub, the Venus, I saw a squadron of Japanese soldiers holding maneuvers in the street and they sneaked up on a car that had a little Chinese fellow in it. The little guy was so afraid that he didn't make a move. The soldiers used the car as if it were a shield and pushed it down the street with the little guy still in it. They pushed it for about a quarter of a mile with about ten or twelve soldiers behind it, then suddenly they all left the car and ran over and hid behind a wall. They were having real maneuvers in the city and I could see that before long the real thing was going to happen. I went to my guys and told them that they had better soon make preparations to go home because Shanghai was going to explode and soon. They all listened and soon we were making bookings to get back home—all except Jonesy, our bass man. He had either married a Filipino girl, or was living with her, and didn't want to go back home, so he stayed.

After most of the guys got their bookings in order we were leaving Shanghai at last. I still loved the city but I didn't want to get caught in a Japanese–Chinese war, so I booked passage on a Japanese boat that I believe was named the "Tayo Maru." Anyway, I left and my traveling companion on the same boat was Clarence of the Five Hot Shots. In less than two weeks after we left the Japanese sailed a warship right down the middle of Shanghai and bombarded the city on both sides. I thanked God that I had got out in time. That was only the beginning. I learned later that Jonesy had been put in a concentration camp and had suffered many physical torments, along with the same correspondent that had stopped the fight with Jack Riley. They both had lost weight and looked very bad.

FOUR

I never heard such swinging music

Clarence and I arrived in San Francisco in pretty good shape and soon we were rejoined with the rest of the band in Los Angeles. I hadn't decided just what I wanted to do. I really had eyes for going on to New York, but some of the fellows persuaded me to stay on in California and re-organize the band. I noticed quite a few changes in Los Angeles during the two years that I had been gone. Lionel Hampton had formed a band. Eddie Barefield had come back to Los Angeles from Cab Calloway's band and had formed a band, and there were several other bands that had come to Los Angeles to find work. There were also musicians who had come on their own: Tyree Glenn, Herschel Evans, Bert Johnson, C. P. Johnson, "Big Chief" Russell Moore and several others. I went about re-organizing my band and had no trouble at all getting the guys together. We worked at the Cotton Club for a while, but every time we worked there we had to use Lionel Hampton on drums as Frank had made him the house drummer. No matter who came in the club, Frank would insist that Lionel be on the drums—unless it was an organized band like Duke Ellington or McKinney's Cotton Pickers who would always use their own drummer, Sonny Greer or Cuba Austin. So I had to use Lionel as I wasn't quite strong enough yet to use my own drummer. I had been using Lee Young, Lester Young's brother, as Baby Lewis had gotten into some kind of trouble in San Diego. Lee was a good drummer and had a sister, Irma, who was a wonderful alto sax player. I guess the whole family of Youngs must have been good musicians because when I met Lester later in Kansas City it was like meeting the cream on top of the cake. We played the Cotton Club and made trips up and down the West Coast. I loved the city of Santa Barbara and we played there many times at a club called the Hacienda. We played in Los Angeles at another club called the Club Araby and there, once again, there was chorus girls and everything. I worked with Miss Sue Hoy, a great singer, and it was a pleasure for me to listen to her sing *Shifting Sands* every night. She was one great singer and I sure dug her. Derb was in the chorus, naturally. It was at the Club Araby that I lost Jack Bratton and had to replace him with Winslow Allen. In fact I had to make quite a few changes in the band, so we lost some of the effect of all of our new uniforms that we had bought in China.

There was another guy who had come to California, a blues singer named Wynonie Harris, a blues shouter. Wynonie and I were about the same size and we both had kinda grayish-green eyes. We became good friends and he was also a good friend of Joe Louis's. I saw Joe one time go to Wynonie's aid. Some guy was gonna punch Wynonie and that's one time I saw Joe Louis, who was champion at the time, get mad and rise up to protect his friend. Naturally that put an end to that, as the other guy took down like a sheep; Joe looked to be fifteen feet tall when he stood up.

After a short time I met the great negro showman Irving C. Miller, who owned the great Brownskin Models show. They had had some kind of trouble with their band and needed a new one. We had a band and no job so I talked to Irving C. and I found him to be one of the nicest men I ever met in show business. I was asked if I would like to play with his show and thought it would be a new experience. I still had never played with a show and always wanted to. Even when I was twelve to fifteen years old I always wanted to play with a circus. So I accepted Mr Miller's offer and we joined the Brownskin Models. I liked it very much once we got started. It was the first time my band had ever played with a show like that, because, as in China, it was something else. There were two left-over musicians from the former band and I was lucky to have had the chance to pick up Red Callender, a wonderful bass man and a great arranger, and a drummer named Kid Lips Hackett. They both already knew the show and were a great help to us and soon we had the show down pat. The first time I ever heard Tommy Dorsey's *I'm gettin' sentimental over you* was late one night when I was with some of the models in a hotel where we were not supposed to be making noise, but somebody had just bought this record and I thought it was, and still think it is, a beautiful record.

We stayed with Irving C. for quite some time and being around the chorus girls was always a pleasure for me. I think that Jo Jones and myself liked to work with chorus girls more than everybody else because to us they seem to be more like sisters than anything else. Finally our engagement came to an end with Irving C. and the girls, but Red and Lips stayed with the band and we went on into other things. We played a burlesque house in Frisco for a few weeks and that too was an entirely new experience for me. I was goggle-eyed as I used to watch those chicks strip on the stage and then walk around backstage with nothing on until they got to their dressing room. Absolutely nothing—because being out West those cowboys would insist that they take everything off, and usually they did. They wouldn't hurry to get back to their dressing room, just walk slowly, and there I was backstage when I wasn't in the pit—which usually I wasn't—and I had to look at them. What an experience.

Kid Lips the drummer always chewed gum with five packages of gum in his mouth while playing. He had at one time been a pugilist. He could fight, and would. He was short but had extra-long arms and was always in some kind of trouble, but I liked him a lot and he liked me too, I think. Whenever I was with Lips I always felt somehow like I had a bodyguard with me. When we played the Cotton Club and I had to lay Lips off because of Lionel being house drummer at the club, I would always pay him his salary just as if he had been working. One day I bought him a new suit as he needed one and couldn't afford to buy one yet, so I got him a new pin-stripe. He was sharp as a pin when the rest of us went to work at the club that night, but when we got back on the avenue after work and saw Lips that suit was in shreds. It looked like he had been mauled by a pack of lions. He had gotten into a fight with some guy and that suit had been cut up so much it looked like a pile of rags. However, Lips had not been cut seriously. Years later his life style of violence came to an end when he was killed by a woman.

Eddie Barefield had a good band—a very good band—but there was no way that Eddie's band could have been anything else with Eddie writing all of those beautiful arrangements. He had trombone man Tyree Glenn, who I had just met since my arrival from China. I tried to steal Tyree from Eddie but I couldn't get him. However, I did steal Herschel Evans from the Lionel Hampton band. Stealing musicians from other bands was commonplace then, because if you had a better band or if you paid a better salary you could steal a lot of guys from bands. When I got Herschel he used to tell me so much about eastern musicians that I had never seen. He told me of Lester Young, Ben Webster, Jo Jones, Basie and a lot of others, including Coleman Hawkins, who was his idol. Sometimes he would call up the Reno Club in Kansas City while Basie was playing on the stand and hold the telephone receiver up to my ears so that I could hear the band swinging, and believe me they were swinging. Then, too, he used to tell me all about different southern musicians with whom he had worked. It was a ball being around "Tex," as we called him, and I was proud to have him in my band. Now I had two hell-of-a-tenor men—Herschel and Bumps Myers.

The Club Alabam was a club that had been built since we had left for Shanghai and there were always new chorus girls. Andy Kirk had just made that fabulous recording of *Until the real thing comes along* and Kansas City people were proud of their Clouds of Joy. I had met Maceo Birch and, being from Kansas City, he was proud as everybody else from KC. There was Ethylyn Sylvester, a chorus girl from Kansas City. There was a group of playboys from Kansas City who gained a lot of prestige after that recording came out: Fuddy, Jim Willie and Salty Dog. Kansas City had come into its own at last as that recording was popular all over the United States.

It seemed to me that Los Angeles was swinging a lot more than when we left for China in 1934. There was so many new people in town and so many new clubs and after-hour joints that had opened up during our absence. There was the Billy Berg Club out in Hollywood. There was a pianist, who led a trio, by the name of Nat Cole, who later became known as Nat "King" Cole because, until Art Tatum came to town, he was the king of Los Angeles piano players. C. P. Johnson was holding forth out in Hollywood and God only knows how many other newcomers there were in town at the time. There was also a new bunch of chorus girls: Deannie Gordon, Garbo and a singer named Billie Yarbo, who used to say to us, "To hell with Billie Holiday. Come on down and listen to me—the real Billie!" Billie Holiday wasn't in town, but her records were becoming more and more popular. Every morning I used to wake up to her recordings that she had made with Teddy Wilson, Benny Morton and Roy Eldridge. Also I'd wake up to Jimmie Lunceford's *I'm walking through heaven with you*.

I worked with my band with the Mills Brothers, Herbie, Don, Harry and John, the first time that they ever played Los Angeles. I don't think that during all the years that have passed I've seen any of them since. I enjoyed working with them very much. They were all young then, and Don used to ride a motorcycle and wore the widest belt that I've ever seen a motorcyclist wear. Our uniform for that engagement was a white silk full dress suit, complete with high hat that we borrowed from a studio for which he had made a movie. Since we were scheduled to go on a tour for the Pantages circuit we were allowed to use the uniforms for the whole trip, including the Mills Brothers' stint, as the suits had been made personally for us.

About this time Harlem decided that it wanted some new girls at the Ubangi Club and sent to Los Angeles for the top chorines that they could get. Derb was selected. Maudine Simmons, Alice "Red" Keyes and Ruth Scott were also selected to go to New York and work with Willie Bryant at the Ubangi Club. Later we gave a big party for all of the departing girls and they all left for the great New York. We read about their success in the *Chicago Defender* a few days after their debut. Also, there came to California a big-time show girl that I had read so much about when I used to sell the *Chicago Defender* in Parsons, Louise "Jota" Cook. She was a big-timer and had been one for some time. She was cute and I think had recently married Herbie Mills of the Mills Brothers quartet. I don't know how I met Louise but somehow it did happen. We became pretty good friends and I considered her to be as great as any movie star and was proud to be seen with her when so many other guys were trying to get to her. One morning, as I was walking down Central Avenue about five o'clock, I heard someone calling me from about a block away. It was a girl's voice so naturally I stopped and waited to see who it was. It was Louise. She had been to a party and was feeling kinda good. She always reminded me of Clara Bow when I'd see her. This morning, as she walked down the street with me, she had a mink coat that she was dragging in the dirt, just dragging it along like it was an old rag. She didn't want to put it on but still she wouldn't lift it up out of the dirt. I think she was showing me that a mink coat didn't mean a damn thing to her as she could buy more if she wanted to. I've seen it done later, but this was the first time that I ever saw anybody drag a mink coat for blocks while I was walking with her. I wanted to pick it up but I wouldn't, I just let her drag it along until we got to wherever we were going, then I picked it up.

Our next engagement was to make a tour of the Pantages theaters up and down the West Coast and our co-star with the show was Roscoe Ates, the funny man from the movies who stammered all the time. The tour was a success, but Roscoe and his old lady argued nearly all the time we were on the tour. I think they had their daughter with them. I met Mr Pantages and worked for him many times later at his theaters. He used to give me some good advice which came in handy later on in my life.

Derb and all of the other California girls were doing a bang-up job at the Ubangi Club in New York and in talking to Willie Bryant she had told him that I was a bandleader and also an arranger. Willie, being one of Harlem's favorite bandleaders, thought it would be nice to have an arrangement by someone other than the arrangers in Harlem, so he sent me a letter and asked me if I'd be interested in making an arrangement for him so that he could feature it at the Apollo Theater with his band. I wrote him back and told him, yes, I'd make one for him. He then wired me to make an arrangement on *Robins and Roses*. This song had been made very popular by Stuff Smith, as he had recorded it in New York. The record was going wild and Willie wanted an arrangement on it. So I made the arrangement for him and sent it to him. He and the band rehearsed it and they liked it very much and got a kick out of playing it.

Next Willie wired me and asked me if I'd be interested in coming to New York and working with his band as a trumpeter and arranger. I answered him by saying, "Well, you know, Willie, I've got my own band out here. I do want to come to New York some day, but we'll just leave it like that until I do decide to come to New York." So I didn't take the job then. After thinking about it for a few days I decided that perhaps I would like New York better than staying out in California, so I went to the band and asked the guys, "Would you cats like to go to New York?" They all said, no, because we didn't have a job lined up in New York—that is, nobody but me, but they didn't even know that. I said, "Are you sure that you don't want to go?" They said, no. I could understand their feeling, though, as they had their homes, their families, in California, and California boys don't like to travel. Frankly I didn't blame them too much. They told me that there was too many good musicians walking around on the streets of New York not making any money and they didn't see why they should go there and increase the population of unemployed musicians. I argued with them, but I could see that it was a losing argument.

Since I couldn't get my band to venture out of California and go to New York, I decided to disband. So I called the guys together and told them that I personally was gonna leave and go to New York by myself and join Willie Bryant's band. I did disband and turned all of my arrangements over to Eddie Beal and started making preparations to leave Los Angeles. I never did work with Lionel Hampton's band, not five minutes of any day in history. I was a bandleader right up to the time I pulled out for New York with Maceo Birch. We left Los Angeles one bright morning in Maceo's car and between us we drove all the way to Kansas City, which was Maceo's home and where he had a mother and a sister. Kansas City looked just the same as it did when I used to go there on weekend excursions from Parsons. There were some nice homes there made of stone that had been quarried from stone quarries outside the city. I was impressed by these beautiful homes and always had a desire to own one some day, but due to the expense of having the stones transported by rail I soon forgot about it.

We drove up to Maceo's home and I met his mother and sister. They were very nice. Maceo's mother suggested that I stay at their home as there was an empty room in their upstairs apartment. She told me that I could stay there as long as I wanted to for only three dollars a week, so I moved in and stayed there for the short time that I was to be in Kansas City. That night Maceo took me to the Reno Club, where I met Count Basie and all the band.

I never heard such swinging music in my life and was spellbound from the very first minute I heard them. There were only nine of them, but that nine could out-swing anything that I'd ever heard. The bandstand was small in the Reno Club and at one time boxing matches were held there. The only thing remaining from the boxing days was the bell that was rung between rounds. This bell was used by Lester and Jo Jones to indicate that someone had goofed in the band. If someone had screwed up something Lester would say, "Ring the bell," and Jo Jones or Jack Washington would ring it.

When I was introduced to Basie I found him to be a nice congenial cat that knew all the answers. He smiled as I was being introduced to him and put that look on me that I knew right away he had experienced quite a bit of life in show business. He had heard of me through our broadcasts from Frank Sebastian's Cotton Club and we talked about that for a few minutes. Then he introduced me to Lester Young. Lester was unique in so many ways. He was a thorough artist, while at the same time enjoyed making people laugh. I never knew anybody that could swing like Lester. The way he ran chords was just fantastic and, coupled with his sense of rhythm, he was the best I had ever heard. When I met him he put those big light-colored eyes on me and said he was happy to meet me. He was everything that Herschel Evans had told me before I left California. He smoked a pipe and was always looking for a jam session. I liked Prez right away and we talked about his brother Lee, who had worked in my band in Los Angeles, and his sister Irma, that I also knew in LA. Then I was introduced to Walter Page, who was the former leader of the famous territory band the Blue Devils, out of Oklahoma. Page, or "Big Un," as he was called, was nice too. When I was introduced to him I asked him, "Are you Lips?"

He said, "No." I hadn't learned yet that Lips Page had quit the band and had left for New York to go on his own as a single, something on the order of Louis Armstrong, under Joe Glaser's direction. So after realizing that he was not the famous Lips Page, we went on to talk about other things such as when I used to hear about the Blue Devils in Parsons, Kansas, and how Lips Page was the star of the band at the time. I had never seen Lips but had heard him play through an open window one time when I was on a weekend excursion to Kansas City and he was playing in the Yellow Front. Walter Page and I became very close in later years. He played string bass in the band and could also play sousaphone and bass- or baritone saxophone and was damn good on all of them. When Bennie Moten died from a tonsil operation there was an election in the band as to who would be the next leader. Basie was noted for his unique and original arrangements that had made Bennie Moten more of an up-to-date band than they had been before he joined them from the Blue Devils. Walter Page was up for election because he had been the leader of the Blue Devils, so the election was between Basie and Walter Page. I, of course, wasn't there, but I was told that the election turned out to be a draw as they both had equal votes. Page, however, thought that the Count was more qualified to be leader due to his original ideas and his improvement of the Bennie Moten band, so he told Basie that he would prefer that he be the leader of the band. He made one exception, which was that if the band ever did become a success it should not forget him, but see to it that he was well taken care of. So Basie took over the leadership, and was true to Page and never forgot him in later years. One of Page's favorite expressions when he was trying to make a chick was, "I'm Walter Page of Count Basie fame."

After meeting Page I was introduced to Jo Jones, the hellion on the drums. Jo was wearing a straw hat, a brim hat. He was lively and always had something going on. He had heard my band broadcast from Los Angeles and had read of my marriage to Derb in the black journals, so we had a lot to talk about. Jo was always full of energy and it sure showed when he sat down behind those drums. He was married and had two young kids, a boy and a girl. Jo was no beginner in show business, and I found out later that he knew a lot of circus and carnival people because of having worked in carnivals and circuses. He could play trumpet, which I didn't know until later, he could dance and he could play piano, so he was perfect for Basie and the band. He and I went through many experiences together when I joined Basie later.

In the evening I met the rest of the band. Jack Washington was one of the four best baritone saxophone players that I had ever heard in my life. (Harris Erwing of the Erwing Brothers' band in Los Angeles, Harry Carney of Duke Ellington's band and Jack Washington were actually my favorite three baritone players, barring none. In later years Gerry Mulligan was to take his place among them.) I met George Hunt, Tatti Smith and Joe Keyes, who was called "Booby Eyes" because of his big eyes. He was first trumpet player in the band and the same Joe Keyes that I had listened to in that small band that I had heard in Parsons when I was aspiring to be a jazz musician. Joe was congenial and actually asked me if I would be interested in taking over Lips's chair in the band. I told him I didn't know if I could fill Lips's shoes because Lips was one hell of a man to follow, so I didn't tell that I would join but I did think about it. Joe was always immaculate in dress and always neat around the collar and tie, and that I liked. He was a good lead man and I respected him very much. He did not have a very good trumpet, though; the one he had was full of strings and rubbers to hold it together. He played a good lead on it, but I always thought it was out of tune because of it being in such bad shape. He wasn't making enough money to buy a new one, so he just kept swingin' along on that one. I'll talk later about a discussion I had with the great jazz writer George Simon about Joe Keyes playing in tune.

After I had met all of the guys in the band Basie invited me over to a table where he was sitting with several friends. As I sat down somebody pulled out a stick of pot and lit it up right there in the club. That surprised me quite a bit because we wouldn't dare do that in Los Angeles. I was quite used to turning on by that time, but I was just surprised that they would do it in public without even thinking anything about it. I found out that anything could be done in Kansas City during the Pendergast regime and nobody would say a word. Even many of the police in Kansas City were former convicts, and they couldn't have cared less about someone smoking pot. Julia Lee was at the table, although I don't know if she turned on or not, and soon the air was blue over our table from the pot. So soon I didn't care if anybody else cared or not and went on to enjoy my meeting with Basie and the boys.

When it came time for the band to go back on the stand I was introduced to Jimmy Rushing. Jimmy had a seat that he always sat on near the bandstand and he was nearly always in that seat. Jimmy and I talked about Los Angeles as he had been there years before I went out and knew many of the musicians that I knew. He used to play piano in small roadhouses and sing. Knowing many of the same musicians that I knew in Los Angeles formed a bond between him and myself. His seat was near the dance floor where the show was staged and sometimes he would pinch the chorus girls on the butt as they would go on to do their dances. There was one chorus girl there that could dance like lightning, Chrystina. She was good. She was also Jo Jones's favorite dancer at the time and even one time later danced with Duke Ellington's band, though she returned to live in Kansas City. "Rush," as he was called by the guys, would run out on the floor and go into his songs and break it up with a dance off of the floor when he finished. He was always in good humor, it seemed to me. I never saw him get angry at any time, even after I joined the band and spent many years working with him. So after meeting Rush, Prez, Jo, Basie, Page, Jack Washington and all of the other guys in the band, I thought that I had spent a very enjoyable evening, and finally Maceo and I went home.

The next day I caught a train to Parsons to see my mother and family. It had been six years since I said goodbye to them and left for Atchison, Kansas, to work in my cousin's rock quarry to get enough money to go to Los Angeles. It was really a happy reunion. My sister Jean had married my idol on the track team, Royter Cherry, and had a new son, Royter, Jr, and a very young daughter, Jacqueline. My dad was very proud of the new little Cherries and wrote a poem to them. My sister Margie hadn't got married yet and was thinking of becoming a singer. She did have a pretty good voice, but later she gave up the idea and moved to Omaha, Nebraska. Everybody was happy to see me. I was a big shot in their opinion. I had been married where the wedding march was played by Duke Ellington's band, I had been to Shanghai, China, I had been in movies, so I was about the biggest thing in Parsons, Kansas.

Dad had gotten a little older and was a little bit less active in church services. Mom was pretty much the same and naturally was pretty proud of my achievements in music, but she still wasn't too fond of jazz music. My Dad's favorite jazz musician was still Fats Waller. I met all of the remaining members of my Dad's chapel orchestra; some had died during my absence and some had moved away from Parsons. Still, at the same time there were some new little guys interested in playing jazz that had come up since I went away. W. S. Davis, son of Walter Davis who sang baritone in my Dad's quartet, was learning to play jazz. He is now known as Wild Bill Davis. Charles Thompson, the son of a preacher who was then stationed in Parsons, was also learning to play piano. One Sunday afternoon they all came to my home to have a jam session with me playing trumpet. I'll never forget that little session. They had called my old buddy Schifford Garner, who came with his alto sax, and he and I were especially glad to see each other. Finally, after some talking and jiving around, we got into the session. All of the kids were happy to play with me, but I, at the time, thought that they all had a lot to learn yet. However, in later years they proved that they did learn everything in the books. Wild Bill became a member of Duke Ellington's band for years and is now one of the top favorites in Europe as well as the United States. Sir Charles later became one of the greats on piano and had his particular style that separated him from all the rest of the piano players. He too became an European favorite and is at present living in Zurich, Switzerland. In 1961 I took Charles to Europe in my band and he liked it so much that he decided to stay over there. He makes periodical visits to the USA but never stays long. Such a change from the little guys who came to the jam session at my home in Parsons. I'd have never thought when I heard them then that they both, Wild Bill and Sir Charles, would become such great jazz musicians as they are now. I can never forget that little jazz session at my home and I don't think they will forget it either.

I stayed about a week in Parsons with my family and then I started thinking of something that Joe Keyes had asked me while I was in Kansas City— would I like to play in Basie's band in Lips Page's place? It was an offer that I couldn't get out of the back of my mind. I had promised Willie Bryant that I was going to play with his band and in fact he was waiting for me to show up in New York, but still, on the other hand, I couldn't forget the way Basie and Jo Jones and Lester Young and the whole band was swinging in Kansas City. I really would have liked to join Basie, but I had too much respect for Lips Page and didn't think I could follow him, though I honestly would have been willing to try. I had been playing the trumpet only four years and I had heard of Lips when I was going to school in Parsons years before: the famous Lips with the famous Blue Devils. So I thought and thought and still was afraid to follow Lips.

At the end of my visit with Mom and Dad I couldn't wait to get back to Kansas City to hear Basie and the guys swinging, and when I heard them I was just as impressed as before. They never let up. They would swing you into bad health. My being from Kansas kinda made a little difference to them as Parsons, Kansas, and Kansas City both had the name Kansas and they took to me like I belonged in Kansas City. Soon we were all really good friends. Basie needed two more saxophones as, at the time I met them, there were only two, Lester and Jack Washington. Basie knew that he was going to New York some time that same year but he was short of two saxophones. He asked me first if I knew any good first alto sax players in California that I could get for him. I thought right away of Caughey Roberts who had gone with me to China, so I recommended him and Basie sent for him to come and join the band. Basie's former first alto man, "Prof," had gone to Texas to live and had left a big hole in the reed section. Then he sent for Herschel Evans, who was in California playing with Lionel Hampton's band. So they both accepted and came to Kansas City to join Basie.

Basie himself had never mentioned to me that he was going to New York, neither had he asked me to join the band. He had left that to Joe Keyes as I think he figured that Joe would have more influence on me by being a trumpet player. Finally, after learning that Joe had asked me, he asked me himself. He told me that they were booked to go to New York for the Music Corporation of America, which was a very high agency. They were to leave in October. I felt honored that he asked me to join that swinging bunch of guys, but I still was thinking of Willie Bryant, Derb, and all of the things that I had planned to do in New York. I told him that I would think about it, but all the time I knew within myself that I was going to accept his offer, especially after learning that Caughey and Herschel were coming in from California. I still hadn't said, yes, and Basie didn't know if I was going to come in or not for a couple of days.

Finally, after deciding that I would like to join Basie instead of joining Willie Bryant, I went to Basie and told him I'd like to join. But when I asked him how much money I'd make working at the Reno Club he told me, "Fourteen dollars a week." I couldn't believe that: a whole week for fourteen dollars, starting at ten o'clock in the evening and working until four or five in the morning. I was really taken aback and, to make it a little worse, he said, "I don't know if I can get Sol to pay any more money, but I'll try." Sol was the boss of the Reno and when Basie came back after seeing Sol he said to me, "Sol says that he can't afford to pay any more money to the band." This would have left me completely out. "But," Basie continued, "I'll ask the guys to chip in and we can make up your salary out of theirs." The guys were making $2.25 a night, so they all agreed to give up their twenty-five cents towards my salary and that made my salary come to the fourteen dollars that they were getting. I still couldn't get over that fourteen-dollar-a-week salary, but one thing I did know was that Basie was going to New York and we wouldn't be making the same salary there. So I accepted, even though it still seemed to me that I was going backwards in the salary department. I made more than twice that much even when I was working in the Red Mill dance hall in Los Angeles. There was no doubt about my liking Basie and I knew that I'd be happy working with him. Besides, Basie had a charm that I liked very much, a nice friendly smile, and he knew how to joke in such a way that it seemed an honor for him to make a joke about you. In other words, I forgot all about the salary and was happy to become a member of the club of Basie, Young, Jones and all the rest.

FIVE

Basie

Kansas City was a beehive of jam sessions; you could find a jam session at almost any hour of the day. The young musicians could be found jamming at the Union during the day. The unemployed musicians were to be found at night jamming at different clubs just to keep in shape to be ready when they did find a job, then at night the pros took over after they had finished their work in various clubs. Many of the pro sessions would begin about six in the morning and go on till eleven o'clock before the guys would stop to have breakfast. Then they'd go home to bed, just in time to wake up and go to their regular jobs.

Lester Young was one of the pros, but he never was too particular about getting into a jam session with Jack Washington. Jack played so much jazz on his baritone and he pushed Prez so much that Prez would rather lay out of a session if Jack Washington was going to be in on a session with him. Jack, however, wasn't the type who would go look for a session after work as he was married and usually would go home. There was nobody in Kansas City who could carve Lester and there would be so many people just waiting for the jam sessions that you would have thought the musicians worked at the jamming places. Lester could play with such clarity that he would be all alone in his field. He could run beautiful chords all over his tenor, chords that nobody else would even imagine. I liked it when he got on one note and pounded it out. The audience would go crazy.

Lips Page was another "carver" who used to invite or, rather, I should say, dare visiting musicians to come down to the Sunset Club on 12th Street and join in a jam session. For example, if Duke Ellington would play Kansas City, Lips would find out at what hotel they would be staying and slip notes under the doors of the trumpet players, such as Cootie Williams or Rex Stewart, and dare them to come down to the Sunset Club after they had finished their engagement. Lips would sometimes get drunk and play all night in the Sunset Club until it closed.

One day, shortly after Maceo and I arrived in Kansas City from LA, Maceo said to me, "Buck, why don't you take your horn out and go jam in some of the clubs so that people will know that you're in town? It is good if all of the guys know you and you can get acquainted with all of the best musicians in Kansas City." I thought it was a good idea so I decided to go down to the Sunset Club and jam with Pete Johnson, who was playing piano there. I went down to 12th Street with my horn and started playing with Pete and pretty soon one lone trumpet player came in with his horn. I thought, "Good, I'll have somebody to jam with." Then after a few minutes about two more trumpet players came in and started jamming. That was OK with me too as I figured we'd all have a ball. Then about a half an hour later in came about three more trumpet players. I thought to myself, "Damn, there's no shortage of trumpet players in Kansas City, that's for sure." Then, as the evening went on, more and more trumpet players came in to blow. To me, it seemed as if they were coming from all directions. Soon the room was just full of trumpet players. They were coming from under the rug, out of the woodwork, behind doors, everywhere. I never saw so many trumpet players in my life. Some had even come from as far as Kansas City, Kansas, because they had heard that the new trumpet player from Los Angeles was going to be there that night, and they all had their weapons (trumpets) with them. They really had blood in their eyes. We all stayed there and jammed until about five in the morning. Then some of them started clearing out and about seven they were all gone. I really had been shown how they jammed in Kansas City. I think, though, that Maceo Birch had put out the word that I was going to be at the Sunset Club that night and from there on things just happened like they always did in Kansas City. Lips Page would have died if he knew that he missed all that. He had left for New York, thank God.

I used to love to hang out in the Sunset Club and listen to Joe Turner and Pete Johnson. Joe was young and had just switched over to being a singer as he formerly had been a bartender. They used to knock me out every night. Listening to Pete Johnson play *Roll 'em Pete* and Joe Turner sing *Piney Brown Blues* was something I'll never forget. I can see now how John Hammond got wrapped up in Kansas City music. Nobody could play boogie-woogie piano like Pete Johnson, nobody in Kansas City that is. There were others in other cities, such as Albert Ammons and Meade "Lux" Lewis, but Pete was the undisputed king of Kansas City boogie-woogie piano men. Joe's favorite, *Piney Brown Blues*, was something else. Piney Brown was a big-time sportsman in Kansas City that everybody loved. He was also the father and the professor of all the pimps in Kansas City and there used to be quite a few of those in town.

One night, in the Sunset Club, I met George E. Lee, the same George E. Lee that had been the leader of that great orchestra that played in Parsons when I was a kid. He was no longer a bandleader but he was as well known as ever by the Kansas City people. I met him and he was pleasant. I told him about hearing his band in Parsons and how I never danced one dance because I couldn't tear myself away from the bandstand. He laughed. Soon another friend of George's came in and I was introduced to him. We listened to Pete Johnson for some time. I was digging George when he didn't know I was digging him. He was dressed more like a businessman in comparison to the glamorous way he was dressed in Parsons—still neatly dressed but not so glamorous. After a couple of hours in the club George and his friend asked me if I'd like to go to another club. I said, "Yes, of course." So we split from the Sunset Club and went out and got into a car. George's friend was driving. We drove up near 18th Street and Vine when all of a sudden George's friend yelled, "There they are."

George looked back out of the rear window and said, "Damn." Me, I didn't know what was happening. Then George said, "Get rid of them. Get rid of them, quick." Then I looked back and saw the headlights of another car following us. George's friend drove up and down different streets and different alleys, but those headlights were still following us. Then, as they continued to talk to each other, trying to dodge the other car, I realized that George had been in trouble with some pimps and it was these same pimps that he was trying desperately to get away from. Then I realized that if they got George they'd probably get me too simply because I was with him and his friend, so I began hoping that soon we could give them the slip. As we turned the corner on 18th and Vine where Matlaw's haberdashery is situated, George said, "Go down another street." We went down the other street, but still there was these headlights behind us. So finally George thought of another idea. He told his friend to drive to a certain place where we could quickly get out of the car, ditch the car in a certain hiding-place and run into the same lady's home where Basie stayed. I don't remember her name but she was a well-known lady. I had been there before to talk to Basie about joining the band when he was at home. We ran into the house and George quickly told her what was happening, so she told us all to be quiet and go into another room and if these pimps did show up she'd tell them that we were not there. So we went into the room but luckily I don't think the guys knew we were in there. After about an hour we came out and I caught a cab and split for Maceo's home. George and his friend got into their hidden car and drove off. That was some experience for me to be in with my first big bandleader that I had ever seen way back in Parsons.

So shortly after, in autumn 1936, I found myself on the Basie bandstand and I was ecstatic. Swinging so much jazz music with Count was like a dream. I had had a good band in California, but we couldn't swing like the Count. Most of Basie's music was "heads." In other words, we did not have music to most of the things that we played; they were made up from playing so long with each other. We did, however, have some arrangements that were held over from the Bennie Moten band made by Basie and Eddie Durham, but they were old and the pages had turned yellow and the corners were dog-eared or lop-eared. But they were swinging just the same. I became quite close to George Hunt—"Rabbit"—our only trombonist, and he and I would drink some kind of lemon-flavored gin which we bought in a nearby store. Rabbit was the one who took that beautiful solo on Basie's first recording of the *One O'Clock Jump*.

In the back of the Reno Club there was an open space where the band used to go out and turn on during intermission. I remember Lester taking me out in the back yard, as we called it, and lighting a stick of pot and then looking at me with those big eyes to see if I really knew how to smoke pot or if I was just pretending. After he scrutinized me for a few minutes he said, "Well, he really knows how." Sometimes when Walter Page would drink a little too much he would go out in the back yard and lie on a bench that was out there, even though there were big rats out there too. Basie wouldn't bother him because he knew that he'd be back on the bandstand as soon as he felt better.

Soon it became such a pleasure working with the band that sometimes I could hardly wait to go to work. Every weekend the guys would chip in their quarters and I'd have a salary. I liked Kansas City more than I thought I would. In the club beer was five cents, whiskey was fifteen cents and scotch was twenty-five cents. There was always guys pushing wagons that were full of sandwiches, boiled potatoes, clams, fried chicken and all kinds of goodies, and they were all cheap. I would always have a good appetite whenever these guys would come around. Sometimes they'd have barbecue too. Everything was cheap in Kansas City at that time. Staying at Maceo's home saved me a lot of money too, as I was only paying three dollars a week rent like I did in Boyle Heights in Los Angeles when I was living with the Willis family. I was fooling around with a waitress in Wolf's Restaurant who wouldn't charge me when I'd have a meal there. I ate nearly all of my meals there in that restaurant on 18th and Vine. Julia Lee was working out in a club which was a little bit out of Kansas City, and she knew that I was not making any money with Basie and would give me all of the silver change that she made every night in tips. She would keep the folding green money but she'd give me all of the silver, sometimes as much as ten dollars a night. There never was anything between Julia and myself, she was just helping me as she knew I was hustling a little bit. I remembered her from the first time I saw George E. Lee's band in Parsons, but I never dreamed I would some day be close to her. I still say that we were only friends and that was all. I had several little girls helping me make ends meet which was no more than everybody else was doing in those days.

When we finally left the Reno Club, as the time got near for us to go to New York, I played piano on different little gigs. One of the clubs was a little honky-tonk dive called the Florida Blossom, where big rough guys would come in and drink beer. Sometimes one would say to me, "Get up, son, let me show you how to play the blues." Then he'd sit down and play some low-down funky blues, which I didn't mind at all because it was less work for me. I met some trumpet players there too. I'll never forget one who had a mouthpiece on the rim of which he had filed notches. He said that the notches made his lips tough. I looked at his lips and they were so scarred up that I said to myself, "That's for you, not for me." He was an old carnival trumpet man. Another time I was Basie's stand-in piano player. We were working at a club called the Movie Chateau and Basie wouldn't show up until after the band had played about an hour. Nearly all of my playing was in the keys of C or F but we were swinging just the same, until Basie would come in and then we'd really start swinging. We were at the Movie Chateau when Herschel and Caughey came in from California. Our biggest competition was the Jay McShann band and of course the Andy Kirk band. Jay had a good band with Charlie Parker, Bo McCain, Gus Johnson and Gene Ramey among the members. Andy Kirk's band was the best known of the Kansas City bands because of his recording of *Until the real thing comes along* with

Pha Terrell doing the vocals. Basie, however, had the swingingest band of all, as McShann's band was mostly a blues band, and Kirk's band was a polished and clean band with people like Dick Wilson on tenor sax, Pha Terrell doing the vocals and Mary Lou Williams on piano. After Herschel and Caughey arrived Basie started looking for more musicians before we started for New York. We were booked into some pretty large clubs and we had to have at least fourteen musicians to play the shows. As for myself, I always preferred the small nine-piece band as it was easier for us to swing with nine, and when we did get fourteen pieces I found that it slowed us down a bit. However, it was something that had to be done.

One of the large clubs that we had been booked into was the Grand Terrace in Chicago. There was no way that we could have gone in there with nine pieces. Along with Herschel and Caughey, we brought in Dan Minor on trombone and we already had Tatti Smith on second trumpet—the same Tatti Smith that made those swinging records under the name of Smith–Jones. Tatti was a nice trumpet player who later moved to one of the Caribbean islands and never returned.

Before we left Kansas City we were told that we were to play a dance at the Paseo Dancing Academy against Duke Ellington and then after the dance we were to leave on our way to New York via a long string of one-nighters. It was Hallowe'en night. I was thrilled at playing against Duke as I hadn't seen him since I got married in 1934. We played first and then the Duke came on. I thought that he played more solid music than we did, but I thought that we out-swung his band. I must have been out of my mind. They played so well and were so sharp in their uniforms. After the dance we all met at the bus to go to some place in Pennsylvania, I think. We all got in the bus and I was sitting next to Claude "Fiddler" Williams and I noticed that, of all our friends and well-wishers, there was not a soul there to say good luck or even goodbye. Not one soul. So we drove off all by ourselves, but at least we were on our way at last for New York City.

I was glad to leave Kansas City, though—not because I hadn't had a very good time there but because I wanted to see so many eastern cities that I had only read about in my life. Believe me, I got my wish, as Basie was booked on so many one-nighters to get the band in shape for New York, especially the new guys that we had hired to enlarge the band. We played all through Pennsylvania, southern states, northern states, and I sure began to see America from a bus window. We had a lot of fun, though, on the bus. We would joke a lot and Basie was always as cool as ever. Sometimes at night, after we had played a gig in some little town and everybody would be asleep, Lester Young would wake up. He always had a pair of dice somewhere on his person. He was always the one who would instigate a crap game in the back of the bus and would always be the first one to get broke and go back to his seat and go back to sleep, leaving all the rest of the band in a big crap game. He would awaken everybody by walking up and down the aisle of the bus clacking his two dice in everybody's ears and at the same time singing, "Sweet, music, sweet music," until everybody would get up and follow him to the back of the bus and the game was on. Then after

Prez would get broke he would go back to his seat and snore like a baby.

Jo Jones and I were health nuts and as soon as we would get in a town we'd find a doctor and go get a checkup. We had a big list of different doctors that we'd go to. Basie and Jimmy Rushing liked to play poker and at times would have a big game in whatever hotel they would be staying. Sometimes they would stay up all night playing poker until it was time for the bus to leave around ten in the morning, and then they would get on the bus and go to sleep. I, too, learned to sleep well on the bus: sometimes I could sleep for three or four hundred miles without waking up and then when I would get in a bed I couldn't sleep. I had gotten used to the rock and roll of the bus.

We played one-nighters for weeks and sometimes there wouldn't be many patrons at the big dance halls that are now parking lots, garages and other modern buildings. But one thing Basie told me, which I've remembered all these years, was when you can spot one person that is patting their feet, just play for that one person and you know you have someone swinging with you, no matter what the other people are doing. I have many times applied that to myself when there is a poor audience. I spot just one swinging person and play the whole rest of the night just to them.

Herschel and I had a lot to talk about as we both had been out in California and he had been in my band. He used to tell me about the bands in Texas, such as Alphonso Trent, Troy Floyd and many others that he had worked with, just as he used to tell me about Lester Young, Ben Webster, Coleman Hawkins and a lot of guys that I had never seen but had heard so much about. Herschel and Lester had great respect for each other. They were a perfect pair to be working together. Lester had a lighter tone and could play very fast, whereas Herschel had a larger tone and specialized in slow numbers. I know that they respected each other even though they didn't talk to each other very much, and when they would sit back to back in the reed section it wasn't any kind of an indication that they didn't respect each other. Sometimes Herschel wouldn't be too happy when Basie would give most of the solos to Lester, but that was because most of the songs that we were playing were pretty fast. Still, when a song like *Blue and Sentimental* came up it was Herschel's time to do his thing. One time Herschel quit speaking to me because he thought that I was giving Prez all the solos in some arrangements that Count and I had made together. He stopped me one time in the Roseland Ballroom on some stairs leading up to the dressing room and asked me why I had given Prez all the solos in the arrangements. I told him that it was Basie's arrangement and Basie thought that Prez could do more on that certain arrangement. Tex didn't say anything else but I knew where his thoughts were. That same thing has happened to me at times. Sometimes we would play a circuit of theaters where we never changed the program and if, during the two or three numbers that were the band specials, you didn't have a solo, you could go for weeks without playing one. I did ask Count about that one time because for weeks I had been playing the same band numbers where I didn't have a solo. The only time I could play was when the vocalist was singing and I would play in a mute behind her. Basie did change later, but it was for that reason that sometimes Herschel wouldn't be too happy.

The bus practically became our second home. Sometimes we would arrive in a town just about fifteen minutes before the dance was to start and that meant we would have to dress in the bus and then run right straight from the bus to the bandstand. Then when we'd get through we'd sleep until it was time to get on the bus the next day and go to another dance in another city. Sometimes when we'd check in at some flea-bitten hotel we'd pick up bugs. There were bugs that would make you itch for weeks. We would pour kerosene on the itch and that wasn't too good either. Most of the time we'd talk about New York and what we were going to do once we got there. Basie and Prez had already been to New York but most of us had only heard about it.

We did some more one-nighters for a few weeks, then we arrived to play the Grand Terrace in Chicago early in November. That was a gas as the Grand Terrace was the home of Earl "Fatha" Hines, who had been there for years, and recently had been occupied by Fletcher Henderson with Roy Eldridge. We were going to be playing for chorus girls again and that was always something to look forward to. We didn't know that we had other people to play for, such as singers, acrobats and different kind of acts. So we swang into Chicago. I was so damn poor that I had borrowed Maceo Birch's raccoon-skin coat, which didn't fit, but still it was better than anything that I had, which was nothing. My heels on my shoes were so run over that sometimes I would back out of a building rather than walk out forwards and let everybody see how bad my heels were. Sometimes, too, I would wait until everybody else had gone out and then I would go out. Those were some pretty tough days, but still we were having a ball just being in Chicago. It was then that I first met Roy Eldridge. He was working at the Three Deuces with Zutty Singleton. It was such a pleasure to meet Roy because, to me, he was the most streamlined trumpet player I'd ever heard, barring none. I don't have to tell you how great Roy was. Just buy his records and you'll know. I think Roy was one trumpet man that Lips Page would have never dared to go to the Sunset Club in Kansas City to have a jam session with.

Came the day for rehearsal at Ed Fox's Grand Terrace. We already had the dance music down so we went right into the show. First we took the chorus girls' routines and went right through them with no trouble. They liked the band and we were playing some arrangements that had been made by Horace Henderson that really were swinging. I always did think that Horace's music was swinging a lot more than Fletcher's arrangements. Not everybody knows that but I always thought so. Fletcher's arrangements are more musical and technically correct, whereas Horace's swing like the devil. So we ran through the chorus girls' music like eating pie. But then—later —came the hard part. The producer of the show had some music that we couldn't make heads nor tails of. Then on came the vocalists with more complicated music. We were stuck. We couldn't get it right to save our lives. Somehow that rehearsal ended with us still not knowing very much about the show. This was the very first show that Basie had run into since we had been booked on the road with the new big band. Finally opening night came. Everything was great until show time. We did get through the chorus girls' music but when we got to the difficult music it was a catastrophe. It was so bad that we didn't want to be seen on the street, especially by the artists whose music we had screwed up. Some of them went to Ed Fox and complained about the band not being able to play their music, but that didn't help. We were booked in there so we had to do the best we could, which was nothing. We abused that show every night we were there. When we left there we were in just as much fog as we were on opening night. But we did discover part of the reason later. We found out, after the disaster in the Grand Terrace, that some of our new members of the band couldn't read—or at least couldn't read well enough—to play that music in the Terrace. It was only some of the new ones that had been added that couldn't read, so Basie had to make a house cleaning to get new musicians that were better readers. Right away he started looking for replacements.

Another incident that I'll never forget was when Basie first played for a dance in Washington, DC. Basie had just left Kansas City and was completely unknown then as he hadn't as yet made any records and really there was only a few people that knew he was Count Basie. Basie always had his "boys," in every town practically, but nobody else knew who Count Basie was. We all went to the dance hall, the Lincoln Colonnade, and as we went in we didn't have any trouble because the guys on the door could see that we were carrying our instruments. We went in and set up our horns and were waiting for Basie to show up. After a few minutes Basie showed up and he was mad as hell. The guys on the door had stopped him as he was strolling past the door to go in the hall. "Hey, fella," one of them called out to Basie, "where do you think you're going?"

Basie said, "I'm Count Basie."

The guy says, "Oh, well now, you're Count Basie."

Basie said, "Yes, I'm the Count."

The guy then says, "Well, Count Basie, you just go over to that window and buy your ticket like everybody else."

Basie insisted that he was Count Basie the bandleader. The guy started calling his fellow workers on the door and they told Basie, "Don't give us that crap. Just go buy your ticket and get out of the way, you're blocking the door." Basie looked at the guy and all of his buddies that were on the door and decided it was best not to argue with them anymore. He had to go out into the street again and walk up and down the street until he saw some one who knew him. When he finally met somebody who could identify him as Count Basie he had to bring him back to the dance hall to verify who he really was. Boy, was he hot when they finally did let him in to his own dance.

After a few more weeks of one-nighters we were told that we were booked into the Roseland Ballroom on Broadway in New York City, starting on 24th December 1936. At the time we hadn't as yet made any changes in the band. So we had to go into the Roseland as we were because there really wasn't enough time to make changes and still be ready to open on Broadway.

Buck's first band: Ronald Wharton (guitar), Jack ? (drums), Theodore Cruz (alto saxophone), LaVern Floyd (piano), Pete Kinard (tenor saxophone)

Buck with his band at the Cotton Club in Culver City, California (left to right): Kid Lips Hackett, Teddy Buckner, Arcima Taylor, Ike Bell, Red Callender, Bert Johnson, Herschel Evans, Buck (in front), Allen Durham, Bumps Myers, Frank Pasley, Winslow Allen, Caughey Roberts, Eddie Beal

Mineola Walker's piano class, 1923: Buck is standing on the extreme right.

The Royal Roosters in Parsons, Kansas (left to right): Clarence Glass, Norene Tate, Danny Shakespear, Fred Henderson

Buck's father, Simeon Clayton

Clayton's Imperial Four (left to right): Clarence Fisher, Marcus Lane, Walter Davis, Simeon Clayton

Left: Buck with his mother, Aritha Dorsey Clayton

Right: Buck aged four

Buck and Gladys (Derb) Henderson on their wedding day in Hollywood with Rev Napoleon P. Greggs and Duke Ellington

Buck in the international settlement, Shanghai

Buck Clayton and the Harlem Gentlemen, Shanghai (left to right): Teddy Buckner, Joe McCutchin, Reginald Jones, Arcima Taylor, Duke Upshaw, Frank Pasley, Buck, Bumps Myers, Jack Bratton, Caughey Roberts, Baby Lewis, Happy Johnson, Eddie Beal

The Count Basie Orchestra, c1941: Harry Edison, Al Killian, Ed Lewis, Buck (trumpets); Eli Robinson, Dicky Wells, Buster ? (trombones); Jo Jones (drums); Freddie Green (guitar); Walter Page (double bass); Buddy Tate, Tab Smith, Earle Warren, Rudy Rutherford, Don Byas (saxophones); Basie (directing)

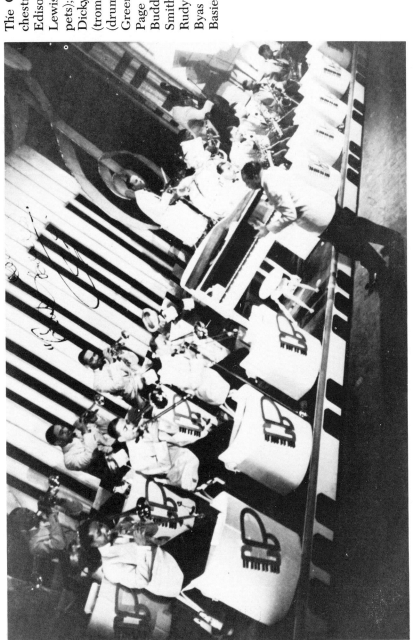

Buck with Herschel Evans

Billie Holiday

But we were very happy to know that finally, after these few months since we had left Kansas City, we were going to the Big Apple.

The last one-nighter before we were to enter New York was something to be remembered and I'm sure I'll never forget it. About seven o'clock one bright sunny morning I awakened on the bus and we were already in New York and were driving down Lenox Avenue in Harlem. We had come through Harlem to get to the Woodside Hotel and on the way we passed the famous Savoy Ballroom, where Chick Webb was playing with Ella Fitzgerald. We were thrilled to even see their name in lights and on the marquee of the building. We all had hopes of playing the Savoy and we stretched our necks looking at it until we turned a corner and it was out of sight. Harlem looked very beautiful to me. The trees in the middle of Seventh Avenue were very impressive and the wide streets intrigued me. "The Big Apple," I thought to myself. At last one of my dreams had come true, but it was a little better than I had anticipated. After congratulating each other on finally arriving in the great New York, as it was in winter we went inside the Woodside Hotel to warm up a bit and to check out everything. Everybody checked in at the hotel except me as Derb was staying at the apartment building at 2040 Seventh Avenue. It was where many theatrical people lived and at all hours of the day and night there would be something happening. It was called the Ranch.

After checking in with Derb in our apartment I was introduced to all the entertainers and musicians in the building and in a few hours we were swinging. It was like Christmas again. Some of our new-found friends had to leave about ten o'clock to go to work at the Apollo Theater, which was only a short distance away. After spending some time at 2040 I caught a cab back to the Woodside Hotel and had a party with all the fellas in Walter Page's room. We had met quite a few New York musicians who were happy to show us around Harlem. Walter Johnson, drummer with Fletcher Henderson's band, was one of the first.

Within a few days we were rehearsing. We rehearsed in the basement of the Woodside Hotel adjacent to the dining room and the rehearsal ended with all of the diners and the waitresses in the room swinging and dancing. We rehearsed some more head arrangements in preparation for our meeting with Woody Herman, who was playing at the Roseland and would be there to welcome our band in that great dancing palace. Woody had a good band but we were not too familiar with his work. After a few more rehearsals we were called together by Basie and he told us that he wanted to make a change in our show-off number, *King Porter Stomp*. We had been playing *King Porter Stomp* the same way since we started playing it some months ago, but Basie wanted to change the ending. He wanted to prolong the ending so we rehearsed it that way, but unfortunately we didn't rehearse it enough. We still were used to playing it the original way and when we played it as our flag-raiser against Woody Herman the inevitable happened. The Roseland was a beautiful ballroom and we were the first to open the night. So we started swinging and soon some of Woody's members came down to get on their stand a little early so they could hear us before they opened up. We had the crowd really dancing and swinging. Jimmy Rushing was an instant success and the band was taking charge on each arrangement. Finally, as we had only one more number to do to finish our first set of the evening, Basie called *King Porter Stomp*. We went into the tune and ran through it like we had been doing on our previous engagements, when all of a sudden we found ourselves in the last chorus and nearing the end that Basie wanted to change. Some of the guys, through force of habit, forgot and played it the way we had been playing it all of the time. The others went into the prolonged ending that Basie wanted, so we ended up our show-off number with two different endings. The ones that forgot ended up about eight or sixteen bars earlier than the ones that remembered. The result was total confusion. Woody Herman's band confused us too because, even before we were through with the number, they picked it up a few bars before we finished it and went on to wash us away with it. We were so embarrassed that we didn't want to face anyone the rest of the night. John Hammond was so upset that he almost pulled all of his crew cut out. He had invited friends, critics, reporters and many others to hear this great band out of Kansas City and we had gotten screwed up on the ending of *King Porter Stomp*, and the band sounded like a cat fight at the end of the number. Willard Alexander almost had a heart attack but recovered in time to get us back on the road as soon as possible after the Roseland.

As for our recordings, my first recording was with Teddy Wilson along with Billie Holiday, just about two weeks before Basie made his first recording with the band. The first recording of my life was *Why was I born?*, which happened to be the first song on the list to be sung by Billie. As I walked with Lester into the studio I was surprised to see so many people that I had never actually seen before. There was Benny Goodman, running up and down on his clarinet, warming up for the session. There was a tall cat sitting on a high stool with a pork-pie hat on that was introduced to me—Freddie Green, guitarist. There was, of course, Teddy Wilson, who I had never seen, and Billie herself. Billie and I immediately became friends and soon we were recording. Such pleasure I had backing up Billie's songs to her vocals. When she would record I would watch her mouth and when I saw that she was going to take a breath or something I knew it was time for me to play between her expressions. It's what we call "filling up the windows." My first recording date was great and I felt so happy that I finally had made a record, especially with Billie. We made several more dates with Billie after that, in fact whenever Basie would be in town we were sure to be called to play with the Lady. John Hammond would be sure to make a date on one of our days in town so that we would be available.

About two weeks later Basie made his own recordings and we made such numbers as *Pennies from Heaven* and some of Jimmy Rushing's originals, like *I may be wrong*. They turned out to be very successful, especially down South where the people really dug the blues. Soon we were a big hit in the recording business and our bookings became better and better all the time. Sometimes Lester and I would get dollars-worth of nickels, as the jukeboxes only took nickels at that time, and pull up two chairs and listen to what we had recorded, sometimes for hours, one nickel after another, and we wouldn't allow anybody to talk while we were digging ourselves. There were jukeboxes everywhere it seemed and we would listen to ourselves on as many as we could find.

Basie told us we had been booked in the Pennsylvania Hotel in Pittsburgh, in the Chatterbox Room. We were pretty happy to be going in a swank hotel like that and we wanted to get off the road as well. Pittsburgh was at that time a pretty smokey town and, if you put some clean white shirts in a dresser drawer, when you opened that drawer to put on the shirt it would be full of soot. I don't think Pittsburgh is like that now, though. I'd like to go back there some day and check it out. In those days we lived in the pawnshops as we were not making enough money to really keep ends going. We were making six dollars a night, per capita. If we only worked four days some weeks our weekly salary would be twenty-four dollars, and that wasn't enough to keep yourself going on the road and a wife in New York or somewhere else. It was impossible. One day Maceo Birch, who was now traveling with the band as our road manager, came in the bus and made an announcement. He says, "Fellows, I've got some good news for you. From now on you will get a raise. Your salary, beginning today, will be six dollars and a quarter every night you work." So it was only natural that we were friends with every loan shark we could find, and between the loan sharks and the pawnshops we were able to make it for a while. We'd pawn everything we had if we were broke—suits, radios, anything. Basie said to me one day, "Don't worry, Buck. One day you'll be wearing an overcoat that will cost a hundred dollars."

We arrived in Pittsburgh and prepared ourselves for our engagement at the Penn Hotel. We checked in at a hotel nearby and there was snow on the ground. Jimmy Rushing always got a room that was near the front door and if any of the guys straggled in late after everybody else had gone to bed, and especially if he had a chick with him, Jimmy Rushing would wake up and peep out and see who it was and who he was with and the next day it would be all over the bus.

We enjoyed our stay at the William Penn even though we did get a pretty bad writeup in the January 1937 issue of *Metronome* by George Simon. John Hammond and Willard Alexander had invited several of the critics and commentators of jazz to come to Pittsburgh to hear the great Basie band that hardly anyone had yet heard in New York. There were quite a few dignitaries of jazz there to hear us and we played our best. We thought everybody was pretty satisfied but I guess we were wrong. After completing our gig there, we were getting on the bus the next morning to go on the road again when Basie comes in the bus with a *Metronome* magazine, the bible of jazz at that time. He opened the magazine and said, "Fellows, I want you to hear this." He opened the magazine to a certain page to an article written by George Simon, in which George in describing the band said, "The whole band is out of tune. If you don't believe the trumpets are out of tune, just listen to the saxophones, and if you don't believe the saxophones are out of tune, just listen to the trombones, and if you don't believe the trombones are out of tune, just listen to the whole damn band." Our feathers dropped when we heard Basie read that. That issue of the *Metronome* wasn't published until about three weeks later after our opening night and we thought all along that we were raising hell. Well somehow we did get on to the next job, but we were pretty upset about that article by George Simon. Although I certainly wouldn't have said it at the time, I did agree with Simon and told him years later that I knew we were out of tune but wouldn't dare say anything to Basie about it. I still say, though, that it was mainly our cheap and over-used instruments that made us play out of tune, especially Joe Keyes. Joe Keyes was one hell of a first trumpet man and could play anything, but having such a bad instrument he was really unable to play in tune, and when the first trumpet player of any band plays out of tune, naturally it makes the whole damn band sound out of tune.

One of the most important changes that Basie made in improving the band shortly after we arrived in New York was the transition of Joe Keyes for Ed Lewis. Ed, in the first place, owned a good trumpet which had a good sound to it and, furthermore, he knew how to play it in leading a brass section. Not only could he lead the section but he was very capable of playing some very good solos. Ed, a good looking cat, had been with the Bennie Moten band for years when Moten was at the height of his career. I believe he was in his early teens when he was a young sharp cat with Moten and played several solos while with the band. He had a big tone and a lead that we all could follow. There was just one thing that seemed strange to me about Ed. When I was so crazy about Louis Armstrong and was really trying to develop myself by playing like him, Ed was admiring Red Nichols. Of course everybody has an idol, especially in jazz, and everyone has his own preference, but I couldn't see Red Nichols being admired over Louis Armstrong. Ed, however, was a wonderful addition to Basie's band and no matter who he admired he sounded good and made the whole Basie band sound strong and in tune. Ed was from Indian extraction like I was and sometimes he and I would drink "kikapoo juice" and go out on some pretty wild, drunk excursions.

One night in Utica, New York, Ed and I got into a fight after going to a party and getting overcharged. I don't even remember why we were fighting but I know that Don Byas had something to do with it. (Don had taken over Lester Young's chair on one of his several departures from the band.) Don had been baiting us both on, until soon we were out of the car and fighting on sleet as it was sleeting. It started in the car as we were being driven home by the host of the party when Ed all of a sudden said, "Stop the car." The driver of the car stopped immediately. I think he wanted to see Ed and I fight. We both got out of the car, just barely being able to stand up as the sleet was so slippery, and I said to Ed, "OK, you big MF, we're out of the car now, so what are you going to do about it?" All of a sudden Ed hit me right between the eyes and knocked me down and when I fell on the sleet I slid right under the car. After I struggled to come out from under the car we started mixing it up. Every time that Ed would swing at me and miss he would fall down on the sleet and slide, and the same thing went for me. I'd miss and then fall and slide. This went on for I don't know how long. When I first got a chance to look up from the fighting I saw about seven spectators. A few minutes later I looked up again and saw about fifteen spectators, then one time later I saw about thirty spectators. It was about three o'clock in the morning. Pretty soon I heard the police siren and soon they were there. They pulled Ed and I apart but Ed was so belligerent that he told one of the cops, "You take that star off and I'll kick your ass." That was the last thing he remembered. One of the cops hit him across the head with a blackjack and he went out. I told them, "Alright! Alright! I'm coming." So they put us in the police car, after Ed came to, and drove us to the police station. They took off my suspenders and put me in a cell. Then they put Ed in a cell next to me, but Ed was still full of fight and as the jailer was turning the key on Ed's cell Ed took off his shoe and threw it at the jailer. The shoe missed and wedged itself between two bars in Ed's cell. The next morning, about seven o'clock, Ed woke up and when he found out that I was in the next cell he said, "Hey, Buck! What happened?"

I said, "I don't know, Ed," even though I did know. I told him that we had been put in jail for disturbing the peace. About an hour later Basie came down to the jail and he was pretty mad at both of us. He said, "I just wish that I had a camera. I'd take both of your pictures and send them to *Down Beat*." Then he left, as we were playing at a theater there in Utica. It was cold as hell in that jail and pretty soon they came around and gave us some coffee. Ed and I were talking to each other through the jail cells and I told Ed that I was sorry about everything. He said he was sorry too. He didn't remember anything and I wasn't mad at him at all. I did provoke the fight by calling him an MF.

About two hours later Maceo Birch came down to the jail to bail us both out. They let me go but they kept Ed several hours after I was released because he had thrown that shoe at the jailer. The shoe was still sticking up there. When I got out I reported to the theater with two big black eyes and my overcoat ripped to pieces, but somehow I had managed to get out of the way of all of Ed's blows that were aimed at my chops. That wasn't the case with him. When he showed up several hours later his lips were all swollen and he couldn't play, so he just went on back to New York and stayed until his chops healed again. Ed and I remained friends and, I think, even stronger friends after we had that fight. We used to eat corn on the cob together with his wife when we lived at the Woodside Hotel a few years ago. Basie used to say that, when he saw Ed Lewis, Buck Clayton, and Don Byas coming down the street drunk, he'd be sure to cross over to the other side of the street.

Another time we were playing the Adams Theater in Newark. As the day ended I went back to the apartment where Derb and I were living at 2040 Seventh Avenue expecting to find her there. After placing my key in the door and opening it I was surprised to look in and find a completely empty apartment. There was only one thing in it, an electric iron. After enquiring from some of her girl friends that lived in the apartment, I found out that she had run off with a pimp and had gone to Detroit. She had taken everything and the only reason that electric iron was still there was because she couldn't put anything else in her suitcase. I was stunned, upset, and could not get myself together, especially after learning that she had told all of her girl friends that she was going to do it. Even they couldn't believe that she had actually done it. They were very sympathetic to me and said, "I told that dumb chick not to do that." But anyway she had done it. I cried like a baby when I was by myself and nobody else around. I don't know why I cried so much because I usually don't cry about anything. I guess I was hurt more than anything else because I really wasn't that much in love with Derb, but since I was married to her, and I did like her, I guess I was hurt because my image as a husband had been tarnished. However, after a few days I began to harden and I said, "To hell with her," and went about my work with Basie. Whenever Basie would have an engagement in Detroit I'd leave the band and go on to Chicago or some other city rather than go to Detroit and see her again or hear about her with that pimp. Basie didn't mind as he had other musicians that wouldn't go to other certain cities because of paternity suits and other reasons.

Shortly after the Roseland we invaded Boston, Massachusetts. We had improved quite a bit during our stay at the Roseland, even after our first night screw-up, so we were in better shape when we played at the Southland in Boston. The Southland had formerly been a church but had been converted into a club. We also played at the Ritz Carlton Hotel on the roof known as the Ritz Roof. We were there when the hurricane of 1938 blew the whole roof off. Fortunately it happened during the day, when we were not playing, but when we reported to work that evening we found it all in shambles.

Boston soon became our second home and we made many friends there that have remained true friends even until today. We stayed at a friendly family restaurant and lodging house called Mother's Lunch. We loved eating at Mother's Lunch because she had those good ol' soul food dinners. Many of the traveling orchestras would end up at Mother's Lunch after their working hours just to chat with other musicians. Charlie Barnet came by one night with his vocalist, who was then the not-so-well-known Lena Horne. Lena sat at the piano and played and sang all night long. It was during those days that I met some great jazzmen and some that I'm proud to have known from Boston. There was Ruby Braff, a young kid blowing up a storm and one who had his own personal style, which means so much. Today he and I are about as close as two trumpet players can be. There was Paul Gonsalves, who later became a member of Count Basie and later Duke Ellington, with whom he remained for years. Also there was Bobby Hackett, a great friend and stylist; Sammy Margolis; Sabby Lewis, the Boston bandleader; and many, many more. After a few more engagements around Boston we were beginning to feel at home when we were informed that we were booked into the Apollo Theater in New York.

The Apollo Theater was a theater like no other, I'm sure of that. Every band that aspired to become famous always had the one and only Apollo Theater in mind. When we first played there we found that it wasn't an elegant theater like some of the downtown theaters such as the Paramount, but what it lacked in splendor it made up in soul. We used to sit in the orchestra pit in front of the stage when we played the various acts (there would always be acts of some kind before the band numbers—balancing acts, juggling acts, trapeze artists, etc). I was designated by Basie to take charge of the acts, which I would do in front of the band. Basie would come on after the acts, when we had moved from the pit to the bandstand on the stage, and then the whole scene changed. We became like a machine bent on nothing but swinging. The chorus girls went crazy, as did everybody else; backstage was swinging as much as on stage. Friday was our opening day and all of the hipsters would stay up all night to catch our show at ten o'clock Friday morning. The whole ten or fifteen first rows in the theater were taken up with guys that we had been hanging out with and who wanted to be on hand for the first show. On the first show they caught the full show, whereas the second show would have a lot of cuts in it. It would seem sometimes that all of the first rows of the theater would be filled up with guys smoking pot. It would drift up on the bandstand but nobody minded. They were all our pals and we were playing just for them. It was really the most enjoyable show of the entire week as the rest of the days were for the normal jazz fans.

At the Apollo I caught up with Derb again. I heard that the pimp had beat hell out of her and had put her in the hospital. She had been on narcotics and things hadn't been like she thought they would when she left New York. One day she had read in the *Chicago Defender* that Count Basie was booked into the Apollo Theater in two or three weeks. So she decided to try to get to New York and get a job in the Apollo as a chorus girl. Being in the chorus line, she knew she'd have to work with me. She intended to get there about three weeks before Basie opened as Basie was doing one-nighters before coming into the Apollo. So one day she slipped away from the pimp, just like she had done with me, and went to New York and got a job at the Apollo, knowing that I'd soon be there with Basie.

On arriving in New York with Count, I was the most surprised trumpet player to find Derb in the chorus line when we reported for rehearsal for the week's show. I found out that everybody in the band, in the show, all the stage hands, everybody knew what was happening. Would she be able to get me to go back with her or not? That was the big question that week in the Apollo. Some were even making bets on it: five dollars I would go back, ten dollars I wouldn't. Everybody it seemed to me was making bets. I still was hurt and angry and for the whole week I wouldn't even speak to Derb, so when the week was about over—I guess she saw that I wasn't going to come around—she got awfully drunk and got fired from the chorus line because she wasn't able to dance. I never saw her again after that. My mother was right again, as she said that my wedding was all glitter and had no substance and she never really did approve of it.

Sometime after the fight with Ed Lewis in Utica I met Singsi. Singsi Kyle. She later married Billy Kyle, but when I first met her I only knew her as Singsi and, even though we were to live together for about four years, I never did know her last name. All I knew was that she was a real beauty—

red hair, big blue eyes, and sexy as hell. Henry Armstrong had been going with a chorus girl that was a very good friend of mine from California, Maudine Simmons, and had given her a whole apartment full of furniture. When he left to go to another city Maudine decided that she too was going out to Chicago, so she asked me if I wanted the furniture. I said, "Hell, yes." So she gave me the whole set of furniture. I had been going with Singsi for some time so now that I had the furniture we decided to get an apartment and live together. So we found an apartment at 75 St Nicholas Place and moved in. I stayed with Singsi for a few years or, rather, until I went into the army some years later. She was always a lot of fun and sexier than any movie actress that was then on the scene. I enjoyed those years then as I had been separated from Derb for some time now. We used to dig all of the nightclubs, jazz clubs, and the after-hours clubs together but when, years later, I was inducted into the army I told her to forget about me because I wasn't ever going to come back. She was one swinging chick, though, I must admit.

The Apollo Theater suddenly became the highlight of all the other swing establishments that we had played. Jimmy Rushing would always bring down the house with his *Goin' to Chicago* and *Good Morning Blues*. Little roly-poly Jimmy always had a lot of lady fans after he would give out with *It's Christmas-time and I want to see Santa Claus*. Sometimes the theater would omit the movie that had been scheduled and we would do extra shows. When we got off the stage from one show, another show was scheduled to go on within a half an hour. We just had time to run across the street and eat and then run right back in the pit.

On Wednesdays, after the last show of the day, there would be the talent show. Basie would retire to his dressing room and an MC, like Willie Bryant or Ralph Cooper, would take over. The band stayed on, however, to play the music for the amateurs, along with a lady pianist who had rehearsed each contender. The star of the amateur show was a plum little guy called Puerto Rico. Puerto Rico had the dirtiest mouth I'd ever heard but still was a likeable guy. He liked to play the "dozens" and sometimes you wouldn't believe what you'd hear between Puerto Rico and some of the musicians just before the curtain went up for the amateur show. When one of the contestants was pretty bad or had no talent, a siren would go off filling the whole theater, and Puerto Rico's job was to do a little dance which he would do in a little short skirt and his underwear. He would come out dancing to his take-off music and run the amateur off the stage while shooting blank bullets in the air. Puerto Rico's little jig dance usually broke up the house. I liked Puerto Rico. We became good friends and when I used to bring my little daughter Candy down to see him he would use nothing but very good language.

Many of today's stars, such as Ella Fitzgerald, Pearl Bailey and others, started by way of that amateur hour. Ella Fitzgerald applied to be a contestant on the amateur show as a dancer when she was very young, but found herself in a spot where she was to follow the Edwards Sisters. The Edwards Sisters were two little geniuses who had been taught to dance by their father and were pretty well known to be the best kid dancers around. When Ella saw that she was to follow the Edwards Sisters, she did the best thing she could have possibly done; she decided to sing, not dance. She realized that she couldn't follow them so she went into her singing and won the prize.

On some of the many times that we played the Apollo Theater I'd talk to Tom Whaley, who was then arranging all of the music that the show needed, such as the music to be played for the chorus girls. I learned quite a few things from Tom Whaley. He looked at an arrangement that I was making during our stay at the Apollo one day and said to me, "Son, you write your trumpets too high. Most trumpet players can't play that high and just because you can do it doesn't mean that everybody can do it." So, from then on, I always wrote my trumpet parts within range unless I was writing for a band full of Cat Andersons or Maynard Fergusons. I once wrote a song called *Tom Whaley*, which he used to sing to me whenever I saw him.

We'd play softball against some of the traveling bands that just happened to be in New York while we were there. We played against Benny Goodman many times in Central Park. Bud Freeman was one of the Goodman all-stars at the time. Prez, naturally, wouldn't think of letting anyone else pitch but himself, but Prez was a pretty good softball pitcher. We played many times against Harry James and his band. Herschel Evans used to hit more home runs than anyone else. I don't know how he did it as he wasn't a big guy— rather on the slim side—but still it seemed that every time he would get up to bat he would hit a home run. I didn't know how he did it. He didn't know how he did it. He did something that was just natural for him which was in his wrists. Like Hank Aaron, I guess, who has a hell of a wrist movement for hitting home runs.

Usually after playing the Apollo we would do what we called the "around the world" circuit, which meant that we would leave immediately for the Howard Theater in Washington, DC, with the same show as that in the Apollo. Then after the Howard Theater in Washington we'd go to Baltimore, then after Baltimore back to New York. When Basie went back to one-nighters the guys started finding hobbies to do sometimes. Freddie Green and I, being roommates, always had some kind of hobbies going to enlighten our lives while living on the bus so much. We once were collecting all of the Mickey Mouses and the Donald Ducks that we could find in different cities. We had a hell of a variety of different kinds of ducks and mice, but we soon gave up this hobby because it got to the place that we didn't have enough room in our suitcases to put our clothes. Who can travel with a couple of suitcases of Mickey Mouses and Donald Ducks? Freddie and I had quite a few interesting things going on while being with Count. We were once going to a dentist in California named Painless Parker. I had broken a tooth in Texas while eating chicken and Freddie and I both went to Painless Parker. It wasn't painless, believe me.

By that time Billie Holiday had joined the band. Billie was great to work with as she was game to do anything that we would do. She would shoot dice with us, joke with us and, in general, do everything that we would do. We all liked Billie. Sometimes on the bus at night, when everybody else would be sleeping, Billie and I would talk. She wanted to know all about China and I related to her all of my experiences that I had there. Then she would tell me all about her life and so many things that had happened to her in Harlem. Sometimes, when we were in New York, she would take me by her mother's restaurant and I'd have some ham hocks and turnip greens and other soul goodies. She had in her room a painting of a severed head of a Chinese that was given to her as a present. To me it seemed rather gruesome but Billie liked it. Sometimes, when Billie would board the bus about ten in the morning to make another ride to another town, she'd say to me, "Buck Clayton, you MF, come over here and let me see what color your eyes are today." Billie always said that if I wore a green suit my eyes would be green that day, if I wore a gray suit they'd be gray, and if I wore a blue suit they'd be blue. Billie called all of her close friends MF. If she loved you she'd call you an MF—unless she was mad and then the MF took on a more serious meaning. Come to think about it, Billie must have loved me quite a bit because she called me an MF in almost every sentence, but I loved Billie and we had a great time together all of the time. One day, surprisingly to me, she left the band and I never knew exactly why. The next thing I knew she was with Artie Shaw and his band. Even she never told me why she left Basie, which I thought was the ideal band for her. After Billie, Basie hired Helen Humes, who was just as popular with the band as Billie and, like Billie, did everything that we would do. She gambled, loved to eat soul food, and would look out for the guys a little bit more than Billie did.

One time, before we left New York to go to Texas on some one-nighters, I bought a brand-new beautiful gray-striped overcoat that Billie admired very much. As we were eating in a diner in Houston, I was a little bit apprehensive about putting my pretty coat on the pile of other coats that belonged to our band, so I picked up all of the other coats and slid my new coat under all the rest and went on to enjoy a chicken dinner. After the meal I went over to the pile of overcoats expecting to find my coat there on the bottom of the pile where I had placed it and I'll be damned if it wasn't gone. Somebody had eased up to that pile of coats while I was wrapped up in chicken and had taken my beautiful coat and had left me with exactly nothing. Another time Buddy Tate and I both had beautiful overcoats and this time I called myself being real cagey about where I put my coat. We were playing a dance in Scranton, Pennsylvania, and both Buddy and I had placed our overcoats right behind our seats on the bandstand. But as the night went on we began to think that wasn't the right thing to do with such pretty coats as someone might steal them at intermission time, so we got up and took them to the cloakroom, where we thought they would be safer after being checked. Then we went back to the bandstand feeling a little better. The dance went smoothly for about an hour and a half, when all of a sudden a fight started. Then about two minutes later they overran the checkroom taking everything they could get their hands on and when Buddy and I got to the checkroom everything was gone. Buddy was able to find an old tattered man's coat but after that all that was left was a dingy old woman's coat, raggedy and all, and that was the coat I had to wear for about two weeks before we played a gig in Pittsburgh and I was able to buy another coat. It was cold as hell and that coat was so thin you could read through it.

When we first met Billie Holiday she made it her business to take Lester Young and myself all around Harlem. We'd go to all the joints in Harlem and if we couldn't make them all in one day then we'd start again the next and go to all of the pads that we had missed the week before. Lester, Billie and myself. You sure couldn't ask for a better chaperone than Billie as everybody in Harlem seemed to know her. From every corner in Harlem there would be talk of Billie Holiday, some of it good and some of it bad, but we three were always pretty tight together. After Freddie Green came in the band Billie showed a great interest in him, but Freddie already knew New York as he was working in a little club called the Black Cat when John Hammond brought him to Basie. Then, later on, after we learned which bars were the ones where you got doubles in and which ones you got singles in, then we were learning New York. I used to go to a place called Monroe's Uptown House. Clark Monroe was the brother of Jimmy Monroe, that married Billie Holiday later. You could go to the Uptown House and see the very latest in all the jazz musicians because at that time there was no restrictions on jamming in clubs as there exist today. You could go to Clark Monroe's Uptown House any night of the week after three o'clock and see Lady Day singing, or Coleman Hawkins, after he returned from Europe, playing sax, or Ben Webster. Don Byas, who had arrived in New York with the Eddie Mallory band (which was really Ethel Waters's band under the direction of Eddie Mallory), Red Allen, Roy Eldridge—they all used to go there and jam till the wee hours of the morning. One night John Hammond took Lester and myself up there. We didn't know that he had also invited Harry James and Babe Russin. They both were playing with Benny Goodman. We went in and sat down but it wasn't long before people began calling for us to get on the stand and jam with each other. Soon we were at it and even in the audience there were great notables in jazz such as Billie herself, Ben Webster and a whole room full of others. There was Bobby Moore, who had played in Basie's band before we got Harry Edison, a wonderful little trumpet player, about sixteen years old and trying to play like Roy Eldridge. He was great but just a little too young for the present company so John Hammond called him out of the session and that left only Harry James and myself jamming on the trumpets. So Harry and I jammed until dawn and I watched him do all of his tricks and he knew quite a few, such as playing the same note in octaves—something I had never seen done before. Harry and I became good friends.

One time when Red Allen and I were jamming at the Uptown House Miles Davis came up and wanted to jam with us. Miles was completely unknown then and just a kid who wanted to sit in with his trumpet. Some of the old timers, Red Allen for one, said, "No, kid, get out. We don't want you up here now." Some others voiced the same feeling. They resented him because they thought that he would mess up the session and I think that I was about the only one that said, "Oh, what the hell, let's let him come up and play. You know he can't hurt anybody." So Miles would come up and play and I don't think that he ever forgot that as far as my part was concerned because he always treated me with a certain amount of respect —which he still does today. That was many years ago, before he became famous.

Another time, shortly after Basie arrived in New York and we didn't know anybody, we were invited by John Hammond to attend a big jam session where Chick Webb was going to play. Duke Ellington was going to be there with his band, Eddie Condon was going to be there with all of his dixieland guys and a lot of other musicians who lived in New York. Basie accepted the invitation and we all went to this big bash downtown somewhere in New York on the 16th floor. I don't remember the address nor the building but there were many, many people there to dig these three big bands and all the other cats. It was there that I first saw Stanley Dance, who had just been in New York a short while from England; he hadn't yet married Helen Oakleigh, who was then very prominent in jazz circles. We arrived at the building where the jam session was being held and went upstairs to our dressing room. We all unpacked and then went downstairs to listen to whoever was playing at the time and before we were to play. I think Duke was playing.

After digging the Duke for a few minutes I noticed that I had forgotten my little bottle of trumpet-valve oil which I needed, so I went back to the dressing room to get it. While I was looking for it in my trumpet case Herschel Evans came in and there were only the two of us in the room. I don't know why Herschel came in but a few minutes later, after we had talked a little about the guys jamming downstairs, he noticed Walter Page's sousaphone mouthpiece laying on a table, where I guess Page had left it before he went downstairs. "Well look here," said Herschel, when he saw Page's piece, "I won't be hearing that damn sousaphone anymore." Herschel hated it when Page would play the sousaphone sometimes in our arrangements. So he goes over to the table, picked up Page's mouthpiece, went over to the window and threw it out. Out the window from sixteen stories up. Then he looked at me and said, "Don't tell anybody."

I said, "Hell, it's none of my business. Why should I say anything about it?" Then he went over to where Freddie Green's pork-pie hat was hanging with Freddie's coat. He walked over to the window again and threw it out of the window too. Then he went on back downstairs to the big session. When it was all over and we went upstairs to put our instruments away Page was fuming about not finding his mouthpiece and Freddie couldn't find his pork-pie hat. Herschel hated pork-pie hats too. So they both just had to come on back to our hotel without the mouthpiece and the hat. I don't think they ever knew what happened. I know I never told them. Herschel just went on and acted as if he didn't know from nothing.

Shortly after the Apollo we were booked into the Savoy Ballroom. When we first saw the Savoy Ballroom we were thrilled, but nothing could be more thrilling than playing there. First, I never saw a ballroom like the Savoy. It was packed to the doors every night—not one night a week, nor four nights a week—but every night. It was unbelievable. When I went there for the first time I had to literally squeeze myself into the upper floor where all the dancing took place. There were always two or three prominent bands on the bandstands and the famous Lindy Hoppers were rug cutting every night. Norma Miller was the leader of the Lindy Hoppers and, you can believe me, some of the gymnastics and the gyrations that they did would do credit to any athletic show on any continent. When we played the Savoy all Harlem turned out to see this great band from the Midwest that was swinging everybody into bad health. First the fans like Buck and Bubbles; then Willie Jones the drummer, who used to yell at Basie, "Count in the Basement"; then, too, all of our new-found friends from downtown; and, last but not least, our musician friends.

The bouncers in the Savoy were the most severe bouncers that ever graced a ballroom. If you were wrong they would throw you out of the Savoy twice. First they would take you to the steps going downstairs and throw you down the steps, then they would come down the steps themselves and finish throwing you out the front door. Many a trouble-maker was thrown out and had to go to Harlem Hospital with broken arms or legs after an encounter with those Savoy Ballroom bouncers. Most of the New York rowdies were as quiet as a mouse when they went to the Savoy because they already knew the reputation of the bouncers, so it was mainly the out-of-town rowdies that usually ended up in the hospital. They were all friendly with us and we treated them with respect and they in turn respected us and we remained friendly with them even after the place closed.

Under the management of Charles Buchanan the Savoy did record business all of the time—never any slow nights. You could never get a table, unless of course you went there very early. Thursday nights were "kitchen mechanics' night" and one of the most popular nights to go there and swing with the maids, cooks, and housekeepers who had Thursday nights off from their jobs. On the bandstand you could always find a good local band, like Lucky Millinder with Bull Moose Jackson doing the vocals, and on another stand there would be a famous traveling band like Tommy Dorsey or Benny Goodman or some band of that caliber. We played there against Chick Webb and that was one hell of a battle. Ella was swinging so beautifully and Chick's band with Taft Jordan on trumpet was really swinging, but Basie kept cool, as he usually did under pressure, and I think we won the battle, but still there were the Chick Webb fans who thought that Chick and Ella won it. It's really hard to say who won a battle like that as all concerned were really putting down some heavy swing. We played a battle there, too, against Lionel Hampton and I'm sure we won that one. Lionel was fresh out of California and really had a good band at that time, but we were laying for him and when he arrived in New York we were waiting. There was also the Savoy Sultans, who used to out-swing anybody that came into the Savoy. They were a small combination, but what a hell of a group. They reminded me of the nine-piece band that we had at the Reno Club in Kansas City. I, and Basie and our whole band, was always glad that we never had to play a battle with them as they would have given us a bit of trouble. We would have gotten to them in the end, but we really didn't want that battle. Besides,

we liked the guys. One could find all of the big bands in battles at the Savoy
Ballroom. It really was the home of happy feet and it's still hard for me to
realize that it doesn't exist anymore.

After the Savoy we returned to our recordings and rehearsals and soon we
were booked into the Paramount Theater. By this time Basie had made quite
a few changes in the band. Earle Warren came in from Ohio and took over
first alto chair replacing Caughey Roberts. Dicky Wells had replaced Eddie
Durham along with the addition of Benny Morton on third trombone. Harry
"Sweets" Edison had taken second trumpet chair replacing little Bobby
Moore, who was a great little kid on trumpet but had some dental work done
on his two front teeth and then couldn't play a note because he didn't have
any more space to play between his teeth because of decays. Freddie Green
had replaced Claude Williams. With the coming Paramount engagement we
had bought some new sharp uniforms, some of the best we had bought so
far, and we went on to become a success in the Paramount along with the
comedy team of Buck and Bubbles and the gospel singer Sister Rosetta
Tharpe. After the Paramount we played various clubs in and out of New
York and our money was increasing until we found ourselves making pretty
damn good money.

From July 1938 we were booked into the Famous Door on 52nd Street,
when 52nd Street was just becoming known as the Swing Street. The Famous
Door was formerly an apartment that had been converted into the club. One
night a woman was sitting in the club when she realized that she was in what
had been her own basement when she had lived there years ago. The band
would always swing in low tones because if we had opened up with our brass
we would have run everybody out of the place immediately. Basie kept us
in mutes and derbys and we were in a groove without being too loud. In the
Three Deuces there was John Kirby and his great little group featuring
Buster Bailey and Charlie Shavers and in the Onyx Club there were Stuff
Smith with Jonah Jones and Cozy Cole.

One time we were kidding Lester about wearing the same suit all of the
time so we finally got him to agree to get some clothes. Prez went out and
bought six nice pretty suits and we were feeling pretty good about that but,
shortly after, on a theater booking down South, someone left the window
open to our dressing room as it was kinda hot in there. So, while the band
is on stage doing a show, somebody slipped into the open window and stole
all of the pants to Prez's suits and left the coats. I guess they wanted to use
them as slacks. Anyway, when Prez came in the room and saw all of his pants
missing he hit the ceiling. He said, "I was happy with my one suit. Now look
what you got me into. Six coats!" Harry Edison and myself cared more for
clothes than most of the other cats and sometimes we'd buy the very latest
in hats, suits and shoes, but even then Harry would always spend more than
I did because he was paying, even then, fifty dollars for a pair of shoes and
I never could seem to get out of the twenty-five dollar class.

We were in Boston, Harry and myself, and one morning after work we
were feelin' kinda good. We were in a restaurant about five o'clock in the
morning when in walked a bakery man with two huge trays of buns balanced

on both hands. He was bald-headed and, as he went by us, I said to Sweets, "Sweets, I bet you can't hit that cat on his bald head with one of those buns."

Sweets said, "Just wait until he passes by here again." So when the guy came back with a second load of buns Harry reached up and got one of them and waited until the guy was about ten feet away, then threw the bun, hitting the guy right on his bald head. Well, after Sweets had been in jail for a couple of hours, Maceo Birch said, "Don't worry, I'll go down and bail him out in a minute." He went down about an hour later and told the judge that he wanted to bail Sweets out. How much was the bail? The judge said, "Five dollars." Maceo searched through his pockets and then turned to the judge and said, "Uh . . . er . . . well . . . I'll be back within the hour to bail him out."

Herschel Evans was one of the neatest dressers that I had ever known and would always take some time to dress. Tex was so immaculate that he wouldn't go out of his room until everything, and I mean everything, was just right. He looked more like a very handsome schoolteacher or a lawyer than a jazz musician. He was very popular with the ladies and didn't either smoke or drink. I should say that he was popular with most ladies, because I can't say that Billie Holiday was in that same category. From the very first day they laid eyes on each other there was a deep dislike for each other. Neither had done anything to the other, they just couldn't stand each other and that was the only reason. Sometimes, when Herschel wouldn't even be aware of Billie looking at him, she would say, "Look at that MF, I can't stand him. Look at him, standing back on his legs and sucking his teeth. He thinks he's cute." And Herschel would do the same when Billie wasn't looking. He'd say, "Look at that old bitch. Who the hell does she think she is?" In other words they got along like a cat and a dog, natural enemies if there ever were any.

Herschel was intensely proud of being a tenor sax man from Texas. He was the first of what is now called the Texas tenors. From Herschel came Buddy Tate, Arnett Cobb, Illinois Jacquet and others. He was prominent in the Basie band making such records as *Texas Shuffle* and *Doggin' Around*— in fact he composed both of those masterpieces by Basie. Of course *Blue and Sentimental* was his high point and still today is the favorite of most tenor sax men. He and I also recorded with Mildred Bailey. We both were on Harry James's first recording after he left Benny Goodman. I of course didn't play a solo on the date but Herschel knocked everybody out as usual. One night we played a battle of music against Benny Goodman in Connecticut and I never heard Herschel play better in my life. He seemed to know that something was going to happen and as soon as the dance was over he had to be taken back to New York by Danny Miller of the Miller Brothers and the band went on without him. On 9th February 1939 he died of complications and we were stunned beyond imagination. His body had accumulated so much fluid that if he was tapped he would have died and if not he would have died.

We all missed Herschel terribly and for some time we used various tenor men, but none could take his place. None had that big sound on tenor that Herschel had. Finally, one day Basie sent for a guy that I didn't know from Nat Towles's band in Omaha—Buddy Tate. I'll never forget when Buddy showed up in New York. He had an overcoat that hung down to his ankles. I was surprised that he could sound so much like Herschel. In a way it was like meeting Herschel's brother and we were all pleased that finally we had found someone to replace Tex. Lester pitched right in and soon began teaching Buddy some of the things that Herschel had done and before long Buddy was just as at home in the Basie band as any one could possibly be.

Later in 1939 we were booked into the San Francisco World's Fair and it was one of the nicest of all our engagements. The exposition grounds were beautiful, with beautiful music being piped to the public through speakers. The 'Frisco nights blended in with the whole scene. We played twice daily and personally I think that was the real beginning of Basie's band. We played like we belonged there and then there was Sally Rand's revue there and we were situated right next to her tent with the whole revue of saloon dancers.

One time, after Tommy Dorsey had made his famous recording of *Marie*, Basie said, "I want to make something with our band singing it." Like Tommy had done with *Marie*. So as we were playing the Adams Theater in Newark, which we played almost as much as we did the Apollo, Basie decides to change our closing theme. Instead of closing with the *One O'Clock Jump* we were going to close with a number that Basie had done years ago with the Bennie Moten band. The number was titled *Goodnight Everybody*. We rehearsed the number, although I don't think that anybody knew the lyrics to the song but Basie and Jimmy Rushing, who had done the number before with Moten. We rehearsed it a couple of times and Basie thought that it would be alright. As it had been a successful closing number with Bennie Moten, why couldn't it be good for us to close the show with? After we had finished the show with all of our swinging band numbers it was time to close, and we all stood up to sing *Goodnight Everybody*. It was horrible. Half of the guys didn't know the words and were just going through the motions of singing and when Lester saw how bad it was sounding he went into his comedy bit and pretty soon had the whole band, except Basie, laughing like hell when we were supposed to be singing. Lester was a natural comedian when he wanted to be and always liked to make the guys laugh, so he continued on with the comedy until it got so bad that half of the guys were laughing and half were trying to sing when, right in the middle of the number, I guess the stage hands said, "This is enough of this," and pulled the curtain down on us. Basie was fuming by then and blamed Prez for screwing up the whole thing. He later said, "The number would have been alright if it hadn't been for Sandy Burns over there doing comedy." After that I don't think Basie made any more singing bits ensemble. We only used vocalists after that.

Shortly after, we hired Snookie Young to play in the trumpet section and the section was then Ed Lewis, Sweets, myself and Snookie Young. It was an improvement to the band as Snookie was a hell of a trumpet man and I was personally glad that he was with us.

One day Basie had to fire Lester and that was something that I would never have imagined when we left Kansas City. We were doing a recording date and after waiting for about two hours for Prez to show up Basie called him at the hotel and got him on the phone. Basie told him that we were all waiting for him to show up and for him to hurry and get his butt down there. Prez said to Basie, "Man, I don't make no records on the 13th of no month." So Basie had to let him go. We made some recording sessions later with Chu Berry and Coleman Hawkins. We made *Feedin' the Bean* as a Hawk special.

The little anecdotes and stories about the Basie band could be endless but I must tell you the one about Earle Warren in the Paramount Theater. Earle had been singing a song which was titled *I struck a match in the dark*. So when Basie was preparing our show to be presented in the Paramount Earle's introduction to his vocal on the song was doctored up in a something like Frank Sinatra style. Before singing the song Earle was to stand in front of the band in complete darkness and just before Basie was to bring the band in on the introduction Earle was supposed to strike a match which would illuminate only his face. Earle was a good-looking guy and Basie figured that this introduction would set off all of the little girls that thought of Earle as a matinee idol. We rehearsed the song until we had it down pat. The fellows who were the light technicians knew that they were not supposed to illuminate the whole stage until Earle had struck that match and the band was going into the introduction.

The first show that morning at the Paramount went down like clockwork. Earle had struck the match in the dark and it really was a nice intro to the song. But the next day Earle went about, as rehearsed, to do the song and as he was out there in the dark all by himself we were waiting to see the match ignite so that we'd be ready for the introduction. We waited and waited but nothing was happening. What really was happening with Earle was that he couldn't get those damn matches to light. He struck one and it went out or, rather, it didn't even light. He struck another one and it fizzled out. Then he started getting panicky as the audience was wondering what was happening in the dark and no music being played. Earle kept striking one match after another and not one would ignite. He was all frustrated as he couldn't sing until the match lit, when somehow Basie dug what kind of trouble he was in and had the band go into the introduction without the lit match. We went into the intro and Earle was saved from his embarrassment. Later I was told that Jo Jones had slipped onto the stage between shows and, when nobody was around, had taken the matches that Earle had placed on the stage as props and had dipped them in a glass of water. Another time, while doing the same number, after striking the match Earle threw it down and it rolled into a crack on the stage and soon there was a wisp of smoke coming up from the crack. After calling the stage hands to get that match and put it out we decided to do away with that introduction.

In the early 1940s we were beginning to be booked in movies and did quite a few. We made *Hit Parade of 1943* and *Reveille with Beverly*, and quite a few shorts also. We were making a movie in 1942 at Columbia Studios in Hollywood when I suddenly became aware of the fact that it was quite possible that I could become a soldier in Uncle Sam's army. Basie was on the stand making this movie and during the breaks between takes Freddie Green strolled out onto Hollywood Boulevard and was window shopping, when suddenly he was confronted by some of Hollywood's finest and asked to show his registration card, his draft card. Freddie had lost his card some time back and had not bothered to get another one, so off he went to jail. Basie, in the meantime, was waiting for Freddie to come back but finally, after a long wait, had to go on and finish without him. The next day Freddie was released and I began to think of my own position. I had lost my card also quite a while back and, like Freddie, I hadn't bothered to get a new one. So I said to myself, "If they arrest Freddie for something like that they'll arrest me too." So on our trip back to New York from California I stopped at my sister's home in Kansas City and wrote to my draft board. I told them that I had lost my draft card and that I would like to have another one. I think that did it. I had opened up a can of worms.

We were coming into New York after being out again on some more one-nighters when someone started a dice game in the back of the bus. I got into the game and soon I found that that day was not my day. Everything that I did was wrong. Basie was in the game too and he was watching me lose all of my money. Finally, after about an hour of losing, Basie said to me, "Buck, you're in such bad luck that I'll bet that you'll be the first one in my band to be called into the army." He didn't know it then, but he was so right. Then I began thinking. What about that letter that I had written to my draft board from my sister's home in Kansas City asking them for a new draft card? What had they done about it? Being on the road almost constantly since I had written it, I really didn't know what they were doing. But I soon found out. When one morning we pulled into New York and I went home I found that letter that everybody never wants to receive that begins with, "Greetings." Just as I had suspected, when I wrote that letter from Kansas City I had really opened a can of worms. When my draft board looked up my record, which they hadn't done until I wrote the letter, and found out that I was eligible to be drafted, they sent me that letter, telling me to be able to report to the army induction center within three weeks. I realized that it was a serious situation when I first got the letter but then, later, it seemed to be more serious when I realized that I would have to leave Count and the band. After being with Count for seven years I finally had to leave and go into the army. I was very unhappy about that as I considered Count and the guys like my family, with Count being the father. I had learned so much from being with him that I just couldn't comprehend what I'd do in the army with a bunch of guys that I didn't know. However, I had three weeks more to be with the Count so I went out again on our tour of one-nighters until my time would be up and I'd have to leave the band. I thought of my father who admired soldiers, then I thought of me, who didn't want to be a soldier at all. I played the three weeks with Count that I had remaining and every day someone would tell me some way to beat the draft. Some would tell me, when I reported to the draft board or induction center, to eat soap. They said that eating soap would cause the medics to cancel you out. So, just before I was to leave the band, I ate a lot of soap. I also was told to break open a benzedrine nasal spray and put the chemical used to make it in a bottle of coca-cola and drink it. I did that. Then I was told to be sure to act like I was gay and they wouldn't want me. I couldn't figure out how to do that but I did keep it in mind.

When the day came for me to leave the band I had taken so much soap that my insides must have been nothing but bubbles and suds. I had taken that benzedrine–coca-cola formula until I hadn't been able to sleep for three days. I had done everything that anyone had mentioned to me about beating the draft. When the morning for me to leave the band came I was so weak that I couldn't carry my trumpet from the train to go back to New York and Snookie Young had to carry it for me. When I arrived back in New York all by myself, which in itself was a new experience for me, I went home and told Singsi that I'd be leaving the next day for the induction center at five o'clock in the morning at the Grand Central Station. I felt so sick and bad that I couldn't sleep that night either. So at five o'clock I was at the induction center and I was feeling like hell. I had a headache, I hadn't been able to sleep for days, and I was just in terrible shape.

At five o'clock in the morning the doctors came in to examine everybody and it seemed to me that all the doctors were evil at having to get up so early. I was with a group of about three hundred guys to be examined. A well-known jazz singer was in the group and he kept telling me what to do to beat the draft but I was half dead already and couldn't take any more advice on how to beat the army. This guy kept telling me, "Do like so-and-so (a famous trumpeter) did. They threw him out yesterday." I don't know what he had done but they did throw him out for some reason. However, I wasn't that lucky. These evil-ass old doctors was going to get me one way or the other it seemed. I was right, because of the three hundred guys only two were exempted. The singer and another guy who had terribly flat feet were excused from military service. After my taking all of that soap and drinking all of the benzedrine–coca-cola stuff I was in such bad shape that the doctors knew that I had been doing something to keep away from them, so they just looked at me and said, "Fine, fellow, you're in the army." When they herded us into the room where we were to take the oath, as I raised my right hand to take the oath I didn't give a damn any more whether I was in the army or not. My head was about to split open. Then they gave us instructions as what to do and one of them was to report to Camp Upton and to bring enough clothes for three days.

I went home and tried to sleep again without much success but anyway I was at the station at train time the next morning. I had brought enough clothes for at least a year it seemed to me after I got on the train. I've always had a tendency to over-pack when it came to clothes. During my last three weeks with Basie I had bought a special tailor-made soldier-suit and a beautiful cap that I wasn't supposed to wear. I had shoes that I really didn't need. I had, oh, so much junk that I could hardly carry it in the bags that they gave us to put everything in. I didn't know that you were not supposed to wear these tailor-made things, only the officers, but anyway I had mine and my bag was so damn heavy that me being in such bad physical shape I could hardly get it in the train that was taking us to Camp Upton.

SIX

In Uncle Sam's army

As we were riding on the train someone told me that John Hammond had
been inducted too and was on the same train as I was and going to Camp
Upton. I wasn't happy to know that John was in the army but if he was on
the train I would have been happy to see him, so I walked all through the
train looking for him but the report turned out to be false. He had been
inducted but he wasn't on the train that I was on. We rode the train not
saying too much to anybody as nobody knew who anyone was. Finally we
arrived at Camp Upton. We were met at the train by some soldiers who
were there especially to bring us to camp and they started hollering at us
just as soon as we stepped off the train, "Fall out! Line up!" So we fell out
and lined up. By this time my head had cleared a little bit and I actually felt
better and I had decided that, since I was already in the army, I would do
my best to be a good soldier, which I knew would make my father happy.

As we got off the train we saw a lot of soldiers who tried so hard to impress
us as being real soldiers just back from the wars, when actually they had
been in Upton maybe a week or ten days and were waiting to be sent to
their basic training camp. Boy, did they give us hell. "Jody! Jody! Jody!,"
they would yell at us as if we were the newcomers and they were the
experienced soliders, hard and tough. "Well, look who we got here. Count
Basie!" they yelled when they saw me. "Well, you're not with Count Basie
now, Jody. You're in Uncle Sam's army." Jody was a name that soldiers used
to ridicule civilians and brand-new soliders and was often used in contempt.
"All you pimps fall in over here," they would yell at us. "Line up over here!"
I remember we followed a private that was from way down home and who
was built like a string bean. He had such long legs that he looked like his
hip pockets were in the middle of his back. Such long legs. He marched us
through the rest of the soldiers hollering at us. It was like running the
gauntlet, Indian style.

We were en route for the camp, which was situated about a mile down
the road. That mile to the camp was the longest mile I'd ever experienced.
Aside from the soldiers heckling us all the way, the big pack of clothes that
I was carrying was beginning to feel like two tons, so I was pretty glad to see
the camp at last as we turned onto a side road in the country. The first soldier
from the camp that I saw was private Cliff Glover and you can believe me
when I tell you that I was glad to see him. Cliff had worked in the Apollo
Theater as assistant leader when Basie first came to New York, since he was

a local musician and New York musicians had to be included with the current show even if they didn't work. I liked Cliff from the Apollo days as he was always a good guy and besides he played alto sax in the little jazz band in Camp Upton along with two other friends of mine, Dave Martin, a wonderful and talented pianist, and McElvaine, a drummer. "Buck," said Cliff when he saw me in that long line of new soldiers, "what the hell are you doing here?" After I talked to Cliff a few minutes he began right away to plan to keep me there in Camp Upton as long as possible so that I'd be able to play in their band. So, along with Dave Martin, they decided to keep me there until something suitable came up for me. For example, if I had a requisition to go to another military band in some other part of the country that would be alright, but if I was scheduled to go to some place to be trained as a combat soldier they were not going to let me go. As they did all of the clerical work at Camp Upton they had access to all of the names of soldiers that were to be shipped out to become combat soldiers and to what state they were to be sent. As my days passed in Camp Upton, Cliff and the boys must have scratched my name from the list to be shipped out at least ten times. Every time my name came up to be shipped to Alabama or some other southern camp for basic training, they would list me as being on weekend pass or on furlough and couldn't be found in time to be shipped away. That way they were sure to have me in their band. They really looked out for me but I hadn't anticipated this at all. I thought that I was going to become a combat soldier, not that I wanted to be one, but I just had expected it. I knew that my father would have preferred, though, that I be a combat soldier. After some days at the camp I began to get the feeling of mixing with other guys that had not been as fortunate as I.

There were, however, some sergeants in Upton who still wanted to make an example of me because, knowing that I had just left Count Basie, they presumed that I'd be more difficult to change from the life of jazzman to soldier. They would give me the dirtiest jobs on the camp, such as taking a hose and washing down the latrines that hadn't been used for weeks, making me get up with all the rest of the soldiers at five o'clock after I had played for an officers' dance until three o'clock and didn't get into my bunk to sleep until after four o'clock in the morning. They would blow the whistle at my bunk first to get me out of bed and sometimes, even though I'd be so sleepy that I could hardly keep my eyes open, I'd get up and get out like all the rest. I knew they were giving me the business but I didn't want to give them the satisfaction of saying that I was a jazz musician and couldn't take it. I would smile to myself when they would give me some ridiculous order and I would obey the order, but there was a dagger attached to every smile. After they saw that they couldn't break me they began coming over to my side and eased up on me. I never did get more than a pack of cigarettes, though, for playing the officers' dances.

Finally, one day, after a long spell at Camp Upton, a requisition came in for me and my buddy Skinny Brown to go to Camp Shanks in New Jersey. A conference was called between Dave Martin, Cliff and McElvaine and it was decided that going to Camp Shanks was good enough for me to report for, so Skinny Brown and myself packed our gear, said goodbye to Cliff and the boys and left for Camp Shanks. Sy Oliver, who was a sergeant by this time, was in charge of requisitions from Shanks and, after learning that Skinny and I were in Upton, had put in the requisition for us to come to Shanks. There were several other musicians in Camp Shanks that we knew, such as Milt Larkin, the bandleader from Texas and a good friend, Mercer Ellington, son of Duke Ellington, and several others.

By this time Lester Young, Jo Jones and Jack Washington had all received their greetings while with the Count, but they had not been as fortunate as I was because they all had been sent to basic training camps as combat soldiers. Poor Prez was in more trouble than anyone else. He could not take the sergeants hollering at him all the time. Like in my case they had intended to make an example of him, but in his case it didn't work and he spent quite a bit of time in the stockade and was even one time in a padded cell. He later wrote a song called *D. B. Blues*, which he wrote from being in the detention barracks. After a few years he was discharged. I've often been asked if the tough life that Prez had been through had affected his playing. My answer is definitely, no! When I worked with him later, after both of our discharges, in Jazz at the Philharmonic, I was particularly interested in knowing how he would play after his tough battle with the sergeants, but to me he seemed to play better than ever, even better than when we had made so many recordings with Basie and Lady Day. Maybe it was because he was relieved to be out of the army but when he played against Coleman Hawkins in the JATP tour he was fabulous.

Being in the army is no picnic for anybody but I thought I was pretty lucky to have a chance to go to Camp Shanks. After we arrived there and were met by Sy and all the other cats we were soon going about our daily duties, which was mostly practicing. We rehearsed Sy's arrangements most of the time. If you know Sy, he is a perfectionist and can write for anybody. When we rehearsed Sy's arrangement on a military number it always sounded just as good as a Tommy Dorsey or a Jimmie Lunceford number. I liked Sy's arranging and really had a ball playing with nine other trumpets, but our main job was to play details such as railheads and embarkations. We'd go to the piers of New York and play for hours at the gangplanks of the boats carrying soldiers to different war zones. Hour upon hour we'd play for hundreds of soldiers until the boat was loaded. Sometimes the soldiers would be drunk or hung over, evil or happy. Believe it or not, there were a lot of soldiers who were glad to get away from their old ladies legally and to be on their way, probably to France. Some of the more evil soldiers from way down home would be especially evil when we'd play *Flying Home*. The idea that they were leaving home and we were playing *Flying Home* put them in a pretty evil mood, especially at us, the musicians, because we were playing it. Some of the other songs we'd play were *Lay that pistol down, babe, St Louis Blues* and others. Sometimes we'd start playing at five o'clock in the morning and play all day, winter and summer. One time at five o'clock in the morning the weather was so cold that after about fifteen minutes of playing the valves on my trumpet froze. When I complained about it the officer in charge of the detail tôld me, "Well, just go on back inside, hold it up to that pot-bellied stove and when the valves thaw out just come on back out here and start playing. And if it happens again just do the same thing." From five o'clock in the morning until late that afternoon I was making a path from the boat to the pot-bellied stove along with all the other trumpets, who were having the same trouble.

Army life in general was pretty routine. When we had nothing to do or no details to make we'd wash windows or do something else. I was known as a pretty good soldier. I'd sometimes pass the whole weekend in camp because I still was tired from the one-nighters that Basie had been doing. I really appreciated the rest in camp. Sometimes on weekends there'd be only myself and CQ (charge of quarters). I used to even wear my leggings around camp, which nobody did but me. I was lucky enough to have a good appetite at that time. I ate everything that the army could dish up. I could eat a boiled gorilla and go back for seconds and thirds. I gained about thirty pounds. I went from 160 pounds to 190 pounds. I found it paid to be in good with the cooks, as at night we could always go to the mess hall and get anything we wanted. I soon began making money by writing arrangements for other big bands, in fact I very soon was making more money writing for bands than I had been making with the Basie band. When I left Basie's band I was making damn good money but now, in the army, I was making more. I had stayed at Camp Shanks for almost a year when I received a requisition to go to Camp Kilmer, also in New Jersey, and in fact not too far from Camp Shanks. Kilmer was near New Brunswick, New Jersey. So one day Skinny Brown, Sy Oliver, Mercer Ellington and others said goodbye to our sergeant that we all liked very much, Sergeant Carrington from Virginia, and left for Camp Kilmer.

At Camp Kilmer we found it to be more like a recreation center than a camp for soldiers. Everything was so relaxed. The soldiers wouldn't salute the officers unless they felt like it and the officers didn't seem to give a damn whether they did or not. In the band was Kenny Kersey, a great jazzman, very talented. There was Jimmy Crawford (Ol' Gal), the famous drummer of Jimmie Lunceford's band, Bo McCain, saxophonist of Jay McShann's band, Charlie Fouquet, one of the original Ink Spots, Joe Turner, a pianist who now lives in Paris, and Bob Carroll, well-known tenor sax man, formerly with Don Redman's band and others. I was pretty happy about joining the new band. We had almost the same duties to perform as in Camp Shanks— the embarkations at the piers. We also had a good dance band, coupled with the military band, that was composed of some of us guys from the military band, and many times we could carve the civilian bands that came to camp to play for us soldiers. I continued to arrange music and compose. Some of the compositions that I wrote were recorded by Duke Ellington and had titles that referred to army life, such as *Khaki Tan, Blues on the Double* and others. I also was recording while being a soldier. I wasn't supposed to, but I was.

The whole time that I was in the army I kept my room at the Theresa Hotel. I was paying thirty-five dollars a week until I left because they could not raise my rent as long as I kept the room, but the moment I did leave the room the rent went up to seventy-five dollars a week. The Theresa Hotel was the place to be during the war if you could be so lucky as to keep a hotel room and be in the army at the same time. Joe Louis was always in the lobby joking with different people. I had met Joe while I was in Basie's band and later saw him at Camp Kilmer when he was on an exhibition tour. In 1941, before leaving Basie, I had recorded a song about Joe Louis with Paul Robeson, called *King Joe*. My mother was happy that I had participated in making a recording of the classical singing of Paul Robeson and the jazz music of Count Basie. Later Joe owned a restaurant on 125th Street near Fifth Avenue in Harlem that was a high spot among tourists. He had three or four jazz combinations going, mainly the small group of Earle Warren and another group headed by my inspiration from Parsons, Kansas, Norene Tate. The restaurant was only a few blocks from the Theresa Hotel and was one of my favorite hangouts. I was at the restaurant when Ray Robinson almost lost the chance to become champion when he fought Tommy Bell. He had been knocked down by Tommy Bell but later went on to win the championship, but I remember how upset Joe was at the time because we did not know whether Ray would weather the storm or not. Ray Robinson practically owned a whole block next to the block where the Theresa was situated and one of his projects was the Ray Robinson Bar just down the street. The Apollo Theater was just across the street and all of the entertainers would come in the bar between shows. My next favorite bar was the Braddock Bar, on Eighth Avenue and 126th Street, where nearly all of the musicians would come between shows.

One morning when I reported to camp I was informed of a new law that was passed only for soldiers. A soldier could file for divorce for only fifty dollars. I immediately put in my application for such a divorce as Derb and I had separated years ago when I was with the Count. In September of that year I was informed that my application had been approved in California and I should be a divorced man within a year and a day, which is the California law.

By this time the war was beginning to come to an end and I found myself back on the piers of New York, only this time we were playing for the soldiers to come back home. We again would play for hours while they disembarked. Since I was probably the last trumpet player to join the band at Kilmer, I was one of the last to be discharged. I noticed that almost every month one of the nine trumpet players would leave the band discharged, because they were inducted before I was in 1943. At first I didn't pay too much attention to their leaving but I eventually found my work increasing as the trumpets dwindled down from nine to six or seven.

I still retained my room at the Theresa and one morning I was surprised to see Fidel Castro and Nikita Kruschev meet in front of the hotel and embrace. The Cubans had registered at the hotel as they had refused to stay at other places or, rather, some of the more elegant hotels in New York. Those were really some strange days in the Theresa Hotel. The Cubans rented several floors of the hotel and wine was flowing everywhere. They even did their own cooking in the hotel rooms, bringing in their own live chickens and cooking them. After their departure the attendants at the hotel were cleaning up chicken feathers and wine bottles for days. I even went up to their floors and looked for myself. Those Cubans really had a ball as there were girls every night at the hotel from different sections of New York.

One of the personal perilous situations that I found myself involved in while being in the army and in Harlem was one that I can never forget. I had been involved with a very pretty girl from the Bronx who at the same time was either married to, or living with, a drummer that I had known ever since Basie arrived in New York. Both were avid fans of Lester Young. I'll only use first names here as I'm pretty sure everybody knows who I'm talking about already. The girl's name was Margie. The drummer's name was Harold (later he changed it to "Doc" for professional purposes). At the time of this incident Harold was working at one of the clubs on 52nd Street which was really swinging. One hot summer night Margie called me at the Theresa and asked me if I'd take her to lunch at Creole Pete's Restaurant any time after nine o'clock, after Harold had gone to work at the club. I agreed to meet her and take her to the restaurant, which I did. When the meal was finished Margie asked me, would I come to her apartment and have a drink? After arriving at the apartment and listening to records and having a few drinks with Margie I naturally found myself in bed with her. My soldier uniform was scattered all over the apartment and I was completely nude with Margie. After two or three hours of having a ball, records, drinks and pot, all of a sudden there were three heavy knocks on the door and a whistle that was used only by members of the Basie band. I knew and Margie knew that Harold was familiar with that whistle from his association with Lester. Looking at my watch, which was the only thing that I had on, I noticed that it was only three o'clock in the morning and not yet time for Harold to come home as the clubs were still open on 52nd Street.

Bang! Bang! Bang! And then this whistle call which Harold used so that Margie would know that it was him at the door. He didn't have a key this particular night and Margie was supposed to let him in but he was at least an hour ahead of his usual time to come home. "Oh my God!," Margie says to me, "it's him." For a while, which seemed to me like an eternity, I couldn't think of what to do. I couldn't run because my clothes were all over the apartment and it would have taken me so long to find them and put them on. Finally Margie thought of opening a window and letting me out. Again, bang! Bang! Bang!, and the familiar whistle, only this time he called her name. "Oh my God! Oh my God!," she kept saying, while at the same time looking for the key to the window gate. The window had an iron gate over it—one of the kind of gates that is widely used in Harlem as a protection against burglars and is locked from the inside with a key. She couldn't find the key and everything was in panic. She was rushing from one dresser to another and still the damn key couldn't be found. At the same time I started putting on my soldier clothes, or at least the ones that I could find. They were under the bed, behind the sofa, everywhere. Finally I found everything but my top underwear and my army shirt. Without my shirt I couldn't go out the window, so I continued to look for it as Margie was looking for the guard key. After not being able to find my shirt and hearing these loud knocks on the door I said to myself, "Well, just get ready to fight," as I was sure that Harold would be through that door in a few more moments and catch me in that terrible predicament.

Finally Margie found the key, while I at the same time had found all of my clothes except my underwear top, which was probably under the sofa or someplace else. As the noise and banging outside the door was getting louder and louder I went through the window onto the fire escape, where I could descend to the courtyard at ground level. Margie's apartment was on the fifth floor and after being on the fire escape leaving her apartment I found that I had to pass four more apartments on the way down to the courtyard. This I hadn't thought of in my hurry to get out of there so I began to go down the fire escape and immediately found myself in another predicament.

On the floor directly under Margie's apartment I found three little kids sleeping in the open window to keep cool on this hot night. I had to pass this window in order to get to the yard below, so I quietly stepped over their heads, one at a time, while at the same time I could hear older people snoring from farther back in the apartment. Probably the kids parents. I didn't realize until then what a situation I was in. If one of those kids had woke up and saw me in their window in the dark at three o'clock in the morning and screamed, I could have easily been shot as a burglar by their parents and that would be the end of it. My mind flashed back to the time when Jack and I were being followed by that five-carload of Texas cops at three o'clock in the morning on a dark road. That seemed to be a hopeless situation then and now going down this fire escape seemed to be another hopeless situation. Finally I made it past the kids and their parents when I found on the very next floor the same thing, only this time it was a man and a woman sleeping in the window. In this case I thought it might be a little bit worse. By them being adults they would shoot first and scream later. I gritted my teeth and started the same tip-toe crossing of stepping over the heads of the man and the woman. I finally and luckily passed them still sleeping. The following two floors on my descent were alright as the windows were closed and there were no sleepers.

I was pretty damn glad when I realized that the trip down the fire escape was over and all I had to do now was to jump down and go into the street and catch a cab back to the Theresa Hotel, but it still wasn't quite that easy. As I got to the bottom rung of the fire escape and was ready to jump down a big black Doberman pinscher dog ran out of somewhere and started raising hell. He barked so loud and had such big white teeth that I just stayed on the fire escape. He was just waiting for me to hit the ground. I thought to myself, "I can't go back up and I can't get down." I really didn't know what to do. Finally a West Indian man came out from somewhere. He was the janitor, I found out, and was mad as hell because his dog had awakened him at that time of the morning and mad as hell at me because I was the cause of it all. "Hey, mon," he yelled at me, "what the hell are you doing up there?" I couldn't think of a decent answer, so I said, "Well, you know how it is when some people come home early." Finally, after a lot of grumbling, he called his dog off and I jumped down. I gave him a five-dollar bill and he allowed me to go into the street, where I caught a cab and went directly to the hotel. I, needless to say, wasn't much good to the army for days after that. I was so nervous about the whole incident that for four or five days I just rested and tried to get my nerves together. I never knew how Margie explained the situation to Harold but she must have succeeded as they stayed together. We never had any more dates after that.

I continued with my army duties at camp and when I wasn't working at camp I'd play jazz concerts every Sunday afternoon for Monte Kaye and Mal Braveman. I had just begun working with Charlie Parker on many of the jazz concerts. He wasn't as big a man in the jazz world as he was to become later—he and Erroll Garner. But I never worked with Charlie again after I had been released from the army. Birdland, the big jazz scene, was at its peak and, though I used to go almost every night that I wasn't working at camp, I wasn't allowed to play there as a soldier like at the jazz concerts on Sundays.

It was around this time that heroin started becoming a fad with many of the modern jazz musicians. Many of the younger musicians were caught up in this latest fad so that they could be, or rather thought they would be, hep musicians. Ten years later some of them, the ones that never tried to quit nor took the cure, began to go into bad health and, in many cases, died at an early age. Many young cats who were hopped up in Birdland, knowing that I was a jazz trumpet man, used to approach me with bleary red eyes and, weaving as if they were going to fall down, would ask me, "Hey, Pops, what school you from?" They were referring to what style I played. They would look down on everybody that didn't play what was then called bebop and later was called contemporary jazz. Later there was a section of bebop that went into a style known as free-form jazz. It's funny, but none of the real giants of modern jazz ever had the idea of superiority—Diz, Parker, Miles—none of them. It was always the imitators that were so damn belligerent. I think they finally ran out of names to call themselves on their form of jazz, but it's still the same as it was in Birdland.

If I was asked to name all of the different kinds of jazz or, rather, the names of different types of jazz, such as most of the critics do, I'd begin with jass, as in the old New Orleans days, then to jazz as a change from jass, then ragtime, then hokum (hokum was a midwestern term), then into swing, then the title originated by Stanley Dance called mainstream. Mainstream was the category to which I belonged, along with swing. Then came the bebop era and after that the contemporary jazz of John Coltrane, Thelonious Monk and Charles Mingus. After contemporary jazz came the free-form jazz where everybody plays his own individual tempo and his own individual key; in fact I personally think that everybody plays his own individual song. It doesn't matter to those guys, they just play anything they want to and when you get ten guys doing that it's unbelievable. If I had known years ago that my jazz that I loved so much would have come to this point, I think I would have stayed in Parsons, Kansas, and would have chosen another occupation.

One day, as I was relaxing in the barracks, I received a call to report to headquarters. I had no idea why I was being called but anyway I left for the main office and, upon arriving, I was told that my Dad, who had been ill for the past two years, had taken a turn for the worse. I was issued a furlough to go to Parsons in order to be at his bedside. I packed a few things and left immediately for Parsons. On arriving home and seeing my Dad in bed I was saddened to find that he was in a coma and didn't recognize me. Poor Pop, I had wanted so much to talk with him, but I just helped in taking care of him as best as I could. There was so many church members that were there helping take care of him that I really couldn't find much to do, so I just sat and waited and hoped that he'd come around enough to know who I was.

One morning I was giving Dad a glass of milk taken through a straw and I had his head cradled in my arms. Suddenly he opened his eyes, saw me, smiled and said, "Buck." Then his head fell over to one side and he was gone. My mother came in the room, looked at him and Mom, always direct to the point, said, "He's dead."

I went out into the hall and stood alone for quite some time. I had mixed emotions about Dad's death. I knew that he had gone through so much pain. Sometimes at night we couldn't sleep because of Dad's moaning, and when I'd hear him I'd wish that it was me instead of him. He had been bedridden for about two years and had to depend entirely on others. So in a way I was glad that at last he was out of his misery. Still, he was my pop and I remembered all of the little troubles that I had as a kid and Dad was always there to help me out with my problems. I cried a little, I couldn't help it, especially as they came to take his body away. As they passed me on the front porch on the way to the hearse with his body I said goodbye to my Dad and tried not to cry any more because I didn't think Dad would have wanted his soldier son to cry. After the funeral all of Dad's cousins, aunts, nephews, nieces and loads of people and relatives from Texas all gathered at my home and, in a somber way, had a big party. I thought it was disrespectful to have all this going on so soon after Dad's burial, but my mother told me that that was the way that Dad would have wanted it. He would rather have his relatives rejoicing than to have them grieving over his death. I think this was another form of a New Orleans funeral that had spread over into Texas, where the funeral procession plays sad music on the way to the cemetery and then plays gay music on the way back from the cemetery.

I returned to Camp Kilmer after Dad's death and went about my army duties. There wasn't too much to do at the time so every day we'd wait for the GIs to come back, and they would tell us stories of the war with the Germans and the Japanese as they passed through our camp on their way to Fort Dix to be discharged. They knew what was happening better than we did. We played all these soldiers off of the boats just as we had played them on the boats when they left. I had now been raised in rank to technical sergeant and I was becoming more and more involved with the duties of the camp. We could see that the war was ending in Europe and, since I was a tech sergeant, I had a lot to do because so many of the others had already split from the army. I was one of the last ones to get out because I was one of the late ones in being inducted. As they used to say, "Last one to go in, last one to get out." Sy Oliver had been discharged, all of the big sergeants had left, it seemed, and quite a bit of responsibility fell on me.

One evening, after I had finished my chores at camp, I went into the city and met Jimmy Crawford, who by now had been discharged also. We were talking in the Palm Gardens on 125th Street and having a few beers, when I noticed a beautiful girl at the bar with several other girlfriends. Some way I got one of the girlfriends to introduce me to her and found her name to be Patricia Roberta DeVigne. She was the prettiest girl that I'd seen the whole time that I had been in the army. She was very pleasaant and seemed to be quite interested in meeting a soldier. Her brother was a combat soldier somewhere overseas and she hadn't seen him for some time. We talked for a short while and then she had to go and we made another date to meet at the same place some days later.

About a week later I met Pat again at the Palm Gardens and she was so surprised when I said, "Hello, Pat." She hadn't expected me to remember her name. She was with her buddy Dottie Turpin, who at the time was passing as Pat's cousin but who really was her very best friend. After a few drinks at the Palm Gardens we decided to go around to the Braddock Bar. After being at the Braddock Bar and enjoying ourselves she invited me to come to her home on 96th Street and meet her parents. I went to her apartment and met her mother and father. Gertrude DeVigne, her mother, was a strong lady that looked out for her kids. She didn't take any lip from any of them, neither did she allow anybody else to intimidate them. Pat had two twin sisters, Hortense (Tony) and Sophia (Jackie), and the brother, Freddie, who was overseas. Her father, Mr DeVigne (Henry), was a light complected gentleman that I thought was an Italian when I first met him. He was nine-tenths white. I thought to myself, "Here's a little girl born in Harlem of a mixed couple." Her father was from down South and he too had a twin brother. He was very, very nice and took to me right away. I don't think that he ever called me anything else other than "sergeant."

After a few more visits to Pat's family and eating Gert's wonderful cooking I began to feel more at ease and pretty soon I was able to take Pat out without having a specific time to have her back home. Pat, aside from being a beautiful girl, had a heart that was just as good as she was pretty. "Pretty Pat," some people called her. Whenever some of her friends had problems they would always ask Pat's advice and she would involve herself with many of her girlfriends' problems. She was liked by everybody, men and women. At first I would have sworn that she was an actress, singer or a dancer, or even a model, but I found out that she was a little girl that adored her family. She wasn't very interested in jazz, although after meeting me she tried to like it. One Sunday afternoon I took her to one of the Monte Kaye sessions at Lincoln Square in New York and after listening to Charlie Parker for a few minutes she turned to me and said, "He sure plays nice trombone." After that I taught her the different instruments so that she would never make that blooper again in public.

After a few months we became very tight and would go to all of the places in Harlem and downtown New York. I was still waiting for my year-and-a-day divorce termination out in California so all we could do would be to enjoy ourselves while waiting. I really was in love this time and pretty soon we got around to talking about getting married as soon as I was free from my first marriage.

One morning, after taking Pat to 52nd Street and listening to Dizzy and Bird, I returned to camp about five o'clock in the morning and found a big brown envelope waiting for me. I opened this envelope and found that it was my divorce papers that I had applied for, the final papers. Derb didn't contest it so I had no alimony to pay, so you know I was a pretty happy solider to get this big beautiful envelope. Actually everything seemed to be coming to an end—the war, my divorce—and it seemed just a matter of time before I'd be discharged and free of the army. Pat and I had talked of getting married but I still had some time to wait. But, unlike my marriage to Derb in California, this time I really had no doubts about getting married. I was proud of Pat and really enjoyed being with her all of the time.

I stayed on with the 373rd ASF band but I noticed that our band was diminishing and fast. When I first joined the band in Kilmer there were about twelve or thirteen trumpets in the band, aside from the other instruments, but when I got my divorce papers there were only about five of us trumpet players left. After another three or four months it got down to where I was the only trumpet player left in the whole band. There were a few clarinets, a few saxophones and scattered other instruments. One day we had a retreat parade on schedule. I went right away to our warrant officer and told him, "You know, I don't really know how you expect me to go out there and play this retreat parade with only one trumpet. I never heard of such a thing."

Our warrant officer, who was always afraid of the big brass in the army, said to me, "Well, we've got to do it anyway, so just go on out there and do the best you can."

I told him, "Alright. But when I get tired I'm gonna stop playing. I have to. I can't play forever."

He said, "Well do the best you can."

So we went out with one trumpet. There were only about eleven pieces in the whole band and as the parade progressed and I got tired I just stopped and there was no lead instrument. When the lead trumpet stops that leaves only the clarinet oodling and fooling around. It was kinda bad, in fact it was very bad. A few hours after the parade that evening we got a message from headquarters that that was our last parade we had to play because of the lack of trumpets. In fact the band was discontinued and we had nothing else to do but regular army duties and wait for our discharge papers to come through. So we just continued with this soldier business until our discharges came individually. I can't tell you how happy we were to be leaving Camp Kilmer forever. However, we were still in the army when V-Day came. The Germans had given up, they had lost the war, and that night in the Theresa Hotel was a night that I'll never forget. People were celebrating down in the streets all up and down Seventh Avenue, in fact all over Harlem, just as they were doing all over the city of New York. Every room in the hotel was swinging. I had my trumpet and I was blowing it out of the window onto Seventh Avenue, down to the people on the streets who were dancing and carrying on, but there was so much noise that I doubt very much if anybody heard me. Anyway, the war in Europe was over and that was the greatest thing in the world. The Japanese were still fighting but that war too was fast coming to an end.

SEVEN

JATP and a trip to Europe

Finally, when we were discharged from the army, I got a message from Norman Granz, whom I had met before. He wanted me, Kenny Kersey and our favorite bass player in Camp Kilmer, Benny Fonville, to make a cross-country tour with Jazz at the Philharmonic, beginning in California and ending in New York. This was to be the first cross-country tour for Norman, though he had made previous tours up and down the coast of California. I was happy at the thought of working for Norman as he paid the best salaries of anyone I knew and he's a beautiful person to work for. He really looks out for his entertainers. He is now one of the biggest agents in the business and has the best in artists. He asked Kenny and I if we'd be interested in making a tour with Coleman Hawkins and Lester Young with myself filling in the third of the three horns that he wanted. Naturally Kenny and myself agreed to make the tour and we signed up right away to begin the first cross-country tour of JATP. We still had to wait about three or four months before the tour was to begin so we continued on with our gigs that we had been doing. These were plentiful because of the fact that we, Kenny and I, had been in the army for the last three years and every bandleader that could use us was glad to have us with them.

Then one day I received at the Theresa Hotel my final papers from California and at last I was free to marry Pat. I received my papers on one day, like a Wednesday, and got married the next day, like Thursday. It wasn't anything like the big Hollywood wedding; in fact it was a simple home wedding that we had with only the family and a couple of Pat's close friends. We were married in Baltimore, where we stayed at the home of Pat's mother's relatives. Pat was very beautiful and her mother was beaming. The wedding went smoothly and we all were pretty happy. We took pictures after the wedding or, rather, I should say we *thought* that we took pictures as we found out later that the photographer had forgot to put film in his camera and didn't discover the loss until he got back to his studio, so Pat and I never had any photos of our wedding after going through all that trouble of posing, cutting the cake, etc. Not one photo.

After the wedding we returned to New York and prepared to go with Norman on the tour. It was kinda like a honeymoon for Pat and myself as she was invited by Norman to make the trip with us. It was a nice trip for Pat to go to California as she had never been there. Especially Hollywood, that was really a great thrill for her—seeing Grauman's Theater and putting her hands and feet in the imprints of the movie stars, the Brown Derby, Hollywood Boulevard—really a big thrill for her. It was on the way to California that we stopped and saw my mother in Parsons and she liked Pat right away.

After arriving in Los Angeles we rehearsed with the rest of the group that was to make the tour. Helen Humes, my Basie buddy, was on vocals and soon we were ready for anything. Coleman was cool so was Prez. These two giants of the tenor got along like they had been together for some time. They knew it was a continued cutting contest but neither one of them doubted his own ability. It was like a weigh-in for the two heavyweight champions of the world. I was knocked out and could hardly wait for the tour to begin. Hawk and Prez were friendly towards each other and never showed any sign of jealousy, which to me meant that they were real professionals. The tour finally started in April 1946. In Hollywood we used several stars on the first night that were not to continue the tour, such as Charlie Parker, Buddy Rich and a few others. Then, after the first night, it was all Hawk, Prez, Kenny Kersey, and myself. The tour was an instant success and Norman was happy. He would play with the guys, joke with them, and sometimes engage them in different kinds of games, such as seeing who could make the most baskets on a basketball court if we had the occasion to find a gymnasium free some day when we arrived early in a town to play a concert. Sometimes he would make bets that he could make more baskets than different guys and sometimes he would. He used to wear a necktie in his trousers instead of a belt—not that he couldn't have a million belts if he had wanted to, but he just liked the style of wearing a necktie instead of a belt.

The tour started out with a bang and every night was something that everybody had been waiting for, to see Coleman Hawkins and Lester Young battle it out. For me it was the greatest thing in the world to be put between these two giants. Kenny and I became buddies on the tour and had a ball, no matter what time of the day it was nor what we happened to be doing. We would begin with all of us playing together with the rhythm section. Hawk would blow his own beautiful solo and bring down the house, then it would be my turn to get into it. After me came Lester with his own unique style of playing, which was totally different from Hawk. They both had something that every other tenor man would have given his life for—their own individual style. Sometimes I'd get so wrapped up in listening to these two that I'd be surprised to find that I had to follow either one of those cats. Kenny was knocking me out too on piano and, to top it all, Helen Humes would come on and sing.

We were a success in almost every city that we played: Hollywood, Kansas City, St Louis, Chicago and finally at Carnegie Hall in New York. We got good raves in all of the journals and finally, when the last concert was played, we were a little sad to see the tour come to an end. However, we knew that Norman was going to call us for the next tour, which was to begin the following year. The next time was a bit different, in that it had become bigger and had more musicians. We had Illinois Jacquet, Willie Smith (the former Jimmie Lunceford sax man), Roy Eldridge, Trummy Young, Rex Stewart and some others added. This tour too was pretty exciting, as Illinois Jacquet would upset the house with his version of *Flying Home*. He'd have the house in an uproar, swinging on one note and stompin' like crazy. It would always bring down the house. The rest of the guys rose to the occasion and everybody received great ovations. On later tours we had Buddy Rich, Flip Phillips and others.

Norman was always a great fighter for equal rights and sometimes he'd have to go to bat for us when we'd get to some city that put prejudice before anything else. Sometimes, when we'd hit a city that would refuse us service in a restaurant, Norman would have us just sit there at the restaurant until they served us, no matter what happened. One time we were doing just that when we noticed that we should be beginning the concert. Norman said, "Hell no, we don't play a damn note until we get served." So, knowing that the concert hall was already fully of people, we just sat in the restaurant and the owner still refused to serve us. Finally we had to give in without getting served because the audience in the hall waiting for us began to raise so much hell. We reluctantly had to leave the restaurant to play the concert, which was already over a half an hour late.

Another time, in Wisconsin, Norman had been to a seafood restaurant and had some beautiful fried shrimps. On arriving at the theater to start the concert he told us all how great these shrimps were. Loving seafood like I do, I decided to go after the show to this restaurant and get some of those crazy shrimps. So, finishing the first show, I caught a cab by myself and went to the restaurant. I went in and sat down. Pretty soon a guy came up to me, the waiter in the joint. He said to me, "Hello, buddy, I see that you're an ex-service man."

I said, "Yes, I am." And in a few minutes he was telling me all about his life in the army and I was telling him about mine. After some time of this I wondered why he didn't take my order for the shrimps. He kept on talking about the army so finally I told him that I'd like to have an order of fried shrimps. He looked at me and said, "Buddy, I know that you're an ex-soldier like me, but I just can't serve you." I asked him why and got the usual answer, "We don't serve colored in here." What a bring down. I went on back to the theater and told Norman about it. He got so mad that he asked me and everybody else to prepare to go right back to this place just as soon as we finished the concert. After the concert Norman, myself, Buddy Rich and a couple of the others got into a cab. We really intended to break up that joint. We were all mad and were ready for a fight. Buddy Rich was with us, as I said, and you know Buddy will fight at the drop of a hat if it's for the right. We finally arrived at the restaurant but it was after eleven o'clock and the restaurant was closed so we had to go back to our hotel with nothing happening. The next day we had to leave town too early to go back to that place. Finally we played our last concert and I was a little sorry about it as I really did enjoy these tours.

A few weeks later Hugues Panassié and Madeleine Gautier visited New York. I had never met Hugues nor Madeleine but was quite familiar with their works in jazz. They were both very capable authorities on jazz in

France. I was asked by Mezz Mezzrow to meet them at the airport with a small band composed of myself, Cliff Jackson, Sidney Bechet, Happy Caldwell and Mezz. We met them and I made friends that I'm happy to say lasted for years. They stayed at the Theresa Hotel and were wined and dined by all the New York cats that were in that bag, such as Zutty Singleton, Mezz, Tommy Ladnier, Bechet and a lot of others. They really were the toast of Harlem. I was playing with Buddy Walker at the time and Hugues would come up to the roof of the hotel on Sundays when we played there and listen to us. It was the first time that he had heard me in person. Before they left to go back to France Hugues asked me if I'd be interested in coming over to their country and make a tour. I accepted the offer immediately and Hugues told me that, after arriving back in France, he would begin making preparations for such a tour. I was so elated that, along with my old army buddy the trumpet man Bobby Williams, I began to take French lessons. We took lessons from a genius on foreign languages, Professor Smith, who had his offices up over Smalls Paradise. I knew that we didn't have long to learn the language, but under Professor Smith we learned to read, write and speak French pretty well before we were to take the boat to France. Smitty, as we called him, was a wonder on languages. He astonished Madeleine and Hugues when they heard him speak French. He could speak it better than most French people and had won many awards for his teaching and speaking. He could speak fluently nine other languages besides French, so in a few weeks he had Bobby and myself learning all about French regular verbs, irregular verbs, first conjugation, second conjugation, etc. In just a few weeks we could both speak pretty good French for beginners.

About this time I had become buddies with a trumpet man by the name of Merrill Stepter. Step was a good trumpet player, about my age and a pretty nice looking cat. We had shared many experiences together, playing together on jam sessions, hanging out, getting juiced together sometimes, so when he learned that I had been asked to go to France he wanted to go too. So I asked Hugues if it would be alright to bring another trumpet, although I really didn't need one. He said, "Yes, by all means bring him." So I told Step and we both began immediately to save our money for the trip to France, as one of the conditions for the tour was that we pay our own passage. It was a brand new adventure for us. Nobody had any money, I was practically unknown in France except for a few people that knew me from Basie, so we agreed to pay our own passage over. I then asked Wallace Bishop if he would come with me and he agreed right away. Bish had played drums for years before with Earl Hines in Chicago and he and I were pretty tight. So Bish, too, started saving his money for the trip over.

Pat, in the meantime, had accepted a job in the Village in New York in a club called the Savannah Club. Pat had never been in show business before. One day I heard from a theatrical producer that this new club was going to open and they needed some chorus girls and show girls. Pat was pretty enough to be able to join anybody's show. She was a strikingly beautiful girl and I kinda thought that she would have liked to be in show business. She had been taking singing lessons. I used to kid her about her singing qualities.

So when I heard about this new club I asked Pat if she'd like to work there. She said, "Well, you know that I can't dance and can't sing. So what can I do in a show?" She wanted so much to be in the business but didn't know what she could do. I told her, "Just go down and sign up as a show girl, because all you have to do is to look pretty and walk out on the stage in a beautiful costume. You don't have to dance nor sing, just walk and keep time with the music." She said she thought she would like that so she went down and applied for the job. She was accepted on the spot and became what I called one of the Savannah Peaches.

Finally the day came for our departure for France. We were to leave on 24th September 1949 on the famous "Ile de France," a beautiful boat that I later became crazy about. One of the girls that worked at the Savannah Club was the ex-wife of Bishop, and when we were ready to get on the boat Bish was still walking up and down the pier. He was looking for his ex-wife to come see him off. He walked, walked and walked, but no sign of Alice his ex-wife. Step and I thought that he was going to miss the boat because they were preparing to pull up the gangplank. Finally, when they actually started pulling up the steps, I ran down and pulled Bish on, crying and everything. We pulled him on just as the boat was about to leave. He almost missed the boat being right there beside it. Finally we were en route for la France.

We enjoyed the four-day trip to France on the "Ile de France." We began to become accustomed to some French ways, such as learning which wine to drink on certain occasions. We soon learned that as soon as one bottle of wine was finished at our table in the dining room another one would be brought soon after, and then another . . . and another. Sometimes Step and I would get up from the table after eating and drinking wine and just barely make it back to our cabins. I didn't know that we could get so looped from drinking that red wine but we did. We naturally hung out at all the bars on the boat but we didn't play on this trip. Soon we pulled in at Le Havre in France and it was quite a sensation to see a country that all my life I had been thinking of and wanted to see. I was comparing it as it was with the France that I had imagined it would be. I liked it and it was really the way that I had imagined that the real France would look. It was beautiful and the people were beautiful. Although I still couldn't understand most of the language, I was in better shape than Bish or Step. They couldn't understand one word. I found out one thing: if you say as much as a simple "bonjour" to a Frenchman, he'll smother you right away because he figures you know all there is to know.

I was glad to see Hugues and Madeleine after we met them in Paris. They had made plans for us to work with some additional French musicians on our tour. There was André Persiany, a beautiful pianist who later came to America and was a member of Jonah Jones's quartet for years. We had Georges Hadjo, a good man on bass, Armand Conrad on tenor sax and George Kennedy on alto sax. Soon we all went to Fontainebleau, where Panassié lived, and were given our rooms where we were to live. There were rooms of different colors—blue, pink, etc. I don't remember which color room I had but anyway soon we were rehearsing the group for the tour.

Aside from that we made recordings for Hugues during our first few days. Bill Coleman was in France and, though I had never met him in person, I knew of him. He was the one trumpet player that I had wanted to see because everybody told me that we sounded so much alike, especially with a mute. Years before, in New York, John Hammond took me in his room one day while I was at his home and said to me, "Buck, come on in. I want you to dig this record." I went in with him and he put this record on the box and the trumpet solo was muted. I thought it was me. I said, "Damn, I don't remember making this record." He played it a couple more times and I couldn't think of where I made it. Finally, seeing that I was really puzzled, John said to me, "That's not even you. That's Bill Coleman playing trumpet." Then I understood why they all thought that I played like Bill or he played like me. I had never seen him nor heard him play, so it was only natural that I was very impressed when I met Bill in person. Eventually we made a recording for Hugues called *B. C. and B. C. Blues*, where we both play together. That's when I made the Louis Armstrong version of *West End Blues*, which nobody had recorded except Pops. I was making quite a few small-band arrangements and we kept pretty busy in Fontainebleau before our tour started. When we did start, in addition to the group we had Armand Conrad's wife with us, Nitoune. She was a beautiful little girl of Vietnamese extraction that would take care of all of the business such as buying tickets, seeing that the band had accommodations and other things that the musicians didn't have time to do.

We had a good concert put together for the tour and we went over pretty well but the audiences were pretty scarce at times. It was from our road manager, Jacques Boulogne, that I learned the French word "inconnu," which means "unknown." We were playing good music but the audiences didn't know me. They hadn't heard too much about Buck Clayton yet so there came the word inconnu. I still had to build up my name. We played the Salle Pleyel in Paris for our initial concert and then went out on the road. It was on this tour that I met some of my best friends in Europe. In Limoges, France, I met Jean Marie Masse, who became one of my very best friends through all these years. He was a real jazz enthusiast who had a wife, Paulette, and two young daughters, Agnes and Sylvie. It was on this tour too that I met Johnny Simmen of Zurich, Switzerland, another great friend whose friendship I cherish very much. He and his wife Liza have invited me many times to have dinner at their home and they know that I love rabbit, stew and chicken. Liza cooks them all equally as well. In Limoges, when I eat at Jean Marie's home, my favorite food is veal kidneys, chicken and pommes vapeur, or steamed potatoes.

On the bus, while making the tour, I was impressed with the beauty of the French countryside: beautiful trees on both sides of the highways, the little restaurants that you see on the highways with the little French cook made of wood standing outside. If we were riding in the bus we would have to stop to eat at certain hours of the day. If you didn't eat between 11 a.m. to 1 p.m., then you'd have to wait until that evening around five o'clock before you could eat again. We made it our business to stop when we were supposed to and eat. I loved French cuisine from the very start and soon I began learning how to order different foods. I learned much from the guys in the band and from Nitoune too, including much slang and things that isn't taught in the books. From Pépé (André) I learned many cuss words.

Don Byas was in France at this time also. He had come over to Europe with Don Redman's band and had remained. I had known Don from the Basie days when he took over Lester Young's chair on one of the few times that Lester had left the band. He spoke fluent French from being there over a year and working with the French musicians, especially slang. I watched him and tried to pick up as much French as I could, until one day something happened when it wasn't too wise to listen to Don too much.

We had been invited to Pépé's home for dinner. His mother was half Italian and naturally was an expert on cooking Italian cuisine, especially spaghetti. All the boys showed up and we were having one great time listening to records, telling jokes, and in general just enjoying ourselves. Don was invited, since we were old friends and it was only natural that he should be with us. Madame Persiany cooked a beautiful dinner and we ate like pigs. When we got up from the table we could hardly do anything else but sit right back down and relax. We were full to the gills.

I went over to Bish and asked him what we could give Madame Persiany as a token of appreciation. Bish suggested that we give her a bouquet of flowers. So I went downstairs to the street where there was a flower vendor and bought a beautiful bunch of roses and brought them upstairs. Without Madame Persiany seeing me I went to Don and asked him to write out a speech for me to say, since I couldn't say that much French yet and Don could. He scribbled out something on a piece of paper and went in the bathroom with me to help me learn it. It began with something like, "Madame Persiany, we hope that you will accept these flowers for such a beautiful dinner, etc." After coaching me a bit Don left and went on back in the room with all of the rest of the guys and I stayed in the bathroom and practiced. I wanted to make good with my first speech I'd ever made in French. I practiced and practiced while everybody else was having a ball in the other room.

Finally, when I thought I had it down pretty well, I came out of the bathroom. I had decided that I was going to give this speech even if it killed me. I had a pretty good idea of what I was saying, even though Don had added one word at the end of the speech that I didn't understand. But I thought that since Don knew more French than I did I'd just say the whole speech as he had coached me. So with everybody watching me, everybody smiling, I began. I said, "Madame Persiany (in French), we have enjoyed this dinner so much that we want you to remember us." She was smiling and beaming as I went on. "We would like for you to accept these flowers . . ." She was still smiling at this point. Then I continued on with the speech until I got to this word that I didn't understand, but anyway I went on and said it. Then I looked at Madame Persiany. She was no longer smiling, her eyes bulged, she got red, and she had that awful embarrassing look on her face. Everybody else, especially the French cats, looked at me like I was crazy or something. Madam Persiany left the room in a huff. Nobody said a word and I got the feeling that I had said something very wrong, and when I looked over at Don and saw him laughing like hell I *knew* that I had said something wrong. Finally Pepe came over to me and said, "Buck, we know that you don't know what you said so we don't blame you for it." Then, after a few minutes, I was told by Nitoune that I had said, "Madame Persiany, we enjoyed that wonderful dinner so much that we hope you will accept these flowers and stick 'em up your ass!" That one word that Don had added to the speech in French was "enculez" and enculez is a bad word in French. You don't say it unless you're either prepared to fight or run. I went over to Madame Persiany and apologized but I really didn't have to because she, like everybody else, knew that I didn't know what I was saying, but she was pissed off at Don. Me too. After that I said to myself, "From now on I'll learn my own French so I'll never have to ask people like Don for assistance."

We traveled practically all over France during our visit and every day we saw something to amaze us. One night we were taken to a castle which Joan of Arc frequented during her reign. The castle was cold, all the walls and hallways were of stone and I was cold, but still it was very interesting to be on the same ground as Joan of Arc. Also, in or near Bordeaux, we saw the actual site where she was burned to death. Bordeaux is a very important city in France and it was there that I discovered that we were not the only ones making a tour of France. When we arrived there one afternoon we were told that we were to share the concert with Sidney Bechet. We were to play the first half of the concert and he and his group were to play the second half. That was OK with us as Sidney at that time was practically the king of France as far as jazz was concerned—with the exception of Louis Armstrong. We went on that evening and played our usual concert, which we ended with the *Muskrat Ramble*. We received a great ovation and left the stage so that Sidney could come on and follow us. I was in my dressing room preparing to go out and listen to Sidney when Nitoune came in and told me that Sidney was furious because I had played *Muskrat Ramble*. He said that I had no business playing *Muskrat Ramble* even if he wasn't going to play it because I had no business playing dixieland. He raised hell and even threatened not to go on. Finally he decided to go on but by that time I had decided not to listen to him and went on out to a nightclub that was near. Now this was the first nightclub that I had been to in France, as we still hadn't spent any time in Paris where all the night life is and especially the Lido Club. As Step and I were sitting listening to the French musicians play soon it was time for the floor show. In a few minutes about eighteen beautiful girls ran out on the floor and they were topless. We watched these little girls out there on the floor bouncin' around when Sidney came in with his group and sat down. We didn't say anything to each other, we just watched the show, which was knocking me and Step out—these pretty little things out there on the floor going through their routines with these exotic French costumes on. They were nude from the waist up. The Frenchmen in the club didn't give a damn about the chicks, though, and pretty soon they were booing the girls off the floor. They wanted them to get off the floor so that we all could start a jam session.

Sidney didn't want to play so I wouldn't play either, and we all cut out and went back to our hotel. The French cats were still booing the girls, which I thought was ridiculous. If these little girls had been in New York bouncin' around like that they would have been an overnight sensation, but these French cats had seen it so often that it didn't interest them in the least.

We continued the tour, which was beginning to swing, and I was now learning more and more about France, especially the life of the country people. The residents of many cities in the south of France wore wooden shoes, which I had expected to see in Holland but not in France. I was beginning to learn the different specialties of food in certain regions. And of course there was the wine. It's impossible to learn all of the different kinds of wine in France, that is unless you're a wine expert. Every section of France has its own wine product. Many of the cities, like Bordeaux and Champagne, are named for wine, which interested me so much. In Fontaine-bleau I had seen the wine cellar of Hugues Panassié and it was amazing. Hugues was a real connoisseur of French wine, as well as many other of my French friends. I couldn't even begin to name half of them.

Finally our tour ended and we were free now to go see Paris, as we had so far only really had time to see Fontainebleau and the countryside and small towns in rural France. We all took up residence in Paris and just lived and thought like French people, all of which was knocking me out. I was around people all the time who spoke only French, so pretty soon I started talking French like everybody around me. Step, myself, and Bish all decided that we were going to stay in Paris for a while. I, myself, had decided to stay in Paris for three more weeks but it got good to me and I stayed there nine months. I had only been married three years now and it wasn't too good to be away from home that long, but I think that if I hadn't been married I would have stayed in Paris like some of my lifelong American friends. We moved into the Hotel Select in Place Pigalle and began our new French life.

Very soon I was getting so many gigs in Paris that I really didn't have too much time to even think of going home. When the European booking agents find out that you're in Europe and that they don't have to pay for your passage over, they all have so much work lined up for you that you just can't do it all, but I sure as hell was trying. I worked many gigs with my good friend Dave Pochonet, a bandleader in France at the time. We played many theater dates in and around Paris. Every weekend for a while I would go to Berne, Switzerland, and work with my buddy Bill Coleman, who had a great group there in the Chiquito Club. That was a gas, working with Bill. I sure enjoyed those gigs because now I was beginning to learn the life of the Swiss people. After the weekends with Bill, though, I'd go back to Paris and get back to my French thinking. I finally learned how to eat French bread without cracking my bridgework.

One week, as I came back from Switzerland, I decided that I wasn't going to live all the time in Paris in the same place. I wanted to really learn the city so I decided to live for a few weeks in different sections of Paris so I'd really be familiar with it. So I moved into a hotel which was near the Eiffel Tower and learned pretty much about that region of Paris. I loved the Eiffel

Tower but all the French cats couldn't understand how I was so crazy about going up to the top and enjoying myself when they, who had been born and lived there all of their lives, had never been up, nor had any desire to go. I guess it's the same everywhere. I had lived in New York all of these years and had never been up in the Empire State Building, but that's one of the first things the French people want to do when they visit America. It was in this section that I met my longtime friend Maurice Cullaz and his family. Some time later I moved to the left bank, where I dug all of the students. The way they lived was still different. Many times when I'd be walking down the streets I could hear a distant rumble and shouting down the street and as it grew louder I found it to be hundreds of students demonstrating against something. I soon found out that it's best to get out of the way when you see this bunch of trouble coming. Those French kids would overturn cars, smash windows, and would fight the French cops to a standstill. I soon learned how to duck because they didn't give a damn who was in the way. It was just best not to be in their way. I worked with my friend Maxim Saury many times in the students' quarter and once I played for the students of La Sorbonne. Everything was cheaper in the students' quarter because the students didn't have too much money. I'd see these kids making love all over Paris because they didn't have enough room for a hotel. I have seen many Parisian lovers kissing each other while crossing the many boulevards of Paris, which was another French custom that I dug.

After a few weeks on the left bank I went back to Place Pigalle, where I found life to be more active than any other section that I had been in. In fact, when all of the other sections of Paris had closed for the night, Place Pigalle was swingin' away. Even when Champs Elysées had finished for the night, which was always after 2 a.m., you could go to Place Pigalle and the streets would be full of life. That's where all of the real action was. I moved back again into the Hotel Select and had a room on the third floor. The first two floors were for the chicks that worked the streets and their johns, all floors above that were for the residentials that were permanent guests. By me being on the third floor I could hear all the noise that would come from the second floor when sometimes the chicks would get into fights with their johns or with each other. Once I heard two girls fighting on the second floor and I went to look down and saw these two chicks, without a stitch of clothes on, fighting all over the joint. It was very interesting. French women, especially the ones that lived in Pigalle, could fight like men. I've seen many Pigalle chicks square off and fight like Sugar Ray Robinson. They're strong. In Pigalle you could also see the pimps knocking their old ladies down in the street and then just walk off and leave them lying there wherever they fell. Those French pimps were pretty rough and heartless. Some of the biggest pimps in Paris, though, were the French motorcycle police. Sometimes early in the morning you could see them checking up with their chicks after the night before. I also knew and hung around some of the cops, or "les flics," as they are called in France, that liked jazz. They used to call me "Monsieur la Trompette" and lots of times when I'd practice my horn lots of people would gather underneath my window and listen. It was like a little concert in jazz. Some of my cop friends had such names as Le Pélican (a cop with a big nose), Beau Garçon (the pretty-boy cop) and Le Catcheur (who was a cop who had been a wrestler). Many of them I knew. I learned too that sometimes, contrary to common belief, the French cops are not as polite as they seem to be when they're making an arrest. I don't know from first-hand experience, because I never was arrested for anything, but I've been told that when making an arrest, a normal arrest, the cops are so polite. When putting you in the black maria they say to you, "Par ici, monsieur" (This way, sir), and they handle you with kid gloves, the white gloves they all wear. They treat you like you're a guest until they get you to the police station, then they take off the gloves and all hell breaks loose. I heard that they turned Sidney Bechet's hair grey overnight as he was being interrogated for a street incident. Madeleine Panassié once told me that she would gladly confess to murder, even if she was innocent, rather than be interrogated by the French cops.

I met a little girl named Jackie that was half Egyptian and half French. A pretty little chick that had just been released from prison the same day that I met her. I liked Jackie because she didn't try to roll me like all the other chicks would if they had the occasion. That's one of the ways of life in Pigalle —you have to watch your wallet at all times. I was an expert, though, on hiding my loot, but even then sometimes I'd get stung. Jackie had been in prison for snatching a woman's purse but with me she never did show any signs of clipping me. So Jackie and I hung out together and we'd go to Leroy Haines's and Gabby's restaurant in Pigalle. I learned a lot of street language from Jackie, too, some more that's not in the books. Haines was an American that had settled in Paris. He had been a football star, in Baltimore, I think it was. He and his wife Gabby had opened this restaurant and all of the Americans in Paris would hang round in their place because it was where you could get all the soul food you wanted. All of the entertaining stars, the American soldiers, everybody would go to Haines's and Gabby's and eat fried chicken, chitterlings, barbecue and all the rest. Many times it was impossible to get near the place for people trying to get to this soul food.

Bishop and Step were gigging too and sometimes we'd make it together, but not too often. Step went to work with Snake Hips Taylor, an American dancer that had become very popular in Paris. He had been a big dancer in Harlem years ago and was a real nice cat. They went to work in a club together in Pigalle. Bish and I would work together sometimes. Once we went to play a mask ball in Lausanne, Switzerland. We didn't sign a contract until the day we were to leave Paris and we really didn't know just how much we were to make but we figured it would be about seventy-five dollars at least. We knew we would be paid because it was for a banker's ball and we were the great jazzmen from America. We went, we played the ball and had a great time. We were treated like kings. That's one gig I'll never forget. When we finished we were paid in Swiss francs, which we didn't mind because you never had any trouble with Swiss francs. You can go to any bank in Switzerland and have your loot changed into any kind of currency that you want. So Bish and I went to the bank the next morning to change our money to dollars. As the clerk was making the change he gave me a hundred dollars, which I thought was all I was going to get, then he gave me a second hundred—very good too—then, without stopping, he gave me another hundred, and another . . . and another . . . and when he finished I had more than five hundred dollars for that one night. Bish too. We were two pretty pleased guys when we went back to Paris with all that bread.

After spending the nine months in Paris I began to think about coming back home. I said goodbye to all my friends and was given a bon voyage party by several of the musicians that I had met. I left Paris with a rather heavy heart because I really did like the city. I was very pleased to have been able to see it just as it was. So in April 1950 I put on my French beret and came back to New York, where I found that Pat had moved from the Hotel Theresa to an apartment on Mount Morris Park in Harlem.

EIGHT

A new phase in my career

The apartment in Mount Morris Park was huge, especially for two people, but in a way it was a different life from living in the Theresa Hotel. Pat had leased it from a friend, Bill Alexander, who was at the time producing black movies in Harlem. Having just come from France it was necessary for me to learn of all the changes that had taken place while I was away and it wasn't too long before I was again familiar with the Harlem scene. Gigs were mostly the thing of the day. There were not too many jobs that were steady unless you belonged with a few chosen musicians that played regularly in the Village at the jazz joints there such as Nick's, Eddie Condon's, etc. It wasn't long, however, before I was in the swim again and traveling all over the big city of New York, as well as in New Jersey and Connecticut. One day I met the great jazzman from New Orleans, Tony Parenti. Tony asked me what I was doing and I told him just what was happening. Now Tony was a dixieland player from way back and I didn't expect him to have any gigs for me, because I only knew about two dixieland numbers and wasn't too sure of those. *Royal Garden Blues*, that I had recorded with Basie with Don Byas, was one; the other was *Muskrat Ramble*, that I had been playing in France. So anyway, Tony says to me, "Buck, I have a group but we only play dixieland. We sure would like to work with you if you'd be interested in learning some dixieland tunes." I thought that this would be a new phase in my career so I thought to myself, "Sure, why not? What have I got to lose?" So I told Tony that I was interested. We made an appointment. I was supposed to meet Tony at his home and, along with Sandy Williams, the great trombonist of Chick Webb's and Duke Ellington's bands, we were to start practicing dixieland.

We met at Tony's and I met his wife and first we all went into the living room where Tony told me of his days in New Orleans and about the different people there that he had played with. His wife was cooking a big dinner of spaghetti while we talked. Pretty soon we took out our horns and I began to get my first lessons in dixieland. We went over and over again such numbers as *That's a Plenty, Fidgety Feet, Struttin' with some Barbecue, Do you know what it means to miss New Orleans?* All of these numbers were new to me but before long I was beginning to get the drift of the things and I kinda liked it. The main thing I learned about dixieland was getting the format together. There are certain routines of dixieland numbers, certain modulations, and once you learn these routines you are on your way, as you can play anything you want on your solos. So I learned the formats, but when it was time for my solo I would play a typical Kansas City style solo. I didn't know how to play a dixieland solo but I made it with the rest of the number. I think that Wild Bill Davison is my favorite man on dixieland songs—not that he can't play other things too—but when he was with Condon's group in the Village I used to admire his playing. Billy Butterfield was another. For some reason black cats never were interested in dixieland music. I never knew why. Only in New Orleans did the black musicians take an interest in dixieland music, and I'm really not too sure that they were really interested in it or if they were playing it simply because it was "home" music. There was very few black guys in New York that played dixieland.

I continued to learn with Tony and sometimes I was glad to get to rehearsals because I knew that Tony's wife was going to have a big spaghetti dinner for us when we finished rehearsal. Sandy Williams was a big help to me in learning because he had also learned how to play dixieland—he sure didn't play it with Chick Webb nor Duke Ellington. Soon we were going on gigs and I was well on my way to playing dixieland. Later I found it quite convenient to know dixieland because now I could accept gigs from other leaders that wanted me to play it. After several gigs with Tony and Sandy I went into a jazz house off-Broadway called Lou Terrassi's.

Lou's place was a swinging joint and was a favorite place for jazz fans that didn't want to go down to the Village. All of the guys from Broadway would come in and listen to such guys as Buster Bailey, Willie "the Lion" Smith, Red Allen, Charlie Shavers and a lot of others. So I went in with Kenny Kersey, Herb Flemming and Sol Yaged, and we stayed there for some time. It was really something else because the room was dark and there was really some good jazz coming out of that place. Lou, however, later sold the place and moved to Florida but it sure was a pleasant gig while it lasted.

I continued my association with Buddy Walker, who played mostly for the different clubs in Harlem and was about the most popular of all the bands there. Buddy was a good guy and often told people that he and I were brothers as we looked quite a bit like each other. He was a tenor man but not a jazzman. He had some good guys and it was always a gas to play with Buddy. Here, again, I had to learn a different style of music and that was the West Indian music that was so popular in Harlem. I learned them all, such as *Sly Mongoose, Small Island, Ugly Woman* and some more. So now I had learned two different kinds of music since I arrived home from Paris —dixieland and West Indian. Buddy used to hire the best cats he could get in Harlem. He used John Strachan, who later became the postmaster general of New York City. John was an alto sax man that had been with me in the army band in Camp Shanks. He used Bobby Williams, trumpet, who went with me to learn French and was also with me in the army. At times he would use Jacques Butler if Jacques happened to be in town from France on a visit. I played many gigs with Buddy and it was always a pleasure. I learned the feeling for music in Harlem at the time. Anytime the dance was going slow and not too many people would dance, all you had to do was to go into a West Indian number and the whole ballroom would begin to move.

Joe Glaser called me one day to go out to Chicago with a group that I thought I'd like: Edmond Hall, Buzzy Drootin, Jess Stacy, Lee Wiley and Wingy Manone. The place was the Rag Doll in Cicero, Illinois. We arrived in town the night that Louis Armstrong was closing, Saturday night, and we all went out to hear Pops. They had such a beautiful show together, Pops, Earl Hines, Jack Teagarden, Barney Bigard and Velma. Their last show was fantastic and the whole club was cheering as Pops played their last number of the gig. That great line of musicians was just too much for us to follow as we hadn't as yet even had a rehearsal. Anyway, the following week we opened in there and we died in there. When we were playing on the stand we could just feel Louis all over the place. Too, Wingy Manone and Lee Wiley didn't like each other and it wasn't long before Lee threw a glass of whiskey in Wingy's face. In a couple of hours they had chosen sides and were going to battle in the alley behind the Rag Doll. Lee had chosen Jess Stacy and Buzzy Drootin was joining Lee because he wanted to be against Wingy. Wingy had even asked Edmond Hall to fight with him, which was so ridiculous. I couldn't imagine Edmond fighting for anybody except himself, and least of all Wingy. However, after choosing up sides, they never did fight. They didn't even ask me to be on one side or the other. That was on a Hallowe'en night and after a few days more I think the club folded. I know that we were let out.

Another time, Jimmy Rushing came to me and asked me if I'd be interested in joining a band that he was getting together to go into the Savoy Ballroom. I said I would and soon we were rehearsing to go into the Savoy for Charlie Buchanan. I made some arrangements and we were on our way. He had, naturally, quite a few Basie cats in the band, such as Dicky Wells, Emmett Berry, Buddy Tate and myself. We knew that, even with all of his experience with big bands, Rush wasn't a musician and didn't know too much about leading a band, but he was an attraction and a good one. We all did our best to make him happy and we had a damn good band. Everybody knew Jimmy Rushing so we stayed in the Savoy for quite some time.

Other than the Savoy Ballroom everything was swinging at Birdland and 52nd Street. Birdland was swinging every night and you couldn't get in the joint half the time. In Birdland there was a girl from Arkansas, a beautiful girl that we all called Birdland Betty. A beautiful blonde girl that loved chitterlings, pig feet, corn pone and all that business. She had come to New York and fell in love with Harlem. She was the queen of Harlem and usually would go out with all of the Harlem bandleaders. No sidemen for the queen, nothing but bandleaders. Her finding Harlem was just like the rabbit finding a briar patch. She was soon the talk of all the musicians and other girls who were jealous of her beauty. I remember once Billie Holiday had a run-in with Betty and didn't like it a damn bit when she found out that her old man was dating Betty. She hit the ceiling. She said to me one night, "Yeah, Buck, guess who that motherfucker was out with last night." I didn't know, so she said, "That bitch, Birdland Betty." She really had gotten under Billie's skin and I don't think it would have been wise to confront Billie at that time.

Joe Bushkin, a little cat that I admired but had never worked with, came to me one day and asked me to open a brand-new club in New York, the Embers Club. He was forming a quartet and I was to play with my two favorite rhythm men, Jo Jones and Milt Hinton. That gassed me so I agreed right away to go with him. We were to open with our quartet and Art Tatum and his trio. Ralph Watkins was one of the owners of the club and was the only one at the time who could get a liquor licence for the new club. When the day for the opening came we were pretty happy and Joe Bushkin was swinging from the start. When Art followed us, there were so many pianists in the place that you couldn't get a seat anywhere near the piano. Sanford Gold was the president of the pianists' club and was there every night. Lou Stein was there, Barbara Carroll, Marian McPartland, Bernie Leighton—in fact it seemed that every piano player in New York was at the Embers Club, and this went on every night.

The Embers was one job that it seemed to me that I should be paying the management for having such a good time every night. The room was ideal for jazz. It was a long room with very soft lights, a nicely lit bandstand and, at the rear, a huge fireplace with the glowing embers that gave the club its name. We played there many times but not always with the same attractions. When we went in the second time we were opposite Eddie Heywood and his trio, who were very popular because of Eddie's song *Canadian Sunset*. It was nice working with him too. At times, when Milt Hinton couldn't make the job, we would use Aaron Bell, a very great man on bass. Aaron and I became running buddies. Sometimes I'd keep Aaron away from home so much that his wife didn't want him hanging around with me, but Aaron would hang out anyway and then catch hell the next day.

The clientele of the Embers was something like seeing so many movie stars together at one time, and they were all jazz-conscious. Any night you could find such greats as Jackie Gleason, José Ferrer and Rosemary Clooney (who were together at the time), Art Carney, John Hammond, Peggy Lee, Bob Preston—everybody. Our little group would swing them all into bad health. One night Pops came in and broke it up by just doing nothing. We were all happy to see him and I was extremely happy because it was the first time that Pops had come to hear me since I met him out in California years ago. Gary Merrill, who then was the husband of Bette Davis, would come in to listen; Bob Rouark the famous traveler would come in and invite us all to his place, as did Jackie Gleason. Bob was a very good friend and he always called me "cousin Buck." Tallulah Bankhead was a very good friend of Bushkin's and would come in nearly every night. Signe Hasso was there often. It was one swinging place and I enjoyed it every night. Sylvia Syms would come in very often and, after my little daughter was born, would bring me little gifts; once she gave me a giant panda that was so big I could hardly get it home. She was a good friend of Billie's and we were very close. Barbara Carroll was a close friend and we used to call each other B. C., just as Bill Coleman and I did in France.

I don't think that during the whole time that I was in the Embers I ever got paid by Joe Bushkin in the normal way. Like, if Tuesday night was our pay night, Joe would go on home after the job or go somewhere else with his many friends and we didn't get paid. Joe was such a flighty little guy and had so many friends and was occupied with so many things on his mind that he never thought of paying us on time. I soon found out that the best thing for me to do was to get my loot in spurts. When I'd see Joe at the bar, I'd walk up to him and borrow two or three hundred dollars. He never remembered it so I would just put it down as money on my salary, but Joe was a nice cat and I liked him a lot. At four o'clock, after the Embers closed, many people would ask us where they could go to finish the night and we'd always take them up to Maggie's to dig the fried chicken and black-eyed peas. Sometimes we'd leave the Embers and go to the Paradise Club on 110th Street and Eighth Avenue and listen to Big Nick (Nicholas) who had a group there, and where all of the jazz cats of Harlem would come and jam. Nick was famous for his singing, which was mostly words like "ooka-lockka," which I never did understand, but he was a friend and popular. A good tenor sax man too.

After being in and around New York for the next couple of years I got a call one day from Mezz Mezzrow. Mezz had written a book, *Really the Blues*, which had been translated into French and which was called in France *Le rage de vivre*. It had become very popular in both countries and Mezz had been asked to form a group and make a tour of France. He was very popular in France and, with the book, he was almost sure to have good audiences. He called me and asked me if I was interested. He had offered to take Pat along with me as his guest. Now you can imagine how elated Pat was to know that she might soon be going to France. I told Mezz that I was interested and soon started planning on going back to France. Mezz also contacted Gene Sedric, Fats Waller's famous tenor man and clarinet, Red Richards, a great pianist and a former bandleader, drummer Kansas Fields, who used to play with the guys like Condon in the Village, "Big Chief" Russell Moore on trombone (a big Pima Indian who made the trombone look small in comparison to his size), and Taps Miller, a top entertainer in Harlem who was a composer, a dancer and a trumpet player. He also hired two Lindy Hoppers to go with the show to demonstrate how they danced in the Savoy Ballroom. Nick and Della were the two. So, along with Pat, we all started getting ready to make the trip to France. We caught the boat and were soon on our way. It was all new to everybody except me but I was glad to be going back to see France again. Pat went to the drug store and bought all of the different kinds of pills for seasickness but she didn't even get seasick one time. She was given a big going-away party by the Savannah Club and the girls.

After the usual crossing we arrived in France in February 1953 and were met by Mezzrow, Panassié and their two organizers for the tour, Yannick Bruynoghe from Brussells and his wife Margo. After some French dinners and seeing some sights of Paris we started rehearsing for the tour and in a few days we had everything all lined out and were ready to go. I used to watch Mezz before each performance. There would be a big club backstage in each theater that we played and Mezz would take this big club and make three loud thumps on the theater floor, which could be heard all over the theater. I never did know what that meant. They used to do it on my tour that I had done three years earlier but I still didn't know what it meant. Anyway the concert could start right after the three loud thumps. We had a good show and as we went along it got better. This is where my dixieland training came in handy because Mezz liked a lot of dixieland. Mezz was known as a Panassié man and at this time there was the serious rivalry of Panassié and Charles Delaunay. You had to belong to one faction or the other. When we got off the boat we were given little buttons to wear in our lapel which read either "Le Hot Club de France," which was Panassié's club, or "Le Hot Club de Paris," which was Delaunay's club. I wouldn't wear either one, though, because I thought it was too bad that these two guys that had done so much for jazz in France should be on opposite sides. But they were really serious about it.

Sometimes when we would be giving our concerts some of the Delaunay faction would yell at Mezzrow when he'd be making an introduction to the next number. They'd tell him to shut up ("Ta gueule"), and he'd yell back, "You shut up!" ("La tienne"). Delaunay's club was more modern than Panassié's and he had the modernists on his side, while Panassié went along with the old New Orleans crowd. I just thought it was a shame that they couldn't have continued to work together instead of splitting. They both seemed to be nice cats. I got along with both of them and was never considered a traitor by either one of them because I played both kinds of music. But, frankly, I hadn't learned too much modern jazz yet. I was to learn it later, right there in Paris, but as of that time I didn't know any. One time, at one of Lionel's concerts in Paris, Hugues was insulted by someone from the Delaunay crowd and Hugues actually hit somebody over the head with his cane that he carried. It was never Hugues nor Delaunay that started any trouble but always their club members. One time, when even Louis was playing a concert in Paris, somebody from the Delaunay club sneaked under the stage and cut all the wires to the microphones and Pops could only be heard about three or four rows back from the stage. They were really serious about the Panassié–Delaunay split.

However, we went on and had great concerts with Mezz. I had seen most of the countryside of France but on this trip I saw so many other things. I saw and visited Carcassonne, which is an old city of the Middle Ages. It's high on a mountain and is preserved, while at the bottom of the mountain is the modern city of Carcassonne with its modern buildings. The old city was amazing. I walked along the whole city with its fortifications, torture chambers, prisons and ramparts. It was very odd for me to realize that many years ago they used to fight on these same walls and pour hot burning oil down on whoever happened to be the invaders. Some of the wooden beams were so old that you could stick your finger right down into a huge wooden beam like it was paper. That beam had probably replaced another beam sometime earlier because I'm sure it wouldn't have withstood the time of the early Carcassonne city.

After the tour of France we were told that we were to go to Belgium so we all prepared to see the country that we had read so much about in our school days. It was also the country of Yannick and Margo so we didn't lack for information and history on the country. Our first gig in Belgium was in Knokke. Knokke is a city on the seashore that has a fabulous gambling casino and we were booked right into that casino. I enjoyed the casino very much and soon we had made friends with all of the Belgian cats that were into jazz. Sometimes, when we'd finish work at the casino, we'd go to all of the places on the beach and play in every joint that we could find that had jazz. Taps Miller and myself would ride bicycles up and down the seashore sometimes early in the morning and sometimes late at night. The casino was a swinging club and soon Mezz was the talk of Belgium. There were many rooms in the casino. I never did visit all of the rooms but we knew practically all of the musicians that played in the different rooms. Once we were playing at the same time that Frank Sinatra was playing in another room. We never saw Frank but we knew the musicians that worked with him and we were told of his concerts there in the casino. The only previous Americans to play the casino that I knew were Sidney Bechet, Bill Coleman, Lips Page and Zutty Singleton. However, we had a good engagement there and soon became popular with all of the jazz fans in Belgium. Knokke reminded me so much of Atlantic City.

We visited Bruges and found it to be one of the most picturesque places in Belgium. It was called the second Venice of Europe because of the water canals there that took the place of streets. I was quite interested in the history of Bruges and the fashion in which the old houses had been built. Then we went to Brussels and I saw for the first time the great city. It knocked me out too but it didn't have the delicious seafood that I used to love in Knokke. After Belgium we were on our way to Morocco.

Our trip to Casablanca was very interesting. I'd never been there before and it was really a different part of the world for me to see. The white buildings impressed me. They're very pretty. In Casablanca there were no factories to pollute the air and all of the white churches and cathedrals were white and remained white. The kids in Morocco were just like everywhere else. They loved jazz but still there were the Delaunay–Panassié crowds. I've always been a camera buff but I soon found out that it's not too wise to take pictures in Morocco. The people there were superstitious of cameras as they believe that cameras steal the spirit of whoever's picture is being taken and they get pretty salty about it. One day I was taking a picture of a little kid sitting in the street, when some big guy ran out to the street and grabbed the little kid in his arms and took him back in the house. He was yelling something at me but I didn't know what the hell he was saying. Anyway, from then on when I'd take a picture I'd be sure that nobody saw me taking it. I'd just shoot the picture without looking at where I'd shot it and sometimes I'd have the camera camouflaged so that people wouldn't realize I was taking their picture. I didn't want any of those curved Moroccan knives aimed at me so I had to be careful. The trip to Morocco was something else. We played Meknès, Fez, Rabat and some other places. The countryside of Morocco was totally different from anything I had seen yet. The little Moroccan merchants sell their goods on the roads, goods such as those big huge Moroccan oranges, different kinds of little meat dishes, chickens, even water from water bags made of pigskins. Nobody would eat the food but myself and Kansas Fields as they thought it might be dirty, which it might have been, but we ate it anyway and nothing ever did happen to us. We also ate couscous, which is a Moroccan corn meal. Pat was with us in the bus and she was digging all this but she wouldn't eat anything from the road.

We went to the Medina, which is a part of Casablanca that is set aside for prostitutes. It is a walled city within a city. To get into the Medina you have to pass through the gate at a police station there and after that you're on your own. I went in with Yannick, Margo and Pat one night and at one time I made a slight turn in one of the crooked alleys and was completely lost. In just two minutes I was so lost that I couldn't for the life of me find the rest of my group and they too were looking for me as it seemed that I had just been swallowed up. After some minutes of this Yannick had to hire a little boy who was familiar with the Medina to go into these alleys and find me. He found me and I sure was glad as hell to see him. In the Medina you can see little girls as young as twelve and thirteen years old who are already prostitutes. They were behind these walls right from their birth, being born of prostitutes, and had never seen the city of Casablanca other than the Medina. After I was found we went on and enjoyed the rest of the trip. They never have much trouble in the Medina, I was told. It's mostly for tourists and I guess the police keep it pretty safe for tourists. It's like the Casbah in Algiers.

After Morocco we went on to Italy. This was new to me too, as I had never been to Italy before. We played so many famous places and cities. We visited the Colosseum in Rome, which really impressed me with its history. It was so interesting, seeing where so many Christians were killed during the days when it was fashionable to kill Christians and the old animal cages and stockades. These were located many miles away by tunnels through which they could goad the animals all the way to the Colosseum underground to put on a show for the old Romans. We saw the prisons for the slaves that were used to fight each other or the animals. It was very impressive. The Colosseum was a beautiful thing when it was first built. It was made of the best marble and had many beautiful statues made by the best sculptors of Italy. The white sand in the arena was imported from Africa so that it would show up better the red blood of the Christians that died there.

I don't think that I have to tell you that Rome is so full of original art works, old ruins, elaborate fountains, cathedrals and churches, that it's almost impossible to see everything there. I tried, though. I visited everywhere that I could possibly go and I still have the desire to go back there some day just to finish the Italian tour of the arts that I started at that time. I went to the club that was owned by the famous Brick Top and was glad to see Brick again, as I hadn't seen her since my early days when I first went to France and she used to talk to me many times in Place Pigalle.

After Rome we went to Genoa, where Pat and I visited the home of Christopher Columbus. That too was very impressive, just to be at the actual site of Columbus's birthplace. It was a very small house that has been preserved and is off-limits to the general public. When Mussolini was in power he had this little small house fenced off from all of the other buildings, so now you see it at the bottom of several modern tall buildings. I found too that the Italian people held a deep affection for Mussolini before he joined up with Hitler, after which it all turned to hate. We went on to Milan, where the great arts of Italy can be found. I was surprised to see so many. I was more surprised when we went on to Florence and I saw even more than in Milan. I think that Florence is the art capital of the world. How those Italian geniuses made so many masterpieces in their lifetime amazed me. Those cats like Da Vinci, Michelangelo, and hundreds of other unsung artists must have painted in their sleep to be able to paint so many beautiful pieces. There was street after street of art works. I had never seen anything like that in my life.

We continued our tour of Italy going on to Bologna. It was great too. In Bologna I had my first taste of octopus and I've been trying ever since to find someone that knows how to cook it. In Bologna we were told that we were to go back to Rome to meet Frank Sinatra, as we were to play a series of concerts with him. Frank was with Ava Gardner at the time and had just left Belgium. We met Frank in Rome and planned our tour. We were to play the first hour of a two-hour concert and he was to sing the remaining hour, "Jazz and Melody." We needed about nine more musicians simply to play the music for Sinatra, which was for fourteen or fifteen musicians, so we hired the nine cats from Rome. They were such nice little guys and couldn't believe that they were playing with us, who they considered to be gods in the world of jazz. I liked them a lot and they were crazy about us. We rehearsed in Rome and got Frank's arrangements down pretty good as the Italian musicians were very good.

After rehearsing, and before we were to leave the next day for Naples, I got a chance to go to the Vatican, where I'd been wanting to go ever since we hit Rome but so far hadn't been able to find the time. The Vatican was something that I couldn't believe. The huge square, the Vatican itself, the statues on the Vatican, the history—it was too much for me. When I went inside it was even more impressive. There was gold everywhere. I never saw so much gold. And there were the wonderful paintings of Michelangelo on the ceiling. I couldn't believe any of it. The Swiss guards there. I'll never forget my impression of the Vatican. It was like being in a different world.

The next day we left for Naples with Frank and the new Italian musicians. They were all very nice and we liked them a lot. Frank and Ava came on down to Naples in a different train. The next day we all met and prepared our first concert in Naples. I know that Naples has some very beautiful scenery and is very important to the Italian people, but I didn't like Naples from the first day because there is so much of the criminal element there. If you put a suitcase down for just a couple of seconds in the railroad station it will be gone when you look for it later. You have to watch everything at all times. Then there are the vendors that sell merchandise while you're leaving on the train, such as watches, pens, jewelry and other things that won't work two hours after you have been on the train. I bought a watch that looked good and seemed to be running when I bought it, but after being on the train for about two hours I looked at it and it didn't work anymore. I opened it up and it had been made to run for about two hours by rubber bands inside. After that it was just junk.

We arrived in Naples and found that we were to play a matinee performance that afternoon. That was OK, so we went to the concert hall where we were to play. On arriving at the hall we found that one of the more ambitious promoters of the concert had advertised that Ava Gardner was to appear with Frank on the bill. We were all surprised to see this as Ava had nothing to do with our concert. She was just with Frank as any wife would be with her traveling husband. When Frank saw this advertisement he told Ava to go on back to the hotel and stay there just in case they tried to make her have something to do with the concert. She went back before we started the concert and we prepared to go on. We all went out with Mezz and were a hit. Italian people don't have the occasion to hear much jazz because it is frowned upon by the church; however, there are many, many people who live there who like jazz. After we finished our part of the concert on came Frank with all the rest of the Italian musicians.

The first three numbers by Frank went down well and we all thought that the tour with Frank was going to be a gas but then little things started happening that made us change our mind and soon. Frank wasn't as popular then as he was to become later in his life. He hadn't made the picture *From Here to Eternity* yet and, actually, Ava was more popular than Frank at this time. Then, too, Frank was having some kind of trouble with his voice and wasn't singing like he had previously nor like he is·singing today. After the third number by Frank someone in the audience yelled up at Frank, "Get off the stage! We want to see Ava." Frank tried to ignore the heckling but as he went on more and more people started booing him and he became very upset about it. Finally the entire audience was calling for Ava. Frank stopped in the middle of his songs and called the theater manager and had him go out on the stage and explain that Ava was not with the show and it had been a mistake to put her name on the bill. We thought everything would be OK and Frank started to sing again, but with his voice not being in perfect condition and with Ava not coming on the stage the boos started all over again. Frank gave up in disgust. The people had ignored the theater manager and raised so much hell that we decided to cancel the rest of that concert. We thought that the evening performance would be much better. So we closed the matinee performance with all of those Italian people raising hell. Some wanted to hear Frank, the others wanted to see Ava Gardner. So we went on back to the hotel and waited until it was time for the evening performance.

About eight that evening we went back to the scene and as we got near the theater we saw lines of pickets around the theater. They carried signs saying, "DON'T GO IN THERE. AVA GARDNER IS NOT GOING TO APPEAR." They were everywhere, these pickets, yelling outside the theater, "Don't go in, don't go in. Ava is not going to show. Don't go in."

We went on backstage to prepare for the concert anyway and we saw a lot of Italian guys backstage that we didn't know. They were all wearing fedora hats, like the famous borsalino hats made in Italy. We said hello to them like everybody else and went on and got on the stage and did our jazz scene and got great applause. After the intermission Frank came on. He had hardly started singing before someone started the same thing as that afternoon, "Get off, get off! We want to see Ava. Bring on Ava." Frank stopped singing and had another little gay fellow, that everybody knew, go out on the stage and announce that Ava was not supposed to show. They listened to the little gay but just as soon as he had finished with his little speech they all started up again. They raised hell. While he was making his little speech I got off the bandstand, as we couldn't play with all this going on. I was standing in the wings looking at the audience raise hell. I turned back to go backstage and I saw all of these Italian musicians and they were fighting with these guys with the felt hats on. That was something I'll never forget. The audience in the hall raising hell and the fighting going on backstage between the musicians and the guys with the hats. It was really bedlam everywhere. After fighting for about ten minutes we all found out that the fellows with the hats were the Italian police. Nobody knew really who they were and in just a matter of minutes they were arresting all of the Italian musicians. Needless to say, that broke up the concert. The musicians were hauled off to jail and we were left with only Frank, Mezz, Ava and ourselves. All the rest were in jail.

The next morning we were to leave Naples for another city but the cops wouldn't let the Italian musicians out of jail. So we were going to try to play Frank's music with our little six-piece band but it never was the same. Before we left Naples, however, Frank went down and paid for all of the musicians to be released but still they couldn't continue the tour and I found myself trying to play first trumpet with Frank's music. I'm really not a first trumpet man but I tried anyway. That reminded me of one time when Bobby Hackett and I both had a recording date and the first trumpet music was passed out. Bobby is not a first trumpet man either; we are both mainly soloists and leave the first trumpet work to the stronger, larger-tone men who make that their business. We both laughed when we both refused to play the first part but, since we didn't have anyone else on the date to play first trumpet, we split the two first parts and I must say they came out pretty well.

The next morning we left Naples and went on to the next town and played Frank's sixteen-piece arrangements with only six men. Somehow we finished the tour and we said goodbye to Frank and Ava and went back to Paris. Most of the band went in different directions. Kansas Fields and myself went and stayed in Paris while, I think, the rest of the guys came on back to America. I wasn't long in Paris before I was asked to appear at the Blue Note, a jazz club there that had been at one time under the direction of the manager of Sugar Ray Robinson. George Gainford, I believe, was his name. The Blue Note was situated near the Eiffel Tower and was very popular. I was happy to go in there and I signed to go in with Don Byas, Kansas Fields, Pierre Michelot, and Raymond and Hubert Fol, two talented brothers. Mary Lou Williams was playing in a club very near and she would come in some nights and jam with us. Hazel Scott was in Paris at the time and she too would come in and jam. Lil Armstrong was there and sometimes they all would meet and jam at the same time with us. I met so many musicians in Paris that it was like being in New York. Pretty soon all of the cats in Paris were coming down to the Blue Note every night. One night Hazel Scott brought Adam Clayton Powell down and we talked a lot about New York and jazz. The Blue Note was a wild scene every night. Hazel would cook chitterlings, pig feet and all the rest of the soul food and would invite all the musicians to her apartment to eat, and it was good to know that we were having home-cooked soul food in Paris.

I was in the Blue Note when Lionel Hampton came to Paris with his big band. When their concert was finished they all came down to the Blue Note and it was there that I met Art Farmer and Clifford Brown, who were playing with Hamp. They had just been kicked off the stage by the French police because Lionel didn't want to stop the concert at the time he was supposed to stop. Lionel still has those same ways, he never wants to stop as long as there is an audience. When the cops warned him to stop at a certain time he just kept on playing. When they warned him again he continued on, jumping up and down on the tom-toms. In France the concerts are scheduled to end at a certain time because people have to catch a bus back to their homes and the buses stop running at a certain time. So when Lionel ignored the third warning and continued to play the cops went up and hauled them all off the stage. Then they came on down to the Blue Note and enjoyed the rest of the night. I had a little friend from Belgium that I had met in Knokke, Monique Dumons, or Nickey as she was called, who used to bring down a contingent of people from Belgium, and the Blue Note would swing. Sometimes the regular guys would send in a stand-in musician and by the end of my time at the Blue Note I knew almost every jazzman in Paris.

After the Blue Note engagement finished I was asked by Babs Gonzales to go with him to Sweden, where he had arranged a tour. I accepted the offer and, together with Kansas Fields, planned on going to Stockholm. Babs is well known in show circles and was one of the forerunners of the scat singers. He was popular in New York and we planned to have a ball with him in Sweden, so we soon were on our way to Stockholm. He had hired some more musicians that we didn't know but they all knew us and soon we were all together on the train for Sweden.

The tour in Sweden went well for a time. We had arranged a nice concert and we played to nice houses. I had met Nils Helmstrong there and at times when we had a day off I would play gigs that Nils had promoted. He at the time was about the biggest jazz promoter in Sweden. One day, however, everything didn't go as smooth as it had been. For some reason that I never knew an argument had sprung up between Babs and Kansas. We were playing in one of the series of parks in Sweden called the Folks parks, which are very popular among the Swedish people in summer. Our dressing room was underneath the stage at the park. When I arrived at the park one afternoon Babs and Kansas were at it. Babs had told Kansas that he wanted a drum solo in the show and Kansas said he didn't want to play a solo. One word led to another and pretty soon Kansas told Babs to play the goddam solo hisself. Babs got huffy and Kansas was just as obstinate. I knew that Kansas had a knife but I was hoping that he wouldn't think of using it. Babs, in the meantime, had given a knife to a girlfriend which was to be given back to him if he needed it. I watched all this. I was concerned because it was my first trip to Sweden and I had never been so far north. Paris seemed to be a million miles away. I knew, too, that Babs had a unique way of getting to somebody that he has an argument with. He had his handkerchief folded in his suit coat pocket in such a manner that he could jerk it out whenever he wanted to but inside the handkerchief was red pepper. If Babs was close enough to whoever he was having the argument with, and if they made a move as if to strike him, he would jerk out this handkerchief with the red pepper right into the eyes of whoever was at odds with him. I watched Kansas and Babs as they got close to each other and, before Kansas could make a move and before Babs could get his handkerchief together, I moved in. I gave them both hell for being so far away from home and acting like two damn idiots. We hadn't even finished the tour yet. So they cooled off and we went on to finish the tour.

Pat had returned to New York after our Frank Sinatra tour and never saw the Blue Note nor Sweden but while in Paris we had met Signe Hasso, the famous Swedish actress. Signe was in Stockholm during the time of our tour there and liked the jazz quite a bit. After the Babs tour Kansas and I remained in Stockholm for a little while and met still other Swedish jazzmen. There are some great jazz cats there, believe me.

One night Signe introduced me to her good friend who was married to the son of the King of Sweden, Gustav VI. I learned later that the king had two sons but the other son I never met. The wife and friend of Signe's was named Christine, or Kirsten. (That depends on where you are and what country you're in; I never knew whether to call her Christine or Kirsten, anyway we became friends.) One night I was invited by Christine to go to a park and listen to some more Swedish musicians. Signe also came with the party and pretty soon we were all wrapped up in the music. After about a half hour Christine asked me, would I play with the guys. I told her that I wouldn't mind but I had left my trumpet at my hotel, which was about three miles from the park. I had locked it in my room. She wanted me to play *Kiss of Fire*, which was her favorite number. So after telling her that my trumpet was at the hotel I forgot all about it and thought that everybody else had too, until I looked up from my table and saw Christine's chauffeur come in with my trumpet. I was surprised, naturally. Christine had sent her man back to the hotel and, when the management of the hotel found out that it was Christine who had sent for the trumpet, they opened up the front door for the chauffeur and he went in and got the trumpet and brought it to me. I believe that the management would have given him anything that he wanted once they learned that the wife of the son of the king wanted something in my room. Anyway, after bringing the trumpet I went on and played with the Swedish guys until about four o'clock in the morning.

After we had jammed for some time Christine asked me if I would like to go to the palace, where there were other friends of hers. I told her, yes, hardly before she could get the question out of her mouth. I had never in my life imagined that I'd be inside the palace of the King of Sweden. Soon we were on our way to the palace. I found out that Christine was a pretty swinging chick—a real swinging jazz lady of royalty. As we entered the palace we went into a large room that reminded me so much of Maggie's after-hour joint in New York, where I used to hang out every night after work and eat fried chicken and black-eyed peas. The room was large with a lot of hassocks on the floor. There were several people in the room, which was dark with soft lights, and in one corner was a pianist, a little gay cat. Everything was quiet as the little guy played and everybody was drinking champagne. I stayed in this room talking to people that I had been introduced to when Christine asked me if I'd like to go to another room and meet her husband. I told her I would consider it an honor and we went into another room, the prince's bedroom. He was asleep and she woke him up. She told him that I was a friend of Signe Hasso's and soon we were talking about jazz. I found out, too, that he was very much interested in jazz and I believe he played an instrument. He asked me about jazz in New York, about Birdland, about different jazz musicians and we had quite a conversation going on when Christine returned to take me back in the room with all of the guests. I was very impressed with the prince, although I never saw him again after that night. I stayed in this large plush room until amost five o'clock when I had to prepare to leave as I had a reservation to leave on a plane for Paris at eight o'clock. Christine called her chauffeur again and he came up in his big Rolls Royce. Before getting in the car I was loaded down with bottles of champagne. I never saw so much champagne in my life. We put them all in the car and shot off for the hotel, as I still had my bags to pack before I left for the airport. We got to the hotel and the chauffeur went on back to the palace and, after packing, I caught another cab for the airport. As I walked in the airport, about twenty minutes before my plane was to leave, all of the loudspeakers in the airport came on, which really surprised me as they all said, "Bon voyage, Buck Clayton. Bon voyage." Christine had sent that message to be broadcasted by the loudspeakers, which I thought was a damn nice send-off from the beautiful city of Stockholm.

I returned to Paris to say goodbye to all my new-found jazz guys and stayed about five days. I hung out with Maurice Cullaz, who was infatuated with Pat's eyes and didn't want to talk about anything else. At the end of five days I caught a plane for New York. When I arrived in New York I was very surprised in a pleasant way to find that Pat was pregnant. She had moved to an apartment on Hamilton Terrace, a beautiful apartment, brand new, that had been built by Dr Delph, a prominent doctor in Harlem who just wanted to be in real estate too. So after seeing Pat I understood why, before leaving Paris, she had had so many fainting spells. She had fainted one day in a department store and was fortunate in having Nitoune with her to help bring her back to our hotel, La Boetie. I arrived in New York with my French beret on just about two days before Thanksgiving. Every Thanksgiving we usually spent with Pat's family because she had two champion cooks in her family, her mother Gertrude DeVigne and her grandmother

Martha Spruill. So we went to Jamaica, Queens, on Thanksgiving day and enjoyed ourselves and that night we stayed there. About four o'clock that morning Pat started having labor pains. I didn't know anything about labor pains then but I soon learned. I had to count the minutes between pains and by nine o'clock we knew that Pat would have to go to the hospital. We called a taxi to take us all the way back to Manhattan and it took so long for the cab to get there that we were wondering if we'd make it or not. We didn't want her to have the baby in a taxi, which has happened many times, so all we could do was to wait for the cab to show up.

Finally the taxi did come and we got Pat in and off we rushed to New York. We arrived at the hospital finally and the nurse took one look at Pat and then had her put on a stretcher and the last I saw of her was being wheeled down a hall. They rushed her into a room and put her under a shower but by this time a little leg was protruding. My little baby was a breech baby. Fortunately, everything went well and Pat had no trouble with the delivery. The baby looked just like me at birth—exactly like someone had made a replica of me and had put it in a baby's crib. I couldn't wait for the attendants to put her in the nursery so I could take a picture of my little girl. When they did I took my camera and took her very first photograph and she looked just like a little Buck lying there in the nursery. I was sorry that my father hadn't lived long enough to see her as he always wondered if or not I'd have children. My mother was ecstatic. I named the little girl Candice, which was later shortened to Candy. I liked the name Candice because it had a French accent to it and I liked the French people. She still resembles me quite a bit but she's thirty-two now and also has many features of Pat's. She is the little girl that you see the picture of, along with me, on a horse on a carousel for an album that I made for Vanguard called *Bucking the Blues*.

NINE

From New York to Australia

One day towards the end of 1953, while in New York, I got a call from John Hammond. He wanted to know if I could make a recording session that he had planned with George Avakian for Columbia. John, I thought, was the most important man in my whole career. He did everything he could for me when I was with Basie, he introduced me to Billie Holiday and Teddy Wilson, he put me on the Carnegie Hall concert "From Spirituals to Swing," and he would encourage me at all times. He had done so many things for me that I just knew the session that he wanted me to do would be a gas, so I accepted.

As I entered the studio I found a lot of guys there that I didn't know. I knew about half of them personally, but the others I had to be introduced to. The great man on trombone Urbie Green was there, and I didn't know him at all. He had just come up from Mississippi, I believe. What John wanted was to record a real jam session in a studio. This is rather hard to do, as most musicians just don't have the same feeling in a recording studio as they have in a nightclub late at night around a bar where everything is swinging. After we learned what he wanted we got into the best mood we could and soon had a genuine session going. Before you knew it we were all playing like we had known each other for years. I enjoyed working with Joe Newman on some of the early sessions, but later I also played with Ruby Braff, Joe Thomas and Billy Butterfield on trumpets and many other greats on different instruments. Sir Charles Thompson was with us and played so beautifully. Everybody did. A few days later I was told that I had been named leader of that group and the albums are known as the *Buck Clayton Jam Sessions*. I think I must credit John Hammond for this too as he still was putting me in the right places.

Jack Bregman, of Bregman, Vocco & Conn, publishers, was another friend that helped me in many ways. He was a publisher of nearly all of my compositions and many times would advance money to me when times were pretty rough, so that I wouldn't have to go to the pawnbrokers. He also made it his business to see that I had my own numbers or compositions made for stock arrangements, so as to be played by students who were interested in playing jazz. What's more, he had me make the stocks myself, and when at first I didn't have any idea how to do it, he made it possible for me to study with other arrangers who taught me many things about making stock arrangements that I didn't know. He was one beautiful fellow and everybody loved Jack, especially us fellows from the old Count Basie band. He did so many good things for Jimmy Rushing, Count and myself.

About this time I made a tour with Frankie Laine which I enjoyed very much. Jack Lesberg was my roomie on that tour and we had some very exciting days. Then I made a tour with Jackie Gleason as a member of the Joe Bushkin Quartet. It was a good show that featured the Honeymooners. Jackie was one hell of a cat to work with and was a real gas the whole time of the tour. We had the De Marco Sisters with us and together with the De Marcos, Art Carney, Jackie and the rest of the cast, we had a good show and played through Chicago and other principal eastern cities. The finale of the show was Jackie Gleason, Joe Bushkin and myself all out in front of the show playing trumpets. Jackie could play a little trumpet and Joe Bushkin was a pretty nice trumpet player too, so we ended it all with the three of us out there screaming on trumpets.

After Jackie's tour I went back to New York and was approached by Ralph Watkins and asked to go into the Royal Roost on Broadway. I opened the Roost with Cozy Cole and Sylvia Syms. After that I went into another of Ralph's places, Basin Street West, which turned out to be a swinging joint. Buster Bailey, Jimmy Crawford and Don Abney were with me on that one. Sometimes we'd play opposite of Benny Goodman and his small group, which included Charlie Shavers at that time.

One morning after I had finished at the Basin Street West I went uptown. I went by the Braddock Hotel just as the place was closing about 4 a.m. to have a last drink for the night with some friends, Marion and Otis. When the bar had closed I was standing in front trying to decide where to go eat at this time of the morning before I went home. As I was standing there I noticed a guy coming up to me that looked like a bum. As I was watching him I suddenly felt my arms being pinned to my side by someone behind me that I couldn't see. The guy that I could see jerked my trumpet out of my hand. I got really mad at this and I noticed the guy's features. He had long hair that was sticking out the back of his old beat-up hat like he hadn't had a haircut in years, and he had a long scar on his face. Then while they were stripping me of my wristwatch I said to the guy, "You know, I'm going to see you on the street one of these days and I sure as hell am going to remember you." The guy looked at me and all he said was, "Oh yeah," and went on about the business of taking my trumpet and watch and wallet. Then, after they got everything they wanted, I got a chance to see the second guy as they joined up and crossed the street on their way to the subway, which was a block away.

I went on back home, which was all I could do at the time as I didn't have any money and couldn't eat. After being there for about fifteen minutes I got a call on my phone. It was from a friend of mine that owned a bar. He said to me, "Buck, did you lose anything this morning?" I told him, yes, I'd lost my trumpet, my watch and my wallet. He then said, "Well, I've got your trumpet. I don't have the other things, but I've got your trumpet. There were two guys in here that asked me to give them some money so they could buy some cocaine and they'd give me the trumpet." He had given them the loot and then, while looking at the trumpet, he had noticed my mouthpiece, which had my name engraved on it. He knew where I lived and called me right away to see if anything had happened to me. I told him that I was alright and he then told me that he had given these guys thirty dollars for the trumpet, and if I wanted it back just give him the thirty bucks that he had put out and just come on and get it. I went and got it that same morning and it was just like getting a million dollars back that I had never expected to see again.

Benny Goodman had his office call me one day to ask me if I'd be interested in making a movie about his life, *The Benny Goodman Story*. I told them I'd be interested and in a few days I received the contract to play in the picture. I was delighted. I was supposed to be one of the trumpet players in Benny's band, along with his old buddies Harry James and Ziggy Elman. I thought this would be interesting so I got myself all ready to go to Hollywood. Myself, Urbie Green and Stan Getz were hired to make the sound track only. When we got to Hollywood it was a gas to see a lot of the guys that I hadn't seen for quite some time, like Harry, Teddy Wilson, Ziggy, and everybody in general. Steve Allen was going to play the part of Benny and, in order to familiarize himself with the clarinet, he hired Sol Yaged to teach him the fingering. So Sol and I were pretty close and we had a ball making that picture. It really was a swinging band that made the track. We had the famous Conrad Gozzo on first trumpet and Conrad was one guy that really sang on his trumpet. One of the best in the world. We had a hell of a lot more fun making the sound track than we did making the actual picture. We made so much good music, but it was to be cut out of the picture in order to show the love-life of Benny. I really was surprised that they would cut out so much of that really good and swinging music, but they did.

I never could understand why I was asked to make the picture in the first place. I thought that since Cootie Williams had played with Benny for quite some time, why didn't they ask Cootie instead? I'm sure Cootie would have been available. One day I asked the director, Val Davies, why I was selected to play in the picture, especially since I had always been in competition with Benny's band by simply being a member of the Count Basie band. He said, "Ah, what the hell. It doesn't make any difference." Not only that, but after we had made the sound track I was asked, and only me, to make the actual picture along with the other actors. The director seemed to take a liking to me and was giving me all the breaks. When there was to be a group picture he would always put me right in front so I'd be on camera, and always with the prettiest girls, like in the scene where Benny's mother was giving him a party in their apartment in New York. I actually wasn't supposed to say anything, but I was given one line to learn. All the really original cats, like Gene, Teddy and Lionel, had lines to learn and were really a part of the picture. Nobody else was to have lines, but some way they figured out some way to give me one line—no, two lines: "Well, how're you going to do it, Benny?" was one: "It looks pretty good to me," was the other. I practiced my lines and got these two famous sentences together, but somehow when I heard them they didn't sound just right to me. I guess it was alright, though, as they didn't have to make any re-takes on my part. They were having trouble with Kid Ory on another set because he couldn't remember his lines. It was there, too, that I saw my old inspiration on trumpet, Red Mack, who was making the picture as part of Kid Ory's old-time New Orleans band. I hadn't even known that Red Mack could play dixieland music, but there he was and sounding pretty good too. We had a great time, usually, making the picture and at the end of the day we would make it to the bar and paint the rest of the evening and jump in the hotel swimming pool. Benny had a continuous fight going on nearly all the time with different musicians on the set. Although he made only the sound track, he still was having fights with different guys. He didn't bother me, though. Steve Allen was nice and I thought he did a damn good job as Benny. Sol had him fingering the clarinet like he really knew what he was doing. When we went to the first showing of the picture we were all invited to a restaurant to have dinner and we all went and celebrated. It was there that I saw Jayne Mansfield order a full sirloin steak for her little dog that she had on a leash.

Some time after the film I was asked by Benny to go to South America as he was going to make a tour there. Away we went. We went to all of the countries, Argentina, Brazil, Chile—all of them. It was a great experience. My hangout buddy on that trip was Tommy Newsom, who then joined the "Johnny Carson Show." Harry Sheppard was on that tour also. We enjoyed South America but on some occasions we were having problems. We were bothered with diarrhoea. I remember eating at a restaurant in Buenos Aires and on the menu was black beans. I ate some, and that did it. I found that most of the South American countries don't have the health standards that we have in the United States. They don't have the strict laws governing the condition of eggs, milk, meat and other things that we take for granted at home. So we ate this stuff and pretty soon we were all making it to the john. Nearly all the trumpet players had diarrhoea and sometimes we didn't know whether it was wise to blow too hard, but still, what could we do? When we went to the toilet we didn't know what end to keep on the seat. We would be erupting at both ends. Not a pleasant feeling. Only Benny had medicine for diarrhoea. We all knew that but, in street words, "he wouldn't give us none."

We met many of the South American musicians and at times we would be invited to nightclubs where they played. My favorite city or, rather, one of my favorite cities was São Paulo, Brazil. It reminded me of Chicago—a Chicago with very gay colors. I sure dug the different vivid colors of South America. The South American guys were good musicians but naturally they were better on the Latin side. Mousey Alexander and myself bought several South American instruments, but only as souvenirs as we had no idea how to play them. The bossa nova was just becoming a fad there and we spent much time getting that rhythm together. I think Mousey Alexander practiced it all the way back to the United States on the plane. One thing that interested me in South America was the dentists who make house calls. I had been introduced to a little South American girl who was very pretty but had a toothache. Instead of going to the dentist she called him on the telephone and he came by and pulled her tooth. One of her front teeth. She had been such a pretty girl before he came but when he left she looked like a jack-o'-lantern.

The tour was a success and Benny received such adoration that we were a little surprised that the South Americans dug jazz that much. Joya Sherrill was our vocalist, which pleased everybody. I hadn't seen Joya since our tour with Teddy Wilson some time before. We had Arvell (the beast) Shaw with us on bass, which in itself is an experience. He and I had been together so many times before and I thought he was a great bass man. He must have been to have remained with Pops so long.

After the trip I came back home and, to my amazement, found that Pat was pregnant again. I began right away to plan for the coming of a new little baby that was due. I could hardly believe it was all happening to me. I didn't think I'd ever be that lucky but still it had been four years since Candy was born. When Pat was due we took her to the hospital and I returned home to wait for a call from the hospital. I had been kinda hoping for a little boy so that I'd have a little fella around to carry on the Clayton name. And then I'd have one of each, a little girl and a little boy. Instead of waiting for the hospital to call me I must have called about ten times for information on Pat, but I was always too early and was told to call back later. After a while of this the hospital did call me and told me that I was the father of a beautiful little boy.

I was about the happiest guy in the world on hearing this good news. I could hardly believe it because Pat and I had gone the first seven years of our marriage without having a baby. Now, four years after the birth of our daughter Candice, we had a little boy and that made what we call a million-dollar family, husband, wife, daughter and son. We named the baby Steven Oliver so as to have the same initials as my father. Steven came into this world looking like a little blond kid. I guess that was because Pat's father was, I'd say, 99 percent white. He was from a French family, the DeVignes. When I first met Pat's father I thought he was Italian. I really don't know why I thought that, but I think it was because at the time there were many more Italians in New York than French. I was sure that he wasn't black, but he was black. Still, he was 99 percent white, if you know what I mean. This can be rather confusing at times.

After going to the hospital and looking at Steven I saw that he was just as blond as any blond baby that I'd ever seen. He was just shining all over like a piece of gold. I asked Pat, "Pat, are you sure that there hasn't been a mistake somewhere? Are you sure that this is our baby?" Pat answered immediately, "You're damn right I'm sure, because I watched everything and this is our baby alright." Even some of the doctors were looking at Steven in amazement because, as I said, he looked just like a piece of gold lying there in his crib. Anyway, I thanked God for having a little boy. Needless to say my mother was extremely happy and now she could rest knowing that I had a little boy and a little girl. He turned out to be a good little fella. He turned to the guitar for his musical career.

After Steven's arrival I spent a few more months working around New

The 37th Army Service Band, New York, 1944: Buck is seated at the extreme right, in front of Sy Oliver.

Buck playing at a concert in Carnegie Hall

Buck with J. J. Johnson and Coleman Hawkins at the Newport Jazz Festival

Above left: Buck with his daughter Candice on the album cover for *Buckin' the Blues* (Vanguard Records); Above right: Patricia Devigne Clayton; Below: Buck with his children Candice and Steven

Left: During record-
ings for the soundtrack
of *The Benny Good-
man Story*; Harry
James is seated behind
Buck; Below: Buck
with Ben Webster

Humphrey
LYTTELTON
Club

WEDNESDAY at the MARQUEE

presents from America the fabulous trumpet of

BUCK CLAYTON

OCTOBER 14, 21, 28.

DOORS OPEN 8.0 p.m. till 11.30 p.m.   Members 6/- Guests 7/6

MARQUEE 90 WARDOUR STREET, LONDON, W.I.

Left: Poster advertising Buck's appearance with the Humphrey Lyttelton band; Below: Buck with Jimmy Rushing

Buck with Hugues Panassié

(left to right): Humphrey Lyttelton, Bud Freeman, Sinclair Traill, unknown, unknown, Buck, Hon Gerald Lascelles

Buck with Jabbo Smith, 1981

During the tour of Africa, 1977

Professor Clayton at a workshop in Hunter College

York. For one thing, I was involved in "Art Ford's Jazz Party," which was a weekly jazz program televised from Newark, New Jersey. It was through this show that I met Nancy Miller, who has collaborated with me on this book. She is now Nancy Miller Elliott and has three young sons who are jazz inclined: Vincent, guitar, Emile, bass, and Tom, drums. Nancy had been doing all of the secretarial work for the show and it was her job to hire all of the musicians that were to be presented. By doing so she met many of the top jazzmen, such as Coleman Hawkins, Red Allen, Billie Holiday, Pee Wee Russell, Charlie Shavers, Lester Young, myself and many others. She'd have to see that they all caught the bus to go to Newark for the show and she was pretty good at it. Nancy was a very beautiful girl, a real beauty. One of those dark complected, mysterious type ladies with long black hair. She was what Leonardo Da Vinci had in mind when he painted the Mona Lisa. Years later, when I ran into her one day on the street, she told me that she had just written an article, "Conversations with Great Jazz Artists," for her studies at Hunter College. After reading the article I found it to be a really good account of jazz people and I was included. It was so good that I asked her if she would help me with my book and she consented.

Then George Wein asked me to go to Brussels to the 1958 World's Fair and play with him, Vic Dickenson, Arvell Shaw, Sidney Bechet and Kansas Fields. I agreed to go with George and that turned out to be the most interesting gig that I'd had for some time. Working at the World's Fair was something else. It reminded me in a way of the fair in San Francisco where I played with Basie years ago. It was just beautiful to see all of these people from so many different lands. Vic Dickenson and I would hang out mostly in the Russian pavilion and the reason for that was that at the Russian pavilion all the vodka you could drink was free. Sarah Vaughan was there too, but not too many more Americans. We went over pretty good as we had a good concert arranged. We recorded one afternoon with Sidney Bechet or, rather, under Sidney Bechet's name and the album proved to be a good one. It was a pleasure to work with Sidney and he and I got along just great. He never reminded me about the time in France when he raised so much hell because I had played a dixieland number in our concert when he was to follow me. Unfortunately, the recording we made with Bechet was to be almost his last recording. I think it is a remarkable album. Everybody played well.

One day, as Vic and I were sitting out on the sidewalk having a little taste at those sidewalk tables that they have so many of in France and Belgium, a telephone call came for me from London. I answered the phone and was told that it was Jack Higgins from the Harold Davison agency there and he wanted to know if I'd like to come to England and bring the same band that I had recorded the *Songs for Swingers* album with in New York some months before. I told him yes, I'd be very happy to come. I had made this album for Columbia under the supervision of Irving Townsend with such guys as Dicky Wells and Buddy Tate. For the tour we also had Emmett Berry, Earle Warren, Herbie Lovelle, Al Williams, Gene Ramey and Jimmy Rushing. This was in 1958 and Jack wanted us to be prepared to make the tour of England in 1959 along with two other groups, Dizzy Gillespie and Dave Brubeck.

Jimmy Rushing was to do the vocals with my group. I told him that I was pretty sure that I could get the guys together. Jack said he'd contact me when I got back to the USA. When I did get back and asked the guys, they all agreed to come as it was the first time that they had been to Europe. So that was no problem. I wired Jack that we would be there the following year. Having a year to continue what we had been doing—mainly gigs and recording dates—we planned and waited for the day to leave for England. I found new people to work with, some I could put up with, others I couldn't. I met a fellow one day by the name of Frank Carey. Frank was a big handsome guy, Italian, that had been on the vice squad of New York. He was a cheerful guy and I liked him as soon as I met him.

Don't get the impression that I like everybody, because I don't. I know some musicians that turn me off completely. Guys that think they're big shots when they're only a big shot in their own conception—would-be big shots. Once in the Basie band we had a trumpet player that I couldn't stand after I heard him bragging one day about how he saved the Basie band by coming in and upsetting the whole world by playing his high notes on *King Porter Stomp*. All that Basie had done before he came in didn't mean a thing. The Basie band was at a standstill until he came in, according to him, and all the nice things that Prez had done, all the things that Sweets had done, the things that I had done—nothing was happening until he came in the band. He was so damn egotistical and arrogant that I wouldn't say hello to that cat for weeks. At times when we'd play a theater, after the last number of the concert he'd rush off the stand, run into the dressing room, put on his makeup and rush out in front of the theater so the people could see him as they passed through the lobby. I guess he thought he was the whole show but, like we all used to say, one monkey don't make a circus.

When I first met Frank I just thought that I had met an ex-cop and didn't know until later that he had been let out of the vice squad for some reason that I guess I'll never know. I just thought he was another one of the guys. One day, however, after not being with the squad, he had decided that he was going to be a bandleader. This just goes to show you how some people think that being a musician is easy work, that you don't have to do anything but look nice, enjoy yourself in playing your horn, be around a lot of groovy chicks and all that business. So Frank hit on the idea of being a bandleader. He didn't know one note from another. He had no idea of music, period. Still, he thought that with his good looks he was going to be able to be a bandleader. Why not? So one day in Brooklyn he went down and bought a bass fiddle, a tuxedo, went down and had some cards made saying "Frank Carey and his Orchestra." Next he came to me and asked me if I'd work with him. I told him, "Why not?" Since I was gigging with everybody else, why not him? Then he went to other guys like Coleman Hawkins, Buster Bailey, Harry Sheppard, Sol Yaged, Marty Napoleon and others. He surrounded himself with all of the best-known musicians in New York and went out looking for gigs. After listening to his spiel he did get quite a few people, bar owners, in Brooklyn to book him and his band. Most of his gigs were on Sunday afternoons. I showed up in Brooklyn for his first gig along with Hawk,

Harry Sheppard, Sol Yaged and others, not knowing just what to expect. But in a few moments I found out. Frank showed up in his brand-new tuxedo with his brand-new bass. He went out in front of the band amid all the yelling of his buddies that lived in Brooklyn and started his speech with jokes to the audience. Then he turned to the musicians and called a number that we were to play. Marty Napoleon was at the piano and made the introduction, after which we went into the number and I got my first taste of working with Frank as a bandleader. Being out in front of the group and with the lights on him he looked like a movie star, but the sound that he produced was awful.

He hit the bass fiddle like it was a drum. To look at him you would think that he really was doing something, but to us he was playing another drum in the band—just a loud boom, boom, boom all through the numbers that we were playing. The note didn't mean a damn thing to Frank; it was just boom, boom, boom. So, naturally, we soon learned to ignore Frank's musicial talent and we did our best to remember what song we were playing. When the gig ended about five in the evening Frank did his finale, which was to get in front of the mike, look pretty and then tear to shreds his pretty tuxedo shirt, which left him showing his undershirt. That was the end of the gig. Just to show you how dumb most people are about jazz, he was regarded by a lot of people in Brooklyn as a great musician and a big-time bandleader. He got a lot more gigs in Brooklyn and we would always help him out. So we played many Sunday gigs with Frank until finally we had other things to do and I had to leave him, as did all the rest of the guys, but just the way some people think of jazz amazed me. I think it's the same way with a lot of music critics. They are or, rather, some of them are no more than frustrated musicians, and the easiest thing that they can do is to sit on their asses and criticize other really good musicians. It's the easiest thing in the world. Anybody can be a critic if he so desires. I don't mean this for all of the critics, because some critics are beneficial to musicians as you can see your weak spots and try to improve yourself. But I've seen critics that just read some books and then go out and criticize someone that they don't like and this to me is just a terrible thing that musicians have to put up with.

I went into the Roundtable Club with Jackie Cooper, which was the first time that I'd ever worked with one of the movie star drummers. There were other drummers that were also movie actors. Jackie was nice, I thought, and I enjoyed my gig there. After the Roundtable it was nearing the time to leave for England so I started rehearsals for the tour about four months before we were to leave. I wanted everyone to know their music by memory so that we wouldn't have to drag out those music stands while on stage. We rehearsed the whole concert so that we knew every note. Most of the band numbers were from the Columbia album *Songs for Swingers*. The only numbers that were not on the album were the special solos and the music for Jimmy Rushing. We got it down to the point where we could just walk out on the stage, no music stands nor music, and blow hell out of each number. Finally, in September 1959, we all caught a plane and went to London.

As we arrived in the big city we found it to be beautiful but still a bit quaint—a lot like the English movies that we see on late-night television. It sure seemed to be a healthy place and most of the girls, or "birds" as they are called in England, had that peaches-and-cream complexion, but what was really strange to us was the way these birds walked down the street with their skirts up almost to their hips. Mini-skirts they were called. Every time we saw a mini-skirt the whole band would give a double take and it's a wonder we didn't all have stiff necks.

When we arrived in London proper we were introduced to Doughy Tolbert who was to be our road manager for the tour. Doughy was a very pleasant cat that knew the business of handling musicians like he was born doing just that. He knew all of the musicians and singers that had been sent to England and before long he was considered just one of the guys and he never gave us any trouble. We all liked him. Then, after we had made our preparations to stay in England, we met the jazz enthusiasts, such as Max and Betty Jones who were covering for *Melody Maker*, Jeff Atterton, Jeff Aldam and a guy who was to become one of my greatest friends, Humphrey Lyttelton. Our tour was combined with the Dizzy Gillespie small group and the Dave Brubeck Quartet and soon we were making the tour and saw so much of England. We had a beautiful tour and we all loved England and I think that they loved us too, because after the tour was finished we were scheduled to return in 1961. Al Williams was replaced by Sir Charles Thompson, Herbie Lovelle by Oliver Jackson on drums, and Jimmy Rushing by Jimmy Withers-poon doing the vocals. This second tour was great also and we made many friends in such countries as Denmark, Sweden, Spain and Switzerland. The tour was going just great until one day I found out that years ago, in California, there had been a bad feeling between Sir Charles Thompson and Jimmy Witherspoon. I don't know what it was all about but it all came to a head while we were playing in Geneva, Switzerland. We had played a concert in Geneva one night and we were all invited to a jazz club there after the concert as guests, and if we wanted to we could have a jam session. We accepted the invitation and after the concert we split for the jazz club. Sir Charles, Gene Ramey, Witherspoon, Emmett Berry, myself, we all showed up and soon were enjoying ourselves being among the jazz fans. After some time we decided to all go up on the bandstand and jam. The crowd was in a good mood that evening and we jammed for about a half hour before Jimmy Witherspoon, who was sitting in the audience listening to the band, was called upon to sing a number with the group. He came up and sang one of his concert numbers and it went down so well with the audience that the crowd was yelling and screaming for more. Sir Charles, sitting at the piano, resented Spoon's getting so much applause from the crowd. While they were still applauding for Spoon and Spoon was trying to decide what to sing next, Sir Charles, all of a sudden, went into the introduction to *C-Jam Blues*, which is not a singing number, and the band followed. We were back into an instrumental number, while Witherspoon couldn't believe that he had been sidetracked by Sir Charles. He had been deliberately cut off, so now he was mad as hell at Sir Charles.

As we played *C-Jam Blues* I could see Spoon with his head down talking to Sir Charles and calling him everything under the sun and, at the same time, Sir Charles, while playing the piano, was calling him everything that he could think of. I wish I could have had a tape of what they were calling each other. Finally the number ended and we got ready to play another song but Sir Charles was mad and didn't want to play anymore so he got up to leave the piano. As he got ready to step down onto the dance floor, Spoon was there looking at Sir Charles like he was gonna kill him. Charles couldn't get past Spoon so he says to Spoon, "Get out of the way, motherfucker."

Spoon glared at him and said, "Go around, you motherfucker." There and then the whole thing blew up. The language got so bad that the little guy that owned the club ran up to me and said, "Mr Clayton, if you don't stop this the police are going to come." Just as he was telling me this Emmett Berry hit Spoon over the head with his trumpet. I turned and looked and saw Spoon lying flat on the floor holding his head. He was yelling, "He hit me, he hit me. That motherfucker hit me." Emmett's trumpet looked more like an accordion and he was screaming at Spoon, "Let that be a lesson to you. You goddam singers don't fuck with us musicians." Spoon got up off the floor and took his coat off, Emmett started taking his coat off, people started running out of the club and I was really afraid that the cops would come. I grabbed Spoon in one hand and Berry in the other and tried to keep them apart, which was a pretty hard thing to do because they're both pretty good-sized cats, but anyway I held them off and made them go back into the dressing room. As soon as they got into the room, off came the coats again and they squared off. I made them listen to me and I told them that they had really messed up everything good that we had done. I gave them hell and told them that the best thing that we could do now would be to shake hands and go on back into that room and play jazz and perhaps the audience would take it like we were brothers and had had a brotherly fight. So they agreed and we all went back out there and the audience applauded when we went on to finish that jam session about five o'clock that morning. That was one jam session that I'll never forget and I don't think the fans of Geneva will either.

Vic Dickenson and I began to work several places in New York about this time. We would work mostly as a team and played in several clubs around the city. We played the Composer Club on 59th Street, when we would go over to Central Park on our intermission and "cool" between sets. Sometimes we'd go out to Vic's home state, Ohio, and play clubs there. We'd go to Boston and play at the Storyville Club, which was owned by George Wein. In fact we almost became permanent fixtures in George's club and made a few recordings under George's sponsorship. We would work with such guys as Jo Jones, Bud Freeman, Pee Wee Russell and others. After a few stints like this with Vic I took a small group into Café Society for Barney Josephson. We worked in there a short time where I used some of my main jazz people like Kenny Kersey, Scoville Brown, and Gus Johnson. On the bill with us was Imogene Coca, who used to interest us with what she couldn't do with a trombone. She was very nice, though, and we enjoyed being there with her. She could make some odd sounds on that trombone.

One day—this was late in 1959—Eddie Condon called me and asked me if I would go into his club as a replacement for Rex Stewart. Rex had been in the club for over a year and was leaving to go into writing items for different magazines on jazz and, too, he was planning on leaving the country. I told Eddie that I thought I could handle the job because, as I said, I had learned nearly all of the dixieland songs. I thought to myself, "If Rex Stewart can hold the job down I sure ought to be able to," because I knew that Rex certainly wasn't a dixieland musician but had learned the songs. So into Eddie Condon's I went. Eddie, by being such a beautiful person and a good friend, made me like the club very much. The first two months, though, that I was there, Eddie kept calling me Rex. He could never remember that Rex had gone and that my name was Buck, so for the longest time I had to get used to being called Rex. But I did like Eddie very much. He had more wit in his little finger than most writers have in their whole body and brain.

I went with Eddie and made many more friends, such as Cutty Cutshall, who I thought was one of the nicest people that I had ever met. I did some commercials in jazz with him. I met Pete Pesci, who was the manager at Eddie's club, and Yank Lawson, one of the stalwarts in the business, who was later to become very close to me as we made several of the Jackie Gleason recordings together. I met and worked with Peanuts Hucko under Condon; Leonard Gaskin was on bass, Gene Shroeder on piano, and Mousey Alexander on drums. Some of our nights at Condon's were pretty wild and the parties that we would go to after work were even wilder. Many times we'd get home some way crawling on our hands and knees. Working at the club was very educational for me as I continued to learn the numbers that I didn't know and I was very thankful to have the great Herbie Hall teaching me the ones that I still didn't know. Eddie didn't play with us too much as his main job was to associate with the customers, so he'd just lay "pork chop" down on his chair and go on out into the room. I stayed at Condon's about a year, only taking other jobs that seemed really good. I could always go back in there any time that I wanted to and between Pete Pesci and Eddie I worked in there so much that I really did begin to dig the dixieland scene. Occasionally I would go out of town. Sometimes I'd go out with Marian McPartland and her trio, where I'd be featured as guest artist. At other times I'd go out with Bud Freeman, who was very active in those days. Bud and I, with Pee Wee Russell, would go to St Louis and play in a hotel there along with Vic Dickenson.

Pee Wee (Charles Elsworth) Russell was a good guy that always made me feel pretty good when I worked with him. He and I did a lot of things together that were interesting. One time we had a recording session together which took place in New Jersey. We didn't know where but we knew that it was in New Jersey so we met one morning and got into a car and left for Englewood Cliffs, New Jersey, where we found that the session was going to take place. When we got to Jersey we continued to drive past the town and soon found ourselves in the middle of a forest. We continued to drive until, in the middle of the forest, we came to a very modern building made of wood. There were no stores around for miles. It was very hot that day and we went on inside this modern building and found it to be the studio where we were to record. It was a beautiful building and a beautiful recording studio.

After getting inside we found that there were no windows in the whole building. Pee Wee and myself had planned to buy some vodka when we got to the city but by continuing on into the woods we had passed all of the liquor stores. So we found ourselves at the studio with no vodka. That seemed to be a major catastrophe at the time and, no matter who we tried to get to go back to the city to buy some vodka, we couldn't find one person who would go. Soon it was time to record and we still didn't have a thing to drink. We even tried to get some beer but couldn't even get that, so we started to make the first song which was to be on the album. We suffered. Pee Wee was so disgusted because it was his date and he had planned on having something there to drink. He grumbled about it as only Pee Wee could grumble, and I agreed with him because I guess this was the only time in our lives that we couldn't get anything to drink before a recording session. So we just knew that the record was going to be a flop because we couldn't get to our favorite booze, but we went on in all this heat, which made it worse, and made the session. Then, just as we were preparing to make the last number of the set, someone came in with two bottles of hot beer and gave it to us. When the session was over we both went home thinking that that was one session that was going to be actually nothing. A few weeks later, when we heard the finished record, we were surprised to find out that it was one of the best recordings that either of us had ever made. It was the Prestige –Swingville record *Swingin' with Pee Wee*. We couldn't believe that we had been cold sober when we made that recording, which shows you, I guess, that you can do something when you have to do it.

Back in New York I worked at the Central Plaza for Jack Chrystal on weekends and at the same time I was working for Bob Maltz across the street at the Stuyvesant Casino. They were both weekend jobs and when I wasn't at one you'd be sure to find me at the other. These Saturday night or, rather, weekend gigs became a way of staying alive for many cats. The Central Plaza was about the best place in town to hear jazz on a Saturday night and the students would flock there every weekend. All of the best musicians in New York played there, such as Shavers, Kaminsky, Red Allen, Barefield, my dixieland teacher Tony Parenti, and loads of others. On trombone, and one of the main attractions there too at the time, was Conrad Janis, who later returned to acting. Every Saturday night the students would get into fights and sometimes it would be pretty hectic but usually it was the swingingest place to go to on weekends. Bob Maltz's place, the Stuyvesant Casino, was on the same street (Second Avenue) but about three blocks away, and it was easy to run from one place to the other between sets. Bob Maltz and his mother ran the place and a lot of guys would just sit close to their telephones during the week and wait for a call from Bob Maltz asking them if they could make the gig the following week. Me included because, as I said, if you didn't have anything to do that week you could usually always depend on either Jack Chrystal or Bob Maltz giving you a call.

The Metropole had opened in New York with a bang and immediately became the most important jazz spot in town. It was a long bar that had previously been used as a gay nineties bar—where the women entertainers dressed in the 1890 style or fashion. They all resembled Mae West in appearance and sang the old barbershop songs, but it had lately been changed to a jazz spot and by being on or very near Broadway it became right away a success for jazz. The Metropole always hired at least two different attractions and when one would finish a set of jazz numbers, half dixieland and half swing, the other group would follow. The bandstand was behind the bar. It was only about four feet wide and many cats would fall off of the bandstand down into the bar below if they were too tipsy. It was a long bar and as one group would finish their set the other group would come up on the stand and join in on one big closing number. Then, after that, the second group would continue on with their own set. We called the whole show "Wall to Wall Jazz" when the two groups would play together. You'd see about fourteen or fifteen musicians elevated on the stand behind the bartenders and all swinging away on the closing number.

Red Allen became one of the first hits at the Metropole and, along with Buster Bailey, became a real attraction at the place with his *Kiss the Baby* composition, where Red would encourage the audience to kiss each other or, rather, he'd encourage the young cats to kiss their girlfriends. There were a lot of people who liked Red and he'd always give them a big greeting, "Nice, nice, nice." I played in the Metropole with so many different people but my main enjoyment was playing with Kenny Kersey, my old JATP buddy. Claude Hopkins was there too and would swing every afternoon. The Metropole had done so much business at night that they had decided on opening up the jazz on afternoons too and the place stayed so full of people that you were lucky if you could get in the doors. Lots of people, after cruising down Broadway, would just stand on the outside of the place and look in at the cats doing their thing. Gene Krupa was a favorite there too and had his trio in there for some time. Practically every musician in New York played the Metropole. Coleman Hawkins, Harold Singer, Ben Webster were some of the tenor sax men who swung in the Met. Charlie Shavers was a favorite. Zutty Singleton was a big draw there and would cut out for the Alvin Hotel, where he lived, when he finished work.

Directly across the street from the Metropole was a smaller bar, the Copper Rail. The Copper Rail was the meeting place for the musicians, who would come over between sets, and their friends who had come down to dig them. It was a swinging place with no music except the jukebox but they had the best soul food downtown. Della, the lady who cooked all the soul food, and Bob, her husband, were the great attractions in the kitchen and were the reason for loads of people coming to the place. The Copper Rail, like the Metropole, stayed so full of people that you were lucky to get inside. I once wrote a number called *Swinging at the Copper Rail*, which was recorded later for Columbia records. Soon people were breaking their necks to get into the Copper Rail before five o'clock in the afternoon when they would be able to get their soul food dinner, as after six o'clock they would always be sold out of ham hocks, collard greens, corn bread and rice.

In November 1962 Eddie Condon asked me to make a tour with him. I accepted and, along with Dick Rath, Kenny Davern and others, started the tour, which was to take us out to Chicago and other midwestern spots before hitting the eastern cities. The tour went fairly nice and we played to nice houses. We played the Colonial Tavern in Toronto and when Eddie said he could not make a return trip, because of his club in New York, I was asked by Goodie Lichtenstein to bring in a group of my own. Goodie was the boss and the owner and the club was a real delight, so I agreed to bring in a group. I was in there maybe three or four times a year and I'd bring up different guys, the best that I could get, and we became quite an attraction there. Later I was teamed up with a great singer, Olive Brown, and between us and my band we had the joint swinging. It was there, too, that I met a man that I admire very much today, Pat Scott. Pat was the foremost critic in Toronto and could be pretty rough on certain guys, but thank goodness he took a liking to me and I liked him. We'd have many meals at his home and he became pretty close to me, but not to everybody.

Most of the time I'd bring Earle Warren or Buddy Tate, Sir Charles Thompson, Tommy Potter or Franklyn Skeete on bass, and on drums Jackie Williams, who I considered the best around—especially for a small group as he played so tasty—and we would swing everybody crazy. There was the Metro Jazz Club there, which was composed of real honest jazz fans, Yvonne and Gordon Patterson, Rupert and Penny Hodge, Jimmy Dean, Mohamid Spencer, Doc Yankou and so many others. We spent many hours with these fans, attending their meetings on jazz, and today it's still a great pleasure to go back to Toronto and have a reunion. Toronto always seemed to be a clean city and modern in every respect. I found a wonderful tailor there and before long I had so many beautiful suits that it took me about three months to wear them all. Nat Salsberg was my favorite tailor since McIntosh's tailor shop in Hollywood, years ago.

Also while working in the Colonial Tavern I met a lady that was to do much to help me in my work in Canada, Tony Maag. Tony was from Holland and had been working at the Colonial as a waitress. She later convinced the owner of a vacation spot to hire me. They had never hired any jazz musicians there before, but after Tony's insistence I was hired. I was to work with a good group, a trio headed by Hughie Clairmont, who was a drummer and at the same time could play trumpet, and it wasn't long before I was teamed up doing trumpet duets with Hughie in this beautiful summer resort. It was great there and soon I learned how to water-ski and scuba-dive which was all new to me. The Muskoka Sands was such a beautiful place, and later I brought my entire family up there to spend an engagement with me. My kids learned how to swim there and Steven especially amazed me as he progressed so well. But Candy had also learned so well that she soon was teaching Steven different strokes. Coleman Hawkins came up occasionally and we would get together. Hawk learned that I liked corn on the cob and, by him being from the next state to Kansas—Missouri—we soon were eating dozens of ears at Hughie's home.

Back again in New York, early in 1964, I went in Condon's club and naturally was asked by Eddie if I'd go to Australia with him. He had a good lineup and I decided right then and there that I'd go. I had worked with all of the guys and I thought it would be great to go to the land of kangaroos with them. He had Pee Wee Russell, Vic Dickenson, Cliff Leeman, Jack Lesberg, myself and Dick Cary on piano and alto horn. Jimmy Rushing was to be our vocalist, so that put the icing on the cake. I said to Eddie, "Hell yes, I'll go." So in a few weeks we were on our way.

We left New York after meeting Bud Freeman, who also was on the lineup, and our first stop was San Francisco, en route for Hawaii. We stopped a couple of days in Frisco and hung out at Turk Murphy's club there, that is when we were not in Chinatown. Then we left for Tokyo, via Honolulu. After arriving in Japan we really turned it on. I was hanging out with Cliff Leeman on this trip and he and I visited quite a few bars in Tokyo. We also went to a bathhouse and took a Japanese bath in water so hot that I felt like a boiled lobster. Then we left for Australia. That was one long trip. One that took weeks to get over the jet lag.

After a couple of days we met some of the greatest jazz fans: Don and Margaret Anderson, Keith Bruce, Allan and Jean Leake, and a great friend and admirer, Dr Roger Currie. Dr Currie and Keith Bruce made it so nice for us. We were making the tour for Kim Bonython, who lives there. After a beautiful reception we were introduced to the town. I thought that Sydney looked a lot like an American city. Their buildings are very similar to ours —even the family homes looked like American houses. We were a hit from the first concert and soon were the talk of Australia. Eddie was popular there as well as Rush, and oh, I guess we were all pretty popular there as the people really dug jazz.

I was fascinated by the funny looking animals that live in Australia and went often to the zoo to dig them firsthand. There's some funny looking things there: the wild dogs called the dingos, the koala bear, the kangaroos, the platypus—the mammal that lays eggs—the Tasmanian devil, the emu and so many others. Then over, or down, in New Zealand is the kiwi bird that has no wings to speak of. These things interested me very much. Also, even the trees were different. Everything was different. Over there it was summer, where back home it was winter time. The skies were different. I looked for the same constellations in the stars at night but I didn't see any constellations that I had been used to seeing, such as the Big Dipper. They were all foreign to me because of my being on the other side of the world. I liked it all, though. In Adelaide I went out on a field where someone was trying to show me how to throw a boomerang. The guy that was showing me threw it so beautifully. It always came back to him, but when I threw it it just kept on going.

We also went to New Zealand. That was a little bit different from Australia in that it was such a small place after seeing Australia. They pull up the sidewalks at ten o'clock at night. Still, we had very nice audiences even after ten o'clock. When we left Australia we were loaded down with gifts, such as kangaroo skins, mohair sweaters, boomerangs and imitation kiwi birds. Some day I hope to return to Australia but it's such a long trip. Not too many people go there too often. Dick Hughes and Don Carless were two friends, too, that I hung out with. On the way back home we were booked to play in Tokyo, which was a gas. The jazz musicians in Japan were fabulous. They can play just like who they want to play like. The Japanese people can imitate anything in the world but they also have their own talent for being original. Those Japanese cats sure surprised me. They sure were modern. Nothing backwards there.

One night in Tokyo, when we were off and had no concert to play, we were hanging around the hotel when Jack Lesberg walked in with two airline stewardesses. They were pretty lively looking chicks and soon Jack suggested that we all go to a nightclub that he had heard about. Jack is a universal playboy and soon Eddie and myself and the two girls were off to this club. It was a huge club with two or three bands in different rooms. There were hostesses everywhere and chorus girls and everything. We all sat down at a table and proceeded to enjoy the show, but after a few minutes of this Eddie and I left and went to the bar leaving Jack alone with the two girls, which was alright with Jack as he knew we would be back. After about an hour we went back to the table to pay the bill with Jack and the waiter told us that we owed one hundred dollars. We didn't think too much of that as it was a plush club and we figured the bill to come to something like that, but we were soon to learn that it was one hundred dollars a person. The table cost one hundred dollars an hour for each person at the table.

By the time we left for the States Eddie had fallen off the wagon. When we first left New York Eddie said, "This is one trip that I'm going to remember everything that happens." He was really on the wagon until Jack Lesberg got him started at that nightclub. One night as we were way out over the ocean, about three o'clock in the morning, Eddie was sitting in front of me on the plane. Everybody was asleep including the hostesses. Eddie had fallen out of his seat so many times that they just tied him in his seat so that he wouldn't be in the aisle and be stepped on. I happened to wake up and I looked at Eddie. He had gotten loose from his seat somehow and was struggling to get up. I just watched him out of the corner of my eye as he got up and went over to the door of the plane. Then he tried to pull on the lever that opened the door of the plane, and I thought it best that I go stop him as everybody else was asleep. I went and pulled him away as he was frantically trying to open the door. I said to him, "Eddie, what the hell are you doing?"

He looked at me and said, "I'm trying to go to the bathroom. Do you mind?" By that time the whole plane had woke up and soon the hostess had Eddie back in his seat under guard. Another time, when we were making a landing in a small plane, we hit an air pocket that threw everybody around like dolls. All the eating utensils, plates and everything went up in the air. One of the hostesses fell in the aisle. Cliff Leeman had a fifth of vodka in his case. He took the bottle out and while we were bothered with this turbulence he drank the whole bottle. I looked at him and said, "Boy, what a hangover you're going to have in a few hours when this is all over."

Finally we got back to San Francisco and everything was great. We had made the trip successfully and nobody had killed anybody, although Eddie and Bud Freeman had gotten into some kind of a disagreement, but I think it was straightened out before we got back to New York. Sometimes being cooped up with the same bunch of guys, day in and day out, can make one be a little touchy at times.

TEN

Humphrey Lyttelton and my English tours

I was doing the gigs at the Metropole and also at Condon's saloon when one day in 1963 I received an offer to go to England and work with Humphrey Lyttelton. I hadn't known too much about Humphrey but I used to hear Pops talk about the cat in England who swings his ass off. I knew he had a band but that was about all I knew about him. I was very happy at the thought of playing with him and I packed my bags and headed for London. This tour was different than the one that I had made with my group before. I had Humph to tell me all about the different places we played and before long I was beginning to know all of the most interesting places in England.

When I met Humph I knew right away that I had met another trumpet player friend. He had just about everything. First of all he was a trumpet player, and a good trumpet player. He was one of the most friendly people that I'd met in a long time. He had a hell of a good sense of humor and a quick wit comparable to Eddie Condon's. He had a beautiful delivery of speech and a good family background. I knew almost right away that I had found a new member for my family of brother trumpet players. So far I had only three what I call "trumpet brothers," but now I had four. I never chose these cats as "brothers"; they just happened. They were men that I had been very close to in my life and, besides that, they all played the way I liked to hear a trumpet played. Sweets Edison is one of the brothers, naturally. After spending so many years together with Count Basie, Harry and I were, and still are, very close. Ruby Braff is a brother. I've known Ruby for such a long time—we have recorded together, played together—and I respect Ruby as being one of the most dedicated trumpet players I ever knew. Ruby constantly improves and today he is one of the really greats. Emmett Berry was one of my brothers. I don't think that Emmett ever got the credit that he was due. He was one swingin' cat, believe me! I never enjoyed working with someone as I did working (playing trumpet) with Emmett on our tour of England. He used to knock me out every show. Now that I had met Humph I knew instantly that I had met another "brother." Four brothers. I wish that I could have played in a trumpet section composed of these four guys.

Humph had a good band and, luckily for me, was playing in the Count Basie style. I met some good guys with Humph: Jimmy Skidmore, Tony Coe, Joe Temperley, Bruce Turner, and the great lady saxophonist of England Kathy Stobart. I met Doug Dobell who at the time was recording

Humph and his band. Doug was what we call "a good cat" and had the swingingest record store in all London.

Soon I was experiencing the English countryside as I drove with Humph to the towns that we were to play. Like the French countryside I enjoyed it very much as it all seemed so different from the American countryside. The shrubbery on the English roads is so green. I've always wished since that I could get my garden and lawn to grow as green as they would if they were in England. I'm not sure, but I believe it's the lime in the English soil that makes everything so green. There were big beautiful rhododendrons—blue, pink and white—that bordered the roads. Just driving along the road with Humph was knocking me out. We'd stop sometimes at the little pubs on the road and have a beer or a meat-pie.

The tour with Humph was so pleasant that I forgot completely about coming back to New York. We played nearly all of the large cities in England and Humph and I had a ball blowing together. I made three more tours with Humph in the following years, and I seemed to commute between London and New York. I was with Humph when we played in Liverpool and I met one of my greatest friends—Steve Voce. Steve was a dynamo in the jazz circles there and was a real fan. He gave classes on jazz and I was guest at one of his meetings. I enjoyed it. Steve and I became pretty tight and we always liked to go to the nearest pub and down a few. I wrote a number for Steve called *Steevos*, which was recorded by Humph later. I have since visited Steve in Liverpool and met more fans as I stayed with him and his wife Jenny. I would walk around Liverpool diggin' the town where the Beatles got their start. I saw many of the clubs where they made their beginning.

We had one bad scare with Humph on the highway one day. At that time there was no speed limit on the roads in England and Humph used to drive so fast that, actually, I would be afraid just sitting there in the seat behind him, but I wouldn't let them know. We wouldn't be able to drive that fast in the States. Humph was a familiar figure sitting at the wheel, talking with everybody, a long cigar in his mouth and his foot upon the dashboard, and driving at least ninety or ninety-five miles an hour. One day, when we were driving at about this same speed, a Jaguar, driving even faster than we were, came on us from behind and cut over in front of us. Humph had to put on the brakes, going at ninety-five miles an hour, in order not to collide with the Jaguar (pronounced in England Jag-you-are). We could only look at that damn fool in the Jaguar and at the same time watch Humph as he tried to slow down and not hit him. Humph was magnificent at the wheel. He pumped the brakes at that speed so that we wouldn't hit the shoulder of the road, because if we had we would have ended up in a field, I'm sure. I could feel the momentum of the car as my knees pressed into the front seat. I looked out of the back window and there was a huge smoke trail where Humph's rubber was burning. Just like a rocket, I guess. Humph stayed with it and soon he managed to get the car down to a speed that he wanted where he could stop. We did stop, but the car was in bad shape from such an experience and we had to knock on to the next town. It messed up the car but we were safe, credit due to Humph's experience at the wheel. We came upon the Jaguar later parked in a roadside eating stop and we had to hold Joe Temperley from going in and punching the guy who was driving it.

In 1965 when I played with Humph, Ben Webster was also a guest star. Ben was in great shape then and was popular in London and had been working at Ronnie Scott's club. On the same tour we used Joe Turner as additional guest star. That was a great tour. Joe had an overcoat that came down to his ankles and, by him being so big, we'd have trouble sometimes getting him in the car with the rest of us, but he made it. I enjoyed working with Joe as it reminded me of Kansas City when I first met him at the Sunset Club. Everybody loved Joe in England. I was glad that he had come over and soon we were talking about the Kansas City of a few years ago. When Joe first came over he didn't have his work permit, or at least he didn't know where it was. When he was stopped at the customs and didn't have it, they just moved him into a little room and told him to wait there until somebody "claimed him." Finally, after hours, the booking office realized that Joe Turner was to arrive in London on that day and so far nobody had seen him. Jack Higgins called the airport and was told that Joe was there so they went out and found him. Joe and I played in many cities with Humph and it was quite an enjoyable tour. We both dug each other professionally and Joe was a lot of fun. The English people couldn't understand half of what he was talking about. He had an accent, I don't know what kind, but it was an accent that the British couldn't understand, so in a way I was his interpreter. And then there was a lot of times when even I didn't understand what the hell he was saying. He kept us laughing all the time and traveling with him was a great experience.

We played at London's Royal Festival Hall in May with the Kansas City Jazz Show, which included (besides myself and Joe) Vic Dickenson, Ben Webster and Ruby Braff. Later in the month the show had split into smaller groups for other engagements and Joe and I stayed with Humphrey. Shortly after that Joe and I were invited to play in Yugoslavia together. Bosko Petrovic, who had a jazz combination, the Zagreb Jazz Quartet, had invited us to a festival in Bled and later to do a radio broadcast from Zagreb. Joe and I left for Yugoslavia and found that we had to make a change of planes in Copenhagen. As we were waiting around in the airport for our plane we walked to the end of the terminal and who should we see but Louis Armstrong and his group on their way to Sweden. There were some guys interviewing Pops at the time with the little tape recorders, so he stopped the interview when he saw us and began talking to us. I was always glad to see Pops and pretty soon the conversation got around to the popular drink in Yugoslavia, Slivovitz, which is a plum brandy and strong as anything that you can imagine. Everybody had warned me about drinking it but I never paid them too much attention because I had never been in a country where it was the national drink before. Even Pops said to me, "Don't fool around with that Slivovitz. That Slivovitz is a bitch."

We arrived in Yugoslavia after leaving Pops and his group still waiting for their plane, and the first thing that Joe and I wanted to do after we checked into a hotel was to go to the nearest bar and have some Slivovitz. We just had to see what it was all about. We went in the hotel bar, sat down and proceeded to order some Slivovitz. When I first tasted it I thought that it was nice, but it tasted so much like apple cider that I said to myself, "This stuff ain't so bad," and, before long, I had ordered many of these bad drinks. When time came that evening for Joe and I to go to the hall, I was still in the bar, trying to imagine what all the big fuss was concerning Slivovitz. It had taken no effect on me at all, so I thought, "This is like drinking apple cider."

Arriving at the festival, we were met by Bosko Petrovic and his group: Davor Kajfes on piano, Kresimir Remata on bass, Silvije Glojnovic on drums. Petrovic played vibraphone. That group was one of the best small groups that I'd met in Europe. I was really surprised to find such musicians in Europe and especially in Yugoslavia. They played with such a feeling of jazz. They could swing like crazy and were very clean in everything they did. A really great group. They can be heard on the Black Lion recording *Feel so Fine!* that was taped by Alan Bates from our concert in Zagreb.

After the festival performance I had the pleasure of listening to a Yugoslavian band, a big band composed of doctors, lawyers, dentists, and whatever. I couldn't believe my ears when I heard these cats swing out. They sounded a bit like Woody Herman's great band and had some of the best arrangements that I'd heard for some time. Great trumpets, great saxes, trombones—everything. They really could play, and I wondered just how they could get that good American big-band sound. I think that there were other bands in Europe composed of non-professional musicians that played big-band arrangements, but here was the best I'd heard so far.

So I continued on with the Slivovitz drinking with these guys, but they were mixing the Slivovitz with rum and that is really dangerous, as I was to find out later. Joe Turner had quit drinking the Slivovitz a long time ago because he only liked Scotch whiskey and the Slivovitz was too tame in taste for him. But me, I kept on drinking with these musicians. I was talking to one of the trumpet players, who was drinking rum and Slivovitz, and right in the middle of a sentence he fell flat on his face. Down on the floor he was —flat on his nose. By this time it was finally getting to me and I started feeling the effects. I wondered, though, if this kind of result happened frequently or whether this was an isolated case. I figured, "These Yugoslavian guys should know already about this stuff so why do they drink it if it's that bad?" Anyway, after they picked the trumpet player up off the floor I stayed with the guys and got worse and worse. When the bar closed at about five o'clock in the morning I was so looped that I didn't want to go home to my hotel, so I went to another hotel that was very near and got another room. I was with a lot of people and musicians and girls so we all decided to go to my new room and have a party. After being in my room for just a few minutes and everybody still drinking this stuff and rum, I don't remember too much what happened. Everybody was having a ball and I went to sleep on the bed in the room. I left everything swinging when I went to sleep. I do remember waking up at one time and I looked up at a boy and a girl dancing over me as I was lying there—dancing right over my body like I wasn't even there. The rest of the bunch were listening to records or still drinking. Finally, when I opened my eyes about seven o'clock, everybody had gone home. I suddenly realized that I was supposed to be at the airport that morning to go back to London as we had some more dates to do with Humphrey. My head was just about ready to split open, but somehow I left that hotel and went back to my original hotel hoping to find Joe Turner and Alan Bates waiting for me.

I entered the lobby of my hotel and the first thing that I saw was all of my bags sitting in the lobby. Joe Turner and Alan Bates had both left for the airport and one of them had gone in my room, packed my bags and brought them down to the lobby just in case I was late. I began to get panicky. Everybody had gone and left me in this strange land and I couldn't speak the language and most of them couldn't understand English either. It was raining cats and dogs, to make matters worse. When I paid my bill I asked the lady to call me a cab and tell the chauffeur to take me to the airport in a hurry as I was already late. She called someone and in a few more minutes a little guy showed up in an old-style automobile. After I had paid my hotel bill I didn't have a cent left, as I had spent too much the night before— renting another hotel room and drinking at the bar—and I had really spent too much money. So I didn't have even enough to pay this little guy to take me to the airport, but I got in the car anyway hoping that I'd be able to catch Joe and Alan before the plane took off and I'd get some more money. The lady at the desk at the hotel talked to the little guy in the car and told him to take me to the airport just as fast as he could get me there. He nodded and away we went in all that rain and my head feeling like a buzz saw.

The little guy had on a straw hat that fitted way down on his head and he looked small in the driver's seat. I don't know what the distance was to the airport but after a while it seemed that we were never going to get there. He was driving, not being able to see too well in all the rain, and I was in the back praying that he'd make it in time for me to catch the plane. I couldn't even begin to think what would happen to me if the plane had left and I was here all by myself in Yugoslavia. Then, too, if this little guy didn't get his money for driving me he would most likely want to kill me and I couldn't blame him. I couldn't talk to him because of the language barrier so I could only hope that he knew where he was going. After what seemed like hours we finally pulled up to a road and through the headlights I could see Joe and Alan, sitting on the edge of the road in the rain. They had held up the plane just as long as they could and the plane was preparing to leave just as we pulled up. They pulled me in the plane and Joe Turner paid the cab bill and we were off for London. My head still swimming around, I learned that if I had missed that plane I'd have had to wait three days for the next one, as there were only limited planes to London. If I had missed it I would have had trouble with the driver, and would probably have had to walk back to the city in the rain to find some Americans at the American Embassy there, as I had no money to eat nor anything else. In other words I'd have been in one hell of a situation. I thanked God that I had made it but I still was having this king-sized hangover, which was to be with me for about three weeks. It was the worst hangover that I'd ever had and I realized what Pops meant when he said, "That Slivovitz is a bitch." I was sicker than a dog and when I got off the plane in England I had turned another color— green I'd say. It was the absolute worst hangover you can imagine but at least I was safely out of Yugoslavia.

While we were in Yugoslavia Humph and the boys had planned a party for Joe and myself and, though I knew about it, I had forgotten about it completely. I checked in at my hotel, at the time thinking that I'd have time to get a good sleep. I had been too nervous to sleep since the Slivovitz and all I'd do at night was toss and turn and stay awake, so after checking in I went right to my room and went straight to bed. I had the chills too. I'd been in bed it seemed to me (although I guess it was a little longer, but not much) about exactly seven minutes before the phone rang and I almost jumped out of my skin. I answered the phone and it was Beryl Bryden, the famous blues songstress of London. She was coming by in a few minutes to get me ("gather me up" in English English) and take me to the party, which was being held at Joe Temperley's home. I agreed to be ready when she came and I still don't know how I had the strength to get out of that cozy bed and put on my clothes again, but somehow I did. Still nervous as a kitten and shaking like a leaf in a thunder storm, I went to Joe Turner's room and together we waited for Beryl to show up, which she did in a few moments, and we were off. I knew that Beryl meant to be nice, and she was, but I was just not fit to be around that day because I was in such bad shape. When Beryl walked us to a street to get a cab I didn't think that I was going to make it without taking time out to rest, and when she told us that we'd have to wait some minutes for the cab to arrive I just had to sit down on the curb. I don't think I could have waited if I'd had to stand up. Finally the cab did show and we all got in and were off for Joe's house. It was a nice party attended by Joe, Tony Coe, Johnny Butts, Dave Green, Eddie Harvey and Joe Turner and myself. As soon as I got in Joe's living room I found the biggest, softest, most comfortable chair in the house and sat in it like I was made of stone. I didn't even want to move so I just sat there and watched all of the cats having a ball. I was shaking so much that I couldn't hold a glass of anything in my hand without it spilling, so Joe T. (Temperley) and myself went behind a door where nobody could see us and, with both hands on the glass, I was able to get a drink down. I had that old feeling that if I took a drink it would make me feel better, but not in this case. I took two or three drinks like that, behind the door with no one looking to see me shaking, but it didn't do any good, so I went on back to my big comfortable chair and stayed there until the party was over and I went home and finally got to bed. The hangover was still there, though, and was to be there for a couple of weeks yet, or more. But now I had a chance to sleep a bit before I was to go to a festival in Sweden, where also Pops was supposed to appear.

I went to Sweden a few days later but I was still shaking. My nervous system was completely wasted and no matter what I did I couldn't stop the shaking. Packing my bags again, I left for Sweden and once again I met Pops and the group at the airport in Copenhagen and we flew together to the festival. It was such a short trip from Denmark to Sweden. Just as soon as you get off the ground you start descending. I was sitting with Billy Kyle and we had no sooner got our seat belts fastened when the plane descended and we were on the ground. Here was the first time that I saw at first hand the popularity of Louis Armstrong in Europe. Pops had told me before that he was tired and as soon as he got to his hotel he was going to "get between them sheets." On the ground at the airport were hundreds of people, all to see Pops. They were behind barriers and when Pops walked the crowd followed. It was just like he was a real saint. The fire-department band was there and one of the firefighters gave Pops one of the department's fire helmets. It was a white helmet and Pops put it on and posed with a lot of dignitaries, who had given him bunches of roses. When Pops left for the hotel where we were staying the whole crowd went crazy and followed on foot. After being assigned to our rooms Pops noticed that my trumpet was in his room. He called me and soon we got that all straightened out. The bellboy had mistakenly put his trumpet in my room, and mine in his.

We went on to the festival that evening and I was to play with a bunch of Danish fellows, Arnvid Meyer and his group. A nice bunch of cats. Arnvid was a trumpet player and in the band was my very good friend John Darville, who played trombone with the group. (Some time later I was to come back to Europe and play with this same group along with Ben Webster.) We played a few concerts in Sweden and in a few days the festival was over. Arnvid Meyer asked me one day why I was shaking so much and why my lips would quiver when I played. I told him in one word, "Slivovitz!"

After the festival I returned to England and went on with Humphrey. We went to Liverpool and once again I could spend some time with my man Steve Voce. Humph and Joe Turner, who was still with us, had a birthday celebration in Liverpool. I had become more and more familiar with Humph now and his playing. Sometimes we'd sound like we had rehearsed in private together but it was all spontaneous. Humph was a guy that you could never take for granted. It was the best thing for me to play with him as he always made me have new ideas. He inspired me all the time we were together. One time, when we were playing at the Royal Festival Hall, Humphrey and the band were to play a few minutes before calling me on as guest artist. They went out on stage while I went to the dressing room to wait for my call. I don't know how I misjudged the time, but sooner than I expected they were calling, "Guest artist, Buck Clayton," on all the loudspeakers backstage. I wasn't in my dressing room as this came on, I was out in a hall, and, realizing that I should be on stage, I ran back to the dressing room to get my trumpet. In the dressing room I saw that my trumpet was not in the room and then I remembered I had left it on stage after arriving and warming up a bit. Then I had to rush down and find the stage, which wasn't familiar to me at all. They were still yelling, "Guest artist, Mr Buck Clayton," on the mike. Finally I found the stage and ran out and picked up the trumpet laying on the piano—late—but I was there. I proceeded to play, *I can't get started with you* and after playing a couple of choruses, just before I was to finish the number, Humph walked out on the stage. Just as I made my last note of the number Humph presented me with a trumpet in front of the entire hall. It was my own trumpet. In my haste to get on stage I grabbed the first trumpet I saw, but it was Humph's trumpet. I had played the whole number with his trumpet and had never noticed the difference. I had given Humph a mouthpiece like mine some time before, which made it easier for me to play his trumpet, but I felt kinda stupid after learning that it wasn't my trumpet. But that shows you how close we were.

We used to play jokes on each other. Sometimes I'd say to Humph, "Say, Humph, I got a sore lip tonight, so I won't play anything too high. Let's just play down in the lower register." He'd say, "OK," and we'd play together. I'd stay down in the lower register of the horn until we got almost to the end, Humph staying down too. Then, just before the song was to end, I'd go way up in the stratosphere and leave Humph still down in the low register without a chance to do anything else because the number was finished. Pretty soon Humph got wise to me and started giving me the business. He'd carve me in a minute if I wasn't on my toes. We called this "wrestler's tricks," where one of us would pretend to be sick and then all of a sudden come to life and win the match. Humph composed a song called *Wrestler's Tricks*, which we recorded later. One day when we were to record we couldn't get the studio because of a mix-up in the booking for the studio. We searched all over London for another studio but couldn't find any that was available. So finally, after hours of searching, we found an empty pub that had in it a piano so we went there and recorded. The recording came out great but we had to take off our overcoats and hang them up all over the pub so as to dull the sound of the room and make it sound more like a studio.

I believe that I could write a book just on all of my experiences with "Sir Humphrey," but I'll try to keep it down. I do believe that when I was playing with Humph I was at the peak of my career. Maybe it was because of my playing with him, I don't know, but I never felt better playing in my life than I did when I made the tours with Humph. The band was great at all times. I found, too, that the English critics never give credit to their own jazz stars like Humph. If he had been an American he would have been compared with the greatest, but by being British he was never credited with being as good as he really was. I could never understand that.

One day, while we drove along the highway, Humph showed me Stonehenge, which I had never heard of before. Humph explained it all to me and we stopped the car and went to visit this place that was so old in history. I looked at these huge stones and wondered where they came from and how they got there, as there was no rock quarries near. I'm still wondering. After taking pictures of Humph trying to lift one of the stones we got back in the car and drove on to the next concert. We played a lot in Manchester, where we would gamble a lot in the casinos. I went to Switzerland with Humph, where we played in Interlaken at a beautiful casino. I had met Red Mack in Paris, the same Red Mack that I admired so much as a kid in Los Angeles, and he went with me to Switzerland with Humph. He no longer played trumpet and was making a tour of Europe as a tourist. He owned a business in Los Angeles and, though I'm not sure about this, I think he owned a bar. I've already told you how much I admired Red Mack when I was a youngster in Los Angeles so now it was my pleasure to have him along with me and to introduce him to Humph and the band. We met Johnny Simmen while there and I introduced them to each other. Johnny was quite interested in Red and tried to get him to return to playing but it never developed.

After that tour with Humph I went to Paris and worked in the Trois Maillets. It was an underground cave that had a long history that began in the French Revolution. It was a favorite spot for jazz and was packed every night. Many greats of jazz played there, such as Bill Coleman, Mezz Mezzrow, Memphis Slim and others. I enjoyed working there, although I hadn't been used to working in these jazz caves before. Madame Calvet was the owner and she'd show me the torture chambers that were below the jazz room. During the time of the revolution they used to torture prisoners who were dropped in the Seine river after being killed. There was a special trapdoor just for that reason. This was quite interesting and I played there many times during my visits to Europe.

In England, in 1967, I also made a tour with another friend trumpet man, John Chilton. It was a nice tour and John and I became pretty tight. I see him now occasionally here in New York, where he plays as leader of the band with George Melly. I don't recall how many tours I've made in England with Humphrey, but it must have been quite a few. I even went to London one time just to be there. I had no work planned, but soon after I arrived I was at work. My working vacation had begun. I'd run into Jimmy Witherspoon occasionally in London—usually at Ronnie Scott's, where many times I'd see Carmen McRae. Annie Ross at one time had a club in London where Witherspoon would do his act. I had known Annie for years and it is always a pleasure to see her when I'm in London. She's made so many discs that I dig. What she did with *Fiesta in Blue*, which I made with Count Basie, is unbelievable. She did my solo word for word, or note for note. She had this club in London called Whisky-a-Go-Go.

ELEVEN

Health problems

It was back in England with Humphrey Lyttelton that I had my very first encounter with the terrible luck that was to follow me for years later. I was playing with Humph one night when I felt a pang in my groin. I did not know at the time what a hernia felt like, but I knew that it hurt to play after about an hour. I told Humph, in earnest, that I didn't feel too well and that I was going to try to take it easy that night. I know that he must have thought that I was pulling a wrestler's trick on him but this time I was really sincere, although I know he didn't believe me. I continued to play with him and it seemed to get worse. Finally I went to the doctor and he told me that I had a hernia—not from playing, but from carrying too heavy suitcases. Sometimes in Europe, when there are no porters around, you have to carry your own luggage and sometimes the distance from the train to the station can be quite long.

At first I didn't take the hernia too seriously, as I'd never had one and didn't know of the dangers it can have, but I was soon to learn. After some days like this I found that I had another hernia on the other side, my right side. Now at last I had succeeded in having a double hernia. I began to wonder just what I had done in life to deserve all this. One thing right after another, and it wasn't through yet. I once knew a girl that had told me that she had put a seven-year hex on a guy, a voodoo curse, and sometimes I wonder . . .

I went in hospital and had both hernias operated on, which didn't bother me too much. I was glad to have them corrected and soon I began to take easy gigs where I didn't have to blow like Cat Anderson, which I never did anyway. I'd work with Joe Kane every Sunday in Long Beach, Long Island, playing weddings, barmitzvahs, anything they had. I liked working with Joe because he was one society bandleader that dug jazz and many times he'd use also Roy Eldridge and Zoot Sims to help him swing the barmitzvahs. I began to learn every Jewish song that I could and soon had a pretty good repertoire. Sometimes I couldn't wait to get to the gig because there would be so much good feeling and the Jewish people always had the greatest food in the world. My playing was still not up to par, but Joe knew it and I wasn't bothered, though within myself I was bothered a lot and you can believe that.

During one tour with Humph I was staying at the White House, which is a big hotel in London. After doing some push-ups in my room my nose started to bleed. I thought it a minor thing until I couldn't stop it. I had a little friend in London, Carole Sylvester, who came and tried to help me stop it, but it was a very stubborn case and soon we thought it best to go to the hospital. We went to the hospital and I sat and bled for about two hours before they got it under control. I was released and told to go back to the hotel and take it easy. I did, and spent a restful night, but the next day it started all over again. Once again I tried to stop it, but couldn't, and away I went again to the hospital, which happened to be very near the hotel. It bled so much that they had to give me transfusions. The medics thought that it would be best for me to remain in the hospital so they could find the reason for the bleeding, so I spent my first time abroad in a hospital.

The hospital wasn't bad. I thought to myself, "I'm glad, though, that it's in England as I can understand what they're saying. But just suppose that I was in hospital in Italy or Germany—somewhere that I didn't understand a word they're saying." In a couple of days I began to talk to the other blokes in the hospital and in the evening we'd watch the English boxing matches on TV. Max and Betty Jones, along with Humph, came by to visit me and perked me up a little. Jack Higgins was concerned and would come by to see if I was alright. My blood pressure was very high and they wouldn't tell me just how high it was, but it was pretty high. This hospital trip reminded me of the time I was in hospital in Canada from the same reason, hypertension. At that time I was using a lot of salt in seasoning my food, which was one factor in bringing on the hemorrhage. Jack Higgins told me that he was surprised to see me use so much salt in having dinner at his apartment, where he had cooked a beautiful roast beef.

After that tour I was to go to Berne, Switzerland, to play in the Chiquito Club with Guy Lafitte, the great tenor man from France. While I had a few days off before the gig started I went to Limoges, France, to hang out with my man Jean Marie Masse. One morning I woke up and when I went to shave I could only feel my razor on one side of my face. Right away I got panicky. Was I paralyzed in the face? Then I found that the entire left side of my face was numb. Even my lips were numb and I could only feel the mouthpiece of my horn on just half of my face and half of my lips. So that was a problem that I didn't understand. Jean Marie took me to a clinic in Limoges and, after X-raying my head and face, I found that I had a deviated septum, which means that there was a blockage in my nasal passage. I didn't know at first what the words deviated septum meant but I was advised to have an operation when I got back to the States. Anyway, I was put back in shape by the doctors in Limoges and soon I was going to the gig in Berne.

As soon as I arrived back in the States, it seemed, I began to have trouble with my top lip, underneath. I had a dental bridge that had been done several years before and, with the years, my gums had receded and the bridge had remained the same. So there was a cutting edge on the bridge that used to cut into my lip every time that I'd put the mouthpiece of my trumpet to my lips. It started out with just a little pain, but the more time that went by the more it cut and hurt. I still was taking gigs, although I began to see how a hurting lip can affect your playing.

I found that the more that I was expected to play the more whiskey I would drink, and sometimes I'd end the gig completely wasted. Of course, this is no excuse for all the other times that I did that, because I used to get wasted, completely wasted, years before that when I was with Basie. Not every day, but when I'd get looped it would be a beauty. Anyway, I'd find myself half drunk on every gig that I'd make. I just couldn't stand the thought that I'd play badly and I'd use the vodka as a crutch. It wasn't doing me any good, but after a few tastes I didn't give a damn. I tried to be brave about it and sometimes play without taking a drink, but it didn't work. I'd come to the gig about two hours early sometimes, to get some practice in so that I'd sound good when the other cats got to the gig, but then instead of practicing I'd just look at that trumpet for minutes before I could get up enough courage to put it to my lips.

I had a previous engagement to play again in Switzerland with Henri Chaix and Ben Webster so, even though I wasn't in the best of shape, I went over and made a beautiful tour even with the cuts under my lip getting larger and larger. I also accepted a recording date with Earl Hines as guest artist with his small group. I played everything in a low profile. I couldn't improvise—in fact I was lucky just to play the straight melody. But anyway, the record *did* come out. Then I had a recording date to make with Jo Jones and Milt Buckner in Antwerp after we had played a concert in Brussels. In Brussels my playing was getting worse and worse and my lip was becoming more and more sensitive and painful. I tried to hype myself into believing that I'd be alright for the recording date the next day, but nothing happened. I sounded bad on the concert—not bad, but I just couldn't do the things that I wanted to do. The next day was the same. I wanted so much to make a record with Milt Buckner, with whom I'd never played. I dig an organ underneath me and I knew that working with Milt would be a gas. I just wished that I'd done it years before when I was in better shape. I had recorded with a couple of great organists, like Marlowe Morris and Sir Charles Thompson, so I was really hoping that I'd be able to make it with Milt Buckner. Jo Jones I wasn't worried about. We'd been through so many things together that I knew he'd understand.

The record date was for the French producer Jean Marie Monestier. When I arrived I found Milt fixing the leg on his organ. He was on the floor underneath it with some pliers or something. Jo was putting up his trap drums. So I took out the trumpet and it took me about a half hour just to get a sound out of it. I became afraid right away. I didn't say anything to Jo nor Milt, but I went in the john and practiced where I wouldn't sound so bad. Soon it was time to begin the date and I came out of the john. Milt was practicing an introduction to something and Jo Jones was sounding so good. They were both fabulous and I really didn't want to get in on their good sounds but finally I had to play something. As I began to play I kept hitting bad notes or, rather, notes that were not in the number that we were making, so we'd start all over again. After a few more minutes of that it was obvious to everybody that I wouldn't be able to make that date. The one that I wanted to make so much. Seeing that I wasn't going to make it, Monestier came over to me and asked me if I wanted to cancel the date. That's where I learned the French word "annuler," which means "cancel." I've never forgotten it. He was very nice about it and I was excused while Jo Jones and Milt went on and made a session with just the two of them. There was nothing for me to do but pack up, which I did. I canceled the recording date and also the rest of the tour that I was to do with Jo and Milt.

I packed my trumpet and went outside the studio and I could hear Jo and Milt in there sounding so damn good and there I was. For the first time in my life I couldn't play enough to make the date with them. I cried like a baby. I cried and cried and cried in the taxi taking me back to the hotel. I went out and bought a bottle of something French—cognac or something— and I got so drunk that I didn't know where I was nor why I was there. I really tied one on. Pretty soon I guess I was too drunk to cry any more and I decided to go out—anywhere—just to get away from the experience of the day. I left the hotel, got into a cab and went to a club, pissy drunk. I had forgotten my passport and left it in my room and didn't know exactly where it was. As I was in the club, Jo and Milt came in after they had finished the record date. Jo looked at me and knew that I was in bad shape. I remember the worried look he had on his face when he saw me. He didn't say anything but I knew he was watching to see that nothing happened to me. Finally he came over and asked me to go back to the hotel with him. I agreed, but when he asked me where I lived I didn't know what hotel I had registered at, and we had to ask a lot of people where they thought I might live. Finally we found it. I went in, found my passport and made plans to come home and probably never play again.

After arriving back in New York I made plans to have something done to my lip, because by now the cuts were so bad that the underside of my top lip looked like a big red hamburger. I was at home one day looking at my trumpet and just wondering why it had turned against me, when the radio came on with a song that had an eight-bar trumpet solo in it. I think it was the recording *Close to You* by the Carpenters. My brother-in-law and his wife were upstairs as I was in the basement and I knew they could hear me as they had done thousands of times before when I'd practice. I listened to the trumpet solo, which was an easy straight melody solo that didn't go any higher than a B-flat under high C. For some reason I decided to see if I could play that same solo so I picked up my horn and started. When I realized that I couldn't make it, that I was sounding so bad, I was ashamed to come back upstairs. I knew my brother-in-law had heard me and I didn't want to see anyone. I knew then that I couldn't accept any more gigs because I just couldn't play. I sneaked back upstairs, past my brother-in-law Freddie, and went into my den and started thinking just what I was going to do. I was thankful that I had been able to play the most part of my life but, still, I wasn't ready to quit. In this case I didn't have any choice. I couldn't play so I just couldn't play. It was just as simple as that.

I knew that the trombonist Marshall Brown had previously had an operation on his lip so I called him and we made an appointment to meet. He was going to refer me to his doctor, Dr Ju, who was a prominent doctor in skin troubles. Dr Ju was an Asian doctor with a wonderful reputation and only did work on people that could afford to pay his prices. His office was downtown in a high-class neighborhood and I was a little bit leery at first to go to him, but after I met him I liked him and very soon we had made an appointment to begin work on my chop. After the first examination he found also a small tumor on the left side of my face that we didn't know if or not it was malignant. I knew that it was there but I didn't take it seriously. At times, when I'd be shaving, I would cut it as the razor went over it and it would bleed. Anyway, after taking a test we found that it wasn't malignant, but just the same it would have to be removed. So now he had my lip *and* the small tumor to contend with. Finally the day came to make the operation. I wanted to be unconscious as he worked on my lip but that wasn't to be the case. I watched him as he used a local anaesthetic. The tumor on my face and the lip were done at the same time. He took thirty stitches under my lip to close up all the cuts. When it was finished he wrapped my entire head in a big bandage and I called a cab and went to stay with a friend who lived in Manhattan, as I didn't want to be seen walking around with this big bandage on my head like Frankenstein. When I knocked on my friend's door and he saw this person at his door with this bandaged head, he didn't know whether to close the door quick or see just who it was. I said, "Hello, this is Buck," just as soon as the door opened and I went inside and he put me to bed in his apartment until I could go to Long Island the next day.

After being at home for just a few days the bad luck still seemed to be following me. Even before Dr Ju had taken the bandages off of my head I cut myself washing dishes as a thin drinking glass broke in my hand, and once again I had to go to the hospital to have stitches put in it. About a week after that I cut my palm on barbwire that I was removing from my garage and away again I went to the hospital to take shots against infection and to have more stitches. Then, to top it off, shortly after the wire cut I was hit by a motorcycle that had run against the light, and my left wrist was broken. I had to wear a cast for some weeks after that. I had hardly got out of the cast when I decided to have the deviated septum taken care of and I went to the New York Eye, Ear and Nose Hospital to have that done. The doctor was good and soon I was able to breathe normally. The bone of the bridge of my nose had grown and had closed the nasal passage on my left side and it had to be opened.

Now that I couldn't play anymore I began thinking about another profession. People were very kind and sympathetic when they heard about all my misfortune. I guess the news must have spread around the world pretty quickly, that I was unable to play any more. I received messages of hope, messages of inspiration, and many friends did their best to offer me all kinds of encouragement. In England there was a benefit for me that was sponsored by my two great friends Humphrey and Steve Voce. It was named "Huckle-Buck." They took up a collection in which Norman Granz gave the biggest contribution and sent the money to me.

Here at home friends rallied around me and offered me so many things, so many jobs. It was very gratifying to see everybody come to my aid in this dark hour. Julian Dash, the famous tenor sax man that had made many of the original *Buck Clayton Jam Session* records for Columbia, tried so hard to get me to work with him as a receptionist at the company where he was working, Merrill Lynch, Pierce Fenner and Smith, the big brokerage company. Frank Cahill, my old army buddy, offered me a job as a projectionist in a theater that he had charge of. Then, too, there were certain people that kept on at me to continue and try to blow the horn, even if it seemed so impossible at that time. Vic Dickenson never gave up and continually pressed me to try to play again. Johnny Letman used to make me a little peeved sometimes because he wanted me to play right away, even if it hurt me, although I loved him for his insistence because I knew he loved me a lot and hated to see my career come to an end. Then there was Len Mash in London, who always encouraged me to think of returning to playing someday and would write me letters of encouragement from England, and Claude and Jean-Pierre Battestini, who encouraged me from France. These particular people I'll never forget because I always kept their thoughts in my mind, even though at the time I had never planned to play again.

I spent some time writing, composing and arranging, and then I received a call from Dick Gibson in Denver inviting me to come and be his guest at his annual birthday jazz party for his wife, Maddie. Dick knew all about my problems and was nice enough to invite me to come with all the other invited guests. Dick's parties are something else. He hires the absolute best musicians he can get and also brings in many of the most popular jazzmen from different countries. One of the men that Dick had brought over was Trummy Young, who had been living for years in Hawaii. I hadn't seen Trummy for years and I was so glad to see him. I was, in fact, glad to see everybody as this was my first time being around so many musicians since I had given up playing some years ago. Soon Trummy and I were talking and, during the conversation, Trummy told me of two dentists in Boston who were great for jazz musicians.

At first I didn't think too seriously about what Trummy was saying to me and I went on to enjoy the party. Dick had arranged a very good show and everyone was superb in their playing. I enjoyed everything and on the last day of the party Dick came to me with a check. I didn't know what it was for but I found out later that he had paid me just as if I had performed. I was surprised, but even more so when I found that he had paid my hotel bill, my bar bill and, in fact, I didn't have to pay for anything, which I thought was pretty nice of him.

On the last day of the party Trummy got hold of me again and I told him that I would go to Boston and see these two dentists that he had so much faith in, but, to tell the truth, I didn't think that any dentist could help me. I had been to some of the best dentists in New York and not one of them had a plan to get my teeth in shape again, so why should I get my hopes up now? As Trummy was preparing to leave for Hawaii he said to me, "Buck, you be sure to go see these guys and I'll bet you five dollars that they will have you playing in three months." When he said that I kinda took him seriously and decided that I really would go to Boston and look them up.

On my return to New York I did go to Boston and looked up the dentists, Dr Tony Minichiello and Dr Norman Becker. I went to their office and I was surprised to find that they knew me already. They were young jazz fans years ago when Basie almost made Boston his headquarters. They were very familiar with me and my playing and they were happy that they could do something for me. Being real jazz buffs, I soon found myself at ease as we talked about jazz. They had worked on some pretty good guys in the business, such as Bobby Hackett, Earl Hines, Trummy of course, Jonah Jones, Jack Teagarden, Cozy Cole and a lot of others. I said to myself, "These guys are for me," and soon I was in the dentist chair.

I would sit in the chair and hold my trumpet and they would study everything. I'd even try to play so that they could get certain particulars on my teeth, gums and jaws. In a few weeks they had constructed a plastic shield over my bridgework that prevented my lip from being cut. Then, as time went by, they finally took the entire bridgework out completely and put in a bridge of their own, where I didn't have to have the plastic shield. Dr Becker did nearly all of the work, as Dr Minichiello was under contract to the teamsters' union and couldn't participate in the actual work being done on me. Dr Becker, however, wouldn't do anything unless Dr Minichiello was there at his side and they would hold conferences to see that I had the best they could offer. Sometimes Dr Becker would call in four or five dentists to have their advice on what he should do or what he shouldn't do. His son was among them as he too is a dentist. Every two or three weeks I'd go to Boston and they would work on me. I may have been one of the very few people that lived in New York and went to Boston for a dental appointment.

Meanwhile I decided to ask Julian Dash to arrange an interview with his company, which he did. I went down to his office in lower Manhattan for the interview and was told to prepare for a physical that was necessary to join the organization. I was deathly afraid of taking a physical as I knew that I was in poor shape, but I did go down anyway early one morning. When I got the results of the physical I found that my pressure was still high and, not only that, one of my hernias had re-occurred. I was rejected from the company because of these two misfortunes and soon I was trying to think of something else that I could do, but there weren't many options. I was a musician, a trumpet player, and that was all. I really couldn't do anything else.

I then went to Shouldice Hospital in Toronto, Canada, which does nothing but hernia operations and is the best in the world in this field. They don't advertise but people come there from all over the world—India, Europe, Japan and from almost every country that I could name. It is a beautiful, spacious hospital that looks like a country club. I was impressed right away with the beauty of the place but more impressed with the technique that they used in their operations. Dr Sweeter was the physician who was assigned to my case as he had been familiar with jazz musicians, especially Peter Appleyard, the Canadian vibraharpist who played for some time with Benny Goodman. He wanted to be in charge of my case and we got pretty chummy after a few minutes of conversation. Soon I was in my hospital room waiting for the operation that was to take place the next day.

The following day, early in the morning, I was prepared to have the operation. Nobody rides around in a wheelchair at Shouldice. You walk to the operation room, you are given a local anaesthetic and you are conscious the whole time of the operation. In fact I talked to the nurse the whole time he was doing me up. When it was over I was sewed up with stainless-steel thread and put on my feet and walked back to my room. The very next day I had calesthenics to do. It was weird, all of us guys who had just got off the operation table out there marching around doing exercises. I stayed there two more days before I was sent home. I was in this hospital when Pops and Charlie Shavers died—they both died within a couple of days of each other —and I couldn't go to the funeral of my two great trumpet friends.

Back in New York I still had the problem of finding something to do. First, I had to find a doctor that could get my pressure down as it sure was an obstinate case. I had a great friend in Ben Wright, who would come to my home and do everything that he could to make life easier for me, and God knows I needed it. He would do carpentry work on my home, he rebuilt my kitchen, paneled the walls, did a lot of painting that I was unable to do. All I did was just help him and when I began feeling a little stronger I would go to his apartment on Central Park West and paint his apartment among other things. I found that I was a pretty good wall painter but surely not good enough to make a living doing it. I was glad to be able to do something for Ben, though.

After a few weeks of doing the home improvement bit I hit upon the idea of working at the Musicians' Union Local 802 in New York. I thought it would be rather nice to be working around guys that I had known for so many years and some guys that I liked to be around when I was having so many difficulties. I knew, too, that I wouldn't have to take a physical to work in the union so I called Cliff Glover, who is one of the most respected men at the union. He was, and is, on the executive board and carries a lot of weight there. Andy Kirk was also there and had been for years. I thought it would be great to be working with my old bandleader and inspiration from the Kansas City days.

Cliff was excited at the prospect of my working there with him and right away began making plans for me to come in. There was no openings at the time for new employees but Cliff put my name high on the list of people looking for jobs there and within two weeks he called me and told me to report to work the following Monday. So, once again, it was me and Cliff Glover just like it was in Camp Upton years ago when I was being inducted in the army. I reported to work and Cliff was delighted to have me meet all of the people at the union. A lot of them I knew, naturally. Some I had worked with previously on gigs but the others I had to be introduced to. Everybody seemed to take me as a celebrity and made it their business to make everything there just as easy as possible. Cliff put me with the insurance department of the union and my first job was to screen all the beneficiaries for the deaths of members of the union. Cliff told me to take it easy, and when I had friends who would come by to see me I could take time off and visit them, even go out on the street and have a beer with them if I wanted to as long as I didn't stay out too long.

Soon the word got out that I was working at the union and many people came down there to see if it was true. I would see different guys peeking at me as I was at my desk but I tried not to notice it. Some of my old friends would come by with words of encouragement, like Eddie Barefield, Red Richards, Jackie Williams, Buddy Tate, Earle Warren and a lot of others. I'd stop work and talk with them as long as I wanted to and nobody said anything. Some guys I'd see that I hadn't seen for years as they came in to pay their union dues. Sometimes it would be like a real reunion there in the office. Every Wednesday was a pretty busy day at the union as many guys came in on that day to go to the floor. The floor was the dance floor of the Roseland Ballroom which was in the same building as the union. On the bandstand in the ballroom sat a guy with a microphone calling out names of different musicians who were wanted by certain bandleaders. The floor was usually packed with guys looking for gigs. The upstairs offices of the union got the overflow of the floor, as usually the guys wandered upstairs to shoot the bull with employees of the union or others of their friends who were there for the same reason. On the floor were jazz musicians, big-band musicians, society band musicians and Broadway show musicians, all hoping that they would land a gig somewhere. After the floor was closed about three o'clock they all went around to the China Song, which was the nearest bar, and stayed there until all hours of the evening.

When I first asked Cliff for the job I didn't even think of a salary or what it would be. I was just so happy to be working around him and the other cats that I said to myself I would go into the salary bit after I was on the job. The main thing for me was just to get started. So finally pay day came and I was brought my check over to my desk. I hadn't expected to make a million dollars at the union, but I thought they had made a mistake with my check. Very soon I found out that it had not been a mistake. What I got was all they paid. When the tax and everything was taken out, I made less than a hundred dollars a week. I thought it was worth that much just to get up in the morning and ride that subway in the rush hour and then ride the same rush-hour crowd again that evening. My next thought was, "Well, maybe if I work exceptionally hard I'll get a raise." I continued to work as hard as I could, which wasn't too very much, until one day I asked a friend (who had been there about ten years) if she ever got a raise. She told me, "No. The union isn't famous for paying good salaries but the guys upstairs, the executives, are the only ones here who make the real bread." However, I decided to stick a while. I told Cliff that when they had my payroll check and I was not at my desk, to please put it on the desk, face down. I didn't want anybody to see it. I had seen the time when I'd make that much money in ten minutes, and now I was working a whole week for it. Pretty soon, too, I found that by my "helping" my co-workers do their work I really was doing a lot of their work that they could have done themselves. Cliff knew they were giving me the shaft but he wouldn't tell me. He had decided to let me find it out myself, which I guess he knew I would. So one day I just balked at anything that was more than what I was supposed to do.

I still did enjoy working around the musicians, though, but I never could get used to that salary. Fess Williams, the Chicago bandleader of the twenties, worked there too and he would relate a lot of stories about early Chicago to me. Still, I had it in the back of my mind to look for something else because I was getting nowhere, and fast. I tried to stay there a year so that I could get unemployment insurance but I just couldn't make it a year. I stayed there eleven months before I told Cliff that, even though I loved working there and that I had had a ball with him every day, I had decided to quit. Cliff understood right away. He knew the salaries that were being paid and he couldn't much blame me if I could make more. So I left Local 802.

Then one day the dentists in Boston finished the job and I was told I could go home and start practicing again. You can't imagine how happy this made me but still I wasn't sure of myself. I had been away from my trumpet now for such a long time and I wasn't really too sure that I'd ever be able to play again, even with all the fine work they had done on me. I didn't have any chops at all. Even when I was playing at my very best I'd always feel insecure when I missed even a few days of playing, but now here I was, not having played for years. I used to wonder, and I still do, if I had become too old to try to play, as a trumpet is a very physical instrument and I thought that perhaps there wasn't a chance of my building up my lip muscles. Clark Terry would encourage me to go ahead and try anyway, so I did.

I'll never forget the first time after the dental work that I picked up that horn. I must have spent a half hour just trying to get some kind of a sound out of it. After what seemed like an eternity a little note peeped out and I was on my way. One of the first things I did was to try to play that solo on *Close to You* by the Carpenters, that I couldn't play before my layoff. Normally it was an easy solo, but for me it was one hell of a challenge. In a few days, however, I had it. It was then that I realized that I might just play again after all. I still couldn't play over two or three bars at a time but it was progress. After some weeks of practice I got a little better and I began to get my courage back, but not entirely. I was afraid to play in public but, still, I sounded pretty good to myself when I practiced.

After several weeks of practicing I was asked to play at the New School, which was a school newly formed to not only teach but to sponsor concerts for the general public in different forms of art. This concert was to feature trumpets. There was to be such names as Ruby Braff, Clark Terry, Howard McGhee, Art Farmer, Jimmy McPartland and myself. Whoever booked this concert must not have known that I hadn't played for some time. However, I decided to try to play anyway, as perhaps I could use this as a steppingstone to continue with my playing. After some weeks of practicing I thought that I would be able to at least make an appearance. I went to the rehearsal the afternoon before the concert and things were not too bad. Everyone played the selections that they were to play at the concert that night, and even I didn't sound too bad, but when the time came for the concert everything seemed to change. The first half of the concert went well and then came the second half in which I was supposed to play. I was to follow Howard McGhee. I went on stage to a thunderous applause and, as the music started, I picked up my trumpet and went on to sound simply awful. I felt so bad that I sneaked out of the concert by the back door, as I just couldn't explain why I sounded like that. I ran into some people that had come out of the building a little early and I told them that my lip was sore, but still I couldn't explain why I had taken the gig in the first place.

After about three months of practice I got a call one day from Wilma Dobie, who had heard that I was practicing again and wanted to know if she could give me a coming-back party with several of my old buddies participating, especially all of my good old trumpet pals. I thought about it for some time. I even dreamed about it and it was weeks before I gave her my decision, which was that I really would like to have the party, which was to be sponsored by the Overseas Press Club where Wilma was one of the executives, especially since I would be playing again and with all my main dudes. At last I was going to play again in public and with all my guys.

When I arrived at the party, which was held at the Biltmore Hotel, I was surprised to see all of these guys. Some I hadn't seen for years, but there they were: Doc Cheatham, Jacques Butler, Scoville Brown, Earle Warren, Eddie Barefield, and loads of other guys. They were so happy to see me and I was overjoyed at seeing them. Wilma had invited my two dentists to attend and sent them a special ticket to be on hand, which they accepted. I spoke with them and after a few speeches the jazz got going and I was actually on the bandstand playing. Dicky Wells came in after a few minutes and soon we were all wrapped up in *Perdido*. Frankly, I was at least playing but I sure wasn't playing too good. Still, I was happy and everybody else was happy, or at least they seemed to be. I guess it didn't matter too much if I wasn't playing good, the main thing was that I was playing. I missed notes all over the place and there was so much missing in the playing. If there's one thing that bugs hell out of me, it's to miss a note.

We jammed for about three hours on all of the favorite standard songs and I hadn't forgotten a single one during my absence from the trumpet. I couldn't play but one chorus at a time before my chops would give out but we were having a ball. I knew what I wanted to do but I just couldn't do it. Still, I was happy and the party ended being a success. Later, in 1977, Wilma gave another concert, "Buck Clayton and Friends Remember Lady Day." This time I was leader again after so many years of hoping that some day I might make the level where I could be leader again. I never did care too much about being a leader but it was nice to know that I was capable.

About this time Ben Wright was still at Clairol. He was one of the executives there who was very much interested in what Clairol did for black people—not only in their products, but for obtaining jobs for black people at the company. My wife Pat was working with Ben as his secretary there, as she was a very good friend of Ben's wife, Jeanne. One day Ben came by my home with a gentleman that I had never seen before, K. C. Coulter. He and Ben had just formed a new black company for advertising in the leading black journals. They were to issue a supplement for these papers, which came out weekly over all of the United States. Ben, knowing that I had just left the union, asked me if I'd like to work with him and K. C. Coulter. He thought that my name might be advantageous in selling the commodities to the leading buyers in the big offices in downtown Manhattan. I told them that I didn't know a damn thing about the business of selling these things like that, but I'd be willing to learn. K. C. Coulter said, "Don't worry about that, I'll teach you everything that you'll need to know. I'll coach you on everything." So I thought that it might be a pretty good idea too. I'd learn something that I knew nothing about and, besides, I wouldn't worry—K. C. Coulter was going to be with me on everything.

I reported to their office on 42nd Street and Fifth Avenue and was given a big book on statistics on black people. I was to learn what percent of black people used a certain brand of cigarettes, whiskey, textiles and other such goods. I was in the office about two days before I found out that K. C. Coulter was the most unpleasant boss I'd ever had. I think he didn't trust me from the first day and at the time I didn't know why. When I'd be in the middle of an appointment, the phone would ring and it would be him asking if I actually showed up at my scheduled appointment, just as if he had expected me to go to a bar or something. I think that he thought that I was put in the office for the sole reason of reporting everything he did back to Ben, but that thought had never entered my mind nor had ever been discussed by me with anyone.

Soon I was making so many appointments a day that I was always on the street downtown in the high-risers. To tell the truth, I never did get too crazy about selling these goods. I would have liked to, but once you go into one of those plush offices, like on Fifth Avenue, and you take one look at the guy sitting behind the desk, looking at you like he's trying to psych you out, you know he's not going to buy a damn thing anyway. Still, you have to try, as they stare at you like you're crazy. All the guys used to call them the real blue-eyed devils. After they'd let you talk as long as you wanted to, they'd say, "OK, we'll give you a call." And that would be the end of it. One time I studied my percentage book all night in order to show this guy the next day that I knew exactly what I was talking about. I think it was for woollen blankets. I knew every percentage there was on black people and woollen blankets. The guy behind the desk let me ramble on and on about why it was necessary for him to place an ad in our papers because it would enlighten more black people to use their brand of woollen blankets. Then, after I had told this cat everything that I had studied the night before, which took about a half hour, he looked up at me with those deadly blue eyes and said, "Gee, son, you really came loaded for bear didn't you?" I think he was secretly laughing at me for being studious for no reason at all. He knew all the time he wasn't going to buy a damn thing. On some of my appointments I'd find people that knew me when I was playing and, sometimes, when I'd go into their office to talk about an advertisement, they'd close the doors and we'd talk about nothing but jazz and jazz musicians that I knew and had worked with.

This went on and on, it seemed. I was walking up and down the streets of New York morning, noon and evening, sometimes. Fifth Avenue, Third Avenue, Lexington and all the big streets. Rain or shine I'd be there, walking most of the time. K. C. Coulter got worse and worse at the office and was always inviting me to find something else to do. I didn't like this at all because it was he and Ben who got me into all this mess in the first place; I'm sure that without his and Ben's insistence I'd have never accepted this job of being a salesman. My attitude towards selling was, "If they don't want to buy anything, then to hell with 'em." I'm sure that this doesn't come up to the standards of a real salesman. There are some very successful salesmen, I know, but they are usually the guys who are "in," to the extent that they play golf with all of the principal buyers and many a deal in selling is made on the links. However, I wasn't in that league by a long shot. I wouldn't have minded being one of those guys but I didn't have the connections and had to do it the hard way, which was to walk, walk, walk.

Finally K.C. had me being an errand boy, which was pretty hard to swallow after once being a great name in music. Still, I did it. He'd send me over to the Greyhound bus station sometimes to pick up a parcel and bring it back to him at the office. I'd go to the post office to buy stamps for the correspondence, and in so many ways he let me know that I was just an errand boy. Finally, one rainy day I was a few minutes late in coming to the office and he proceeded to bawl me out in front of everybody, so it was then that I told Idi Amin to shove it.

I went on back to Long Island, not having a job now, and tried to think of something else that I could do, but by this time I had decided that all I could really do was stay in the music field. While I had plenty of time to think about it, I sometimes would pass my time in a neighborhood bar around the corner from my home in which there was a pool table.

I soon found myself spending hours and hours in this bar. There was only one person there who knew who I was, and that was the barmaid, Joyce. Joyce had at one time aspired to be a vocalist in Baltimore and she knew me from my Count Basie days. She never told any of the guys that hung out in there who I was because, I guess, she didn't want to drag me by saying that I had once been in the same league with all of the popular musicians of the day. So she just let the other guys learn from me what my name was and all that jazz. Very soon I was a regular patron at the bar and sometimes I would shoot pool for ten or twelve hours a day. I learned the names of all the guys: Smiley, Al, Roy, Owens, Randy, Flowers, and so many others. I became pretty good at shooting pool, although it wasn't the kind of pool I learned in my early days in Los Angeles as we played on what they call three-quarter tables, which aren't as large as a standard-size table. I became pretty good and as a result I would come home blind every evening because it was a rule that the winner of a game would win a drink, and you could tell by seeing me come home that I had won a lot of games. There was one cat, though, that nobody could beat. His name was Indian. He was a little West Indian guy whose real name was Morgan. I could never beat him and I knew it, but I would play him just for the experience. I figured, "It's better to play someone that you can't beat so that you can pick up something that you didn't know." Naturally, my name in the bar was "Cat Eye," which was an appropriate name for a poolroom hustler. At night when I'd go to bed I'd think to myself, "Well, here I am just where I was forty years ago, shooting pool."

I decided to continue my practice but had decided not to take any more gigs until I got better so I passed up quite a few jobs. I still was arranging for different bands and one day Hank O'Neal of Chiaroscuro records called me to ask me about reviving the *Buck Clayton Jam Sessions* that I had made for Columbia years ago. This time they were to be a little different in that we would have half arranged music and half solos. He and George Avakian, who was so influential in the early *Buck Clayton Jam Sessions*, along with John Hammond, wanted to know if I would do all of the arranging and we would have a big session. I liked the idea and soon we were with it.

I made four originals and in such a way that every man had a riff, or rhythm pattern, under his solo when he played. I myself was not going to record for a while but, still, the recording was to be under my name and I was to make all of the arrangements. "Good," I thought to myself, and we went about seeing just who we could get for the session. Earl Hines happened to be in town at the time and we grabbed him real quick. We had Joe Newman and Doc Cheatham on trumpets, Urbie Green on trombone, Zoot Sims and Budd Johnson on tenor saxes, Earle Warren on alto sax, Joe Temperley, my old buddy from Humphrey Lyttelton's band, on baritone sax, Milt Hinton on bass and Gus Johnson on drums. It was a gas. We all ended up swinging like crazy. Later we made more sessions, but with different guys. One thing that I found out was that it had become increasingly more difficult to find jazz artists as so many had passed on, and sometimes the few who were still on the scene were under contract to other companies and were not available to us. However, we did get some very good guys on later recordings, such as Sweets and Bob Wilber. I had decided to wait at least a year before I would blow on the sessions.

One day after spending the whole afternoon at the bar with my pool-playing buddies, I came home and I felt a little bit more tired than I had been usually. I went to the drug store and bought some vitamin pills and thought no more about it. However, after two or three weeks I still felt no better and, besides, people were beginning to tell me that I looked pale and had no color. I guess I should have taken more precautions concerning my health, but I really didn't think there was anything seriously wrong and went on with my daily routine, which wasn't too much of anything. I even visited my home town, Parsons, with my sister Jean and her husband, as we had some unfinished business there of selling our old house. Our old home had gone into decay and it was cheaper to sell it than to pay taxes on it, so we all went to Parsons and I was never so surprised in my whole life when I saw how Parsons had changed since I was a kid there.

As we drove into town, I couldn't believe it. There were no more railroad buildings, no stations, in fact there were no more trains running in or out of Parsons. The only transportation was by bus or by car, except for a small airport on the outskirts of town. The center of the town was a beautiful mall. The streets were beautiful. There was no traffic in the center of town. Main Street was just one beautiful street that seemed more like a dream. As I walked down these streets I recalled so many of the devilish things that we used to do there. It just didn't seem real someway, but there it was. As I walked with my sis, there was beautiful music being piped from the buildings that led to a kinda heavenly atmosphere. All day there was this beautiful music. It wasn't jazz music, of course, but it was beautiful. The shops were modern and had the latest in men's wear and women's. I really was proud of my home town.

I visited my old piano teacher, Mrs Walker, and some of my old teachers that were still with us. While I was visiting one of my former teachers she sent for someone to come to her house and fix a broken window. As we were all talking about when I was a kid, a rather young man came and began to repair the window. When he was finished I was introduced to him and it turned out that he was the mayor of the town. I asked my former teacher how in hell did she get the mayor of the town to come and fix her window. She told me that he would have felt slighted if she hadn't called him because his hobby was fixing things like that.

On returning to New York I still felt a little weak. I just couldn't understand it. Too, I was gaining weight. I seemed to become heavier every day and still weaker. Then one day, on a Sunday morning, I went to shave myself sitting down in a chair. Then, about an hour later, I had to go to the toilet. When I got up off the toilet stool it was a bright bloody red. It looked like someone had slaughtered an ox, there was so much blood. I almost had a heart attack as I looked at all that blood but still I didn't know what was happening nor why. I was so scared. My first thought was that perhaps I had swallowed some glass in some way and was bleeding inside, but still I couldn't think of ever having done anything like that. I guess it was from panic that I thought that but still it was there, all that blood. I flushed the bowl as I didn't want Pat to see it. Right away she called a cab and we were on our way to Jamaica Hospital, which was the nearest hospital to our home.

When we arrived at the hospital I was almost too weak to walk to the emergency room and had to be helped out of the cab. Once in the emergency room I saw patients waiting in the room with tubes in their noses. I remember thinking to myself, "Gee, I hope they don't put those things in my nose." Soon a nurse came over to me and began taking some tests on me, such as my blood pressure, my blood count and everything. I laid on that bed, it seemed, for hours. There were several patients there before me and they too were waiting their turn. By it being on a Sunday, there were not too many doctors there and all I could do was wait. I waited and waited with Pat but still nobody came. I began to get very drowsy and felt like I should go to sleep. I told Pat to please go and see if she could get someone to come and look at me, because I felt that if I went to sleep I wouldn't wake up.

Just as she was going up some stairs to inquire about a doctor, two doctors came running down the stairs. They were yelling, "Mr Clayton, Mr Clayton. Which one of you is Mr Clayton?" When they learned that I was Mr Clayton, one of them, a Chinese doctor, rolled up my coat and shirt sleeve and started giving me a blood transfusion right there on the spot. They had to cut deep into my arm to find an artery, as all of my veins had collapsed and they were forced to dig deep. In a few minutes they had that tube in my nose that I had dreaded so much, and I was on my way to intensive care. When they rolled me into the intensive care unit there was a nurse there, Miss True, that I later found to be the most efficient, dedicated and the kindest nurse that I had ever seen. She really seemed to love her patients and never tired of helping them at all times. As they rolled me in she looked down on me and said, "Well, look here, we have a gray-eyed bleeder." Soon several doctors were working on me—East Indian doctors, Chinese doctors, American doctors and one French doctor. They all looked like a miniature League of Nations around my bed. I was in shock I was told later, but still I remember everything that happened. My heart was pounding like a triphammer and soon they had all kinds of machines around my bed. One of the machines, that they used to try to regulate my heart, looked like a piano.

I noticed that they were not talking to me but were talking to Pat in a corner all by herself. I thought to myself, "This must be pretty bad because when they don't talk directly to you, and talk to your kin, you can bet it's pretty bad. Finally, after a couple of hours, Pat was able to talk to me before she went back home. All she said was, "You're pretty sick." I told her that I knew that, but how sick?

I was put on the critical list and I stayed on that critical list for over two weeks. The doctors told me that I had been very lucky because, in the first place, if I had gone to another hospital it would have been necessary to transfer me to Jamaica Hospital because they were the only ones with the proper equipment that was vital to my case. And if I had been transferred I probably wouldn't have made it in time and would have been DOA at the hospital. I only went to Jamaica Hospital because it was nearest to my home. My blood count was low enough to be considered fatal.

Soon I had tubes—tubes everywhere. The intensive care unit was a pretty dismal place. All hours of the day and night patients would moan and cry—sometimes scream. There were so many different kinds of sounds coming from those very sick people. I guess I myself was just about as sick as they were, but to me it didn't seem that way—not yet. I knew that I had been bleeding internally for weeks but the symptoms hadn't shown until that Sunday morning. The bleeding was not showing in my digestive tract but was going into my body without being shown until that black Sunday morning. I was distended where I thought I was gaining weight. I didn't have any kind of color and my complexion was like a sheet of white paper.

As I settled down in intensive care I tried to make the best of it. At the time I had no intentions of dying but still, every day it seemed, someone in intensive care would die and soon I wasn't too sure that I would walk out of that hospital alive. Only my close kin could visit me and even then only two persons at a time. I sure felt isolated by not being able to have a telephone. Candy came to visit me with Pat and she started crying at the sight of me with all these tubes in me. She had never before seen me like that and she just couldn't control her feelings, even though she did try.

Soon, after a couple of days of trying to stop the bleeding, I was given tests to determine the cause of the bleeding. I was found to have a gastric ulcer. I was treated for this ulcer, and when the bleeding did stop I had to make the decision as to whether or not I wanted to have an operation. If I had chosen to keep the ulcer and not have an operation I would have had to treat it by being on diet. It would have been necessary to treat it all the rest of my life, and I would not have been able to eat so many things that I liked. I didn't like that idea so much so I decided to go ahead and have the operation. I had known some guys that were treating their ulcers and at times had to eat baby food.

I selected Dr W. V. Cordice to be my surgeon. He had been recommended to me by Ben Wright and was one of the best surgeons in the business. He had operated many times before at Jamaica Hospital but was not on their staff. He had his own private business and stayed so busy that I considered myself lucky that he would be my doctor. He had been chief medical doctor on Doctor Martin Luther King when he was stabbed once in Harlem by a distraught woman. In a few days after getting my blood pressure down, which had been pretty high, Dr Cordice decided that my physical condition would have to be built up before having an operation because in my present condition I was far too weak. So I was given everything possible to build up my strength. I ate ice cream for days.

As I remained in the ICU I saw so many people die, that I think it got to me psychologically. I began more and more to feel that I wasn't going to make it either. There was a man who looked a lot like Coleman Hawkins, who entered intensive care on a Friday. He came in with his wife and young daughter and one son. Another son who lived out of New York came in later. When he came in he was joking with the nurses and his family. He had a history of bleeding and it wasn't too long before they were working on him and there were no more jokes. They hooked a long rope to a weight and in some way attached this rope in his nose and let it dangle over the curtain rod of his bed that was used to shield him for privacy. When he saw this he raised hell. He said, "I can't stand this. I can't stand it. I'd rather be dead than have this thing in my nose. I can't stand it." Finally his wife left with her kids and he was still complaining. I was watching all this as I was just across the room from his bed. In less than two days he started to become delirious. I thought to myself, "Poor guy." I think I'd have been delirious too if they put that contraption in my nose. I listened to him talk to himself at night when everybody else was asleep. I remember him talking about a lock on his door at home. I thought, too bad. This fellow who came in so cheerful with his family just a couple of days ago was now just a human mass of misery. The next day they took this thing off of him but by this time I don't think he knew it nor cared anymore. The next day, Mother's Day, he erupted again and for hours the nurses and docs tried unsuccessfully to stop the bleeding. They never did get it under control and he got worse and worse. I heard the head nurse tell one of the other nurses to call his wife on the phone. I knew this wasn't good as they wouldn't call his wife unless it was very serious. His wife wasn't at home. I suppose that she was at Mother's Day services at church, anyway they never could contact her as he got worse. He was now bleeding inwardly *and* outwardly. The head nurse put in an emergency call on all of the loudspeakers in the hospital and in just a few minutes the room was filled with every doctor that was available or, rather, every doctor that was not busy with a patient. There were so many doctors around his bed that I could no longer see him but I could hear them call out for suction, suction, suction.

When the nurses saw me looking they made arrangements to get me out of the room, as they didn't want me to see all of this. They called for a wheelchair to move me out of the room and into another hall where I couldn't see, but before they wheeled me out I could see, over all of these doctors' heads, his hands waving in the air and he was yelling, "Oh, my heart, my heart . . ." Then silence. I could see the docs giving him artificial respiration, but he was gone before they could get me out of the room. When they did put me back in my bed he was just lying there dead. They finally contacted his wife and she came back with her daughter and two sons and they started making preparations to take him to a funeral parlor. After he was removed from the room on that death wagon, I called it, where he was placed and strapped, another young girl patient was brought in for internal bleeding and placed in that same bed that he had occupied, and in just another couple of days she died too of the bleeding.

There was another young girl there, next to my bed, that had been in an automobile accident and had been in a coma for weeks and was only kept alive by machines. Her boyfriend used to come by to see her, but she wasn't really alive and he would just look at her for long moments and silently cry. One day, quite suddenly, she started to bleed. Blood was spurting everywhere and once again came this call for suction. In a few more minutes she was dead and I could hear the nurse call the office to say there was another expiration there.

These things were really getting to me and I began to think of Duke Ellington, who was in another hospital at the time. Duke had entered the hospital some time before I entered and nobody knew for sure if he'd make it or not. There was so much death around me that it really made me wonder if I was going to make it or not. It had such a psychological effect on me that I finally came to the conclusion that I was going to die on May 6. I don't know why I had that day in mind, but I just knew that on May 6 I'd be gone. I even began to wonder which one of my dark suits would be used to put me in my coffin. I began to have strange dreams about so many former friends who had died, such as Herschel Evans, Lips Page, Prez and so many others. I dreamed that I could see their names in the night sky. One night when everyone in ICU was asleep, about two thirty in the morning, I woke up and heard a very soft sound coming from a small radio that belonged to one of the nurses. It was playing a melody that I'd never heard and it was sure a haunting melody. Then came the vocal. It sounded just as if I were listening to Billie Holiday singing. It seemed that Billie was singing this song and at the same time beckoning for me to join her. It seemed that Billie was saying, "Come on, Bucket, come on with me."

When I did wake up the next morning I just couldn't forget this. I kept hearing that voice and that tune and hearing Billie calling me. (Some time later, after I had left the hospital, I made it my business to find out what the name of that song was and who was singing it, as I'd never heard Billie sing it. After I visited several music stores in Manhattan and had sung the song to clerks who didn't know the name of it, I finally hit on it and found the song to be *Midnight at the Oasis* and the singer was Maria Muldaur, who I didn't know at all.)

After a couple more weeks I began to take on more weight and get stronger. It was then that Dr Cordice decided that the operation could be performed with no danger and the day finally came for the operation. I was operated on early in the morning and the operation was successful. When I woke up in the recovery room I was taken back to ICU for more treatment. In about a week I was informed that I no longer required intensive care and, happily, I was transferred to another room to recuperate. I was really happy as so many people never get out of ICU. It still wasn't May 6, though, and I still had that feeling that I wouldn't be here after the 6th. I was placed in a room with a fellow who had had a stroke and couldn't move. I felt so sorry for the guy. He couldn't eat, he couldn't move, he couldn't go to the bathroom by himself, in fact he couldn't do anything by himself. I felt terribly sorry when his brother would come to visit him and cry and say to me, "I might just as well be coming to see you, as he doesn't seem to even know that I'm here."

Finally the night of May 5 came and I wondered what would happen to me during the night, but when I woke up the next morning, May 6, I was still alive and I said to myself, "Well, it's May 6 and I'm still here, so I just might as well try to get well." After that I really began to look forward to being on the scene again and in a few more days I was placed in another room, which was still considered to be an improvement, but when I was wheeled into this room I found it to be more like a pool hall. The guys in there were doing everything that they shouldn't have been doing. They were smoking in bed, cussing, talking like convicts and I soon saw that I wasn't going to like that room at all. There was one guy there who had raped a woman and was trying to convince everybody that some women want to be raped. He said that some women had been alone for so long that they enjoyed being raped and he was doing them a favor by raping them. He was crazy, really crazy. One time when a nurse was trying to give him an injection in his hip he jerked the needle from her hand and stuck it in her. I can't forget the sight of that nurse running down the hall with that syringe sticking out of her hips. He wasn't there much longer after that. The next morning I saw cops all over the place and they told this cat that he was going home to Brooklyn, but once they got him in the ambulance they took him to Creedmore, which is a hospital for crazy people. I know he must have raised hell on arriving there but he was in the company of a lot of policemen.

The rest of my stay at Jamaica Hospital was pretty normal. I improved from the critical list to the serious list and finally from the serious list to the stable list. Finally the day came when I could go home and I packed my stuff and rode home with my brother-in-law Freddie. Being back home was so strange to me. I was so weak I could hardly stand but at least I was considered well. I tried to walk two blocks away from home and got so tired that I thought for a while that I'd have to call someone to help me back home, but somehow I made it. I felt like I was a little chicken who had just been hatched from the egg. I had spent five weeks in that hospital and had lost weight like crazy but I was well and considered myself very lucky. Now I could get on with the business of living.

TWELVE

Still swinging

After some more weeks of recuperating I began to think of making arrangements, which was the easiest thing I could think of, so I let people know
that I had begun arranging again. Soon I received a call from my good friend
Earl Hines. Earl had known of my troubles and had decided that he
wanted me to make some arrangements for his small group. I was happy to
hear this and soon I was making the charts for Earl. I was back in music
which was the main thing. Even after that, when I made an arrangement for
Earl, I never charged him the same as I would other people. Sometimes I
charged him about as half as much as other bandleaders. The same goes for
Humphrey Lyttelton. I'd never charge him like other people because he did
everything in his power to get me back into music by having me make
arrangements for his band.

I continued to arrange and soon found myself making more money than I
could have ever made doing something else. I wondered why I ever went
to work at the union in the first place. By arranging I was my own boss. I
could get up when I wanted to, work when I felt like it, have no one to tell
me what to do nor when to do it. I was happy again. I don't mean to say that
arranging is easy, it's not. I work when I feel like it, but still some days I
may work fifteen hours a day if I'm into it. I may get up at 2.30 a.m. and
work until noon the next day if it's something that I really dig. When people
would see me going to a movie in the afternoon they'd never know that I
had just spent maybe ten or twelve hours making an arrangement. Sometimes
I've seen the sun come up as I was writing and set that evening as I was still
writing, but I loved every minute of it. I don't know how many arrangements
I've made that I've never heard played. I have made arrangements for bands
in Europe that I've never heard, because when I'd send them off to whoever
ordered them that would be the last of it—unless perhaps they were recorded
and I'd hear my work long after I had made it. I'd never know if I had made
mistakes or not but I never got any complaints, so I guess they were alright.

I still hadn't given up hope of playing again and continued to practice;
even though I sounded worse than any amateur, I was at least blowing
something. Then I got a telephone call from a friend of mine, Dave Burns,
who was a government official in Washington and also a musician on the
side. He had his own jazz band in Washington called the Hot Mustard Band,
where he played bass. He called me and told me that he had chosen me to
make a State Department tour of Africa and asked me if I'd agree to go. I

had only ever been to North Africa, when I played Morocco and Algiers with Mezz Mezzrow several years before, but I wanted so much to see what is called black Africa. So, even though I wasn't playing much, I accepted the tour but I told Dave that I surely wasn't playing my best. It didn't matter to him; he thought I should make it anyway. So we signed with the State Department to make the tour. The executive officer was Mrs Corinne Heditsian who was stationed in Paris, France.

Soon we, Dave and I, had hired the fellows we were going to use on the trip. We had John Phillips, who was a very talented pianist from Washington, DC. Then there was Bull Moose Jackson, who was an excellent performer and a beautiful singer with a rich voice that had captivated audiences in New York in previous years with Lucky Millinder and several other bands at the Savoy Ballroom in Harlem. He played tenor sax and, along with his beautiful voice, could be nothing short of a sensation in Africa. On the drums we asked Jackie Williams, who was one of my favorite drummers, to make the trip, to which he readily agreed. So, after rehearsing several weeks at Dave's home in Washington, we finally boarded the plane for Africa on 29th April 1977. We were met in Paris by Mrs Heditsian and given the list of countries we were to play. We were to start in Athens, Greece, which for some reason was on the State Department list. Then we were to play Khartoum, Sudan; Cairo, Egypt; Algiers; Conakry, Guinea; Monrovia, Liberia; Abidjan, Ivory Coast; and Nouakchott, Mauritania.

In Athens we were met by the promoter that I had met before in the States by the name of Luis Vilas. Naturally, the first thing we did was to visit the Acropolis with its beautiful ruins. We all took pictures of the surroundings and the Parthenon, which impressed us immensely. Mr Vilas invited us to several dinners and showed us a great time. I was given a beautiful dinner of sardines, which is a standard dinner in Greece, but to me it was an experience because the only sardines I'd ever seen were in cans. These were fresh and too large to be put in cans. The Greek music also was very interesting to me as they play in so many different tempos, which was so different from American music. Another thing that was so different was that, when we went to a nightclub and the entertainers completed their act, instead of applauding as we do in America the audience would throw their glasses that they had been drinking from onto the stage. There would be a little guy to come on the stage with a broom and sweep up all the broken glass. Then at the next show the same thing would happen. So, just to be in line, the next act I threw my glass on the stage and nobody even noticed or looked at me as they were all doing the same thing. The breaking of the glasses was one way of showing the actors that they had been well received. The concert that night was a complete success. It took place in a sports palace and it was filled to the rafters. When we first arrived in Greece we were a bit apprehensive about going through with the concert, as we had been told that there was an anti-American movement going on at the time, but the audience loved the jazz. I thought of my wrestler idol who had showed me so many things when I was a kid in Parsons; he was a Greek, Billy Hallas.

The next day, before leaving, we revisited the Acropolis and took more photographs and that night were given a farewell dinner, which this time was a delicious meal of liver cooked in a special way. I don't know how they cooked it as it is a special recipe that only the Greek people use and, although I've tried since to cook liver the same way, I was nowhere close.

In Khartoum Jackie and myself toured the city on our first day of arrival. Jackie and I were running buddies as we were the only ones from New York and, too, we had been good friends for years. We were so impressed with the way the Africans dressed, the bright colors, the way everybody looked, the way many of them walked on the highways, as there was no way of transportation except by wagons drawn by horses and by foot, which was the way most people traveled. We visited the museums and went to all the historical places and in general enjoyed ourselves very much. The concerts went well also, which made me very happy. The color of the skin of so many Africans in Khartoum impressed me. They ranged from a light tan to an almost blue-black, and in the countryside they hardly wore any clothes and lived in huts with no electric lights. In the market square there were hundreds milling about buying their daily needs. We bought a few souvenirs, which I treasure very much today. After all, this was the continent where my ancestors came from and I was occupied in seeing so many people that looked like they had just came from Harlem except for their dress. Some even looked like relatives of mine.

In Cairo we really could hardly wait to get to Giza, which is near Cairo and the site of the Sphinx and the pyramids. Before even unpacking our bags we were in the street hailing a cab to take us to Giza. We were all jubilant at the thought of seeing these wonders of the world. In the cab going to Giza we could see in the distance these huge things that looked like mountains, only they were pointed at the top. As we left the cab we were immediately surrounded by camel drivers urging us to take their camels and make the trip through the desert to the pyramids. Riding a camel was something I had never expected to do in my life, but in a matter of seconds there I was on top of a camel. It certainly wasn't easy getting on these big desert caravans but, still, it was worse when we tried to dismount. The camels bend their front legs and it is really complicated as you feel that you are going right over the camel's head and land in the sand, but somehow no one fell.

Again, Jackie and I went and marveled at these pyramids that we had heard of all of our lives and, after taking hundreds of photographs, we decided that we would do more by going into the center of the pyramids. We found a guide that would take us to the interior of the pyramid Khufu, which was the largest. We went down some steps with a very low ceiling where we had to bend over to get to the bottom and we were shown large rooms where at one time the kings and pharaohs of Egypt had kept their valuables. These had long since been burglarized by thieves. We were also shown where they lived in very large rooms. It was very cool down there as that, I guess, was the forerunner of air conditioning. While moving from place to place in this underground I almost slipped over a deep pit, which I was told was the burial pit of slaves that died during the making of these pyramids.

Once again on the outside, we just looked in amazement at the structure of these monuments and, I guess, like all other people of the world, wondered just how they managed to get these huge two-ton stones all the way up to the top. There seemed to be millions of them. We were told that at one time the pyramids were beautiful. After placing the large stones, which came from miles away as they certainly didn't come from the desert, they were all covered by a beautiful layer of special white sand. Today there is only a section of this white sand that remains at the top of some of the pyramids. We rode around the Sphinx with its broken nose, which was a result of the war with the Turks years ago. Going back to take the cab, we were followed by these desert hustlers who were trying to sell us everything including the Egyptian beetles called scarabs, which are supposed to bring good luck. Before taking the cab back to Cairo we all went in the souvenir stores and bought all kinds of camel-skin luggage and other reminders of this great trip.

In Algiers I didn't make any excursions as I had already been there before, but Bull Moose just had to see the Casbah so the other guys went out on their own.

In Conakry, Guinea, we were met by officials from the American embassy and taken to an apartment building where we were lodged. I didn't see a single hotel the whole two days that we were there. In fact, I didn't see even a post office. Guinea was a rather poor country and it showed. Dave acted as our manager, as he had been there before, and we all settled in our rooms in this apartment building. At the break of day the following morning we were awakened by the roosters in the neighborhood. It was a very peculiar feeling as the roosters seemed to have special timing to crow. First one would crow, then some distance away another one would crow, and this went on for some time. But the strangest thing was that they didn't crow like American roosters; they had an entirely different accent. I had previously thought that all roosters sounded the same, but there was just as much difference between the Conakry roosters and American roosters as there was between the Guinea language and the American language. Then, too, many of the Conakry citizens would keep their roosters on a leash like we keep dogs on a leash in America.

We started out to take photos of the city, but were quickly advised not to try because of the Castro influence there. Everywhere we looked we would see signs of Castro and the taking of photos, especially by Americans, was absolutely forbidden, so we went back to the apartment. All we could do was to sneak taking pictures out of our windows. We were advised not even to carry our cameras over our shoulders as they might be taken to the Cuban soldiers.

The second night of our concerts there we noticed a flurry of action and excitement and we wondered why. About an hour before we were to begin we were told that the President of Guinea was to come to the concert. I had been speaking French so far to the African audiences and I was asked to make a welcoming speech to the President. We couldn't start the concert until President Ahmed Sekou Tourré arrived, so while everyone was running around like crazy we waited. Finally the military band started playing the president's anthem and in he came with about fifty people in his party. As we went on stage to begin I made a special speech to the president in French, welcoming him to the concert. He seemed to like that very much as he hadn't expected to hear this coming from an American. At the end of the concert he had some of his staff come backstage and invited me to come to his table, where he talked briefly to me about how he liked the show and thanked me for making the welcoming gesture. I thought when I went to his table that there would certainly be champagne there as he was the president, but all they had was orange juice and that wasn't even cold. However, he liked everything. Then we left for the next city.

In Monrovia we were again met by officials from the American embassy, and taken on a trip to see the city. We were in a beautiful hotel and it was a pleasure just being there where everyone spoke English, the only city we had played where English was the spoken language, due to the fact that it was founded by American slaves in 1822. The only mishap occurred one night when my passport was stolen, along with my wallet, but fortunately, being in the capital, and thanks to Dave and other officials, I was able to get another passport in a couple of days.

In Abidjan, on the Ivory Coast, we were reminded so much of the gay cities like Paris and New York, except that all decorations and architecture were strictly African. One of the most beautiful hotels I've ever seen was all in African design, with huge elephant tusks and water brooks running all through the hotel. Again we loaded ourselves down with souvenirs, especially myself. I think I could have opened up a souvenir shop in New York if I was lucky enough to get back with all of my souvenirs. Every evening there would be all kinds of animal skins sold by hunters that had made their daily hunting results, and you could buy anything from leopard skins to huge snakeskins. After seven o'clock in the evening you would literally have to step over so many animal pelts and skins to get to a taxi in the street.

In Mauritania, where I'd never been, everything was strange. By being in the Sahara Desert, everyone wore masks over their faces and in a sandstorm they resembled ghosts walking around in the streets. The sandstorms seemed to be every few hours and at times you couldn't see over a few feet in the distance, but anyway it was a new experience to us Americans who had never seen so much sand except at the beaches.

After arriving back in New York from Africa, nothing earth-shattering happened for a while until one day I was asked if I'd be interested in taking over a jazz class at Hunter College. Milt Hinton, my old friend who at that time lived near me in St Albans, Queens, had been the jazz professor at Hunter College before me, but had had to quit the position because of his many other businesses. Nancy Elliott had submitted my name to her professor of oral jazz, Charles Schwartz. In just a matter of days I received a call from Louis Martin, who was chairman of the jazz projects at Hunter, asking me to come by the school for an interview with some of the faculty. I made the appointment and the interview took place. The order of professors all were enthusiastic that I was going to be with them. There were some jazz fans who were professors there, including Dean Hugh Scott and Dick Smallens, who was a math teacher but also sang in some of the popular spots in New

York when he wasn't too busy with the numbers and decimal points. So in 1978 I started to be Professor Jazz at the swank Hunter College of the City University of New York, CUNY.

Not having been a teacher before, I had planned already just how I was going to proceed with the classes of green kids that had never played in any kind of group before but still knew how to play their horns. I had planned to form a jazz band by making some simple arrangements so that they would experience the feeling of playing together. The first day of class things went pretty well. The kids were all scared that they wouldn't make the grade, playing with someone else. However, in a few minutes I had them all playing standard songs with the feeling that they were part of a team. I had little girls who aspired to be singers, who had never sung in front of a band nor any other group. They quickly became used to playing and singing with a group. I had some pretty good singers that I think will be famous some day in the future if they continue to carry on, such as Angela Bullock, Terry Haas, and Bob Meyers. I expect to see their names in the papers someday doing what they did best, singing.

One day my good friend Red Richards asked me to make some arrangements for a recording session that he was going to make and to play in the group as well. The arrangements were easy and I think I made them in a matter of hours, but I asked him to find another trumpet player as I didn't know if I was capable of even playing my own arrangements. He told me that he didn't want anyone else to play on his session but me and, even after explaining to him my condition, he still insisted that I play with him on this date. I finally had to agree to play, so back to the woodshed I went with the practicing bit.

The night before the session, in February 1979, I was on the subway coming from New York to Jamaica about seven o'clock in the evening, and there wasn't enough room to hardly get into the subway car, much less to find a seat. In fact it was so crowded that once I was in the car I couldn't move, nor even turn my body to shift to an easier position. If I moved even my feet I would bump into someone else's feet and they would give me a stare that in itself would be enough to kill. However, I still rode through all this to get home and prepare myself for Red's session. After this terrible experience of not being able to move for about forty minutes, the train stopped. I didn't have a straphanger to balance myself, as the hundreds of people had taken them long before I had gotten on the train, so when the train lurched the whole group of standing people would lurch into each other, and soon everybody was annoyed and arguments started, but still the worst was to come. As the train went under the river between Manhattan and Queens, it stopped completely. Now I and, I guess, most people were used to trains stopping for a few minutes on the transit line, so I just knew we'd be there only for a few minutes at the most. After a while the minutes turned into an hour and by this time, being in such a cramped position, everyone was really annoyed. I wanted so badly to get off the train but, naturally, I couldn't as we were under the river and the doors were closed. The hour turned into two hours and then three hours. By this time it wouldn't have been safe to say even hello to the passengers, as you would have probably been cursed out. We all were stuck there and all were tired and it was torture to have to be standing without being able to make the least bit of movement. After about three and a half hours the conductor announced that we would all have to get out of the train, under the river, and take another train that would take us to another train underground, that would take us on the rest of our trip. Then the riders were really upset. Half were glad to get out of the overcrowded train and the other half resented getting off the train and walking underground by flashlight for miles, it seemed, to get to the other train. It took another hour to evacuate the hundreds of people on the train. Finally, when we did find the new train and continue the trip, I was in a terrible condition and in no way relaxed as I wanted to be for the session. This was now supposed to start in a few hours, as I didn't get home until far after one o'clock in the morning from a trip that I had started at seven o'clock the previous evening. However, I did get up and made the trip back to Manhattan for the date, but my nerves were just a frazzle and after the first number was recorded I knew this date would be, for me, another disaster. We started with one of my own arrangements and I couldn't even play it. Everybody was kind to me, even though I knew myself that I was screwing up everything. Then, to make matters even worse, my hernia re-occurred and I began to hurt when I tried to play. I didn't tell this to anyone but finally I was asked to let the group finish without the trumpet, which they did. I was happy for that but sorry for Red Richards, as I couldn't live up to his expectations. The record was made but to this day I hate to even think about it, and when some people play the record you can be sure that I won't be in the room to listen to it.

After being at Hunter about three years I took some time off and hired my old standby Jackie Williams to replace me during my absence. I was to be away for three weeks and all the kids liked Jackie and I knew that he would keep charge of everything. So in 1981 I boarded a plane for Sweden, where I was booked for three weeks, also playing in Finland, Poland, Italy and Denmark. The trip to Helsinki was great as I was playing with some good musicians that I'd never heard of. Matti Oilling, who was a great drummer and in fact was a drum professor that had his own school, was one of the guys that I played with. In Poland there were some excellent musicians that surprised me with their ability to play jazz with such a good feeling. Zbigniew Jaremko and Wysocki Bogda were great musicians and wonderful arrangers. They really gassed me.

In Bari, Italy, I was booked with a big band that was all jazz, Paolo Lepore and his Jazz Studio Orchestra. On arriving in Bari I was met by the whole band and I immediately fell in love with this pretty little city with the beautiful blue water. The main speaker for the group was one of the trumpet players, Mario Andriulli. Mario was the hot man in the trumpet section and I thought he was a very good jazzman. He was a young cat and since has visited New York several times, as he has relatives who live in New Jersey. One of the most dedicated jazz fans in the world, I think, was a pharmacist in Bari, Mike Ambrosi. I spent some time at Mike's home listening to records that I had made with Basie and other groups. Mike wakes up every morning to jazz and goes to bed at night with jazz coming from rooms all over his home. After Bari I went to Rome, where I met Luigi Toth. Luigi was either the manager or the owner of the Mississippi Jazz Club, which was a great club for jazz. I never knew for sure if he was the owner or the manager but I did know that whenever he spoke around the club everybody listened. He also was a trumpet player and knew right away that I wasn't playing like I did when I was with Basie. Later we became very good friends and at the end of the gig he took me to the airport for a flight to Copenhagen, where I was to go on to another tour for Bo Johnson, who was a jazz promoter there and was responsible for the entire Scandinavian tour.

In Denmark I played with a great group, of which the most famous was the great tenor saxophonist Jesper Thilo and an American pianist who had come to Denmark to live, Kenny Drew. The tour went along pretty good and, thanks to Jesper and Kenny Drew, the audiences were very enthusiastic. Jesper was top tenor man in Copenhagen and Kenny really showed me that he ranked among the best, not only in Denmark but in the USA as well. So many pretty things came out of that piano or, I should say, *those* pianos, as we were on tour and every night Kenny had a different piano. The last night of the tour was at the Monmartre Club in Copenhagen and my good buddy John Darville came to see me, along with his wife Maj-Britt. John and I talked of Ben Webster, who was really the greatest tenor man to hit Denmark and was loved by everybody. I saw there Ernie Wilkins, the great arranger for Count Basie who also now lived in Denmark. After the tour ended John Darville took me to the airport to go to Warsaw, where I was to take the Polish airline for New York.

In Poland I had a couple of days before the flight, so I called a very good friend, Piotr Lawski, who was a student there and spoke perfect English. He took me around the city for the two days I had there and I bought more souvenirs. He took me all over the city and showed me the ghetto that had been destroyed by the Germans in World War II. It was amazing how the Polish people had reconstructed the entire ghetto, brick for brick, the way it was before the war. Poland is famous for amber and good leather products, so after buying some of these items I met Piotr and he took me to his home to meet his mother, who was holding some souvenirs that I had bought previously when I played the Polish Jazz Festival.

I can never forget how I felt when I saw how the Polish people were forced to stand in line for hours just to buy a small amount of bread and meat. The Polish soldiers were everywhere and when the day for my flight came I was at the airport about three hours too early. Piotr had a girlfriend who worked at the airport and they were very helpful in getting me through the miles of red tape that one has to go through to leave Poland. I must have bugged the hell out of the airport clerks about my flight as I would ask them for information about every five minutes. I couldn't understand the Polish language and I wasn't going to take a chance on misunderstanding the calls, which were in Polish, but they spoke to me in English.

After leaving Poland I found myself wondering what was happening at

Hunter College. I knew Jackie had the class under control but still I wanted to see what had developed during my absence. I went to class the following Friday, which was the day of class, and Jackie was trying so hard to get the little singers to sing *It don't mean a thing if it ain't got that swing*. They were having so much trouble with the "doo-wa, doo-wa, doo-wa" part. They were all glad to see me, however, and I had to relate to them my tour in these countries. The following week I returned to class and found that some changes had taken place while I was gone. There had been a big-band program under the direction of Bob Montesi, and I found that most of the instrumentalists had signed to play in the big-band program and I had been left with nothing but singers and a million guitarists.

Professor Montesi was a good choice to head the newly formed big-band program; he played trumpet and trombone and probably other instruments that I didn't know about. Still, I must admit that, secretly, I wished that I could have had that assignment. That would have been right up my alley, to work with a big band with all the trombones, trumpets, saxes and rhythm. However, Mr Montesi was very capable. He was the senior professor in jazz studies at Hunter and I was an adjunct professor, but I just couldn't help wanting that job of teaching a big band.

As I continued on with my little class of singers and guitarists I began to become more and more disenchanted with the school. It finally got to the point that I had only one instrumentalist, a little girl sax player, and, though she played exceptionally well, there was no one whom she could team with. Gone were all of my trumpet players and sax players, and there wasn't too much that I could do as far as calling that a band. The final exam for the year was to play a concert in the large concert hall, where the kids' parents could come and encourage them and to hear what progress they had made during the semester. So, after the final concert in 1982, I began thinking of leaving Hunter, as trying to teach guitar players and singers wasn't exactly my cup of tea. Then one day Professor Michael Griffel, who had been elected to the chairmanship of music at Hunter, called me in his office and regretfully told me that someone who had been checking the files for some reason had noticed that my birthyear was 1911, which made me two years over the age limit to be a professor at Hunter. He explained that other professors had been dismissed for the same reason and it wouldn't have been fair for me to be an exception. However, he wanted me to continue as consultant and to make speeches at various schools in New York. I agreed to do this but actually I was secretly happy that I was leaving, as I didn't think I'd be happy just teaching and coaching young singers and guitar players. So after finishing my last semester I said goodbye to Hunter College.

Shortly after leaving Hunter I was hired by Jean-Pierre Vignola, a French promoter, to make the arrangements and direct a band of former Count Basie musicians for whom he was planning a five-country tour. Once again I was happy at the thought of working with some of my old Count Basie buddies. Vignola had brought my favorite first trumpet player, Ed Lewis, out of retirement as well as Eddie Durham, who had played with Count Basie when they all were members of the great Bennie Moten band. Ed

Lewis was a member of that band even before Basie joined. Ed had never been to Europe before and I knew I'd have a ball in just watching his reaction to the sights of Europe.

I began making the charts for the tour and I made all of the favorite numbers of Count Basie: 9:20 *Special, Blue and Sentimental, Jive at Five* and all the rest of such numbers. After writing for some months the arrangements were finished, and in November 1983 we all met in New York and took the plane to Paris. We were billed as The Count's Men. This had been the name of a group led by Earle Warren a few years before when we worked at a jazz club in New York called the West End, which was managed by Phil Schaap who knows more about the history of jazz than any musician. Later we were called the Basie Alumni Band. Basie had excused Freddie Green for the three weeks to make the tour with us, which I thought was a nice gesture as Freddie would have been a great attraction to the band as he had been with the Count over forty years.

The tour went well. We played in France, Switzerland, Italy, Ireland and England. We happened to be in Limoges, France, on the day of the anniversary of the Hot Club of Limoges and some of us were invited to a great celebration and banquet. I met a lot of my old friends, such as Jean Marie Masse, who was the president of the club, Johnny Simmen with his wife Liza, Jean-Pierre Battestini and his wife Claude, and André Vasset, who I hadn't seen since I went to France with Mezzrow in 1953. It was so nice to see all of these old friends. The tour went exceptionally well and after the three weeks of traveling we returned to Paris, where we played the last night of the tour at the swank Meridian Hotel. There I met more old friends, such as Moustache (I never knew his real name), who had now become the big wheel in promoting jazz in the Meridian. He was a drummer that I had worked with in my early years in France. Maxim Saury also dropped by to see me with his young trumpet player Alain Bouchet, who I admired very much. I had heard him for the first time in Nice and was very impressed with his playing—good tone, good ideas and a great feeling for jazz. He reminded me so much of Mario Andriulli that I had met in Italy. Maxim Saury and I had been friends for many years when I was working around Paris with Dave Pochonet. In those years we kept bumping into each other as we both liked the same little girl in Paris, but now, both being senior citizens, we were very happy to see each other. He later brought his group to New York, which made me very happy when I went to visit him. Also at the Meridian we were visited by my old friend Memphis Slim, who was very successful in Paris, writing several compositions such as *Every day I get the blues* and *There's an awful lot of shakin' going on* among others. He took us all to his restaurant, where we listened to French musicians playing jazz and ate some of his own concoctions in the food department, which was very good. The following day we boarded the plane for our trip back to New York.

On our arrival at Kennedy airport we found that all of our luggage had been left in Brussels, so after hanging around the airport filling out forms for our luggage to be delivered, which we hoped it would, we all split for our homes. When I arrived home that afternoon there was no one at home, which wasn't unusual at that time of the day, so I lay down without even starting to unpack the couple of smaller bags that I had carried with me in the plane. (Our other bags did arrive the next day.) After a couple of hours Steven, my son, came in and had a big smile on his face. "Hello, Pops," he greeted me, "when did you get in?" After a few minutes of chit chat he went to his room and lay down. In a few hours Pat came home from work and we discussed the tour and I told her of the gifts that I had bought for her and Steven that were packed in the bags that I hoped would be delivered the next day.

A couple of hours later she called me to tell me that Steven didn't seem to be well and that he had a temperature. I went to look at him and he was beginning to become delirious. A couple of hours later we called a friend, Peggy Castro, and she and Pat took him to the Mary Immaculate Hospital, which was near where we lived in Jamaica. The next day I went to see him and he was in the intensive care unit. It all seemed so quick to me. Steven had never been sick one day in his life and now I was looking at him in bad shape. He had been diagnosed as having double pneumonia. As Steven was lying in the hospital bed one of the last little jokes that he was trying to tell me was, "Everyone else can come to the hospital with a usual case of pneumonia, but me, I have to have double pneumonia." We visited him every day for a while, hoping that he would get better, when he went into a coma.

After a couple of weeks I went on to arranging music for various bands in New York. There was a young guy, Loren Schoenberg, a tenor saxophonist who had formed a good band, and I had decided to help him as much as I possibly could because he was trying to keep the big-band tradition going. He was a protégé of Benny Goodman and I knew he had a good beginning in that field, as who could ask for a better mentor than Benny Goodman? Loren's band was not an organized group, but they were all some of the best musicians in New York and would go to Loren's rehearsals simply because they liked him and knew that they would be playing good jazz and having a ball away from their daily jobs in the studios. Nearly every big band that had been popular in the big-band days was represented in Loren's band—Artie Shaw, Stan Kenton, Benny Goodman, etc. I gave Loren two arrangements that I had made for the Count Basie Alumni Band, *Down for double* and *Blue and Sentimental*, which he later recorded after pushing the recording session with some of his own money. The arrangements came out later and they sounded much better than even the Basie All-stars played them.

In Loren's band was a wonderful young guitarist that I met at one of his rehearsals, Howard Alden. He later formed a five-piece group with a great young trombonist, Dan Barrett, who had been working with Joe Bushkin at the St Regis Hotel on Fifth Avenue. It was a great combination, these two, with a great modern alto sax man, Chuck Wilson, and Frank Tate on bass. My old buddy Jackie Williams was on drums and I promised to make them some small-band arrangements. I made eight or ten, and I was startled the way these young cats could play. They were, even in the beginning, the closest thing that I had heard to the John Kirby band of the thirties. I knew that if they continued they would be a great group someday. So, between Loren Schoenberg and the Howard Alden–Dan Barrett group, I became more and more interested in composing and arranging charts. At the same time I was doing things for Nat Pierce, who had a similar big band in California. Nat, in my opinion, is a master arranger, and for me it was an honor that he wanted me to make some charts for him as he really didn't need anyone to arrange for him. However, he liked my charts and recorded some of them. I was also writing for such guys as my friend Humphrey Lyttelton in England.

One day I went to one of Loren's rehearsals and was told by Paul Cohen, one of the great trumpet players in Loren's group, that he had heard that Count Basie had been rushed to the hospital somewhere in Florida. Paul had played in the Basie band for years and was naturally concerned, as was I, about the health of our former boss. We both thought it was something very serious because they would not issue any reports on his health, nor would they state just what the illness was. The last time that I saw Basie, before he took to his little wheelchair, was at the Village Gate. There he told me that arthritis was bothering him so much that sometimes he could hardly move. The next time, a few months later, he was in the little mobilized chair.

Two days later, while listening to music on the radio, I happened to hear the announcer say, "After leaving Kansas City . . .' He went on to say that whoever he was speaking of came to New York and became an instant hit in the jazz world. I said to myself, as he continued, "Damn, this must be it." Then at the end of the report came the words I didn't want to hear, "Count Basie died yesterday in Florida at the age of seventy-nine. He would have been eighty in August." So on 26 April 1984 the Count left us. His funeral services were held at Abyssinia Baptist Church in Harlem and, needless to say, there were thousands waiting in line to pay tribute to the real King of Swing. Notables came from all over the country and there were so many flowers that they had to hire different rooms in the church to place them on exhibit. John Hammond came with Willard Alexander, and as I was talking to Willard he told me that he too was concerned about himself, being almost in the same condition as Basie was. He was walking with a cane and said to me, "Buck, I get the feeling that I'm going through the same thing that Bill went through." Then a few days later he went to California. I wrote a letter to him in California asking about making some more arrangements for the band. He answered me saying that I should contact Aaron, Basie's adopted son, as he was going to take over the business of running the band. He advised me, however, to wait until he got back to New York and talk to him about making the charts before I talked to Aaron. Then, while I was waiting for him to return, I received the news that he too had passed, so I guess he too went through the same thing that Basie went through.

Six months after Basie's death came the most heart-breaking experience of my whole life. My son Steven, who had been in the hospital since November, had steadily deteriorated and didn't appear to be making any progress. Pat and I had visited him practically every day for the eleven months he was confined. We both had prayed so hard for him to come through but he only continued to get worse. It was so painful to watch him for eleven months go from a healthy young kid to just a mere shadow of his former self. He had suffered brain damage and, though he didn't seem to be in pain, I cried so much just seeing him like this. He hadn't eaten anything for eleven months (he had been fed intravenously), and he hadn't uttered a word in eleven months. His weight had gone from 175 pounds to 91 pounds and the brain damage had twisted his body into a grotesque shape that even therapy couldn't have helped. Sometimes, when I looked at him, I wondered if he would have wanted to live in such a condition after being so athletic and full of life. In fact I began to understand how people who love someone so dearly could commit a mercy killing. I could have never done that to Steven but I did begin to understand just how people who committed that act felt. I could just visualize Steven saying to me years later as he was wheeled in his chair because he couldn't walk, "Dad, why didn't you let me die?"

It was the most terrible experience of my life. We moved him from Mary Immaculate Hospital in Queens, hoping that he would do better, to Mount Sinai Hospital on Fifth Avenue in Manhattan. Even there he didn't make any progress. One morning after being in Mount Sinai I was up early at about five o'clock, when the telephone rang. Immediately I stopped in my tracks as I began to think, "Now just who would be calling at this time of the morning?" Pat answered the phone and after talking for about a minute she hung up the receiver and said just three words that will remain with me all the rest of my life. She simply said, "Steven is gone."

Steven's funeral services were very tearful as everyone loved him so much. Candice came in from California with her little family, husband Donald Bryson and their four kids. Steven had been scheduled to go out to visit them just before he became ill. After the services were over we all went to our home. The house was full of people for the next three days trying to console us. Even now, every time I see a picture of Steven or even think of him, I say to myself, "God bless you, Steven." As much as we loved him, God must have loved him more and took him away from this world where he will have no more pain, suffering and worldly troubles.

After a few weeks in which I wasn't able to do very much of anything, not even answer letters from my friends nor write music, I received a call from Professor Samuel Roberson of Hampton Institute in Hampton, Virginia. He had been referred to me by Stanley Dance. He was looking for someone who knew Count Basie very well and could be consultant to him, as he was going to sponsor a review called the One O'Clock Jump featuring the life of Basie. He invited me to come down to Hampton and discuss the whole idea with him, so, along with the great playwright Leslie Lee, I went to Hampton. With the faculty we planned the show, which was to be composed of students and the faculty with a few professional musicians to augment the orchestra under the leadership of a former professional trumpet player, Bob Ransom. He was musical director at Hampton. Professor Roberson was extremely happy to learn that I could arrange the music for the show, as he hadn't known before that I had arranged for Basie when I was in the band. So we came back to New York and I began to score the musical numbers for the show, which took my mind off of Steven, at least in a small way. After making the scores we went to Hampton and rehearsed the show, and on 11th March 1985 we presented it. The show went well with the public as it seemed that all of Count's fans came to Virginia for the opening. Professor Roberson hopes to put the show on Broadway as was done with Fats Waller's *Ain't Misbehavin'*, Eubie Blake's *Eubie* and Duke Ellington's *Sophisticated Lady*.

Coming back to New York I was surprised to hear that my very good friend Gene Ramey had passed in his sleep in Texas. Gene had been my favorite bass player and had gone several times with me to Europe and Canada. In fact, 1984 and 1985 were very bad years for prominent jazzmen, such as Ramey, Trummy Young, Bill Pemberton, Budd Johnson, Vic Dickenson, Zoot Sims, Eddie Beal (my pianist who went with me to China in 1934), Jo Jones, and Alberta Hunter the great blues singer. There had been other bad years for musicians but I think that those were two of the worst. I had had my brush with the grim reaper but now, thanks to my good doctor, Dorothy Kunstadt, I am in pretty good shape. Roy Eldridge had his brush also but is now in good shape, but the others were not so lucky as we were.

Nancy Elliott had now become a professional photographer and had added her maiden name, so she is now known as Nancy Miller Elliott. She had been hired by Phil Schaap to take photographs of Doc Cheatham on his eightieth birthday in which Roy Eldridge, Jonah Jones, Jabbo Smith and myself were to participate. Doc Cheatham is a phenomenon. How anyone can play trumpet like that at the age of eighty is beyond me. In fact, after seeing and talking to Doc, I gave up all hope of playing again and decided to continue composing and arranging. He is a marvel. At my age of seventy-three, I'd be a hundred years old before I could even start playing like Doc Cheatham. Anyway, after taking pictures of all of us old geezers, we all split. The next time I saw Doc was when we did the Kool Jazz Festival for George Wein at Avery Fisher Hall.

George had dedicated the festival to Max Gordon, the famous owner of the Village Vanguard, which I thought was a nice gesture. As one of the first musicians to play the festival for George Wein (it was then known as the Newport Jazz Festival), I was amazed at how he had promoted the festival from an open field in Providence, Rhode Island, to a festival which covered the entire city of New York, including such sites as Avery Fisher Hall, the Blue Note, Carnegie Hall, Fat Tuesday's, St Peter's Church, Small's Paradise, the Staten Island Ferry, Town Hall, the Village Gate, the Village Vanguard and many others.

I participated in a tribute to John Hammond which took place at Avery Fisher Hall on 25th June 1985. John had been ill and was confined to his home. However, the tribute was a great honor to the greatest talent scout in the history of entertainment. I had to make a short speech and, along with my buddies such as Sweets Edison and Gus Johnson, we all had a ball. Freddie Green was there too. Then in August 1985 I was invited by my man

Humphrey Lyttelton to be his special guest at the Edinburgh Jazz Festival in Scotland. After the festival I spent a week at Steve Voce's home in Liverpool with him and his wife Jenny. My life still goes on.

Discography
Compiled by Bob Weir

Notes

1) The discography excludes Clayton's recordings with Count Basie and Billie Holiday during the period 1937–43 (readers are referred to Chris Sheridan's *Count Basie: a Bio-discography* (Westport, CT, and London, 1986) and Jack Millar's *Born to Sing: a Discography of Billie Holiday* (Copenhagen, 1979), for these details). Clayton maintains, however, that his first recordings were made in New York with Teddy Wilson and Billie Holiday (the date given by discographers as 25 January 1937) and not with Basie (given as 21 January 1937); he is sure that Basie's first date was about two weeks after that with Wilson and Holiday. Every other known recording by Clayton, including radio and television broadcasts, transcriptions, film soundtracks and "live" tapes, is listed. (At many sessions in the discography other items were recorded on which Clayton did not play; these are not listed.)

2) Only the first record issue is given. Microgroove issues (shown in italics) are 12″ LPs unless otherwise indicated.

3) Where more than one take of a title has been issued, the takes are listed in the sequence of issue.

4) Where a vocalist is listed in the recording group title or at the head of the personnel details, he or she sings on every item in the session. Elsewhere those items with vocalists are indicated by initials immediately after the titles.

5) A question mark after a record company name indicates that the item was issued on a 78, but the record number is not known.

A large number of collectors, discographers, writers and record companies have assisted generously with information for the discography. I am grateful especially to Steve Voce (who originally suggested the project) and Chris Sheridan, who have helped me at every stage.

Abbreviations

AFRS	Armed Forces Radio Service		th	tenor horn
ah	alto horn/mellophone		tb	trombone
alt	alternative take		ts	tenor saxophone
as	alto saxophone		v	vocal
bj	banjo		vc	cello
bs	baritone saxophone		vib	vibraphone
c	circa		vn	violin
c	cornet/trumpet-cornet		xyl	xylophone
cel	celeste		†	arrangement by Buck Clayton
cl	clarinet		*	composition by Buck Clayton
d	drums		*Record types*	
db	double bass		45	45 rpm single play
eb	electric bass guitar		EP	45 rpm extended play
eg	electric guitar		10″	33⅓ rpm long play
f	flute		ET	electrical transcription
fh	french horn		*Country of record origin*	
g	acoustic guitar		B	Belgium
ldr	leader		C	Canada
mar	marimba		D	Denmark
mst	master take		E	England
nar	narrator		F	France
o	organ		G	West Germany
p	piano		I	Italy
pc	percussion		Sw	Sweden
ss	soprano saxophone		Sz	Switzerland
t	trumpet			

1937
June 29   New York
Mildred Bailey and her Orchestra
Mildred Bailey (v); Buck Clayton (t); Edmond Hall (cl); Herschel Evans (ts); James Sherman (p); Freddie Green (g); Walter Page (db); Jo Jones (d)

21332-1	If you should ever leave	Vocalion 3615
21333-1	The moon got in my eyes	Vocalion 3626
21334-1	Heaven help this heart of mine	Vocalion 3615
21335-1	It's the natural thing to do	Vocalion 3626
21335-2	It's the natural thing to do	Unissued

NB: there is no alternative take of 21334; the one usually listed as 21334-2 is identical to 21334-1.

1937
Dec 1   New York
Harry James and his Orchestra
Harry James (t); Buck Clayton (t); Earle Warren (as); Herschel Evans (ts); Jack Washington (as, bs); Jess Stacy (p); Walter Page (db); Jo Jones (d); Helen Humes (v)

B22083-1	Jubilee (HH:v)	Brunswick 8038
B22083-3	Jubilee (HH:v)	*Tax(Sw) m-8015*

B22084-2	When we're alone	Brunswick 8035
B22084-1	When we're alone	*Tax(Sw) m-8015*
B22085-1	I can dream can't I? (HH:v)	Brunswick 8038
B22086-2	Life goes to a party	Brunswick 8035
B22086-1	Life goes to a party	*Tax(Sw) m-8015*

NB: Eddie Durham (tb) is usually listed for this session but no trombone is audible.

1938
Jan 5   New York
Harry James and his Orchestra
Harry James (t); Buck Clayton (t); Vernon Brown (tb); Earle Warren (as); Herschel Evans (ts); Jack Washington (as, bs); Jess Stacy (p); Walter Page (db); Jo Jones (d); Helen Humes (v)

B22249-1	Texas Chatter	Brunswick 8067
B22249-2	Texas Chatter	*Tax(Sw) m-8015*
B22250-1	Song of the Wanderer (HH:v)	Brunswick 8067
B22251-1	It's the dreamer in me (HH:v)	Brunswick 8055
B22251-2	It's the dreamer in me (HH:v)	*Tax(Sw) m-8015*
B22252-1	One O'Clock Jump	Brunswick 8055
B22252-2	One O'Clock Jump	Columbia 37142

1938
March 18   New York
Eddie Durham and his Base Four/Kansas City Five
Buck Clayton (t); Eddie Durham (eg); Freddie Green (g); Walter Page (db); Jo Jones (d)

P22580-1	Laughing at life	Commodore 510
P22581-1	Good Morning Blues	Commodore 511
P22582-1	I know that you know	Commodore 510
P22583-1	Love me or leave me	*Columbia CG33566*

1938
Sept 27   New York
Kansas City Six
Buck Clayton (t); Lester Young (cl, ts); Eddie Durham (eg, tb); Freddie Green (g, v); Walter Page (db); Jo Jones (d)

P23421-2	Way down yonder in New Orleans	Commodore 512
P23421-1	Way down yonder in New Orleans	*Tax(Sw) m-8000*
P23422-1	Countless Blues	Commodore 509
P23422-2	Countless Blues	*Tax(Sw) m-8000*
P23423-1	Them there eyes (FG:v)	Commodore 511
P23423-1	Them there eyes (FG:v)	*Tax(Sw) m-8000*
P23424-1	I want a little girl	Commodore 509
P23424-1	I want a little girl	*Tax(Sw) m-8000*
P23425-1	Pagin' the Devil	Commodore 512
P23425-2	Pagin' the Devil	Tax(Sw) m-8000

1939
Sept 5   New York
The Quintones with Buck Ram's Orchestra
The Quintones (v); Buck Clayton (t); George Koenig (cl); Clark Galehouse (ts); Les Burness (p); Walter Page (db); Jo Jones (d)

WM1076-A	Sly Mongoose	Vocalion 5509
WM1078-A	When my sugar walks down the street	Vocalion 5172

1939
Dec 24   Carnegie Hall, New York
Kansas City Six
Buck Clayton (t); Lester Young (ts); Charlie Christian (eg); Freddie Green (g); Walter Page (db); Jo Jones (d)

Way down yonder in New Orleans	*Vanguard VRS8523/4*
Good Morning Blues	*Vanguard VRS8523/4*
Pagin' the Devil	*Vanguard VRS8523/4*

NB: Clayton was also recorded with Count Basie's Orchestra at this "From Spirituals to Swing" concert.

1941
April 23   Carnegie Hall, New York
Jam session—Café Society Concert
Buck Clayton (t); J. C. Higginbotham (tb); Buster Bailey (cl); Tab Smith (as); Buddy Tate (ts); Count Basie (p); Pete Johnson (p); Freddie Green (g); Walter Page (db); Jo Jones (d)

One O'Clock Jump (Jam Session at Carnegie Hall, part 1)
(16″ ET) AFRS NOJ 15

1944
March 22   New York
Kansas City Seven
Buck Clayton (t); Dicky Wells (tb); Lester Young (ts); Count Basie (p); Freddie Green (g); Rodney Richardson (db); Jo Jones (d)

HLK21-2	After Theatre Jump	Keynote K1302
HLK22-3	Six Cats and a Prince (*)	Keynote K1303
HLK22-2	Six Cats and a Prince (*)	*Queen-disc(I) Q-051*
HLK24-2	Destination K.C. (*†)	Keynote K1303
HLK24-1	Destination K.C. (*†)	*EmArcy MG26010*

1944
Oct 12   New York
Coleman Hawkins and his All American Five
Buck Clayton (t); Coleman Hawkins (ts); Teddy Wilson (p); Slam Stewart (db); Denzil Best (d)

HL64	I'm Yours	*EmArcy MG26011*
HL65	Under a Blanket of Blue	Keynote K655
HL66-1	Beyond the Blue Horizon	Keynote K622
HL66-2	Beyond the Blue Horizon	Keynote K622
HL67	A Shanty in Old Shanty Town	Keynote K622

NB: take 1 of Beyond the Blue Horizon is the usual version on Keynote K622 but a few rare copies contain take 2.

1944
Dec 1   New York
Leonard Feather and his All Stars
Buck Clayton (t); Edmond Hall (cl); Coleman Hawkins (ts); Leonard Feather (p); Remo Palmieri (eg); Oscar Pettiford (db); Specs Powell (d)

9001	Scram	Continental C-6016
9002	Esquire Stomp	Continental C-6009
9003	Esquire Jump	Continental C-6009
9004	Thanks for the Memory	Continental C-6016

1944
Dec 4   New York
Trummy Young and his Orchestra
Buck Clayton (t); Trummy Young (tb); Milt Yaner (cl, as); Don Byas (ts); Ernie Caceres (bs); Bill Rowland (p); Hy White (g); Al Lucas (db); James Crawford (d)

SRC154	Let me call you sweetheart	Signature 15005
SRC155	Lame Brain	Unissued
SRC156	Please, please, please	Signature 15005
SRC157	Flogalapa	Unissued

1945
Jan 17   Broadcast Playhouse, New York
Buck Clayton (t) as soloist with unknown radio studio big band
Sweet Lorraine   (16″ ET) AFRS ONS 490

NB: from the New York location of the Second Esquire Jazz Concert; there were simultaneous concerts in New Orleans and Los Angeles.

1945
March 16   New York
Horace Henderson and his Orchestra
Buck Clayton (t); Eddie Bert (tb); Hank D'Amico (cl); Aaron Sachs (cl); Horace Henderson (p); Hy White (eg); Billy Taylor (db); Specs Powell (d)

HL86	'Deed I do	Jamboree 908
HL87	Make love to me	Jamboree 909
HL88	A Bunch of Rhythm	Jamboree 909
HL89	Smack's Blues	Jamboree 908

1945
May 2   New York
Trummy Young and his Lucky Seven
Buck Clayton (t); Trummy Young (tb, v); Ike Quebec (ts); Ken Kersey (p); Mike Bryan (eg); Slam Stewart (db); James Crawford (d)

DU4900-A	Good and Groovy	Duke 110
DU4900-B	Rattle and Roll (*)	Duke 111
DU4901-A	I'm living for today	Duke 110
DU4901-B	Behind the Eight Bar	Duke 111

1945
May 7   New York
Freddie Green and his Kansas City Seven
Buck Clayton (t); Dicky Wells (tb); Lucky Thompson (ts); Sammy Benskin (p); Freddie Green (g); Al Hall (db); Shadow Wilson (d); Sylvia Syms (v)
DU4907	I'm in the mood for love (SS:v)	Duke 113
DU4909	Sugar Hips	Duke 113
DU49??	Get Lucky	Duke 114
DU49??	I'll never be the same	Duke 114

1945
June 7   New York
Buck Clayton's Quintet
Buck Clayton (t); Flip Phillips (ts); Teddy Wilson (p); Slam Stewart (db); Danny Alvin (d)
MR105	Diga diga doo (†)	Melrose 1201
MR106	Love me or leave me (†)	Melrose 1201
MR107	We're in the money (†)	Melrose 1202
MR108	B.C. Blues (Melrose Blues) (*†)	Melrose 1202

1945
June 27   New York
Don Byas's All Star Quintet
Buck Clayton (t); Don Byas (ts); Johnny Guarnieri (p); Eddie Safranski (db); Denzil Best (d)
J7005	Little White Lies	Jamboree 902
J7006	Deep Purple	Jamboree 903
J7007	Them there eyes	Jamboree 903
J7008	Out of Nowhere	Jamboree 902

1945
July 17   WOR Studios, New York
Ike Quebec Swing Seven
Buck Clayton (t); Keg Johnson (tb); Ike Quebec (ts); Ram Ramirez (p); Tiny Grimes (eg); Grachan Moncur (db); J. C. Heard (d)
BN246-1	I found a new baby	(10″) Blue Note BLP5027
BN246-0	I found a new baby	Mosaic MR4-107
BN247-0	I surrender dear (omit Grimes)	(10″) Blue Note BLP5001
BN247-1	I surrender dear (omit Grimes)	Mosaic MR4-107
BN248-1	Topsy	Blue Note 515
BN249-0	Cup-mute Clayton	Blue Note 515

1945
July 18   New York
Trummy Young and the Guys from V-disc
Buck Clayton (t); Trummy Young (tb, v); Henry Wells (tb, v); Willie Smith (as; 1); Bill Stegmeyer (as; 2); Don Byas (ts); Ken Kersey (p); Mike Bryan (eg); Bob Haggart (db); James Crawford (d)
| VP1519-XP35151 | Four or five times (TY:v) (1) | V-disc VD538 |
| VP1563-843898 | I want a little girl (TY, HW:v) (2) | V-disc VD559 |

1945
Summer   Central Park, New York
Buck Clayton Trio
Buck Clayton (t); Sammy Price (p); possibly Bob Haggart (db)
| Love me or leave me | (16″ ET) AFRS AJ 24 |

1945
Aug 14   Barbizon Plaza Hotel, New York
Teddy Wilson Sextet
RBuck Clayton (t); Ben Webster (ts); Teddy Wilson (p); Al Casey (g); Al Hall (db); J. C. Heard (d)
5296-5	If dreams come true	Musicraft 336
5296-1	If dreams come true	MGM(G) 65055
5297-1	I can't get started	Musicraft 332
5297-2	I can't get started	(10″) MGM(E) E-129
5298-2	Stompin' at the Savoy	Musicraft 332
5298-3	Stompin' at the Savoy	(10″) MGM(E) E-129
5299-3	Blues Too	Musicraft 336

1945
Aug 15   New York
Charlie Ventura Sextet
Buck Clayton (t); Charlie Ventura (ts); Bill Rowland (p); Eddie Yance (g); Al Hall (db); Specs Powell (d)

T13(mst)	C.V. Jam	Black & White 37
T13(alt)	C.V. Jam	Savoy SJL2243
T14	Tammy's Dream	Black & White 38
T15(mst)	Let's jump for Rita	Black & White 38
T15(alt)	Let's jump for Rita	Savoy SJL2243

1945
Aug 17   New York
J. C. Heard Quintet
Buck Clayton (t); Flip Phillips (ts); Johnny Guarnieri (p); Milt Hinton (db); J. C. Heard (d)
HL105	Why do I love you?	Keynote K682
HL106	All my life	Keynote K623
HL107	Groovin' with J.C.	Keynote K623
HL108	What's the use?	Keynote K682

1945
cSept   New York
Hot Lips Page and his Orchestra
Hot Lips Page (t, v); Buck Clayton (t); Benny Morton (tb); J. C. Higginbotham (tb); Sandy Williams (tb); Earl Bostic (as); Don Byas (ts); Ben Webster (ts); Rufus Webster (p); Buford Oliver (d); plus unknown (t, as, g, db)
W3397	Lady in debt (HLP:v)	Continental C-6015
W3398	Corsicana (*†)	Continental C-6025
W3399	They raided the joint (HLP:v)	Continental C-6017
W3400	Sunset Blues (HLP:v)	Continental C-6015
W3401	Willie Mae Willow Foot (HLP:v)	Continental C-6061

NB: Clayton's presence is not absolutely certain.

1945
Sept 4   New York
Sir Charles Thompson and his All Stars
Buck Clayton (t); Charlie Parker (as); Dexter Gordon (ts); Sir Charles Thompson (p); Danny Barker (g); Jimmy Butts (db); J. C. Heard (d)
R1030	Takin' Off	Apollo 757
R1031	If I had you	Apollo 757
R1032	20th Century Blues	Apollo 759
R1033	The Street Beat	Apollo 759

late 1945
New York
Skip Hall and his Band
Buck Clayton (t); George Stevenson (tb); Vincent Bair-Bey (as); Buddy Tate (ts); Dave McRae (bs); Skip Hall (p); Walter Page (db); Herbie Lovelle (d); Warren Evans (v)
J1001-2	Two Left Feet	Jamboree 1001
J1003	Skip a Page	Jamboree 1001
J1005	Hey Bruz	Jamboree 1002
J1006	The Spot	Jamboree 1002
J100?	So deep in love (WE:v)	Jamboree 1003
J100?	I still love you (WE:v)	Jamboree 1003

1946
April 22   Embassy Auditorium, Los Angeles
Jazz at the Philharmonic
Buck Clayton (t); Charlie Parker (as); Willie Smith (as); Coleman Hawkins (ts); Lester Young (ts); Ken Kersey (p); Irving Ashby (eg); Billy Hadnott (db); Buddy Rich (d)
101,2,3,4	JATP Blues (parts 1–4)	Clef 101, 102
135,6,7,8	I got rhythm (Parts 1–4)	Mercury 11084, 11085, 11086
142,3	I surrender dear (Parts 1–2)	Mercury 11084, 11085
139,40,41	I found a new baby	Verve 815.149.1

Buck Clayton (t); Ray Linn (t); Willie Smith (as); Corky Corcoran (ts); Coleman Hawkins (ts); Babe Russin (ts); Lester Young (ts); Ken Kersey (p); Billy Hadnott (db); Buddy Rich (d)
| 156,7,8 | Bugle Call Rag | Unissued |

NB: Parker not present on I surrender dear or I found a new baby

1946
April   NBC Studios, Hollywood
Jubilee All Stars (JATP)
Buck Clayton (t); Coleman Hawkins (ts); Lester Young (ts); Ken Kersey (p); Irving Ashby (eg); Billy Hadnott (db); Shadow Wilson (d); Helen Humes (v)

One O'Clock Jump (theme)   (16″ ET) AFRS Jubilee 190
I got rhythm   (16″ ET) AFRS Jubilee 190
Lady be good   (16″ ET) AFRS Jubilee 190
One O'Clock Jump (theme)   (16″ ET) AFRS Jubilee 192
My Old Flame (omit Hawkins, Young) (16″ ET) AFRS Jubilee 192
Don't blame me (omit Hawkins, Young) (16″ ET) AFRS Jubilee 192
Unlucky Woman (HH:v)   (16″ ET) AFRS Jubilee 192
Sweet Georgia Brown   (16″ ET) AFRS Jubilee 192

1946
*c*May   Los Angeles
Helen Humes (v) with Buck Clayton and All Stars
Buck Clayton (t); Charlie Beal (p); Barney Kessel (eg); Red Callender (db); unknown (d)

BW414-5	One Hour (If I could be with you)	Black & White 114
BW415	I don't know his name	Black & White 114
BW416-2	Drive me daddy	Black & White 112

1946
May 27   Carnegie Hall, New York
Jazz at the Philharmonic
Buck Clayton (t); Coleman Hawkins (ts); Illinois Jacquet (ts); Lester Young (ts); Ken Kersey (p); Al McKibbon (db); J. C. Heard (d)

107,8,9,10	Carnegie Blues	Verve(E) 825.101
111,112	Lady be good	Jazz Archives JA-18
113,114	I can't get started (omit Jacquet)	Jazz Archives JA-18
131,132	Sweet Georgia Brown	Phoenix LP8
133,134	Slow Drag (omit Jacquet)	Clef 103 (edited)

1946
June 3   Carnegie Hall, New York
Jazz at the Philharmonic
Buck Clayton (t); Georgie Auld (ts); Coleman Hawkins (ts); Illinois Jacquet (ts); Ken Kersey (p); Ray Brown (db); J. C. Heard or Buddy Rich (d)

	How high the moon	Unissued
	I found a new baby	Unissued

1946
June 17   Carnegie Hall, New York
Jazz at the Philharmonic
Buck Clayton (t); Trummy Young (tb); Lester Young (ts); Ken Kersey (p); John Collins (eg); Rodney Richardson (db); Doc West (d)

206	Blues	Verve (E) 825.101 (excerpt)
207	Just you, just me	Unissued
204	It's the talk of the town	Unissued
208	I got rhythm	Verve(E) 825.101 (excerpt)

1946
June 26   New York
Buck Clayton's Big Four
Buck Clayton (t); Scoville Browne (cl); Tiny Grimes (eg); Sid Weiss (db)

1042-1	Dawn Dance	HRS 1024
1043-3	Well's-a-poppin'	HRS 1025
1044-2	On the Sunny Side of the Street	HRS 1026
1045-2	It's dizzy	HRS 1024
1046-2	Basie's Morning Bluesicale	HRS 1025

1946
July 24   New York
Buck Clayton's Big Eight
Buck Clayton (t); Dicky Wells (tb); Trummy Young (tb); George Johnson (as); Billy Taylor (p, cel); Brick Fleagle (g); Al McKibbon (db); James Crawford (d)

1047	Saratoga Special	HRS 1027
1048	Sentimental Summer (Taylor: cel)	HRS 1027
1049	Harlem Cradle Song	HRS 1028
1050	My Good Man Sam	HRS 1028
1051	I want a little girl	HRS 1029

1946
late July   New York
Trummy Young's Big Seven
Buck Clayton (t); Trummy Young (tb); Buster Bailey (cl); George

Johnson (as); Jimmy Jones (p); John Levy (db); Cozy Cole (d)

1052	Fruitie Cutie	HRS 1030
1053	Blues Triste	HRS 1030
1054	Johnson Rock	HRS 1031
1055	Lucky Draw	HRS 1031

1946
Aug 19   New York
Teddy Wilson Octet
Buck Clayton (t); Scoville Browne (cl, as); Don Byas (ts); George James (bs); Teddy Wilson (p); Remo Palmieri (g); Billy Taylor (db); J. C. Heard (d); Sarah Vaughan (v)

5652	When we're alone (SV:v)	Musicraft 505
5653	Don't worry 'bout me (SV:v)	Musicraft 421
5654	I want to be happy	Musicraft 421
5655	Just one of those things	Musicraft MVS-2001

1946
Aug 23   New York
Benny Carter and his Chocolate Dandies
Buck Clayton (t); Al Grey (tb); Benny Carter (cl, as); Ben Webster (ts); Sonny White (p); John Simmons (db); Sid Catlett (d, v)

D6-VB-2694	Sweet Georgia Brown	Swing(F) 258
D6-VB-2695	Out of my way (SC:v)	Swing(F) 226
D6-VB-2696	What'll it be?	Swing(F) 226
D6-VB-2697-1	Cadillac Slim	Swing(F) 258

1946
Oct 7   Shrine Auditorium, Los Angeles
Jazz at the Philharmonic
Buck Clayton (t); Howard McGhee (t); Trummy Young (tb); Willie Smith (as); Illinois Jacquet (ts); Ken Kersey (p); Barney Kessel (eg); Charlie Drayton (db); Jackie Mills (d)

167,168	How high the moon	Unissued
164,5,6	Shrine Blues	Unissued
	The man I love	Unissued

1946
Oct 24   Civic Opera House, Chicago
Jazz at the Philharmonic
Buck Clayton (t); Trummy Young (tb); Illinois Jacquet (ts); Ken Kersey (p); Charlie Drayton (db); Jackie Mills (d)

	Blues	Unissued
	How high the moon	Unissued
215	The man I love	Unissued
	Sweet Georgia Brown	Unissued

Helen Humes (v); possibly Buck Clayton (t); Ken Kersey (p); Charlie Drayton (db); Jackie Mills (d)

	Be-baba-leba	Unissued

(4 further items performed and probably recorded)

Buck Clayton (t); Ken Kersey (p); Charlie Drayton (db); Jackie Mills (d)

	My Old Flame	Unissued
	Blues	Unissued

Buck Clayton (t); Roy Eldridge (t); Rex Stewart (c); Trummy Young (tb); Coleman Hawkins (ts); Illinois Jacquet (ts); Ken Kersey (p); Charlie Drayton (db); Jackie Mills (d)

	C-jam Blues	Unissued

1946
Nov 3   Music Hall, Detroit
Jazz at the Philharmonic
Matinee concert: *Buck Clayton (t); Illinois Jacquet (ts); Ken Kersey (p); Charlie Drayton (db); Jackie Mills (d)*

159,60,61	Detroit Blues	Unissued
	How high the moon	Unissued
216	Just you, just me	Unissued
	The man I love	Unissued
185	Sweet Georgia Brown	Unissued

Evening concert: *Buck Clayton (t); Trummy Young (tb); Illinois Jacquet (ts); Ken Kersey (p); Charlie Drayton (db); Jackie Mills (d)*

	How high the moon	Unissued
162,163	Music Hall Blues	Unissued
	The man I love	Unissued
	Sweet Georgia Brown	Unissued

1946
Dec 4   New York
Esquire All-American Award Winners
Charlie Shavers (t); Buck Clayton (t); J. J. Johnson (tb); Coleman Hawkins (ts); Harry Carney (bs); Teddy Wilson (p); John Collins (eg); Chubby Jackson (db); Shadow Wilson (d)

D6-VB-3369-1	Indiana Winter	RCA-Victor 40-0137
D6-VB-3371-1	Blow me down	RCA-Victor 40-0134
D6-VB-3372-1	Buckin' the blues	RCA-Victor 40-0134

1947
Feb 15   Carnegie Hall, New York
Jazz at the Philharmonic
Buck Clayton (t); Trummy Young (tb); Willie Smith (as); Flip Phillips (ts); Ken Kersey (p); Benny Fonville (db); Buddy Rich (d)

105,106	Bell Boy Blues	Clef 2001
169,70,71	Flying Home	Unissued
116,7,8,9	How high the moon	
	(add Coleman Hawkins, ts)	Clef 107,108

1947
cMay   New York
Helen Humes (v) and Buck Clayton's Orchestra
Buck Clayton (t); George Matthews (tb); John Hardee (ts); Ram Ramirez (p); Mundell Lowe (g); Walter Page (db); Jo Jones (d)

859	Jet Propelled Papa	Mercury 8047
860	Blue and Sentimental	Mercury 8047
861	I just refuse to sing the blues	Mercury 8056
862	They raided the joint	Mercury 8056

1947
Nov 19   New York
Canada Lee (nar); Buck Clayton (t); Edmond Hall (cl); Teddy Wilson (p); Sid Weiss (db); James Crawford (d)

The Story of Jazz, part 2: Jazz Band		Young Peoples Records YPR410

NB: the band plays 2 musical illustrations to Lee's narration of the history of jazz.

1947
Dec 3   New York
Teddy Wilson Quartet
Buck Clayton (t); Teddy Wilson (p); Billy Taylor (db); Denzil Best (d)

5998	The Sheik of Araby	Musicraft 547
	Limehouse Blues	Vernon VM-505
	Georgia on my Mind	Vernon VM-505
	After you've gone	Vernon VM-505
	Unknown title	Unissued

late 1947
New York
Helen Humes (v), with Buck Clayton (t); Scoville Browne (cl); Rudy Williams (ts); Teddy Wilson (p); Jimmy Butts (db); Denzil Best (d)

1641	Mad about you	Mercury 8074
1642	Jumpin' on Sugar Hill	Mercury 8077
1643	Flippity flop flop	Mercury 8074
1644	Today I sing the blues	Mercury 8077
	Lover Man	Unissued

1948
April   WOR Guild Theatre, New York
Peanuts Hucko and the All Stars
Buck Clayton (t); Fred Ohms (tb); Peanuts Hucko (cl); Bill Vitale (ts); Ernie Caceres (bs); Joe Bushkin (p); Jack Lesberg (db); Morey Feld (d)

J609/USS1039	The Sheik of Araby	Unissued
J628/USS1058	The song is ended	V-disc VD874

1948
Nov 15   New York
Frankie Laine (v) with Carl Fischer and his Orchestra
Big band, possibly including *Buck Clayton (t); Eddie Bert (tb); Eddie Barefield (cl); Carl Fischer (p); Mundell Lowe (g); others unknown*

Rosetta	Mercury 5227
It only happens once	Mercury 5227

1948
New York
Buddy Tate and his Orchestra
Buck Clayton (t); Eli Robinson (tb); Burnie Peacock (as); Buddy Tate (ts); Skip Hall (p); Jimmy Butts (db); Harold Austin (d); Dick Barrow (v)

158	Swingin' with Willie and Ray	Supreme 1514
159	Unknown title	Unissued
160	Unknown title	Unissued
161	Dear Mary (DB:v)	Supreme 1514

1949
Jan 12   New York
Milt Larkins
Buck Clayton (t); Milt Larkins (tb, v); Hal Singer (ts); George Rhodes (p); Walt Buchanan (db); Joe Harris (d)

S23017	She ain't with me no more	Unissued
S23018	Early Morning Boogie	Unissued
S23019	Easy Going Baby	Unissued
S23020	Rainy Weather Blues	Unissued

1949
Feb 17   New York
Sy Oliver and his Orchestra
Bernie Privin (t); Tony Faso (t); Buck Clayton (t); Mort Bullman (tb); Henderson Chambers (tb); Sy Schaffer (tb); Johnny Mince (as); Hymie Schertzer (as); Wolfie Tannenbaum (ts); Wilford Holcombe (bs); Billy Kyle (p); Joe Benjamin (db); James Crawford (d); Sy Oliver (ldr, v); Charles McCormick (v); The Aristokrats (v)

74766	Just in case (CM, TA:v)	Decca 24594
74767	Gran'ma plays the numbers (SO, TA:v)	Decca 24594

1949
July 7   New York
Sammy Price and his Rocking Rhythm
Buck Clayton (t); Vincent Bair-Bey (as, bs); Buddy Tate (ts); Sammy Price (p); Billy Taylor (db); Sid Catlett (d); Jesse Perry (v)

W75046	'T ain't nobody's business if I do (JP:v)	Vocalion 55023
W75047	In the Middle of the Night (JP:v)	Unissued
W75048	Bash Street	Vocalion 55023
W75049	Hold me baby (JP:v)	Unissued

1949
Aug 17   New York
Billie Holiday (v) with Buster Harding and his Orchestra
Emmett Berry (t); Jimmy Nottingham (t); Buck Clayton (t); Dicky Wells (tb); George Matthews (tb); Rudy Powell (as); George Dorsey (as); Lester Young (ts); Joe Thomas (ts); Sol Moore (bs); Horace Henderson (p); Mundell Lowe (g); George Duvivier (db); Shadow Wilson (d)

W75147-A	'T ain't nobody's business if I do	Decca 24726
W75148-A	Baby get lost	Decca 24726

1949
Sept 1   New York
Louis Armstrong (t, v) with Sy Oliver and his Orchestra
Buck Clayton (t); Ivor Lloyd (t); Henderson Chambers (tb); George Dorsey (as); Artie Baker (as); Budd Johnson (ts); Freddie Williams (ts); Horace Henderson (p); Everett Barksdale (eg); Joe Benjamin (db); Wallace Bishop (d)

W75221	Maybe it's because	Decca 24751
W75222	I'll keep the lovelight burning	Decca 24751

1949
Sept 8   New York
Billie Holiday (v) with Sy Oliver and his Orchestra
Buck Clayton (t); Shad Collins (t); Bob Williams (t); Henderson Chambers (tb); George Stevenson (tb); Pete Clarke (as); George Dorsey (as); Budd Johnson (ts); Freddie Williams (ts); Dave McRae (bs); Horace Henderson (p); Everett Barksdale (eg); Joe Benjamin (db); Wallace Bishop (d)

W75241-A	Do your duty	Decca 48259
W75242-A	Gimme a pigfoot and a bottle of beer	Decca 24947

1949
Oct 10   Paris
Buck Clayton Sextet/Quintet/and his Rhythm
Buck Clayton (t); Merrill Stepter (t); Don Byas (ts); Charlie Lewis (p): Georges Hadjo (db); Wallace Bishop (d)

RJS900-2 High Tide   Royal Jazz (F) 719
RJS901-1 At Sundown   Vogue(F) V5063
RJS902-3 Who's Sorry Now?   Royal Jazz(F) 720
RJS903-2 Sugar Blues (omit Stepter)   Royal Jazz(F) 720
RJS904-1 Blues in First (omit Stepter, Byas) (*)   Royal Jazz(F)
                                                                   721
RJS904-2 Blues in Second (omit Stepter, Byas) (*)   Royal
                                                          Jazz(F) 721
RJS905-2 Don's Blues   Royal Jazz(F) 719

1949
Nov 4   Poste Parisien Studio, Paris
Earl "Fatha" Hines's All Stars Quintet
*Buck Clayton (t); Barney Bigard (cl); Earl Hines (p); Arvell Shaw (db);
Wallace Bishop (d)*
RJS908-1   Chicago   Royal Jazz(F) 724
RJS909-3   Night Life in Pompeii   Royal Jazz(F) 725
RJS909-2   Night Life in Pompeii   (10″) Vogue(F) LD 053
RJS910-1   Japanese Sandman   Royal Jazz(F) 726
RJS911-2   Rhythm Business   Royal Jazz(F) 726
RJS913-2   Air France Stomp   Royal Jazz(F) 725
RJS913-1-3 Air France Stomp   (10″) Vogue(F) LD 053

1949
Nov 21   Paris
Buck Clayton and his Orchestra
*Buck Clayton (t); Bill Coleman (t); Merrill Stepter (t); Alix Combelle
(ts); Armand Conrad (ts); George Kennedy (as, bs); André Persiany (p);
Georges Hadjo (db); Wallace Bishop (d)*
RJS919   Uncle Buck (*)   Royal Jazz(F) 734
RJS920-2 Buck Special   Royal Jazz(F) 731
RJS921   Night Life (*)   Royal Jazz(F) 731
RJS922-2 Perdido   Royal Jazz(F) 734
RJS923-4 B.C. and B.C. (omit Stepter, saxes) (*)   Royal Jazz(F)
                                                                   738
RJS924   Sweet Georgia Brown (omit saxes) Royal Jazz(F) 738

1949
December   Paris
Coleman Hawkins–Buck Clayton Quintet
*Buck Clayton (t); Coleman Hawkins (ts); Raymond Le Senechal (p);
Pierre Michelot (db); Wallace Bishop (d)*
Mop mop   Europa Jazz(I) EJ-1020
I'm in the mood for love   Europa Jazz(I) EJ-1020

1949
Dec 24   Paris
Willie "the Lion" Smith Quartet/Buck Clayton Trio
*Buck Clayton (t); Claude Luter (cl); Willie "the Lion" Smith (p, v);
Wallace Bishop (d)*
RJS938-1 Darktown Strutter's Ball (WS:v)   Royal Jazz(F) 742
RJS938-2 Darktown Strutter's Ball (WS:v)   Mode(F) 9736
RJS939   Ain't Misbehavin' (WS:v)   Royal Jazz(F) 742
RJS940   Stormy weather (omit Luter)   Vogue(F) V5063
RJS941   Get Together Blues   Royal Jazz(F) 743
RJS942   Nagasaki (WS:v)   Royal Jazz(F) 743

1950
Autumn   New York
Patti Page (v) with Jack Rael's orchestra, incl. Buck Clayton (t)
3951 Boogie Woogie Santa Claus   Mercury 5534
3952 Tennessee Waltz   Mercury 5534

1951
April 1   New York
Benny Goodman Trio with guests
*Buck Clayton (t); Benny Goodman (cl); Teddy Wilson (p); Johnny
Smith (eg); Eddie Safranski (db); Gene Krupa (d)*
XTV14889-2b Honeysuckle Rose   Columbia MB1000
XTV14889-2d One O'Clock Jump (add Lou McGarity, tb)
                                          Columbia MB1000

NB: Clayton not on 8 further items; all 10 titles were originally
issued as a limited edition album in aid of the Fletcher Henderson fund.

1951
April 28   Birdland, New York
Count Basie Seven with Buck Clayton
*Buck Clayton (t); Clark Terry (t); Marshall Royal (cl); Wardell Gray
(ts); Count Basie (p); Freddie Green (g); Jimmy Lewis (db); Gus
Johnson (d)*
Jumping at the Woodside Ozone 6/Music Room Special MRS-5006
How High the Moon
Lady be good
Golden Bullet
One O'Clock Jump

1951
July 10   New York
Peggy Lee (v) with Mel Tormé (v, d) and his Orchestra
*Buck Clayton (t); Bernie Privin (t); Buddy Morrow (tb); Lou McGarity
(tb); Warren Covington (tb); John Lewis (p); Barry Galbraith (eg); Joe
Shulman (db); Billy Exiner (d)*
7294 Don't fan the flame (PL,MT:v)   Capitol 1738
      Telling me yes and telling me no (PL:v)   Capitol 1738

1951
July 31   New York
Joe Bushkin Quartet
Buck Clayton (t); Joe Bushkin (p); Eddie Safranski (db); Jo Jones (d)
CO 47005   If I had you   Columbia 39621
CO 47006   They can't take that away from me   Columbia
                                                                   39621
CO 47007-1 At Sundown   Unissued—rejected
CO 47008   California here I come   Columbia 39618
CO 47009   Dinah   Columbia 39620

1951
cAugust   The Embers Club, New York
Joe Bushkin Quartet
Buck Clayton (t); Joe Bushkin (p); Eddie Safranski (db); Jo Jones (d)
The Sheik of Araby   Foxy(I) 9002
Blue Moon
I can't get started
On the Sunny Side of the Street
'S wonderful
I've got a crush on you
Wrap your troubles in dreams
At Sundown
Perdido

1951
cAugust   The Embers Club, New York
Joe Bushkin Quartet
Buck Clayton (t); Joe Bushkin (p); Eddie Safranski (db); Jo Jones (d)
If I had you   Private tape
Portrait of Talullah
The best thing for you
You're just in love
Medley: Easy living/Sing a blue song/
    I surrender dear
Medley: Sugar/Squeeze me

NB: the Joe Bushkin Quartet with Clayton played several engagements at the Embers Club in the 1950s and further amateur
tapes of radio broadcasts are probably available.

1951
Aug 7   New York
Joe Bushkin Quartet
Buck Clayton (t); Joe Bushkin (p); Sid Weiss (db); Jo Jones (d)
CO 47007-2 At Sundown   Columbia 39619
CO 47022   Old Man River   Columbia 39618
CO 47023   Once in a while   Columbia 39619
CO 47024   High Cotton   Columbia 39620

1951
Aug 18   New York
Patti Page (v) with the Joe Reisman Orchestra
*Billy Butterfield (t); Jimmy Maxwell (t); Buck Clayton (t); Buddy
Morrow (tb); Bob Alexander (tb); Sam Marowitz (as); Charlie O'Kane
(as); Paul Ricci (as, bs); Romeo Penque (as, bs); Lou Stein (p); Mundell
Lowe (g); Eddie Safranski (db); Sol Gubin (d)*

One sweet letter from you   Mercury 5706
That's all I ever ask   Mercury?
And so to sleep again   Mercury 5706
Jingle Bells   Mercury 5730

1951
Sept 12   New York
Rita Moss (v) with Neal Hefti and his Orchestra
Buck Clayton (t); Kai Winding (tb); Artie Baker (as); George Berg (ts); Bernie Leighton (p); George Barnes (steel g); Art Ryerson (g); Irv Manning (db); Don Lamond (d)
Darlin'   Decca 27873
Love me or please let me be   Decca 27873

1951
September   New York
Bernie Leighton and his Swing Seven
Buck Clayton (t); Kai Winding (tb); Peanuts Hucko (cl); Bernie Leighton (p); Barry Galbraith (g); Sid Weiss (db); Morey Feld (d); Johnny Davis (v)
Smooth Sailing (JD:v)   Mello-Roll 5004
Whispering   Mello-Roll 5004
Sixty Minute Man (JD:v)   Mello-Roll 5005
The world is waiting for the sunrise (JD:v)   Mello-Roll 5005

1951
Oct 16   New York
Titus Turner (v) with Howard Biggs and his Orchestra
Buck Clayton (t); Joe Thomas (ts); Pinky Williams (bs); Howard Biggs (p); Jimmy Cannady (g); Abe Baker (db); James Crawford (d)
CO 46966   It's too late now   OKeh 6938
CO 46967   Don't take everybody to be your friend   OKeh 6844
CO 46968   What'cha gonna do?   OKeh 6883
CO 46969   The Same Old Feeling   OKeh 6844

1951
Oct 25   New York
George Siravo's Orchestra
Chris Griffin (t); Yank Lawson (t); Bernie Privin (t); Buck Clayton (t); Warren Covington (tb); Bob Alexander (tb); Hymie Schertzer (as); Bill Shine (as); Al Klink (ts); Yano Salto (ts); Ernie Caceres (bs); Bill Rowland (p); Mundell Lowe (g); Frank Carroll (db); Don Lamond (d); Trudy Richards, Ray Charles Singers (v)
I'll see you in my dreams (TR,RCS:v)   Mercury 5746
The Song is Ended   Mercury 5746
West End Ramp   Mercury?

1951
Nov 3   New York
Jesse Powell and his Orchestra with Fluffy Hunter (v)
Buck Clayton (t); J. J. Johnson (tb); Jesse Powell (ts); Cecil Payne (bs); Bill Doggett (p, o); Johnny Jones (eg); Jam Smith (db); Herbie Lovelle (d)
F190   My natch'l man   Federal 12060
F191   Love is a fortune   Federal 12056
F192   As long as you're satisfied   Federal 12060
F193   The Walkin' Blues   Federal 12056

1952
Jan 30   New York
Paul Quinichette and his Orchestra
Buck Clayton (t); Dicky Wells (tb); Paul Quinichette (ts); Count Basie (p); Freddie Green (g); Walter Page (db); Gus Johnson (d)
YB4815-1   Shad Roe   Mercury 8287
YB4816-2   Paul's Bunion   Mercury 70020
YB4817   Crew Cut (*)   (10") EmArcy MG26022
YB4818-1   The Hook   Mercury 8287

1952
Feb 7   New York
Ace Harris (v) and his Orchestra
Buck Clayton (t); Dick Jacobs (vc); Billy Kyle (p); Everett Barksdale (g); Sandy Block (db); Rudy Traylor (d)
81517   At your beck and call   Brunswick 84020
    That's how it goes   Coral?
    One for my Baby   Coral?
    Sentimental Tears   Coral 60666
    Two wrongs don't make a right   Coral 60666

1952
March 11   New York
Billy Daniels (v) with Russ Case Orchestra
Jimmy Maxwell (t); Bernie Privin (t); Buck Clayton (t); Jack Lacy (tb); Bobby Byrne (tb); Eddie Barefield (as); Andy Brown (ts); Benny Payne (p); Barry Galbraith (g); Milt Hinton (db); Specs Powell (d); Artie Malvin, Steve Steck, Gene Steck (v group)
My thrill is loving you   Mercury 5822
Must you go?   Mercury 5868
That's how it goes   Mercury 5822
Don't want that woman   Mercury?

1953
Feb 18   New York
Buck Clayton with the Marlowe Morris Trio
Buck Clayton (t); Marlowe Morris (o); Jerome Darr (eg); Les Erskine (d)
CO 49002-1   I want a little girl   OKeh 6968
CO 49003-1   Blue Moon   OKeh 6968
CO 49004   Basic Organ Blues, part 1   (EP) Epic EG-7009
CO 49005   Basic Organ Blues, part 2   (EP) Epic EG-7009
CO 49006   Hammond stomp   Unissued
CO 49007   'S wonderful, part 1   (EP) Epic EG-7009
CO 49008   'S wonderful, part 2   (EP) Epic EG-7009
CO 49009   It's only a paper moon   Unissued

1953
March 1   Théâtre des Champs-Elysées, Paris
Mezz Mezzrow and his Orchestra
Buck Clayton (t); "Big Chief" Russell Moore (tb, v); Mezz Mezzrow (cl); Gene Sedric (cl, ts); Red Richards (p); Kansas Fields (d); Taps Miller (v, t, tap dancing)
Matinee concert:
    Indiana   Vogue(F) DP14
    On the Sunny Side of the Street
    Swingin' with Mezz
    Perdido Street Stomp
    Honeysuckle Rose   (10") Vogue(F) LD137
    Boogie Special   (10") Vogue(F) LD137
    West End Blues (omit Sedric)   Vogue(F) DP14
    Buck Clayton Special
    I ain't got nobody (TM: tap dancing)
    Royal Garden Blues
    Tommy's Blues
    I can't believe that you're in love with me
    Clarinet Blues   Unissued
    Ain't Misbehavin' (omit Mezzrow)   (10") Vogue(F) LD137
4606   Wabash Blues   Vogue(F) V5161
4607   When the saints go marching in (RM, band:v)   Vogue(F) V5161
    When the saints go marching in (encore)   Unissued
    Liza   Unissued
    Liza (encore)   Unissued
    Wham and hold tight (TM: tap dancing, v, t)   Vogue(F) DP14
    Sweet Georgia Brown   Unissued
Probably from this concert:
    Really the Blues   Vogue(F) DP14
Evening concert:
    Indiana   Unissued
    Squeeze me
    Swingin' with Mezz
    Perdido Street Stomp
    Honeysuckle Rose
    Boogie Special
    West End Blues
    Buck Clayton Special
    I ain't got nobody (TM: tap dancing)
    Christopher Columbus   Vogue(F) DP14
    Royal Garden Blues   Unissued
    I can't give you anything but love   (10") Vogue(F) LD137
    Clarinet Blues   Unissued
    Someday Sweetheart
    Wabash Blues
    When the saints go marching in (RM, band:v)
    Liza
    High Tide (TM: tap dancing, v)

Boogie Blues   Unissued
Muskrat Ramble   (10") *Vogue(F) LD137*
Probably from this concert:
    I can't believe that you're in love with me   (10") *Vogue(F) LD137*

1953
April 2   Paris
Mezz Mezzrow and his Orchestra/Buck Clayton and his Orchestra
Buck Clayton (t); "Big Chief" Russell Moore (tb); Mezz Mezzrow (cl); Gene Sedric (ts); Red Richards (p); Pierre Michelot (db); Kansas Fields (d); Taps Miller (tap dancing)

53-V-4497	Wrap your troubles in dreams	*Vogue(F)* V5153
53-V-4498	Rose Room	*Vogue(F)* V5153
53-V-4499	Sweethearts on Parade (omit Mezzrow, Sedric)	*Vogue(F)* V5154
53-V-4500	Patricia's Blues (omit Mezzrow, Sedric) (*)	*Vogue(F)* V5154
53-V-4501	Special B.C. (omit Mezzrow, Sedric) (*)	*Vogue(F)* V5178
53-V-4502	She's funny that way (omit Mezzrow, Sedric)	*Vogue(F)* V5178
53-V-4503	Lazy River (omit Mezzrow, Sedric)	*Vogue(F)* V5182
53-V-4504	West End Blues (omit Sedric)	*Vogue(F)* V5182
53-V-4505	Swingin' with Mezz	*Vogue(F)* V5159
53-V-4506	St Louis Blues	*Vogue(F)* V5159
53-V-4507	Big Butter and Egg Man	*Vogue(F)* V5164
53-V-4508	I ain't got nobody (TM: tap dancing)	*Vogue(F)* V5164

1953
May 26   Paris
Clayton–Sedric Sextet
Buck Clayton (t); Mezz Mezzrow (cl); Gene Sedric (cl, ts); Red Richards (p); Georges Hadjo (db); Kansas Fields (d)

53-V-4588	Blues for Fats Waller	*Vogue(F)* V5165
53-V-4589	Catchin' the Boat Train	*Vogue(F)* V5165

mid-1953
Belgium
Taps Miller and Orchestra
Taps Miller (v, t); Buck Clayton (t); unknown (tb, reeds); possibly Red Richards (p); unknown (db); Kansas Fields (d)

18571	Some of these days (TM:v)	Ronnex (B) 1016
18572	Ferme la bouche (TM, band:v)	Ronnex (B) 1016
18599	How about me (TM:v)	Ronnex (B) 1020
18604	Manneke pis boogie (TM:v)	Ronnex (B) 1020
18611	Hot Dog (TM, band:v)	Ronnex (B) 1024
18612	There's nothing like a woman (TM:v)	Ronnex (B) 1024
18644	Boogie Woogie Drummer (TM:v)	Ronnex (B) 1027
18645	Bird Song	Ronnex (B) 1027

1953
Oct 9   Yverdon, Switzerland
Buck Clayton Quartet
Buck Clayton (t); George Voumard (p); Al Jacquillard (db); Mike Thevenot (d)
I'm confessin' that I love you   Private tape
Tea for Two
One O'Clock Jump
These Foolish Things
Perdido
B-flat Blues

1953
Oct 20–21   Paris
Buck Clayton with the Alix Combelle Orchestra
Buck Clayton (t); Alex Rénard (t); Pierre Selin (t); Aimé Hanuche (t); André Simon (t); René Godard (as); Jean-Jacques Lèger (as); Alix Combelle (ts); Henri Bernard (ts); Henri Jouot (bs); Jean-Claude Pelletier (p); Roger Chaput (g); Yvon Le Guen (db); Christian Garros (d)

53-V-4758	Qui? (Who?) (†)	*Vogue(E)* V2330
53-V-4759	Relax Alix	*Vogue(E)* V2330
	Sahiva Boogie (†)	(10") *Vogue(F) LD182*
	Promenade Blues (Strolling Blues) (†)(10") *Vogue(F) LD182*	

Bonds et rebonds
   (Jumping on the Rebound) (†)   (10") *Vogue(F) LD182*
Blues en cuivres (Blues in Brass) (†)   (10") *Vogue(F) LD182*

Pulsation du rhythme
   (Beatin' the Count) (†)   (10") *Vogue(F) LD182*
Chocs sonores (Basie Days) (†)   (10") *Vogue(F) LD182*

1953
Nov 6   Paris
Gérard Pochonet All Stars with Buck Clayton
Buck Clayton (t); Guy Longnon (t); Michel de Villers (cl, bs); André Persiany (p); Jean-Pierre Sasson (eg); Buddy Banks (db); Gérard Pochonet (d)

OLA6727	Blues for Hazel	(EP) *VSM(F)* 7EMF57
OLA6728	Stompin' at the Savoy	(EP) *VSM(F)* 7EMF57
	(add Benny Vasseur, tb)	

Buck Clayton (t); Roger Guerin (t); Benny Vasseur (tb); Charles Verstraete (tb); José Germain (as); André Ross (ts); Michel de Villers (bs); André Persiany (p); Charlie Blareau (db); Gérard Pochonet (d)
Swingin' the A. P. Blues   (10") *VSM(F) FFLP1022*

1953
Nov 12   Paris
Gérard Pochonet All Stars with Buck Clayton
Buck Clayton (t); Benny Vasseur (tb); André Ross (ts); Michel de Villers (bs); André Persiany (p); Jean-Pierre Sasson (eg); Buddy Banks (db); Gérard Pochonet (d)
Some of these days (†)   (10") *VSM(F) FFLP1022*

Buck Clayton (t); Benny Vasseur (tb); José Germain (as); André Ross (ts); Michel de Villers (bs); André Persiany (p); Charlie Blareau (db); Gérard Pochonet (d)
I'm confessin' that I love you (†)   (EP) *VSM(F)* 7EMF57

Buck Clayton (t); Michel de Villers (as, bs); André Persiany (p); Jean-Pierre Sasson (eg); Charlie Blareau (db); Gérard Pochonet (d)
Buck's bon voyage   (10") *Club Français du Disque(F)* J6
Fast but Soft
Please don't talk about me when I'm gone (omit Sasson)
Easy to Riff (omit de Villers)
I found a new baby (as Gift for the Club) (†)

1953
December   The Embers Club, New York
Joe Bushkin Quartet
Buck Clayton (t); Joe Bushkin (p, v); Milt Hinton (db); Jo Jones (d)

I can't get started	(16" ET) AFRS ONS 3511	
Undecided	(16" ET) AFRS ONS 3511	
Medley: Stars fell on Alabama/Georgia on my Mind/		
Oh look at me now (JB:v)	(16" ET) AFRS ONS 3511	
Love me or leave me	(16" ET) AFRS ONS 3511	
Goody goody	(16" ET) AFRS ONS 3511	
Medley: I've got a crush on you/		
Stompin' at the Savoy	(16" ET) AFRS ONS 3511	

NB: Clayton does not play on Stars fell on Alabama; Stompin' at the Savoy is incomplete.

1953
Dec 14   New York
Buck Clayton Jam Session
Buck Clayton (t); Joe Newman (t); Urbie Green (tb); Benny Powell (tb); Lem Davis (as); Julian Dash (ts); Charlie Fowlkes (bs); Sir Charles Thompson (p); Freddie Green (g); Walter Page (db); Jo Jones (d)

CO 50436	Sentimental Journey	(10") *Columbia CL6325*
CO 50437	Moten Swing	(10") *Columbia CL6325*

1953
Dec 16   New York
Buck Clayton Jam Session
Buck Clayton (t); Joe Newman (t); Urbie Green (tb); Henderson Chambers (tb); Lem Davis (as); Julian Dash (ts); Charlie Fowlkes (bs); Sir Charles Thompson (p, cel); Freddie Green (g); Walter Page (db); Jo Jones (d)

CO 50531	Lean Baby	*Columbia CL882*

CO 50532   The Huckle-buck   *Columbia CL548*
CO 50533-1 Robbins' Nest ⎫ (splice from
CO 50533-2 Robbins' Nest ⎭ both takes)   *Columbia CL548*
CO 50534   Christopher Columbus (edited)   *Columbia CL614*

1953
Dec 30   New York
Mel Powell Septet
Buck Clayton (t); Henderson Chambers (tb); Edmond Hall (cl); Mel Powell (p); Steve Jordan (g); Walter Page (db); James Crawford (d)
'S wonderful   (10") *Vanguard VRS8004*
It's been so long
I must have that man
You're lucky to me

early 1954
The Embers Club, New York
Joe Bushkin Quartet
Buck Clayton (t); Joe Bushkin (p); Milt Hinton (db); Jo Jones (d)
Love me or leave me   (16" ET) AFRS ONS 3520
Medley: If I had you/Dinah   (16" ET) AFRS ONS 3520
California here I come   (16" ET) AFRS ONS 3520
Undecided   (16" ET) AFRS ONS 3520
Medley: Our love is here to stay/The very
     thought of you/Don't blame me   (16" ET) AFRS ONS
                                       3520
You're driving me crazy (part)   (16" ET) AFRS ONS 3520

early 1954
The Embers Club, New York
Joe Bushkin Quartet
Buck Clayton (t); Joe Bushkin (p); Milt Hinton (db); Jo Jones (d)
Indiana   (16" ET) AFRS ONS 3548
You're driving me crazy   (16" ET) AFRS ONS 3548

1954
Feb 28   NBC Studios, New York
"Excursion in Jazz" (television broadcast)
Buck Clayton (t); Vic Dickenson (tb); Edmond Hall (cl); Paul Quinichette (ts); Mel Powell (p); Mundell Lowe (bj, eg); Walter Page (db); Osie Johnson (d)
'S wonderful (dixieland style)
Unknown title (slow blues) (t, bj, db, washboard only)
That's a plenty (dixieland style) (omit Quinichette)
Backwater Blues (accompaniment to record by Bessie Smith)
Lady be good (dance band style)
Lady be good (swing style)
Lady be good (bop style) (omit Hall, Powell)
Stompin' at the Savoy (add Count Basie, p; Louis Bellson, d)

1954
March 31   New York
Buck Clayton Jam Session
Buck Clayton (t); Joe Thomas (t); Urbie Green (tb); Trummy Young (tb); Woody Herman (cl); Lem Davis (as); Al Cohn (ts); Julian Dash (ts); Jimmy Jones (p, cel); Steve Jordan (g); Walter Page (db); Jo Jones (d)
CO 51243   How hi the fi   (10") *Columbia CL6326*
CO 51244   Blue Moon   (10") *Columbia CL6326*
CO 51245-1 Jumpin' at the Woodside   (EP) *Columbia B2089*

1954
April 9   Carnegie Hall, New York
Mel Powell and his All Stars
Buck Clayton (t); Ruby Braff (c); Urbie Green (tb); Vernon Brown (tb); Tony Scott (cl); Lem Davis (as); Buddy Tate (ts); Mel Powell (p); Steve Jordan (g); Milt Hinton (db); Jo Jones (d); Martha Lou Harp (v)
CO 51386   When day is done (MLH:v;
       add Jay Brower, t; Romeo Penque, as, bs)   *Columbia*
                                            CL557
CO 51387   I found a new baby
CO 51388   Lighthouse Blues
CO 51389   After you've gone (add Gene Krupa Trio)

NB: Krupa Trio: Eddie Shu (ts); Teddy Napoleon (p); Gene Krupa (d)

1954
July 1   New York
Buck Clayton's Band featuring Ruby Braff
Buck Clayton (t); Ruby Braff (c); Benny Morton (tb); Buddy Tate (ts); Jimmy Jones (p); Steve Jordan (g); Aaron Bell (db); Bobby Donaldson (d)
Kandee (*)   (10") *Vanguard VRS8008*
I can't get started
Love is just around the corner
Just a Groove (omit Morton, Tate) (*)

1954
Aug 13   New York
Buck Clayton Jam Session
Buck Clayton (t); Joe Newman (t); Urbie Green (tb); Trummy Young (tb); Lem Davis (as); Coleman Hawkins (ts); Charlie Fowlkes (bs); Billy Kyle (p, cel); Freddie Green (g); Milt Hinton (db); Jo Jones (d)
CO 51245-2 Jumpin' at the Woodside (splice) *Columbia CL701*
CO 52505   Don't be that way   *Columbia CL614*
CO 52506   Undecided   *Columbia CL614*
CO 52507   Blue and Sentimental   *Columbia CL701*

NB: all 12" LP issues of Jumpin' at the Woodside contain a spliced version of Jumpin' from 31 March 1954 and part of take 2.

1955
March 15   New York
Buck Clayton Jam Session
Buck Clayton (t); Ruby Braff (c); Benny Green (tb); Dicky Harris (tb); Coleman Hawkins (ts); Buddy Tate (ts); Al Waslohn (p); Freddie Green (g); Milt Hinton (db); Jo Jones (d); Jack Ackerman (tap dancing)
CO 52630   Rock-a-bye Basie (JA: tap dancing) *Columbia CL701*
CO 52631   Out of Nowhere   *Columbia CL882*
CO 52632   Blue Lou   *Columbia CL882*
CO 52633   Broadway   *Columbia CL701*

1955
April   New York
Teddy Wilson Trio with Coleman Hawkins and Buck Clayton
Buck Clayton (t); Coleman Hawkins (ts); Teddy Wilson (p); Milt Hinton (db); Jo Jones (d)
One O'Clock Jump   (16" ET) AFRS Teddy Wilson No. 7
I'm confessin' that I love you
  (omit Hawkins)   (16" ET) AFRS Teddy Wilson No. 7

1955
May 6   Carnegie Hall, New York: "Lighthouse Concert"
Billie Holiday (v), with Buck Clayton (t); Lester Young (ts); Count Basie (o); Carl Drinkard (p); Walter Page (db); Jo Jones (d)
Stormy Weather   *Society (E) SOC1027*

Count Basie and his Orchestra with guests
Buck Clayton (t), Lester Young (ts), as featured guests with:
Wendell Culley (t); Renauld Jones (t); Thad Jones (t); Joe Newman (t); Henry Coker (tb); Bill Hughes (tb); Benny Powell (tb); Marshall Royal (as); Bill Graham (as); Frank Wess (ts); Frank Foster (ts); Charlie Fowlkes (bs); Count Basie (p); Freddie Green (g); Eddie Jones (db); Sonny Payne (d)
Lady be good   *Hall of Fame/Jazz Greats JG-629*

1955
July 1   Hollywood   "Steve Allen in Movieland" (NBC television broadcast)
Benny Goodman Septet
Buck Clayton (t); Urbie Green (tb); Benny Goodman (cl); Stan Getz (ts); Teddy Wilson (p); Steve Allen (p); George Duvivier (db); Gene Krupa (d)
Slipped Disc   Unissued

1955
early August   Universal-International Studios, Hollywood
Benny Goodman and his Orchestra "The Benny Goodman Story" (film soundtrack)
Conrad Gozzo (t); Chris Griffin (t); Irving Goodman (t); Buck Clayton (t); John Best (t); Ray Linn (t); Urbie Green (tb); Murray McEachern (tb); Jimmy Priddy (tb); Benny Goodman (cl); Hymie Schertzer (as); Blake Reynolds (as); Babe Russin (ts); Stan Getz (ts);

Teddy Wilson (p); Allan Reuss (g); George Duvivier (db); Gene Krupa (d); Martha Tilton (v)
89016 Let's dance   *Decca DL8252/3*
89017 Down South Camp Meeting
          (saxes double cl)
89018 King Porter Stomp
89019 It's been so long
89020 You turned the tables on me (MT:v)
89021 Bugle Call Rag
89022 Don't be that way
89023 Roll 'em
89024 Goody goody
89026 Stompin' at the Savoy
89027 One O'Clock Jump
89033 And the angels sing
          (MT:v; add Manny Klein, t)
89034 Jersey Bounce
89035 Sometimes I'm happy
89036 Shine (add Harry James, t)
89037 Sing sing sing (add Harry James, t)

Benny Goodman Octet
Buck Clayton (t); Urbie Green (tb); Benny Goodman (cl); Stan Getz (ts); Teddy Wilson (p); Allan Reuss (g); George Duvivier (db); Gene Krupa (d)
89025 Slipped Disc   *Decca DL8252/3*
NB: The following item appeared in the film but not on records:
Benny Goodman Septet
Buck Clayton (t); Urbie Green (tb); Benny Goodman (cl); Teddy Wilson (p); Allan Reuss (g); George Duvivier (db); Gene Krupa (d)
Sensation Rag

1955
Aug 18   New York   "Cat Meets Chick"
Buck Clayton, Jimmy Rushing, Ada Moore with Buck Clayton's Orchestra
Jimmy Rushing (v, nar); Ada Moore (v, nar); Buck Clayton (t); Emmett Berry (t); Dicky Wells (tb); Eddie Barefield (cl, as); Budd Johnson (ts); Willard Brown (ts, bs); Sir Charles Thompson (p); Steve Jordan (g); Aaron Bell (db); Jo Jones (d)
Any place I hang my hat is home (AM:v) (†)   *Columbia CL778*
Pretty little baby (JR:v) (†)
I've got a feeling I'm falling (AM:v) (†)
One hour (JR,AM:v) (†)
Ain't she sweet? (†)

1955
Aug 19   New York   "Cat Meets Chick"
Same personnel as session of 18 Aug 1955
You're my thrill (AM:v) (†)   *Columbia CL778*
Between the devil and the deep blue sea (AM:v) (†)
Gee baby, ain't I good to you? (JR:v) (†)

1955
Aug 23   New York   "Cat Meets Chick"
Same personnel as session of 18 Aug 1955 except Ken Kersey (p); Milt Hinton (db); Osie Johnson (d) replace Thompson, Bell and Jones
Any place I hang my hat is home (AM:v) (†)   *Columbia CL778*
Cool Breeze Woman (JR:v) (†)
I can't give you anything but love (†)
The Blues (†)
Any place I hang my hat is home (AM:v) (†)
After you've gone (JR:v) (†)
Closing Theme (†)

1955
Oct 24   New York
Frankie Laine (v) with Buck Clayton and his Orchestra
Buck Clayton (t); Ray Copeland (t); Urbie Green (tb); Hilton Jefferson (as); Budd Johnson (ts); George Nicholas (ts); Dave McRae (bs); Sir Charles Thompson (p); Skeeter Best (g); Milt Hinton (db); Jo Jones (d)
ZEP 37276 Baby baby all the time (†)   *Columbia CL808*
ZEP 37328 S'posin' (†)
ZEP 37329 That Old Feeling (†)
ZEP 37330 You can depend on me (†)
ZEP 37331 Stars fell on Alabama (†)

1955
Oct 25   New York
Same personnel as session of 24 Oct 1955 except Lawrence Brown (tb); J. J. Johnson (tb); Kai Winding (tb) replace Green
ZEP 37277-1 Taking a chance on love (†) Rejected—unissued
ZEP 37278   Roses of Picardy (†)   *Columbia CL808*

1955
Oct 26   New York
Same personnel as session of 25 Oct 1955 except Bobby Donaldson (d) replaces Jo Jones; omit Lawrence Brown
ZEP 37277-2 Taking a chance on love (†)   *Columbia CL808*

Buck Clayton (t); Urbie Green (tb); Dicky Wells (tb); Hilton Jefferson (as); Budd Johnson (ts); Al Sears (ts); Dave McRae (bs); Sir Charles Thompson (p); Skeeter Best (g); Milt Hinton (db); Bobby Donaldson (d)
ZEP 37342 Until the real thing comes along (†) *Columbia CL808*
ZEP 37343 If you were mine (†)
ZEP 37344 My Old Flame (no vocal) (†)

1955
Nov 14   New York
Benny Goodman Sextet with Rosemary Clooney
Buck Clayton (t); Urbie Green (tb); Benny Goodman (cl, v); Dick Hyman (p); Aaron Bell (db); Bobby Donaldson (d); Rosemary Clooney (v)
CO 54293-1 It's bad for me (BG,RC:v) (10") *Columbia CL2572*
CO 54294-1 Goodbye (RC:v)
CO 54295-1 That's a plenty

1955
Dec 6   New York
Benny Goodman Sextet
Buck Clayton (t); Urbie Green (tb); Benny Goodman (cl); Claude Thornhill (p); Aaron Bell (db); Bobby Donaldson (d)
CO 54220   Can't we talk it over?   (10") *Columbia CL2572*
CO 54221-1 A Fine Romance   (10") *Columbia CL2572*

1955
Dec 12   New York
Benny Goodman and his Orchestra
Bernie Glow (t); Doc Severinsen (t); Buck Clayton (t); Urbie Green (tb); Lou McGarity (tb); Benny Goodman (cl); Hymie Schertzer (as); Milt Yaner (as); Peanuts Hucko (ts); Boomie Richman (ts); Sol Schlinger (bs); Morris Wechsler (p); Al Caiola (g); George Duvivier (db); Don Lamond (d)
20932   Don't be that way   *Capitol S-706*
20946-1-2   King Porter Stomp   Unissued

1955
Dec 14 (afternoon)   New York
Benny Goodman and his Orchestra
Same personnel as session of 12 Dec 1955 plus Benny Goodman (v)
20946-3-8   King Porter Stomp   Unissued
20947   It's been so long   *Capitol S-706*
20948   Let's dance   *Capitol S-706*
20951   Sometimes I'm happy   (45) *Capitol F-3331*
20952   Goody goody (BG:v)   (45) *Capitol F-3331*

1955
Dec 14 (evening)   New York
"The Tonight Show" (NBC television broadcast)
Benny Goodman Sextet with guests
Buck Clayton (t); Urbie Green (tb); Benny Goodman (cl); Teddy Wilson (p); unknown (db); Don Lamond (d)
Honeysuckle Rose   *Giants of Jazz GOJ-1010*
Memories of You   Unissued

add Doc Severinsen (t); Lou McGarity (tb); Sol Yaged (cl); Sid Caesar (ts)
One O'Clock Jump   Unissued
Stompin' at the Savoy   Unissued

1956
New York
Vic Damone (v) with Camarata and his Orchestra
Buck Clayton (t); string section; unknown (p, cel, vib, eg, db, d)
39651 You stepped out of a dream   *Columbia CL900*

Out of Nowhere (unknown female: v)
Time on my Hands
The Touch of your Lips

1956
March 5   New York
Buck Clayton Jam Session
Buck Clayton (t); Billy Butterfield (t); Ruby Braff (c); J. C. Higginbotham (tb); Tyree Glenn (tb, vib); Coleman Hawkins (ts); Julian Dash (ts); Ken Kersey (p); Steve Jordan (g); Walter Page (db); Bobby Donaldson (d); Jimmy Rushing (v)
CO 55544   All the cats join in   *Columbia CL882*
CO 55545   After hours   *Meritt 10*
CO 55546   Don't you miss your baby?
                 (JR:v; omit Glenn)   *Columbia CL882*

1956
March 21   New York
Johnny Mathis (v) with Gil Evans and his Orchestra
Jimmy Maxwell (t); Buck Clayton (t); J. J. Johnson (tb); Tommy Mitchell (bass tb); John LaPorta (cl, as); Hank Jones (p); Bill Pemberton (b); Billy Exiner (d)
CO 55650   Love, your magic spell is everywhere   *Columbia CL887*
CO 55651   It might as well be spring
CO 55652   Easy to love

1956
March 26   New York
Boyd Raeburn and his Orchestra
Billy Butterfield (t); Buck Clayton (t); Jerry Laubach (t); Mike Shain (t); Eddie Bert (tb); Phil Giacobbe (tb); Harry DiVito (tb); Ray Beckenstein (as); Sam Marowitz (as); Eddie Scalzi (as); Sam Taylor (ts); Frank Socolow (ts); Danny Bank (bs); Nat Pierce (p); George Barnes (g); Oscar Pettiford (db); Gus Johnson (d)
CO 56387   Tonsilectomy   *Columbia CL957*
CO 56388   Blueberry Hill
CO 56389   I'll see you in my dreams
CO 56390   Get out of town

1956
July 6   Newport Jazz Festival
Buck Clayton All Stars
Buck Clayton (t); J. J. Johnson (tb); Coleman Hawkins (ts); Dick Katz (p); Benny Moten (db); Gus Johnson (d)
CO 56793   You can depend on me   *Columbia CL933*
CO 56794   In a Mellotone
CO 56795   Newport Jump (*)

1956
July 12   New York
Buck Clayton Band
Buck Clayton (t); Lawrence Brown (tb); Buster Bailey (cl); Coleman Hawkins (ts); Nat Pierce (p); Freddie Green (g); Eddie Jones (db); Gus Johnson (d); Leonard Bernstein (nar, v)
Trumpet Cadenza (Clayton only)   *Columbia CL919*
Rhumba (Clayton with Latin rhythm section)
Trumpet Mutes (Clayton only)
MacBeth Blues (LB:v; full band minus Hawkins)
Happy Blues (full band)
Sweet Sue (Clayton, Bailey and rhythm section)
Sweet Sue (full band minus Hawkins)

NB: this session provided some of the musical illustrations for the "What is Jazz" LP.

1956
July 19   New York
Boyd Raeburn and his Orchestra
Ernie Royal (t); Al Maiorca (t); Buck Clayton (t); Nick Travis (t); Lawrence Brown (tb); Johnny Messner (tb); Sam Russo (tb); Buster Bailey (as); Sam Marowitz (as); Charlie O'Kane (as); Coleman Hawkins (ts); Frank Socolow (ts); Walter Bettman (bs); Nat Pierce (p); Freddie Green (g); Eddie Jones (db); James Crawford (d)
CO 56386   Sweet Sue (1938 style: extract)   *Columbia CL919*
CO 56820   A little bit square but nice   *Columbia CL957*
CO 56821   One Hour (If I could be with you) *Columbia CL957*

1956
July 28   Connecticut Jazz Festival
The Jazz Festival All Stars
Buck Clayton (t); Jimmy Hamilton (cl); Paul Gonsalves (ts); Hank Jones (p); Sidney Gross (g); Jimmy Woode (db); Sam Woodyard (d)
Tea for Two   *Queen-disc(I) Q-044*
Jazz Festival Blues

Willie "the Lion" Smith and his Quartet
Buck Clayton (t); Willie "the Lion" Smith (p); Walter Page (db); Art Trappier (d)
Perdido   *Queen-disc(I) Q-044*
Squeeze me

1956
Nov 6   New York
Jimmy Rushing (v) with Buck Clayton and his Orchestra
Buck Clayton (t); Ernie Royal (t); Vic Dickenson (tb); Hilton Jefferson (as); Buddy Tate (ts); Danny Bank (bs); Hank Jones (p); Skeeter Best (g); Milt Hinton (db); Jo Jones (d)
CO 56714   Careless Love (†)   *Columbia CL963*
CO 56715   Doctor Blues (†)
CO 56716   Rosetta (†)

Jimmy Rushing (v); Buck Clayton (t); Vic Dickenson (tb); Tony Parenti (cl); Cliff Jackson (p); Walter Page (db); Zutty Singleton (d)
CO 56717   New Orleans (†)   *Columbia CL963*
CO 56718   Baby won't you please come home? (†)

1956
Nov 7   New York
Jimmy Rushing (v) with Buck Clayton and his Orchestra
Buck Clayton (t); Vic Dickenson (tb); Buddy Tate (ts); Cliff Jackson (p); Walter Page (db); Jo Jones (d)
CO 56719   Piney Brown Blues (†)   *Columbia CL963*
CO 56720   'T ain't nobody's business if I do (†)
CO 56721   I'm gonna move to the outskirts
                 of town (†)

1956
Nov 8   New York
Jimmy Rushing (v) with Buck Clayton and his Orchestra
Buck Clayton (t); Ed Lewis (t); Billy Butterfield (t); Urbie Green (tb); Dicky Wells (tb); Hilton Jefferson (as); Rudy Powell (as); Budd Johnson (ts); Dave McRae (bs); Hank Jones (p); Steve Jordan (g); Milt Hinton (db); Jo Jones (d)
CO 56723   Old Fashioned Love (†)   *Columbia CL963*
CO 56724   Lullaby of Broadway (†)
CO 56725   Some of these days (†)

1956
Nov 10   Carnegie Hall, New York
Billie Holiday (v), with Buck Clayton (t); Tony Scott (cl); Al Cohn (ts); Carl Drinkard (p); Kenny Burrell (eg); Carson Smith (db); Chico Hamilton (d); Gilbert Millstein (nar)
Yesterdays   *Verve V8410*
Please don't talk about me when I'm gone
I'll be seeing you
My Man
I cried for you
Fine and Mellow
I cover the waterfront
What a little moonlight can do
Lover Man   *Unissued*
I only have eyes for you
Strange Fruit
Easy Living
I love you Porgy

1957
Feb 10   New York   "Ed Sullivan Show" (television broadcast)
Benny Goodman and his Orchestra
Jimmy Maxwell (t); Buck Clayton (t); Nick Travis (t); Rex Peer (tb); Frank Rehak (tb); Benny Goodman (cl); Al Block (as); Red Press (as); Budd Johnson (ts); Sol Schlinger (ts); Hank Jones (p); Steve Jordan (g); Irv Manning (db); Mousey Alexander (d)
Let's dance (theme)   *Giants of Jazz GOJ-1010*
Sing, sing, sing

1957
March 14   New York
Buck Clayton Septet
Buck Clayton (t); Vic Dickenson (tb); Earle Warren (as); Hank Jones (p); Kenny Burrell (eg); Aaron Bell (db); Jo Jones (d)
Buck Huckles (*)   *Vanguard VRS8514*
Claytonia (*)
Cool Too (*)
Squeeze me
Good Mornin' Blues
Ballin' the Jack
Blues Blase (*)
The Queen's Express (*)

1957
July 20   Great South Bay Jazz Festival, Great River, Long Island
Buck Clayton's Kansas City Six with Jimmy Rushing
Buck Clayton (t); Vic Dickenson (tb); Paul Quinichette (ts); Hank Jones (p); Walter Page (db); Bobby Donaldson (d); Jimmy Rushing (v)
First set:
    Lester Leaps in
    'S wonderful
    Birth of the Blues
    On the Sunny Side of the Street (JR:v)
    Goin' to Chicago (JR:v)
    How Long Blues (JR:v)
    Blues (JR:v)
    Sent for you yesterday (JR:v)
Second set:
    I found a new baby
    The Huckle-buck
    Blue Skies (JR:v)
    Baby won't you please come home (JR:v)
    Blues (JR:v)

NB: These sessions were recorded by Voice of America radio but were not broadcast. It has been reported that the tapes of this festival were confiscated by the AFM.

1957
August   RCA Studios, New York
Nat Pierce Orchestra featuring Buck Clayton
Buck Clayton (t); Doug Mettome (t); Al Stewart (t); Don Stratton (t); Skip Reider (t); Jim Dahl (tb); Bill Elton (tb); Frank Rehak (tb); Dick Meldonian (as); Anthony Ortega (as); Dick Hafer (ts); Paul Quinichette (ts); Gene Allen (bs); Nat Pierce (p); Turk Van Lake (g); Bill Takas (db); Gus Johnson (d)
Stompin' at the Savoy   *RCA Victor LPM2543*
Seventh Avenue Express (*†)
Love Letters
Pepper Green (*†)
Whaddaya know?
Moody Chant (†)
After Glow
Middle Man

1957
Oct 4   New York
Buck Clayton All Stars
Buck Clayton (t); Vic Dickenson (tb); Buddy Tate (ts); Dick Katz (p); Walter Page (db); Bobby Donaldson (d)
CO 59022 Jive at Five   *Philips(E) BBL7217*
CO 59023 Cookin' Joe C. (*)
CO 59024 Love Drop (*)
CO 59025 Wooster-shire (*)

1957
Oct 8   New York
Same personnel as session of 4 Oct 1957
CO 59030 Thou Swell   *Philips(E) BBL7217*
CO 59031 I hadn't anyone till you
CO 59032 At Sundown
CO 59033 Makin' Whoopee
CO 59034 You Can't Fight the Satellite Blues (*)

1958
New York
Mae Barnes (v), with Buck Clayton (t); Ray Bryant (p); Aaron Bell (db); Jo Jones (d)
Blues in my Heart   *Vanguard VRS9039*
They raided the joint
Old Man River
Up on a Mountain
I don't want to cry anymore
Willow weep for me
True Blue Lou

1958
New York
Mae Barnes (v), with Buck Clayton (t); Ray Tunia (p); Aaron Bell (db); Jo Jones (d)
Somebody's wrong   *Vanguard VRS9039*
'S wonderful
Summertime
Paris is my Old Kentucky Home
A Foggy Day
Umbrella Man
You came a long way from St Louis

1958
Jan 27   New York
LaVern Baker (v) and her All Stars
Buck Clayton (t); Vic Dickenson (tb); Paul Quinichette (ts); Sahib Shihab (bs); Nat Pierce (p); Danny Barker (g); Wendell Marshall (db); Joe Marshall (d)
2935 Nobody knows you when you're down
         and out   *Atlantic ATL/SD-1281*
2936 Gimme a pigfoot and a bottle of beer
2937 Baby Doll
2938 On Revival Day

1958
Jan 28   New York
LaVern Baker (v) and her All Stars
Same personnel as previous session except Jimmy Cleveland (tb) replaces Dickenson
2939 Money Blues   *Atlantic ATL/SD-1281*
2940 Empty Bed Blues
2941 I ain't gonna play no second fiddle
2942 There'll be a hot time in the old town tonight

1958
Jan 29   New York
LaVern Baker (v) and her All Stars
Same personnel as previous session except Urbie Green (tb) and Jerome Richardson (bs) replace Cleveland and Shihab
2943 Backwater Blues   *Atlantic ATL/SD-1281*
2944 After you've gone
2945 Young Woman's Blues
2946 Preaching the Blues

1958
Feb 4   RCA Studios, New York
Dicky Wells and his Orchestra
Buck Clayton (t); Dicky Wells (tb); Rudy Rutherford (cl, bs); Buddy Tate (ts, bs); Skip Hall (p); Everett Barksdale (eg); Major Holley (db); Jo Jones (d)
Take 3 Come and get it   *Felsted FAJ-7006/SJA-2006*
Take 3 Stan Dance (*)
Take 3 Hello Smack

1958
Feb 12   New York
Buddy Tate All Stars
Buck Clayton (t); Dicky Wells (tb); Earle Warren (as, bs); Buddy Tate (ts); Skip Hall (p); Lord Westbrook (eg); Aaron Bell (db); Jo Jones (d)
Take 5 Moon Eyes   *Felsted FAJ-7004/SJA-2004*
Take 3 Rockin' Steve (*†)
Splice Rompin' with Buck

1958
Feb 18   RCA Studios, New York
Coleman Hawkins All Stars
Buck Clayton (t); Coleman Hawkins (ts); Hank Jones (p); Ray Brown (db); Micky Sheen (d)
Take 5 Vignette   *Felsted FAJ-7005/SJA-2005*
Splice Get set
Take 1 You've changed
Take 4 Bird of Prey Blues
Take 2 Ooh-wee Miss G. P.
Take 1 My One and Only Love

1958
Feb 20   New York
Jimmy Rushing (v) and his Orchestra
Mel Davis (t); Bernie Glow (t); Buck Clayton (t); Emmett Berry (t); Vic Dickenson (t); Urbie Green (tb); Dicky Wells (tb); Earle Warren (as); Rudy Powell (as); Buddy Tate (ts); Coleman Hawkins (ts); Danny Bank (bs); Nat Pierce (p); Danny Barker (g); Milt Hinton (db); Jo Jones (d)
CO 60472 I'm coming Virginia   *Columbia CL1152/CS8060*
CO 60473 Mister Five by Five
CO 60474 June Night
CO 60475 Rosalie (†)

1958
Feb 25   New York
Benny Goodman and his Orchestra
Doc Severinsen (t); Bernie Glow (t); Buck Clayton (t); Chauncey Welsch (tb); Eddie Bert (tb); Billy Byers (tb); Benny Goodman (cl); Hymie Schertzer (as); Walter Levinsky (as); Al Klink (ts); Boomie Richman (ts); Sol Schlinger (bs); Hank Jones (p); Tony Mottola (g); George Duvivier (db); Roy Burns (d)
CO 60487 Back in your own Backyard   (45) Columbia 4-41148
CO 60488 Swing into Swing   (45) Columbia 4-41148

1958
Feb 26   New York
Jimmy Rushing (v) and his Orchestra
Mel Davis (t); Doc Cheatham (t); Buck Clayton (t); Emmett Berry (t); Frank Rehak (tb); Urbie Green (tb); Dicky Wells (tb); Earle Warren (as); Rudy Powell (cl, as); Buddy Tate (ts); Coleman Hawkins (ts); Danny Bank (bs); Nat Pierce (p, cel); Danny Barker (g); Milt Hinton (db); Osie Johnson (d)
CO 60476 Knock me a Kiss   *Columbia CL1152/CS8060*
CO 60477 Jimmy's Blues (†)
CO 60478 Someday Sweetheart (†)
CO 60479 Harvard Blues

1958
Feb 27   New York
Jimmy Rushing (v) and his Orchestra
Same personnel as session of 26 Feb 1958
CO 60480 It's a sin to tell a lie   *Columbia CL1152/CS8060*
CO 60481 Trav'lin' Light
CO 60482 When you're smiling
CO 60483 Somebody stole my gal (†)

1958
April 9   New York   "Texaco Swing into Spring" (NBC television broadcast)
Benny Goodman and his Orchestra
Doc Severinsen (t); Bernie Glow (t); Billy Butterfield (t); Buck Clayton (t); Lou McGarity (tb); Urbie Green (tb); Eddie Bert (tb); Benny Goodman (cl, v); Hymie Schertzer (as); Walter Levinsky (as); Zoot Sims (ts); Al Klink (ts); Sol Schlinger (bs); Hank Jones (p); Kenny Burrell (eg); Russ Saunders (db); Roy Burns (d); Ella Fitzgerald (v); Jo Stafford (v); Ray Eberle (v); The McGuire Sisters (v); add Ralph Burn's studio orchestra (1), studio chorus (2)
Let's dance (theme)   *Giants of Jazz GOJ-1010*
Riding high (EF:v)
Sometimes I'm happy   *Sandy Hook SH-2057*
Don't be that way
Medley: Careless / Moonlight Serenade / Blue Champagne (RE:v)/I'm getting sentimental over you/Let's get away from it all (JS:v)
King Porter stomp (add Harry James, t) *Giants of Jazz GOJ-1010*

Spring rhapsody (1)   *Sandy Hook SH-2057*
Blue skies (1; MS:v)
I'd rather lead a band (MS:v)   Unissued
Gotta be this or that (2; BG,JS,EF,MS:v) (add Harry James, t; Teddy Wilson, p; Red Norvo, vib) *Giants of Jazz GOJ-1010*
Goodbye (theme)
Swing into spring (theme)   *Sandy Hook SH-2057*

1958
April 23   New York
"The Subject is Jazz" (NBC TV education film), program 5: "Swing"
Buck Clayton (t); Doc Severinsen (t); Benny Morton (tb); Jimmy Cleveland (tb); Tony Scott (cl); Sid Cooper (as); Ben Webster (ts); Paul Quinichette (ts); Billy Taylor (p); Mundell Lowe (eg); Ed Safranski (db); Ed Thigpen (d)
For Dancers Only   Unissued
King Porter Stomp
One O'Clock Jump (†)

Buck Clayton (t); Benny Morton (tb); Ben Webster (ts); same rhythm section
Flying Home   *Jazz Archives JA-35*

1958
April 30   New York
"The Subject is Jazz" (NBC TV education film), program 6: "The Blues"
Buck Clayton (t); Vic Dickenson (tb); Paul Quinichette (ts); Billy Taylor (p); Mundell Lowe (eg); Ed Safranski (db); Ed Thigpen (d); Jimmy Rushing (v)
Sent for you yesterday (JR:v)   Unissued
Goin' to Chicago (JR:v)
St Louis Blues (JR:v)
I want a little girl (JR:v)
Billie's Bounce
Boogie Woogie (JR:v)
Blues in a Minor Key (theme)

1958
June 10   New York
The Big Eighteen
Rex Stewart (c, ldr); Billy Butterfield (t); Buck Clayton (t); Charlie Shavers (t); Lawrence Brown (tb); Vic Dickenson (tb); Lou McGarity (tb); Dicky Wells (tb); Walter Levinsky (cl, as); Hymie Schertzer (as); Sam Donahue (ts); Boomie Richman (ts); Ernie Caceres (bs); Johnny Guarnieri (p); Barry Galbraith (eg); Milt Hinton (db); James Crawford (d)
J2JB 4446 Swingtime in the Rockies   *RCA Victor LPM/LSP-1983*
J2JB 4447 Easy does it   *LPM/LSP-1921*
J2JB 4448 Five O'Clock Drag   *LPM/LSP-1921*

1958
June 17   New York
Same personnel as session of 10 June 1958 except Peanuts Hucko (cl, as) replaces Levinsky
J2JB 4585 Feet Draggin' Blues   *RCA Victor LPM/LSP-1983*
J2JB 4586 Summit Ridge Drive   *RCA Victor LPM/LSP-1983*
J2JB 4587 Tuxedo Junction   *LPM/LSP-1921*
J2JB 4588 Blues on Parade   *LPM/LSP-1921*

1958
June 24 New York
Same personnel as session of 17 June 1958
J2JB 4987 Okay for Baby   *RCA Victor LPM/LSP-1983*
J2JB 4988 March of the Toys   *LPM/LSP-1921*
J2JB 4989 Skyliner   *LPM/LSP-1983*
J2JB 4990 Parade of the Milk Bottle Caps   *LPM/LSP-1983*

1958
July 5   Newport Jazz Festival
Newport Blues Band
Buck Clayton (t); Lennie Johnson (t, on 1st set only); Jack Teagarden (tb); Georgie Auld (ts); Buddy Tate (ts); Rudy Rutherford (cl, bs); Pete Johnson (p); Kenny Burrell (eg); Tom Bryant (db); Jo Jones (d); Big Jo Turner (v); Big Mabelle (Mabel Smith) (v); Chuck Berry (v, eg)

First set:
Pete's Boogie Woogie	*Jackson(D) LP1206*
Feeling happy (BJT,band:v)	*Jackson(D) LP1206*
Let the good times roll (BJT:v)	Unissued
Corinne Corinna (BJT:v)	*Jackson(D) LP1206*
Honey Hush (BJT:v)	Unissued
Shake Rattle and Roll (BJT:v)	

Second set:
Baby please don't go (BM:v)
Cherry (BM:v)
One Hour (BM:v)
I ain't mad at you (BM:v)

Third set:
School Days (CB:v,eg)
No Money Down (CB:v,eg)
Sweet Little Sixteen (CB:v,eg)
Johnny B Goode (CB:v,eg)

NB: Sweet little sixteen and I ain't mad at you were included in the feature film *Jazz on a Summer's Day*.

Jack Teagarden All Stars
Buck Clayton (t); Jack Teagarden (tb); Pee Wee Russell (cl); Lester Young (ts); Don Ewell (p); Tom Bryant (db); Jo Jones (d)
Royal Garden Blues	Unissued
I cover the waterfront	*Unique Jazz(I) UJ-14*
Muskrat Ramble	Unissued
Jump the Blues	*Unique Jazz(I) UJ-14*

NB: all 4 sets were recorded by Voice of America for radio broadcasts.

1958
July 8   New York
The Big Eighteen
Same personnel as session of 10 June 1958 except Yank Lawson replaces Butterfield
J2JB 5329	Celery stalks at midnight	*RCA Victor LPM/LSP-1983*
J2JB 5330	I'm praying humble	*LPM/LSP-1921*
J2JB 5331	Hors d'oeuvres	*LPM/LSP-1921*
J2JB 5332-1	Liza	Unissued—rejected

1958
July 15   New York
The Big Eighteen
Same personnel as session of 8 July 1958 except Bob Ascher (tb), Sy Berger (tb), Russ Saunders (db), Don Lamond (d) replace Brown, Dickenson, Hinton, Crawford
J2JB5332-2	Liza	*RCA Victor LPM/LSP-1921*
J2JB 5488	The Campbells are swinging	*RCA Victor LPM/LSP-1983*
J2JB 5489	Organ Grinder's Swing	*LPM/LSP-1983*
J2JB 5490	Ton o'Rock Bump	*LPM/LSP-1983*
J2JB 5491	Quaker City Jazz	*LPM/LSP-1983*

1958
July 25   Newark, New Jersey   "Art Ford's Jazz Party" (WNTA television broadcast)
Billie Holiday (v) with Mal Waldon's Group
Buck Clayton (t); Tyree Glenn (tb); Paul Quinichette (ts); Mal Waldron (p); Mundell Lowe (g); Joe Benjamin (db); Jo Jones (d)
Easy to remember	*Nostalgia Greats (Amalgamated) 132*
Moanin' low	
When your lover has gone	

1958
July 29–Aug 3   American Theatre, Brussels World's Fair, Belgium
Sidney Bechet and his All Stars
Buck Clayton (t); Vic Dickenson (tb); Sidney Bechet (ss); George Wein (p); Arvell Shaw (db); Kansas Fields (d)
Indiana	*Vogue(F) SB-1*
Society Blues	
St Louis Blues	
Swanee River	
In a Sentimental Mood	
All of me	
When the saints go marching in	

I found a new baby	Unissued
Basin Street Blues	
South	
Birth of the Blues	

1958
Sept 5   Hackensack, New Jersey
Paul Quinichette and his Orchestra
Buck Clayton (t); Shad Collins (t); Paul Quinichette (ts); Jack Washington (bs); Nat Pierce (p); Freddie Green (g); Eddie Jones (db); Jo Jones (d)
1577	Blues I like to hear	*Prestige PRLP7147*
1578	Roseland Shuffle	
1579	John's Idea	
1580	Love jumped out (*)	
1581	Baby don't tell on me	

1958
Sept 9   Persian Room, Plaza Hotel, New York
Billie Holiday (v), with Buck Clayton (t); Mal Waldron (p); Jimmy Woode (db); Sam Woodyard (d)
Don't explain	*Columbia C32471*
When your lover has gone	

1958
Sept 26   Oakdale Musical Theatre, Wallingford, Connecticut
The Seven Ages of Jazz Concert
Buck Clayton (t); Don Elliott (t); Tyree Glenn (tb); Dick Hyman (cl); Willie "the Lion" Smith (p); Milt Hinton (db); Don Lamond (d)
Dippermouth Blues	*Metrojazz 2-E1009*

Buck Clayton (t); Tyree Glenn (tb); Coleman Hawkins (ts); Dick Hyman (p); Milt Hinton (db); Don Lamond (d)
It don't mean a thing	*Metrojazz 2-E1009*

Buck Clayton (t); Georgie Auld (cl, ts); Don Elliott (vib); Dick Hyman (p); Milt Hinton (db); Don Lamond (d)
Stompin' at the Savoy	*Metrojazz 2-E1009*

Billie Holiday (v); Buck Clayton (t); Mal Waldron (p); Milt Hinton (db); Don Lamond (d)
I wished on the moon	*Metrojazz 2-E1009*
Lover Man	

Buck Clayton (t); Tyree Glenn (tb); Coleman Hawkins (ts); Georgie Auld (bs); Don Elliott (ah, mar); Dick Hyman (p); Milt Hinton (db); Don Lamond (d)
One O'Clock Jump	*Metrojazz 2-E1009*
Jazz Lab	

Buck Clayton (t); Dick Hyman (p); Milt Hinton (db); Don Lamond (d)
Blue and Sentimental	*Metrojazz 2-E1009*

1958
Oct 16   Nola Studios, New York
Harry Edison–Buck Clayton Group
Harry Edison (t); Buck Clayton (t); Jimmy Forrest (ts); Jimmy Jones (p); Freddie Green (g); Joe Benjamin (db); Charlie Persip (d)
22505	Memories for the Count	*VerveMGV-8293/MGVS-6016*
22506	Come with me	
22507	Critic's Delight	
	(Eddie Costa, vib, added later)	
22508	It all depends on you	
	(Clayton and rhythm only)	
22509	Oh how I hate to get up in the afternoon	
22510	Unknown title	Unissued

1958
Oct 28   New York
Vic Dickenson and his All Stars
Buck Clayton (t); Vic Dickenson (tb); Herbie Hall (cl); Hal Singer (ts); Al Williams (p); Danny Barker (g); Gene Ramey (db); Marquis Foster (d)
3178	Has anyone here seen Corinne? (†)	Unissued
3179-1	The lamp is Low (†)	*AtlanticATL/SD-1303*
3179-2	The lamp is Low (†)	Unissued
3180	Under Plunder Blues (†)	
3181	Harlem Nocturne (†)	

3182   Undecided (†)   *Atlantic ATL/SD-1303*
  -1   Blues for Mac (†)   Unissued
  -2   Blues for Mac (†)

1958
Nov 25   New York
Buck Clayton and his All Stars
Buck Clayton (t); Emmett Berry (t); Dicky Wells (tb); Earle Warren (cl, as); Buddy Tate (ts); Al Williams (p); Gene Ramey (db); Herbie Lovelle (d)
CO 61795 Sunday (†)   *Columbia CL1320/CS8123*
CO 61796 Swingin' along on Broadway (*†)
CO 61797 Night Train (†)
CO 61798 Buckini (*†)
CO 61799 Moonglow (†)
CO 61800 Swinging at the Copper Rail (*†)
CO 61801 Mean to me (†)
CO 61802 Outer Drive (*†)

1959
New York
Bob Wilber All Star Jazz Band
Buck Clayton (t); Vic Dickenson (tb); Bob Wilber (cl); Bud Freeman (ts); Dick Wellstood (p); Ahmed-Abdul Malik (db); Panama Francis (d)
Tin Roof Blues   *Music Minus One MMO-1009*
Wolverine Blues
The man that got away
Keepin' out of mischief now
When the saints go marching in
Do you know what it means to miss New Orleans?
High Society   *Music Minus One MMO-1010*
Chimes Blues
Milenberg Joys
Wild Man Blues
Basin Street Blues

NB: The 2 LPs, with instruction booklets, were in a series for amateur musicians providing accompaniment for "living room practice"; Basin Street Blues is included twice on MMO-1010, with different editing of the breaks.

1959
Feb 23–4   RCA Studios, New York
Pee Wee Russell and his Orchestra
Buck Clayton (t); Vic Dickenson (tb); Pee Wee Russell (cl); Bud Freeman (ts); Dick Cary (p); Eddie Condon (g); Bill Takas (db); George Wettling (d)
Pee Wee's Blues   *Dot DLP-3253/DLPS-25253*
What's the pitch?
Dreamin' and Schemin'
Cutie Pie
Oh no
Pee Wee's Tune
Oh yes
Missy
Are you here?
Write me a love song baby
This is it
But why?

1959
March 16   Washington Jazz Jubilee Concert, Washington, DC
Dick Cary Band
Buck Clayton (t); Pee Wee Russell (cl); Bud Freeman (ts); Dick Cary (p, t, ah); unknown (db); Jo Jones (d)
Unknown titles

NB: This concert, entitled "A History of Jazz from Congo Square to Carnegie Hall", was recorded in stereo by Mercury Records but not issued.

1959
March or April   New York   "Jazz from Studio 61" (CBS television broadcast)
Ben Webster Sextet

Buck Clayton (t); Vic Dickenson (tb); Ben Webster (ts); Hank Jones (p); George Duvivier (db); Jo Jones (d)
Mop mop   *Extreme Rarities LP-1004*
C-jam Blues

1959
April 10   New York   "Texaco Swing into Spring" (CBS television broadcast)
Benny Goodman and his Orchestra
Buck Clayton (t); John Frosk (t); Irwin Berger (t); Allen Smith (t); Urbie Green (tb); Hale Rood (tb); Buster Cooper (tb); Benny Goodman (cl, v); Hymie Schertzer (as); Gerald Sanfino (as); Babe Clark (ts); Herb Geller (ts); Pepper Adams (bs); Hank Jones (p); Kenny Burrell (eg); Jack Lesberg (db); Roy Burns (d); Phil Kraus (perc); Ella Fitzgerald (v); Peggy Lee (v); The Hi Los (v); Donna Musgrove (v); add studio vocal chorus (1)
Let's dance (theme)   *Giants of Jazz GOJ-1011*
Medley: 'S wonderful (EF,PL:v)/
   Things are swinging (PL:v)
Medley: Bach goes to town/
   Swing low sweet chariot (1)   *A&R 2000/1*
Why don't you do right? (PL:v)
Like young (1; Andre Previn, p)   Unissued
Mountain greenery (EF:v)   *A&R 2000/1*
Let's dance (theme)
Medley: A String of Pearls/Goody goody (HL:v)/
   You turned the tables on me (DM,HL:v)/
   One O'Clock Jump
Swing into Spring (1;PL,EF,HL:v)
'S wonderful (1;PL,EF,HL:v)
Goodbye (theme)
Swing into Spring (theme)

1959
May or June   Essen Jazz Festival (radio broadcast)
Buck Clayton with Humphrey Lyttelton and his Band
Buck Clayton (t); Humphrey Lyttelton (t); Johnny Picard (tb); Tony Coe (as); Jimmy Skidmore (ts); Joe Temperley (bs); Ian Armit (p); Pete Blannin (db); Eddie Taylor (d)
Christopher Columbus
That's my home
In a Mellotone
Blues

1959
June   Boston
Dixieland All Stars
Buck Clayton (t); Vic Dickenson (tb); Pee Wee Russell (cl); Bud Freeman (ts); Lou Carter (p); Champ Jones (db); Jo Jones (d)
Embraceable You   *Omega OSL-52*
Somebody loves me
Someone to watch over me
Fascinating Rhythm
St James Infirmary
Ballin' the Jack
Sweet Sue, just you   *Coronet CX-14*
Strike up the band   *Omega OSL-52*
Muskrat Ramble
Bugle Call Rag
When the saints go marching in   *Omega OSL-63*
Synthetic Blues
Billboard March

1959
June   Boston
Newport Jazz Festival All Stars
Buck Clayton (t); Vic Dickenson (tb); Pee Wee Russell (cl); Bud Freeman (ts); George Wein (p); Champ Jones (db); Jake Hanna (d)
4017-1 Royal Garden Blues   *Atlantic ATL/SD-1331*
4018   Rose Room
4019-1 You took advantage of me
4020   Sunday
4021   Dinah
4022   'Deed I do

4023-1 Pee Wee Russell's Unique
  Sound   Unissued—breakdown
4023-2 Pee Wee Russell's Unique Sound   *Atlantic*
                                                    ATL/SD-1331

NB: there were 5 takes of 4021 and 2 takes of 4022; the take
numbers of the issued versions are not known. 4017 and 4019
were single takes.

1959

July 2   Newport Jazz Festival
Newport Jazz Festival All Stars
Buck Clayton (t); Vic Dickenson (tb); Pee Wee Russell (cl); Bud
Freeman (ts); Ray Bryant (p); Freddie Green (g); Champ Jones (db);
Buzzy Drootin (d)
Avalon   Unissued
Wrap your troubles in dreams
Sweet Sue, just you   *Europa Jazz(I) EJ-1023*

add Ruby Braff (c), Jimmy Rushing (v)
I'm gonna sit right down
Goin' to Chicago
St Louis Blues

NB: recorded by CBS and Voice of America for radio broadcasts

1959

Sept 17   Concert, Copenhagen
Buck Clayton All Stars with Jimmy Rushing (v)
Buck Clayton (t); Emmett Berry (t); Dicky Wells (tb); Earle Warren (cl,
as); Buddy Tate (ts); Al Williams (p); Gene Ramey (db); Herbie Lovelle
(d)
Outer Drive (*†)   *Steeplechase(D) SCC-6006/7*
Swinging at the Copper Rail (*†)
Moonglow (†)
Night Train (†)
Swingin' along on Broadway (*†)
Exactly like you (JR:v)
I want a little girl (JR:v)
Every day I have the blues (JR:v)
'Deed I do (JR:v)
Goin' to Chicago (JR:v)
Sent for you yesterday (JR:v)
Sent for you yesterday (JR:v) (encore)

1959

Sept 26   Concert, Free Trade Hall, Manchester
Same personnel as session of 17 Sept 1959
Swinging the Blues (†)   Private tape
Moonglow (†)
Airmail Special
On the Sunny Side of the Street (JR:v)
I want a little girl (JR:v)
Goin' to Chicago (JR:v)
Sent for you yesterday (JR:v)
Night Train (†)

1959

Oct 17   Concert, Olympia Theatre, Paris
Same personnel as session of 17 Sept 1959
Swinging the Blues (†)   (10") Palm Club(F) LP-26
Goin' to Chicago (JR:v)
Sent for you yesterday (JR:v)
On the Sunny Side of the Street (JR:v)
Night Train (†)
Outer Drive (*†)
Moonglow (†)   Unissued
I want a little girl (JR:v)

1959

Nov 16–17   Paris
Buck Clayton Quintet
Buck Clayton (t); Jean-Claude Pelletier (p, o); Jean Bonal (eg); Roland
Lobligeois (db); Kansas Fields (d)
Lonesome (Si tu vois ma mère)   *Pop(F) POMS 71.005*
I've got my love to keep me warm
Premier bal
Louise

Tenderly
Black and Blue
These Foolish Things
I'm in the mood for love
Rosetta
Sugar
Pennies from Heaven
Stompin' at the Savoy

1960

March 29   Rudy Van Gelder Studio, Englewood Cliffs, New
Jersey
Pee Wee Russell Quintet
Buck Clayton (t); Pee Wee Russell (cl); Tommy Flanagan (p); Wendell
Marshall (db); Osie Johnson (d)
2094 Wrap your troubles
   in dreams   *Prestige–Swingville SVLP-2008*
2095 What can I say dear?
2096 Midnight Blue
2097 I would do 'most anything for you
2098 Englewood
2099 Lulu's back in town
2100 The very thought of you

1960

July 7   New York
Jimmy Rushing (v) with Buck Clayton All Stars
Buck Clayton (t); Benny Morton (tb); Dicky Wells (tb); Buster Bailey
(cl); Coleman Hawkins (ts); Claude Hopkins (p); Everett Barksdale
(eg); Gene Ramey (db); James Crawford (d)
CO 65017 Shipwrecked Blues   *Columbia CL1605/CS8405*
CO 65018 Muddy Water (Mississippi Moan)
CO 65019 Gulf Coast Blues
CO 65020 Everybody loves my baby
CO 65021 Trouble in Mind

1960

July 13   New York
Same personnel as session of 7 July 1960
CO 65059 Downhearted Blues   *Columbia CL1605/CS8405*
CO 65060 Squeeze me
CO 65061 How come you do me like you do?
CO 65062 Crazy Blues
CO 65063 Arkansas Blues

1960

Aug 28   Quaker City Jazz Festival, Philadelphia "World
Series of Jazz" (CBS television broadcast)
Gene Krupa Quartet with Buck Clayton and Pee Wee Russell
Buck Clayton (t); Pee Wee Russell (cl); Eddie Wasserman (ts); un-
known (p, db); Gene Krupa (d)
I found a new baby   *Sunbeam SB225*

1960

Oct 5–6   New York
Tommy Gwaltney's Kansas City Nine featuring Buck Clayton
Buck Clayton (t); Bobby Zottola (t, ah); Dicky Wells (tb); Tommy
Gwaltney (cl, as, vib, xyl); Tommy Newsome (cl, ts); John Bunch (p);
Charlie Byrd (g); Whitey Mitchell (db); Buddy Schutz (d)
Hello babe   *Riverside RLP-353/S-9353*
Just an Old Manuscript
Kansas City Ballad
The Jumping Blues
Walter Page
Midnight Mama
John's Idea
Steppin' Pretty
Dedicated to you
The New Tulsa Blues

1960

Nov 2–3   New York
Nancy Harrow (v) with Buck Clayton's Jazz Stars
Buck Clayton (t); Dicky Wells (tb); Tommy Gwaltney (cl, as); Buddy
Tate (ts); Danny Bank (as, bs); Dick Wellstood (p); Kenny Burrell (eg);
Milt Hinton (db); Oliver Jackson (d)

Can't we be friends? (†)   *Candid CJM-8008/CJS-9008*
On the Sunny Side of the Street (†)
omit Burrell
Take me back baby (†)
All too soon (†)
Wild women don't have the blues (†)
I've got the world on a string (†)
I don't know what kind of blues I've got (†)
Blues for Yesterday (†)

1960
Dec 20   Rudy Van Gelder Studio, Englewood Cliffs, New Jersey
Buck Clayton–Buddy Tate Quintet
Buck Clayton (t); Buddy Tate (ts); Sir Charles Thompson (p); Gene Ramey (db); Mousey Alexander (d)
2766 High Life (*)   *Prestige–Swingville SVLP-2017*
2767 Can't we be friends?
2768 Birdland Betty (*)
2769 Kansas City Nights (*)
2770 When a woman loves a man (omit Tate)
2771 Thou Swell

1961
April 10   New York
Buck Clayton All Stars
Buck Clayton (t); Emmett Berry (t); Dicky Wells (tb); Earle Warren (cl, as); Buddy Tate (ts); Sir Charles Thompson (p, cel); Gene Ramey (db); Oliver Jackson (d)
Night Ferry (*†)   *Columbia(E) 33SX-1390*
I can't give you anything but love (†)
One for Buck
Mr Melody Maker (*†)
Blue Mist
Prince Eagle Head

1961
late April   Belgium
"Buck Clayton and his All Stars" (film soundtrack)
Same personnel as session of 10 April 1961 plus Jimmy Witherspoon (v)
Outer Drive (*†)   Unissued
Stompin' at the Savoy
Blue and Sentimental
When I've been drinking (JW:v)
Night Train (†)

1961
late April   Palais des Beaux Arts, Brussels (radio broadcast)
Same personnel as session of 10 April 1961
Perdido   Unissued
Swinging the Blues (†)
Swinging at the Copper Rail (*†)
Outer Drive (*†)
Robbins' Nest
Moonglow (†)
Night Train (†)
Stompin' at the Savoy (Clayton and rhythm)

1961
April 22   Olympia Theatre, Paris
Same personnel as session of 10 April 1961 plus Jimmy Witherspoon (v)
Swinging at the Copper Rail (*†)   *Vogue(F) LD544*
Outer Drive (*†)
Robbins' Nest
Moonglow (†)
Swinging the Blues (†)
I'll always be in love with you (JW:v)   *Vogue(F) LD546*
Gee baby, ain't I good to you (JW:v)
See see rider (JW:v)
I make a lot of money (JW:v)
Blowin' the Blues (JW:v)
'T ain't nobody's business if I do (JW:v)
Everything you do is wrong (JW:v)
Roll 'em Pete (JW:v)

Night Train (†)   Unissued
Stompin' at the Savoy

1961
May 2   Casino, Basel (radio broadcast)
Same personnel as session of 10 April 1961 plus Jimmy Witherspoon (v)
Robbins' Nest   Unissued
Outer Drive (*†)
Everyday I have the blues (JW:v)
'T ain't nobody's business if I do (JW:v)
Everything you do is wrong (JW:v)
Moonglow (†)
Swinging the Blues (†)
Night Train (†)
I'll always be in love with you (JW:v)
See see rider (JW:v)
St Louis Blues (Clayton and rhythm)
Roll 'em Pete (JW:v)

1961
May 15–16   "Le Fagon" Cinema Studio, Paris
Buck Clayton Quintet
Buck Clayton (t); Sir Charles Thompson (p, o); Jean Bonal (eg); Gene Ramey (db); Oliver Jackson (d)

	I can't believe that you're in love with me	*Pop(F) POMS-71009*
	I surrender dear	
	Them there eyes	
	When your lover has gone	
	Georgia on my Mind	
	I've got the world on a string	
	I cried for you	*POMS-71007*
	I cover the waterfront	
Take-A	Night and Day	*POMS-71009*
Take-B	Night and Day	
	Body and Soul	*POMS-71007*
Take-A	I want a little girl	*POMS-71009*
Take-B	I want a little girl	
	Baby won't you please come home?	*POMS-71007*
	Sleepytime Gal	
	My Funny Valentine	
Take-A	Rose Room	*POMS-71009*
Take-B	Rose Room	
	I gotta right to sing the blues	*POMS-71007*
	Ma gigolette	
	Green Eyes	
	You go to my head	*POMS-71009*
8984	Passport to Paradise	*POMS-71007*
	Please be kind	
	Petite fleur	*POMS-71009*
8985	Tangerine	*POMS-71007*
	Nous deux	Unissued

1961
Sept 15   Rudy Van Gelder Studio, Englewood Cliffs, New Jersey
Buck Clayton–Buddy Tate Quintet
Buck Clayton (t); Buddy Tate (ts, cl); Sir Charles Thompson (p); Gene Ramey (db); Gus Johnson (d)
3209 Dallas Delight (*)   *Prestige–Swingville SVLP-2030*
3210 Blue Ebony (*)
3211 A Swinging Doll (*)
3212 Don't mind if I do
3213 Rompin' at Red Bank
3214 Blue Creek
3215 Blue Breeze (*)

1962
Feb 8   New York
Marlowe Morris Sextet
Buck Clayton (t); Edmond Hall (cl); Buddy Tate (ts); Marlowe Morris (o); Jo Jones (d); Ray Barretto (bongos)

CO 69380 No, no, no   *Columbia CL1819/CS8619*
CO 69381 Moonlight in Vermont
          (omit Barretto)
CO 69383 Stompy Jones
CO 69384 Marlowe's Blues

1962
April 11–12   Plaza Sound Studios, New York
Odetta with Buck Clayton's All Stars
Odetta F. Gordon (v); Buck Clayton (t); Vic Dickenson (tb); Herbie Hall (cl); Dick Wellstood (p); Ahmed Abdul-Malik (db); Shep Shepherd (d)
Hard, oh Lord   *Riverside RLP417/S9417*
Believe I'll go
Oh, papa
How Long Blues
Hogan's Alley
Leavin' this morning
Oh, my babe
Yonder comes the blues
Make me a pallet on your floor
Weeping Willow Blues
Go down, sunshine
Nobody knows you when you're down and out

1962
April 25   RCA Victor Studio B, New York
Odetta
Odetta F. Gordon (v); Buck Clayton (t); Vic Dickenson (tb); Buster Bailey (cl); Dick Wellstood (p); Leonard Gaskin (db); Panama Francis (d)
N2PW1933 Poor Man   *RCA Victor LPM/LSP-2573*
N2PW1934 Special Delivery   *RCA Victor LPM/LSP-2573*
N2PW1935 Misery Blues   Unissued—rejected

1962
April 26   RCA Victor Studio B, New York
Same personnel as session of 25 April 1962
N2PW1928 Pretty Woman   Unissued
N2PW1936 House of the
          Rising Sun   *RCA Victor LPM/LSP-2573*
N2PW1937 If I had wings
N2PW1992 Empty Pocket Blues (omit
          Dickenson and Bailey)

1962
Nov 3   Chicago   "Apartment 7A: Marty's Place" (television broadcast)
Ella Fitzgerald (v); George Kirby (v); Buck Clayton (t); unknown (p)
'S wonderful   Unissued
Buck Clayton (t); Father Joseph Dustin (bj); unknown (p); George Kirby (brushes); Ella Fitzgerald, Marty Faye (v, hand clapping)
Satin Doll   Unissued

1962
Dec 15   Paris   "La Nuit du Jazz" (radio broadcast)
Buck Clayton Quartet
Buck Clayton (t); Georges Arvanitas (o); Pierre Sim (db); Charles Bellonzi (d)
Indiana   *Europa Jazz(I) EJ-1014*
St Louis Blues   *Europa Jazz(I) EJ-1014*
Stompin' at the Savoy   *Europa Jazz(I) EJ-1023*
Buck Clayton with Jacques Denjean and his Orchestra
Buck Clayton (t); George Bence (t); Pierre Dutour (t); Yvan Julien (t); Henry van Haeke (t); Michel Poli (t); Jean-Marie Chauval (tb); Pierre Dandonbere (tb); Raymond Fonseque (tb); Christian Guizien (tb); Jean-Louis Chautemps (as); Jo Hrasko (as); Dominique Chanson (ts); Robert Pautrat (ts); William Boucako (bs); Henri Renaud (p); Pierre Sim (db); Rene Nan (d)
C-jam Blues   Unissued
I want a little girl
Swinging the Blues
Honky-tonk

1962
Dec 17   Paris
Buck Clayton Band
Buck Clayton (t); Georges Arvanitas (o); Harry Kett (eg); Pierre Urban (eg); Georges Megalos (eb); Pierre Sim (db); Charles Bellonzi (d)
Barbara   *Pop(F) POMS-71010*
September Blues
Daniel (omit Megalos)
Cavalier
Grand-mère
C'est à l'amour auquel je pense
Blueberry Hill   *Mode(F) CMD.INT-9409*
La colline du delta
Frankie and Johnny (omit Megalos)
That's my Home

1962
Dec 18   Paris
Buck Clayton Band
Buck Clayton (t); Georges Arvanitas (p, o); Harry Kett (eg); Pierre Sim (db); Philippe Combelle (d)
Nuages (omit Kett)   *Pop(F) POMS-71010*
Tous les garçons et les filles
(omit Kett)
Girl's Dance
En flanant dans les rues de Paris
Laura (add Roger Terrien, eg) *Mode(F) CMD.INT-9409*
The way you look tonight
(omit Kett)
Full of dreams
(add Georges Megalos, eb)
It ain't necessarily so
(add Georges Megalos, eb)
La vie en rose   Unissued

1962
Dec 19   Paris
Buck Clayton Band
Buck Clayton (t); Georges Arvanitas (p, o); Roger Terrien (eg); Pierre Sim (db); Charles Bellonzi (d)
La vie en rose   *Pop(F) POMS-71010*
Promenade aux Champs-Elysées
I'm confessin' that I love you *Mode(F) CMD.INT-9409*
Flamingo (add Georges Megalos, eb)
Stardust
Goodnight Sweetheart
(add Harry Kett, eg)

1963
February   Colonial Tavern, Toronto
Buck Clayton with the Count Basie All Stars
Buck Clayton (t); Earle Warren (f, as); Sir Charles Thompson (p); Tommy Potter (db); Jackie Williams (d); Olive Brown (v)
Canadian Capers   *Discus(C) DS-MM/DS-VS 63/2*
Blue Goose Special
Canadian Sunset
North Atlantic Squadron
Alouette (OB:v)
Thousand Islands Song
Saskatchewan
Squid Jiggin' Ground

1963
Feb 2   New York   "Music Spectacular" (WNEW radio broadcast)
Count Basie Septet
Buck Clayton (t); Dicky Wells (tb); Earle Warren (as, v); Buddy Tate (cl, ts); Count Basie (p, o); Rodney Richardson or Gene Ramey (db); Jo Jones (d)
Every Tub   Unissued
Swinging the Blues
These Foolish Things (EW:v)
Jumping at the Woodside
Blues
One O'Clock Jump

1963
July 5   Lansdowne House, London
Buck Clayton with Humphrey Lyttelton and his Band
Buck Clayton (t); Humphrey Lyttelton (t, th); Danny Moss (ts); Joe Temperley (bs); Ian Armit (p); Pete Blannin (db); Eddie Taylor (d)
Tam (*)   *World Record Club(E) T/S-324*
Fondu Head (*)
Sentimental Journey
Cotton Tail
Stardust (omit Lyttelton, Temperley)
Autumn Leaves (omit Lyttelton, Temperley)
Humph and Me (omit Moss, Temperley) (*)
Me and Buck (omit Moss, Temperley)

1964
late January   Toronto
Phyllis Marshall (v) with Buck Clayton and his Quintet
Buck Clayton (t); Buddy Tate (cl, ts); Norman Amadeo (p); George Tucker (db); Jackie Williams (d)
I ain't got the man I
thought I had   *Columbia(C) FL314/FS614*
Trust in me
How deep is the ocean?
That old black magic
Romance in the Dark
Bei mir bist du schön
Don't worry 'bout me
I'm gonna put you in your place
Happiness is a thing called Joe
Day in, day out (omit Tate)
I cried for you

1964
March 11   Festival Hall, Melbourne (Radio Northern 3AW broadcast)
Eddie Condon All Stars
Buck Clayton (t); Vic Dickenson (tb); Pee Wee Russell (cl); Bud Freeman (ts); Dick Cary (p, ah); Eddie Condon (g); Jack Lesberg (db); Cliff Leeman (d); Jimmy Rushing (v)
I can't believe that you're in love with me
Stompin' at the Savoy (Clayton with rhythm)
Am I blue? (JR:v)
St Louis Blues
Caravan
Medley: Goin' to Chicago/I'm gonna move to the outskirts of town/Harvard Blues/St Louis Blues (JR:v)
I can't get started (Clayton with rhythm)
There'll be some changes made (JR:v)
Love is just around the corner

1964
March 14   Sydney Stadium, Sydney   "9 O'Clock Special" (radio broadcast)
Same personnel as session of 11 March 1964
Caravan
St Louis Blues
Sugar (omit Dickenson, Freeman)   *IAJRC 28*
Stompin' at the Savoy (Clayton with rhythm)
I can't get started (Clayton with rhythm)
Am I blue? (JR:v)
When you're smiling (JR:v)
Medley: Goin' to Chicago/I'm gonna move to the outskirts of town/See see rider/St Louis Blues (JR:v)
Medley: Sent for you yesterday/Rock and Roll/Sent for you yesterday (encore) (JR:v)
That's a plenty

1964
March 24   Tokyo (radio broadcast)
Same personnel as session of 11 March 1964
Muskrat Ramble   *Chiaroscuro (J) UPS 2069-CH*
Do you know what it means to miss
New Orleans?   Unissued
Rose Room   *Chiaroscuro CR-154*

Caravan   Unissued
I would do 'most anything for you   *Chiaroscuro CR-154*
St Louis Blues   *Chiaroscuro (J) UPS 2069-CH*
Basin Street Blues   *Chiaroscuro (J) UPS 2070-CH*
I can't believe that you're in
love with me   *Chiaroscuro CR-154*
Stompin' at the Savoy
(Clayton with rhythm)   *Chiaroscuro CR-154*
I can't get started (Clayton with rhythm)   Unissued
All of me (JR:v)   *Chiaroscuro CR-154*
Am I blue? (JR:v)   *Chiaroscuro CR-154*
When you're smiling (JR:v)   *Chiaroscuro CR-154*
Medley: Goin' to Chicago/Every day
I have the blues/See see rider/St Louis Blues (JR:v)Unissued
Royal Garden Blues   *Chiaroscuro CR-154*

1964
March 27   Festival Hall, Osaka (radio broadcast)
Same personnel as session of 11 March 1964
Muskrat Ramble   *Plain label LP*
St Louis Blues
Basin Street Blues
Caravan
Stompin' at the Savoy
(Clayton with rhythm)
All of me (JR:v)
Am I blue? (JR:v)
When you're smiling (JR:v)
Medley: Goin' to Chicago/I'm gonna
move to the outskirts of town/
See see rider/St Louis Blues (JR:v)
Medley: Sent for you yesterday/
Rock and Roll/Sent for you yesterday/
(encore) (JR:v)

NB: The limited edition LP was issued in the mid-1970s with a plain sleeve, no record company name or record number.

1964
April 24   South Shore Jazz Festival, Milton, Massachusetts
Buck Clayton (t); Yank Lawson (c); Vic Dickenson (tb); Edmond Hall (cl); Dick Wellstood (p); Russ Best (db); Walt Gifford (d)
At the jazz band ball   Private tape

NB: Clayton was a featured star at the festival, playing with a rhythm section and with various pick-up groups. This material was taped but no further details are known.

1964
July 5   Newport Jazz Festival   "Jazz Hour" (VOA radio broadcast)
Newport Jazz Festival All Stars
Buck Clayton (t); Al Grey (tb); Ben Webster (ts); Sir Charles Thompson (p); Slam Stewart (db); Ben Riley (d)
Take the 'A' Train
Stardust
Perdido

1964
November   White Horse Pub, Willesden, London
Buck Clayton with Humphrey Lyttelton and his Band
Buck Clayton (t); Humphrey Lyttelton (t); Tony Coe (ts); Joe Temperley (bs); Eddie Harvey (p, tb); Pete Blannin (db); Eddie Taylor (d)
The Green Tiger (*†)   *77 Records(E) 77-LEU-12/11*
Red Barrel Blues (*†)
Unbooted Character
It's the talk of the town
Blues in the Afternoon (†)
The Huckle-buck
One Hour
Carole's Caper (*†)
You can depend on me
The Wrestler's Tricks (omit Coe, Temperley)

late 1964
Marquee Club, London   "Jazz 625: Buck and Humph" (BBC television broadcast)
Same personnel as session of November 1964

The Green Tiger (*†)
One Hour
Cotton Tail
(Buck Clayton interviewed by Steve Race)
Red Barrel Blues (*†)
Me and Buck (omit Coe, Temperley)
Carole's Caper (*†)
Carole's Caper (encore) (*†)
Swinging at the Copper Rail (*†)
It's the talk of the town
Robbins' Nest
Unbooted Character
Blues in the Afternoon (†)
The Huckle-buck
The Huckle-buck (encore)

NB: the session was broadcast in two parts on 9 Jan and 24 March
1965.

late 1964
Dancing Slipper Ballroom, Nottingham
Same personnel as session of November 1964
First set:
  Stompin' at the Savoy
  (Clayton with rhythm)   Private tape
  One Hour (If I could be with you)
  In a Mellotone
  Unbooted Character
Second set:
  These foolish things
  (Clayton with rhythm)
  Me and Buck (omit Coe, Temperley)
  Shiny Stockings
  Blues in the Afternoon (†)
  The Huckle-buck
Third set:
  I want a little girl (HL:v)
  Jive at Five
  It's the talk of the town
  Cotton Tail
  Robbins' Nest
  You can depend on me (HL:v)

1965
May 13   Studio 102, Paris
Buck Clayton Quintet
*Buck Clayton (t); Vic Dickenson (tb); Joe Turner (p); Jimmy Woode
(db); Kenny Clarke (d)*
Keeping out of mischief now   Unissued
All of me   Unissued

Buck Clayton's All Stars
add Benny Waters (ts), Alix Combelle (ts)
Perdido   *Europa Jazz(I) EJ-1023*

Big Joe Turner's All Stars
*Big Joe Turner (v); Stuff Smith (vn); Buck Clayton (t); Vic Dickenson
(tb); Benny Waters (ts); Alix Combelle (ts); Joe Turner (p); Jimmy
Woode (db); Kenny Clarke (d)*
Shake rattle and roll   *Europa Jazz(I) EJ-1014*

1965
early May   Dancing Slipper Ballroom, Nottingham
Buck Clayton and Big Joe Turner with Humphrey Lyttelton and
his Band
*Big Joe Turner (v); Buck Clayton (t); Humphrey Lyttelton (t); Tony
Coe (ts); Joe Temperley (bs); Eddie Harvey (p, tb); Dave Green (db);
Johnny Butts (d)*
First set:
  The Green Tiger (*†)   Private tape
  I can't get started (Clayton with rhythm)
  Perdido (omit Lyttelton)
  Unbooted Character
Second set:
  Feeling happy (BJT:v)
  Flip flop and fly (BJT:v)
  Cherry Red (BJT:v)
  Hide and go seek (BJT:v)

Third set:
  This old man (omit Coe, Temperley)
  Mood Indigo
  'Deed I do
Fourth set:
  Wee Baby Blues (BJT:v)
  I know you love me baby (BJT:v)
  Roll 'em Pete (BJT:v)
  TV Mama (BJT:v)
  Low Down Dog (BJT:v)

1965
May 16   London   "Jazz 625" (BBC television broadcast)
Buck Clayton, Vic Dickenson and Big Joe Turner with Hum-
phrey Lyttelton and his Band
*Buck Clayton (t); Humphrey Lyttelton (t); Vic Dickenson (tb); Tony
Coe (ts); Joe Temperley (bs); Eddie Harvey (p); Dave Green (db);
Johnny Butts (d)*
Swinging at the Copper Rail (*†)
The Green Tiger (omit Dickenson) (*†)

omit Lyttelton, Coe, Temperley
Jeepers Creepers
Love is just around the corner

*Big Joe Turner (v); Buck Clayton (t); Humphrey Lyttelton (t); Vic
Dickenson (tb); Eddie Harvey (tb); Tony Coe (ts); Joe Temperley (bs);
Johnny Parker (p); Dave Green (db); Johnny Butts (d)*
Low Down Dog
Low Down Dog (encore)
Roll 'em Pete
Roll 'em Pete (encore)
Morning Glories (omit Lyttelton, Harvey, Coe, Temperley)
Cherry Red (omit Lyttelton, Harvey)

NB: the session was broadcast in 2 parts on 16 June and 3 Nov
1965.

1965
June 2   Zagreb, Yugoslavia
Buck Clayton and Big Joe Turner with the Zagreb Jazz Quartet
*Buck Clayton (t); Bosko Petrovic (vib); Davor Kajfes (p); Kresimir
Remeta (db); Silvije Glojnaric (d); Big Joe Turner (v)*
Honeysuckle Rose   *Black Lion(E) 2460.202*
I can't get started
Perdido
Too late, too late (BJT:v)

1965
JJ's, Connecticut
Buck Clayton Septet
*Buck Clayton (t); Vic Dickenson (tb); Tommy Newsome (ts); Hank
Jones (p); Kenny Burrell (eg); Milt Hinton (db); Osie Johnson (d)*
In a Mellotone   Private tape
Sweet Georgia Brown
Just you, just me
I cover the waterfront
How high the moon
Sunday
Thou Swell

1966
March 14   Schlieren, near Zurich
Buck Clayton and his Swiss All Stars
*Buck Clayton (t); Raymond Droz (tb); Werner Keller (cl); Michel Pilet
(ts); Henri Chaix (p); Alain Dubois (g); Isla Eckinger (db); Johnny
Burrows (d)*
Clayton Place   *Decca(Sz) SLK 16-431P*
Casa Bar
I want a little girl
Tune for Buck
Candy's Tune
Topsy
Swinging the Blues (Vince Benedetti replaces Chaix)

1966
March 16   Paris
Buck Clayton and Friends
Buck Clayton (t); Hal Singer (ts); Joe Turner (p); Mickey Baker (eg);
Roland Lobligeois (db); Wallace Bishop (d)
Groovy Sunday (*)   *Polydor(G) INT(S)623.221/(M)423.221*
I can't think
Georgia on my Mind (omit Baker, Singer)
Boo boo (*)
Just you, just me
One for Bonnie (*)
Blue Boy
Pat's Party (*)
Juggi Buggi (Bernard de Bosson replaces Turner)
Come with me   *Polydor(F) LP-74566*
These foolish things   Unissued
Spanish Fly   Unissued
Rosetta   Unissued

1966
May 25   White Horse Pub, Willesden, London
Buck Clayton with Humphrey Lyttelton and his Band
Buck Clayton (t); Humphrey Lyttelton (t); Chris Pyne (tb); Kathy
Stobart (ts); Eddie Harvey (p, tb); Dave Green (db); Tony Taylor (d)
Say forward, I'll march   *77 Records(E) 77 LEU 12/18*
Russian Lullaby
Talkback
One for Buck
An evening in Soho (*)
The Jumping Blues
Blue Mist (†)
The Swingin' Birds (*†)
Poor Butterfly (omit Lyttelton, Pyne)
Bernie's Tune
(omit Lyttelton, Stobart)   *Harlequin(E) HQ-3002*

1966
June 29   Union Debating Hall, Oxford
Jazz from Chicago to Kansas City   "Jazz Goes To College"
(BBC television broadcast)
Buck Clayton with Humphrey Lyttelton and his Band
Buck Clayton (t); Humphrey Lyttelton (t); Chris Pyne (tb); Tony Coe
(ts); Eddie Harvey (p); Dave Green (db); Tony Taylor (d)
Russian Lullaby
The Swingin' Birds (*†)
Blue Mist (†)

Buck Clayton, Rex Stewart, Bud Freeman and Earl Hines with
Humphrey Lyttelton and his Band
add Rex Stewart (c), Bud Freeman (ts); Earl Hines replaces Harvey
The Jumping Blues
The Jumping Blues (encore)

Buck Clayton, Rex Stewart, Bud Freeman and Earl Hines with
Alex Welsh and his Band
Buck Clayton (t); Rex Stewart (c); Alex Welsh (c); Roy Williams (tb);
Bud Freeman (ts); Johnny Barnes (bs); Earl Hines (p); Jim Douglas
(eg); Ron Mathewson (db); Lennie Hastings (d)
St Louis Blues (splice from 2 takes)

NB: this session was broadcast in 2 parts on 17 Nov 1966 and 23
Jan 1967.

1966
Sept 16   Hotel Jerome, Aspen, Colorado
Dick Gibson's Aspen Jazz Party
Buck Clayton (t); Edmond Hall (cl); Teddy Wilson (p); George Van Eps
(g); Jack Lesberg (db); Mousey Alexander (d) (Eddie Miller, ts, added
for some items)
Georgia on my Mind (add Dick Cary, p)   Private tape
I can't get started (add Dick Cary, p)
Sweet Georgia Brown (add Cliff Leeman, d)
plus several unknown titles

1966
Sept 17   Hotel Jerome, Aspen, Colorado
Dick Gibson's Aspen Jazz Party
Buck Clayton (t); others unknown
Several unknown titles   Private tape

1966
Sept 18   Hotel Jerome, Aspen, Colorado
Dick Gibson's Aspen Jazz Party
Buck Clayton (t); Yank Lawson (t); Billy Butterfield (t); Lou McGarity
(tb); Cutty Cutshall (tb); Edmond Hall (cl); Matty Matlock (cl); Ralph
Sutton (p); Clancy Hayes (bj); Milt Hinton (db); Cliff Leeman (d)
That's a plenty   Private tape
plus several unknown titles

1966
cNovember   New York
Roberta Peck (v), with Buck Clayton (t); Willie Ruff (fh); Frank Wess
(f, ts); Pat Rebillot (p); George Benson (eg); Aaron Bell or Reed
Wasson (db); Jimmy Lovelace (d)
Body and Soul   *Columbia CL2658/CS9458*
The more I see you
In my arms (omit Ruff)

1967
Jan 15   Carnegie Hall, New York "Spirituals to Swing" concert
Café Society All Stars
Buck Clayton (t); Edmond Hall (cl); Buddy Tate (ts); Ray Bryant (p);
Milt Hinton (db); Jo Jones (d); Big Joe Turner (v); Willie Mae "Big
Mama" Thornton (v)
Swinging the Blues
(Count Basie, p, replaces Bryant)   *Columbia G-30776*
I'm going away to wear you off my
mind (BJT:v)   *Columbia G-30776*
Hide and go seek (BJT:v)   Unissued
Roll 'em Pete
(add Pete Johnson, p; BJT:v)   *Columbia G-30776*
Mother-in-law (WMT:v, harmonica)   Unissued
Sweet Little Angel (WMT:v)   *Columbia G-30776*
Backdoor Blues (WMT:v)   *Columbia G-30776*
Hound Dog (WMT:v)   *Columbia G-30776*
Unknown title (WMT:v)   Unissued
Unknown title (WMT:v)   Unissued

Count Basie and his Orchestra with guests
Al Aarons (t); Gene Goe (t); Sonny Cohn (t); Harry Edison (t); Richard
Boone (tb); Harlen Floyd (tb); Bill Hughes (tb); Grover Mitchell (tb);
Marshall Royal (as); Bobby Plater (as); Eric Dixon (ts); Billy Mitchell
(ts); Charlie Fowlkes (bs); Count Basie (p); Freddie Green (g); Norman
Keenan (db); Jo Jones (d); plus Buck Clayton (t); Edmond Hall (cl);
Buddy Tate (ts); Big Joe Turner (v)
Blues for John (edited)   *Columbia G-30776*

1967
March 6   Zurich
Buck Clayton and Ben Webster
Buck Clayton (t); Ben Webster (ts); Henri Chaix (p); Alain DuBois (g);
George Furrer (db); Romano Cavicchiolo (d)
Blues in F   Private tape
Satin Doll
It all depends on you (omit Webster)
I want a little girl (omit Webster)
Perdido
The Huckle-buck
Wrap your troubles in dreams (omit Webster)
Unknown title (omit Webster)
Sunday
C-jam Blues

1967
March 12   Paris
Jazz from a Swinging Era
Buck Clayton (t); Roy Eldridge (t); Vic Dickenson (tb); Earle Warren
(as); Bud Freeman (ts); Sir Charles Thompson (p); Bill Pemberton
(db); Oliver Jackson (d)
Into the Blues Bag (*†)   *Fontana(E) DTL/STL-200*
Swingville (*†)
Night-cap (*†)
Swinging the Blues (omit Eldridge, Freeman) (†)
Jive at Five (omit Eldridge, Freeman) (†)
Très chaud (omit Dickenson, Warren, Freeman) (†)
Indiana (omit Dickenson, Warren, Freeman) (†)

1967
March 17   Copenhagen
Jazz from a Swinging Era
*Buck Clayton (t); Vic Dickenson (tb); Earle Warren (as); Sir Charles
Thompson (p); Bill Pemberton (db); Oliver Jackson (d)*
Swinging the Blues (†)   *Pumpkin 101*

NB: No details known of further material presumably taped at
this concert

1967
March 24   Ronnie Scott's Jazz Club, London   "Something
Special" (BBC television broadcast)
Jazz from a Swinging Era
Same personnel as session of 12 March 1967
Swingville (*†)   *Pumpkin 101*
Night-cap (*†)   Unissued
Into the Blues Bag (*†)
Into the Blues Bag (*†)
Jive at Five (omit Eldridge, Freeman) (†)
Swinging the Blues (omit Eldridge, Freeman) (†)
Très chaud
(omit Dickenson, Warren, Freeman) (†)   *Pumpkin 101*
Indiana
(omit Dickenson, Warren, Freeman) (†)   Unissued

NB: this session was broadcast in two parts on 6 April and 1 June
1967.

1967
April 3   Liederhalle, Stuttgart (Suddeutscher Rundfunk radio
broadcast)
Jazz from a Swinging Era
Same personnel as session of 12 March 1967
Into the Blues Bag (*†)   *Pumpkin 101*
Jive at Five (omit Eldridge, Freeman) (†)   Unissued
Indiana (omit Dickenson, Warren, Freeman) (†)   *Pumpkin 101*
Très chaud
(omit Dickenson, Warren, Freeman) (†)   Unissued
Buck's Blues (Clayton, rhythm section)   *Pumpkin 101*
All of me (Clayton, rhythm section)   Unissued
St Louis Blues (Earl Hines, p,
replaces Thompson;
add Budd Johnson, ts)   *Pumpkin 101*

1967
April 4   Munich (Bavarian Radio broadcast)
Jazz from a Swinging Era
Same personnel as session of 12 March 1967
Into the Blues Bag (*†)
Indiana (omit Dickenson, Warren, Freeman) (†)
Très chaud (omit Dickenson, Warren, Freeman) (†)
Buck's Blues (Clayton, rhythm section)
All of me (Clayton, rhythm section)
St Louis Blues (Earl Hines, p, replaces Thompson; add Budd
Johnson, ts)

1967
June 16   Antwerp Jazz Club, Belgium
Buck Clayton and Ben Webster
*Buck Clayton (t); Ben Webster (ts); Camille de Ceunynck (p); Tony
Vaes (db); Charlie Pauwels (d)*
Perdido   Private tape
Blues
Sunday
I want a little girl (omit Webster)
All of me (omit Webster)
C-jam Blues
Avalon
Sweet Georgia Brown (omit Webster)
Blues
How high the moon
I can't get started (omit Webster)
In a Mellotone
B-flat Blues

1967
Sept 15   Casino Vail, Colorado
Dick Gibson's Colorado Jazz Party
*Buck Clayton (t); Lou McGarity (tb); Bob Wilber (ss); Phil Woods (as);
Lou Stein (p); Johnny Smith (eg); Milt Hinton (db); Nick Fatool (d)*
Just you, just me   Private tape
Several unknown titles

1967
Sept 16   Casino Vail, Colorado
Dick Gibson's Colorado Jazz Party
*Buck Clayton (t); Lou McGarity (tb); Bob Wilber (ss); Ernie Caceres
(bs); Lou Stein (p); Eddie Condon (g); Major Holley (db); Cliff Leeman
(d)*
Afternoon session:
   Them there eyes   Private tape
   In a Mellotone
   Limehouse Blues

*Buck Clayton (t); Urbie Green (tb); Matty Matlock (cl); Ernie Caceres
(bs); Dick Hyman (p); Milt Hinton (db); Mousey Alexander (d); Dick
Gibson (v)*
Evening session:
   Baby won't you please come home? (DG:v)   Private tape
   Several unknown titles

1967
Oct 30   Fine Studio A, Great Northern Hotel, New York
Jimmy Rushing All Stars
*Buck Clayton (t); Dicky Wells (tb); Julian Dash (ts); Sir Charles
Thompson (p); Gene Ramey (db); Jo Jones (d); Jimmy Rushing (v)*
MJR Blues   Master Jazz Recordings MJR-8104
Who's sorry now? (JR:v)   Master Jazz Recordings MJR-8104
Broadway   Unissued
St James Infirmary (JR:v)   *MJR-8104*
C-jam Blues   *MJR-8120*
Good Morning Blues (JR:v)   Rejected—Unissued
'Deed I do (JR:v)   Unissued
These foolish things   *MJR-8104*
You can depend on me (JR:v)   Unissued
The Sheik of Araby   Unissued
Gee baby, ain't I good to you? (JR:v)   *MJR-8104*
Moten Stomp   Unissued
Baby won't you please come home? (JR:v)   *MJR-8120*
All of me (JR:v)   *MJR-8120*
Old Man River   Unissued
On the sunny side of the street (JR:v)   Unissued
Boogie Blues   Unissued
I ain't got nobody (JR:v)   Unissued
I surrender dear (JR:v)   *MJR-8120*
One O'Clock Jump   Unissued
I'm gonna move to the outskirts of town (JR:v)   Unissued
Stormy Monday Blues (JR:v)   *MJR-8120*
Jelly jelly (JR:v)   *MJR-8120*
Perdido   Unissued
Good Morning Blues (JR:v)   *MJR-8104*
Tin Roof Blues   Unissued
I'm gonna sit right down and write myself a letter   Unissued

1968
March 8   New York
Earl Hines Quartet with Buck Clayton
*Buck Clayton (t); Budd Johnson (ss, ts); Earl Hines (p, v); Bill
Pemberton (db, eb); Oliver Jackson (d)*
120.028 Rhythm Sundae   *Decca DL75048*
120.029 The one I love belongs to
         somebody else
120.030 Back in your own backyard
         (EH:v)
120.032 For me and my gal

1968
March 11   New York
Earl Hines Quartet with Buck Clayton
*Buck Clayton (t); Budd Johnson (ss, ts); Earl Hines (p); Bill Pemberton
(eb); Oliver Jackson (d)*

120.033 Nobody knows and nobody seems to care
(omit Johnson)   *Decca DL 75048*
120.035 Shine on harvest moon
120.036 Thinking of you
120.037 I love my baby, my baby loves me

1968
Sept 13   Casino Vail, Colorado
Dick Gibson's Colorado Jazz Party
Buck Clayton (t); Vic Dickenson (tb); Matty Matlock (cl); Red Norvo (vib); Teddy Wilson (p); Howie Collins (g); Eddie Safranski (db); Cliff Leeman (d)
Yesterdays   Private tape
Sweet Georgia Brown
Several unknown titles

Buck Clayton (t); Yank Lawson (t); Ralph Sutton (p); Jack Lesberg (db); Morey Feld (d)
St James Infirmary   Private tape

Buck Clayton (t); Yank Lawson (t); Lou McGarity (tb); Urbie Green (tb); Bob Wilber (cl); Ralph Sutton (p); Howie Collins (g); Bob Haggart (db); Morey Feld (d)
Chinatown   Private tape

1968
Sept 14   Casino Vail, Colorado
Dick Gibson's Colorado Jazz Party
Buck Clayton (t); Dave McKenna (p); Howie Collins (g); Jack Lesberg (db); Don Lamond (d)
St Louis Blues   Private tape
Kansas City Blues
(add Clancy Hayes, bj, v)
Several unknown titles

Buck Clayton (t); Vic Dickenson (tb); Matty Matlock (cl); Bud Freeman (ts); Dave McKenna (p); Howie Collins (g); Jack Lesberg (db); Cliff Leeman (d)
'S wonderful   Private tape
Several unknown titles

1968
Sept 15   Casino Vail, Colorado
Dick Gibson's Colorado Jazz Party
Buck Clayton (t); Yank Lawson (t); Lou McGarity (tb); Carl Fontana (tb); Bob Wilber (cl); Bud Freeman (ts); Ralph Sutton (p); Jack Lesberg (db); Morey Feld (d)
Limehouse Blues   Private tape

1969
April 20–21   Otto Mønsted College, Copenhagen
Buck Clayton and Ben Webster with Arnvid Meyer's band
Buck Clayton (t); Arnvid Meyer (t); John Darville (tb); Jesper Thilo (ts); Hans Aspøck (p); Hugo Rasmussen (db); Hans Nymand (d)
I want a little girl   Private tape
Hi'ya
In a Mellotone
Buck in Copenhagen
Perdido

Buck Clayton (t); Ben Webster (ts); Hans Aspøck (p); Hugo Rasmussen (db); Hans Nymand (d)
Body and Soul (fragment)
Perdido

Buck Clayton (t); Arnvid Meyer (t); John Darville (tb); Ben Webster (ts); Jesper Thilo (ts); Hans Aspøck (p); Hugo Rasmussen (db); Hans Nymand (d)
Buck in Copenhagen
Buck in Copenhagen (encore)

1969
April 23   Copenhagen   (Danish radio broadcast)
Buck Clayton with Arnvid Meyer's Band
Buck Clayton (t); Arnvid Meyer (t); John Darville (tb); Jesper Thilo (ts); Hans Aspøck (p); Niels Henning Ørsted Pedersen (db); Hans Nymand (d)
These Foolish Things
Buck in Copenhagen

1969
late April   Copenhagen   (Danish radio broadcast)
Buck Clayton with Arnvid Meyer's band
Buck Clayton (t); Arnvid Meyer (t); John Darville (tb); Jesper Thilo (ts); Hans Aspøck (p); Hugo Rasmussen (db); Hans Nymand (d)
Buck in Copenhagen
These Foolish Things (Clayton and rhythm section)
Elephant Romp
Sugar (Clayton and rhythm section)
Hi'ya

1969
May 6   Antwerp
Milt Buckner Group
Buck Clayton (t); Milt Buckner (o); T-Bone Walker (eg; 1); Jo Jones (d)
Broadway   Private tape
I want a little girl
That's my weakness now
C-jam Blues (1)
These foolish things
Willow weep for me (1)
Blues (unknown title) (1)
Satin Doll
Swinging the Blues
Unknown title (1)

1970
May   Half Note Club, New York   "L'Adventure [sic] du Jazz" (film soundtrack)
The Panassié Stompers
Buck Clayton (t); Vic Dickenson (tb); Eddie Barefield (as); Budd Johnson (ss, ts); Sonny White (p); Tiny Grimes (eg); Milt Hinton (db); James Crawford (d)
Chez Panassié (*)   *Jazz Odyssey(F) JO-001*
Montauban Blues   *Jazz Odyssey(F) JO-001*
Basin Street Blues   *Jazz Odyssey(F) JO-002*

1974
March 25–6   New York
Buck Clayton Jam Session
Buck Clayton (conductor, arranger, composer); Joe Newman (t); Doc Cheatham (t); Urbie Green (tb); Earle Warren (as); Budd Johnson (ss, ts); Zoot Sims (ts); Joe Temperley (bs); Earl Hines (p); Milt Hinton (db); Gus Johnson (d)
Boss Blues   *Chiaroscuro CR-132*
Case Closed
Easy Blue
Jayhawk   *Chiaroscuro CR-163*

1975
June 6   New York
Buck Clayton Jam Session
Buck Clayton (conductor, arranger, composer); Joe Newman (t); Harold "Money" Johnson (t); Vic Dickenson (tb); George Masso (tb); Earle Warren (as); Lee Konitz (as); Budd Johnson (ss, ts); Buddy Tate (ts); Sal Nistico (ts); Tommy Flanagan (p); Milt Hinton (db); Mel Lewis (d)
Sidekick   *Chiaroscuro CR-143*
Change for a Buck
The Duke we knew
Glassboro Blues   *Chiaroscuro CR-163*

1976
July 7   Montreux Jazz Festival   "Jazz from Montreux" (BBC television broadcast)
Swinging Sextet with Humphrey Lyttelton
Buck Clayton (t); Humphrey Lyttelton (t); Jim Galloway (ss); Buddy Tate (ts); Jay McShann (p, v); Danny Mastri (db); Paul Rimstead (d)
Swinging the blues
Kansas City (JM:v)
Moten Swing

NB: Clayton also played at the festival with the Jim Galloway All Star Sextet, which was probably taped.

1976
July 8–17   Nice Jazz Festival
July 8   Jim Galloway All Star Sextet
Buck Clayton (t); Jim Galloway (ss, as, bs); Buddy Tate (ts); Jay McShann (p, v); Danny Mastri (db); Paul Rimstead (d)
Several unknown titles   Private tape

July 8   Jam session
Buck Clayton (t); Francis Williams (t); Eddie Daniels (ts); Gerard Badini (ts); Milt Buckner (p); Michel Gaudry (db); David Lee (d)
I may be wrong   Private tape
Pennies from Heaven

July 9   Jim Galloway All Star Sextet
Swinging the Blues   Private tape
My Melancholy Baby
Undecided

July 10   Jim Galloway All Star Sextet
Several unknown titles   Private tape

July 10   Jam session
Buck Clayton (t); Jimmy Maxwell (t); Gene Connors (tb); Zoot Sims (ts); Buddy Tate (ts); Illinois Jacquet (ts); Harold Mabern (p); Bucky Pizzarelli (eg); George Duvivier (db); Alan Dawson (d)
Several unknown titles   Private tape

July 11   Jim Galloway All Star Sextet
I'm gonna sit right down and write
 myself a letter   Private tape
Just you, just me
I've got a secret (JM:v)
Moten Swing
C-jam Blues

July 11   Teddy Wilson Trio with guests
Buck Clayton (t); Zoot Sims (ts); Teddy Wilson (p); Michel Gaudry (db); Bobby Rosengarden (d)
On the Alamo   · Private tape

July 12   *Carrie Smith (v), with Buck Clayton (t); Teddy Wilson (p); George Duvivier (db); Alan Dawson (d)*
Several unknown titles   Private tape

July 12   Jam session
Buck Clayton (t); Doc Cheatham (t); Dick Sudhalter (c); Norris Turney (as); Milt Buckner (p); Rodney Jones (eg); Michel Gaudry (db); Sam Woodyard (d)
Several unknown titles   Private tape

July 13   Jam session
Buck Clayton (t); Gene Connors (tb); Buddy Tate (ts); Raymond Fol (p); Rodney Jones (eg); Benjamin Brown (db); Mickey Roker (d); Carrie Smith (v)
What is this thing called love?   Private tape
Stompin' at the Savoy
Stormy Monday (CS:v)
Crazy Rhythm

July 13   Jam session
Buck Clayton (t); Joe Newman (t); Ed Hubble (tb); Gene Connors (tb); Haywood Henry (cl, bs); Jim Galloway (cl, as); Eddie Daniels (ts); Harold Mabern (p); George Duvivier (db); David Lee (d)
Crazy Rhythm   Private tape
Sunday
Take the 'A' train

July 14   Jim Galloway All Star Sextet
Swinging the Blues   Private tape
Untitled boogie-woogie
Broadway

July 14   Jam session
Buck Clayton (t); Francis Williams (t); Harry Edison (t); Jim Galloway (ss, bs); Jay McShann (p); Danny Mastri (db); Paul Rimstead (d)
Several unknown titles   Private tape

July 15   Jim Galloway All Star Sextet
Several unknown titles   Private tape

July 17   Jam session
Buck Clayton (t); Zoot Sims (ts); Marian McPartland (p); Major Holley (db); David Lee (d)
Several unknown titles   Private tape

July 17   Jam session
Buck Clayton (t); Jim Galloway (ss, bs); Harold Mabern (p); Percy Heath (db); David Lee (d)
Several unknown titles   Private tape

NB: all sessions at the festival were taped by the Black and Blue Records team as well as by countless amateurs.

1976
Sept 13   New York
Buck Clayton Jam Session
Buck Clayton (conductor, arranger, composer); Harry Edison (t); Marvin "Hannibal" Peterson (t); Vic Dickenson (tb); Jimmy Knepper (tb); Bob Wilber (ss); Lee Konitz (as); Earle Warren (as); Budd Johnson (ts); Buddy Tate (ts); Hank Jones (p); Richard Davis (db); Bobby Rosengarden (d)
Jazz Party Time   *Chiaroscuro CR-152*
Kansas City Style
Even Steven
Bandwagon

late 1977
Municipal Auditorium, Kansas City (television videotape)
Kansas City Seven
Buck Clayton (t); Harry Edison (t); Zoot Sims (ts); Eddie "Lockjaw" Davis (ts); unknown (p, db); Jo Jones (d)
Moten Swing
Several unknown titles

1979
Feb 21 or 22   New York
Red Richards and Friends
Buck Clayton (t); Norris Turney (as); Red Richards (p, v); Johnny Williams (db); Ronnie Cole (d)
In a Mellotone   *West 54 WLW-8005*
I've got a feeling I'm falling (RR:v) (†)
More than you know (RR:v) (†)
I can't give you anything but love (RR:v) (†)

1979
July 6–12   Nice Jazz Festival

July 6   Jam session
Buck Clayton (t); Barney Bigard (cl); Peanuts Hucko (cl); Maxim Saury (cl); Hank Jones (p); Slam Stewart (db); Shelly Manne (d)
Several unknown titles   Private tape

July 6   Jam session
Buck Clayton (t); Spiegel Wilcox (tb); Jim Galloway (cl, ss, as); Roland Hanna (p); Jack Sewing (db); Bobby Durham (d)
Several unknown titles   Private tape

July 7   Jam session
Buck Clayton (t); Spiegel Wilcox (tb); Peanuts Hucko (cl); Jim Galloway (cl, ss, as); Roland Hanna (p); Major Holley (db); Bobby Durham (d)
Several unknown titles   Private tape

July 8   Les Haricots Rouges (French New Orleans-style band) with Buck Clayton (t)
Several unknown titles   Private tape

July 8   Jimmy Witherspoon Quartet with guests
Jimmy Witherspoon (v); Buck Clayton (t); Erskine Hawkins (t); Vic Dickenson (tb); unknown rhythm section
Several unknown titles   Private tape

July 10   Jimmy Witherspoon Quartet with Buck Clayton
Jimmy Witherspoon (v); Buck Clayton (t); unknown rhythm section
Several unknown titles   Private tape

July 10   Jam session
Buck Clayton (t); Vic Dickenson (tb); Peanuts Hucko (cl); Jim Galloway (cl, ss, as); Ray Bryant (p); Slam Stewart (db); Bobby Durham (d)
Several unknown titles   Private tape

July 11   Jam Session
Buck Clayton (t); Spiegel Wilcox (tb); Peanuts Hucko (cl); Bob Wilber (cl, ss); Ray Bryant (p); Slam Stewart (db); Major Holley (db); Duffy Jackson (d)
Several unknown titles   Private tape

July 12 Jay McShann Quintet with guests
Buck Clayton (t); Al Grey (tb); Claude Williams (vn); Barney Bigard (cl); Buddy Tate (ts); Jimmy Forrest (ts); Jay McShann (p); Gene Ramey (db); Gus Johnson (d)
Several unknown titles   Private tape

NB: all sessions unissued but available on tape

1983
Nov 7 Grand Theatre Municipal, Limoges (French radio broadcast)
The Count's Men
Buck Clayton (leader, arranger, conductor); Harry Edison (t); Joe Newman (t); Al Aarons (t); Ed Lewis (t); Curtis Fuller (tb); Eddie Durham (tb); Mel Wanzo (tb); Earle Warren (cl, as); Preston Love (as); Buddy Tate (ts); Skip Williams (ts); Haywood Henry (bs); Nat Pierce (p); Freddie Green (g); Eddie Jones (db); Frankie Capp (d)
Down for Double
9:20 Special
Mes amis de Limoges (†)
It's sand man

Doggin' Around (†)
Jive at Five (†)
Blue and Sentimental (Warren:cl)
Jumping at the Woodside
Tickle Toe (†)
One O'Clock Jump

NB: this band also appeared at the Cork Jazz Festival on 29 Oct 1983 (where the performance was televised), at the Chichester Festival on 30 Oct, and at concerts in France and Spain; it is likely, therefore, that further tapes are available.

1984
June 30 Carnegie Hall, New York Kool Jazz Festival: "A Salute To Count Basie"
The Reno Club Band
Buck Clayton (leader, conductor); Harry Edison (t); Grover Mitchell (tb); Earle Warren (as); Illinois Jacquet (ts); John Lewis (p); Freddie Green (g); Ed Jones (db); Gus Johnson (d)
Rompin' at the Reno   Unissued
Kansas City Blues
Cherry Blossom

Index

Davison, Wild Bill, 142
D. B. Blues, 119
Dean, Jimmy, 169
'Deed I Do, 20, 22
Delaunay, Charles, 146, 147
Delesega, John, 22
De Marco Sisters, 157
Denmark, 164, 179, 208, 209
Denver, 16, 187
Detroit, 39, 101, 102
DeVigne, Freddie, 126, 185, 200
DeVigne, Gertrude, 126, 129, 154
DeVigne, Henry, 126, 160
DeVigne, Hortense (Tony), 126
DeVigne, Sophia (Jackie), 126
Dickenson, Vic, 161, 165, 166, 170, 175, 187, 215
Diggs, Mae, 56
Dinah, 22
Ding Dong Daddy from Dumas, 45
Dobell, Doug, 173, 174
Dobie, Wilma, 192
Doggin' Around, 111
Dorsey, Aritha (Mrs Spotts) [cousin], 13
Dorsey, Lucille: *see* Kerford, Lucille
Dorsey, Monroe [uncle], 13
Dorsey, Tommy, 80, 112, 119
——, band, 109
Down for double, 212
Do you know what it means to miss New Orleans, 141
Drake and Walker minstrel show, 19
Drew, Kenny, 209
Drootin, Buzzy, 143
Drop me off in Harlem, 38, 50
DuBois, W. E. B., 14
Dukes, 38
Dumons, Monique (Nickey), 152
Durham, Eddie, 91, 110, 210

Early, Thomas D., 18
East St Louis Toodle-oo, 38
Echols, Charlie, 42–4, 49–51, 55
——, band, 42, 44, 53
Edinburgh Jazz Festival, 216
Edison, Harry (Sweets), 107, 110–12, 162, 173, 195, 215
Edwards Sisters, 104, 105
Eldridge, Roy, 81, 95, 107, 130, 182, 215
Eleven-thirty Saturday Night, 21
Ellington, Duke, 21, 30, 38, 41, 49–51, 54, 60–65, 70, 93, 108, 119, 120, 142, 199, 215

——, band, 11, 64, 79, 85–7, 89, 93, 102, 108, 141
Ellington, Mercer, 119, 120
Elliott, Emile, 161
Elliott, Nancy Miller, 161, 206, 215
Elliott, Tom, 161
Elliott, Vincent, 161
Elman, Ziggy, 158
Empty Bed Blues, 20
England, 161, 163, 164, 173, 178, 181, 182, 186, 187, 211
Englewood Cliffs, New Jersey, 166, 167
Erwin, Pee Wee, 23
Erwing, Dorchester, 41
Erwing, Harris, 41, 85
Erwing, James, 41
Eubanks, Logan, 37, 40
Eubanks, Teddy, 40
Eubie (show), 215
Evans, Herschel (Tex), 79, 81, 84, 87, 88, 92–5, 105, 108, 111, 112, 199
Every day I get the blues, 211
Every Tub, 49

Fain, Elmer, 51
Farmer, Art, 152, 191
Farrell, Glenda, 54
Feedin' the Bean, 113
Feel so Fine!, 176
Ferguson, Maynard, 105
Ferrer, José, 144
Fetchit, Stepin, 50
Fez, 147
Fidgety Feet, 141
Fields, Kansas, 145, 148, 151–3, 161
Fiesta in Blue, 181
Finland, 208
Fitzgerald, Ella, 97, 104, 105, 109
Five Foot Two, Eyes of Blue, 21, 22
Five Hot Shots, 74, 78
Flagstaff, Arizona, 28
Flemming, Herb, 142
Florence, 149
Florida, 142, 213
Floyd, LaVern, 38, 39
Floyd, Troy, 94
Flying Home, 119, 131
Fol, Hubert, 151
Fol, Raymond, 151
Fonville, Benny, 129
42nd Street (film), 43
Fouquet, Charlie, 120
Fourteen Gentlemen from Harlem, 53
Fox, Ed, 95, 96